Lecture Notes in Computer Science 6400

Commenced Publication in 1973
Founding and Former Series Editors:
Gerhard Goos, Juris Hartmanis, and Jan van Leeuw

Mark Chignell   James Cordy
Joanna Ng   Yelena Yesha (Eds.)

The Smart Internet

Current Research and Future Applications

IBM CAS Research

Springer

Volume Editors

Mark Chignell
University of Toronto
Ontario, Canada
E-mail: chignel@mie.utoronto.ca

James Cordy
Queen's University
Kingston, Ontario, Canada
E-mail: cordy@cs.queensu.ca

Joanna Ng
IBM Canada Software Laboratories
Markham, Ontario, Canada
E-mail: jwng@ca.ibm.com

Yelena Yesha
University of Maryland Baltimore County
Baltimore, Maryland, USA
E-mail: yeyesha@cs.umbc.edu

Library of Congress Control Number: 2010936901

CR Subject Classification (1998): H.4, H.3, H.5, C.2, D.2, I.2

LNCS Sublibrary: SL 3 – Information Systems and Application, incl. Internet/Web and HCI

ISSN 0302-9743
ISBN-10 3-642-16598-2 Springer Berlin Heidelberg New York
ISBN-13 978-3-642-16598-6 Springer Berlin Heidelberg New York

springer.com

Printed in Germany

Typesetting: Camera-ready by author, data conversion by Scientific Publishing Services, Chennai, India
Printed on acid-free paper 06/3180

Foreword

I love the idea of a Smart Internet that lets users improve many parts of their lives, pulling together data and services from around the internet. This won't happen with large unwieldy programming requirements...it will happen because we're moving towards integrated, simple tasks that users can do on an every day basis. With services available on the cloud, with analytics available, with data that has meaning to the user and not just to some protocol parser - with all of these, users at all levels will be able to do a better job. The users may be small and large enterprises, local governments, individuals, etc. All of this means that as the world is becoming more intelligent, instrumented and more interconnected, we'll be headed towards smarter health care, smarter cities, and smarter lives."

— Gennaro A. Cuomo, IBM Software Group Vice President
and IBM Fellow, WebSphere Chief Technology Officer

Congratulations to the team on the publication of this first volume of the IBM CAS Research book series! This is a significant milestone for IBM CAS Research. This series not only captures the innovations resulting from the collaboration across IBM technical leaders, IBM CAS faculty members, as well as our network of distinguished academic partners, it also lays the foundation for ongoing commercialization of future research initiatives."

— Judy Huber, IBM Software Group Vice President
and Director of IBM Canada Lab

Preface

It is our great pleasure to introduce this first volume in what we hope will be a series of books presenting research results from the IBM Canada Centre for Advanced Studies; (CAS), which was established in 1990 at the IBM Toronto Software Laboratory. It performs a significant role in bringing together IBM researchers and technical leaders with academic and government research organizations from around the world. The publication of this book coincides with the 20th anniversary of CAS and also the 20th Annual International Research Conference hosted by the Centre for Advanced Studies at the IBM Canada Software Laboratory (CASCON 2010). The CASCON "Meeting of Minds" provides an exciting annual forum for exchanging ideas and experiences in the ever-expanding and critical fields of software engineering and computing.

The origins of this book began with ideas concerning the next generation internet developed by Joanna Ng [1], which were further elaborated in an NSERC Strategic Workshop on the Smart Internet (SITCON 2009). SITCON was organized by James Cordy, Joanna Ng and Mark Chignell, and co-sponsored by the IBM Canada Centre for Advanced Studies. It was held in Markham, Ontario as part of CASCON 2009. The workshop brought together prominent researchers from a diverse set of research areas whose expertise was relevant to the advancing the science base of the Smart Internet vision. Workshop participants included computer scientists, psychologists, practitioners and others from a range of engineering disciplines, who presented position papers on a wide range of topics related to the Smart Internet vision and its realization.

Following the SITCON 2009 workshop, contributors were invited to submit extended versions of their position papers as potential chapters for this book. Each submission was formally reviewed by at least two members of the Program Committee, consisting of the 14 senior members of the research community listed below; the editors selected papers for acceptance based on this advice. Following a round of revisions in response to the reviewers' concerns, accepted papers were reviewed once again by the editors, and the final selection of chapters is what you see presented here.

The chapters in this book represent a snapshot of current research and conceptualization of the Smart Internet. The Smart Internet initiative has been

[1] A summer afternoon in 2008 at Uffizi, Florence: it dawned on me that what would have been thought of as obvious advancement in art from flat imagery of Madonna by Pietro Lorenzetti, 1340 to a realistic 3D imagery of Madonna by Raphael, 1505 actually took almost two centuries. Studying the progression of these images of Madonna inspired me to imagine the obvious advancement that the 20 year old internet needed, thus came the idea of Smart Internet. I was hoping that it would not even take a decade! — Joanna

spearheaded by IBM and aims to extend and transform the Web so that it is centered on the user, with the Web as a "calm" platform ubiquitously providing cognitive support to its users and their tasks. In addition to some initial motivating chapters, the chapters in this book are concerned with two major research areas for enabling the Smart Internet, namely, smart interactions and smart services. Many of the chapters in the book grew out of earlier papers presented at the workshop.

We would like to thank the workshop participants for bringing their expertise and enthusiasm to this event and we would particularly like to thank the authors who chose to share their research in this book. We could not have produced a quality result without the incisive reviewing of the Program Committee members, who we thank for their hard work and dedication. The preparation of this book benefited greatly from the preparatory work done at the workshop itself, and we are very grateful for the generous support of both NSERC and the IBM Canada Centre for Advanced Studies in making the workshop possible. A number of people put a lot of effort into organizing the workshop, and we would particularly like to thank Emilia Tung, Stephen Perelgut, Debbie Kilbride, Jimmy Lo, and Leho Nigul of the IBM Canada Laboratories for their help. Finally, we would also particularly like to thank Ryan Kealey for his help in the final editing and formatting of the chapters, as well as Danielle Nicholls for her editing assistance. For doing the illustration for the book, we would like to thank Robyn Ng. Special thanks go to Alfred Hofmann and the team at Springer for their assistance in the preparation of this book.

August 2010

Mark Chignell
James R. Cordy
Joanna Ng
Yelena Yesha

Dedications

Joanna To my Heavenly Father who affirms that I am His beloved, to my late father, who always took joy in finding smart solutions to day-to-day problems and to Terry, Robyn and Evelyn, who are very special people in my life.

Yelena To my mother Valentina

Program Committee

Marsha Chechik	University of Toronto
Mark Chignell	University of Toronto
James R. Cordy	Queens University
Hans-Arno Jacobsen	University of Toronto
Patrick Martin	Queen's University
Joanna McGrenere	University of British Columbia
Hausi Müller	University of Victoria
Joanna Ng	IBM Canada Centre for Advanced Studies
Kamran Sartipi	McMaster University
Ian Spence	University of Toronto
Margaret-Anne Storey	University of Victoria
Eleni Stroulia	University of Alberta
Jens Weber-Jahnke	University of Victoria
Yelena Yesha	University of Maryland, Baltimore County

About the Editors

Mark Chignell is a professor of Mechanical and Industrial Engineering at the University of Toronto, where he has been on the faculty since 1990. Prior to that he was an assistant professor in Industrial and Systems Engineering at the University of Southern California from 1984 to 1990. He has a PhD in Psychology (University of Canterbury, New Zealand, 1981), and an MSc in Industrial and Systems Engineering (Ohio State, 1984). Mark is currently President of Vocalage Inc., a University of Toronto spinoff company, director of the Interactive Media Lab, and a visiting scientist at both the IBM Centre for Advanced Studies and Keio University in Japan.

James Cordy is a professor and past Director of the School of Computing at Queens University, Kingston, Canada, where he has been on the faculty since 1985. From 1995 to 2000 he was Vice President and Chief Research Scientist at Legasys Corporation, a software technology company specializing in legacy software system analysis and renovation. Cordy received his PhD from the University of Toronto. He is the author of more than 130 refereed contributions in programming languages, software engineering and artificial intelligence. Cordy is an ACM Distinguished Scientist, a senior member of the IEEE, and an IBM Visiting Scientist and Faculty Fellow.

Joanna Ng is currently the Head of Research at IBM Canada Software Laboratories, Centre for Advanced Studies. She is also a Senior Technical Staff Member of IBM Software Group. She has held various senior management and architect positions in product development teams and software strategy division. Joanna is a an IBM Master Inventor with a long track record of profitable innovations. She has been granted over 25 patents from various countries in research areas such as mobile commerce; voice-enabled portal; commerce portal; retail industry solutions; service-oriented architecture (SOA); asset repository; and semantic and Web technologies.

Yelena Yesha received a BSc degree in Computer Science from York University, Toronto, Canada in 1984, and the MSc and PhD degrees in Computer and Information Science from The Ohio State University in 1986 and 1989, respectively. Since 1989 she has been with the Department of Computer Science and Electrical Engineering at the University of Maryland Baltimore County, where she is currently a professor, and Director of the UMBC NSF Center for Hybrid Multicore Productivity Research. Yesha served as the Director of the Center of Excellence in Space Data and Information Sciences at NASA (1994–1999).

Table of Contents

Part I: Motivation

Part II: Smart Interactions

Part III: Smart Services

Part I
Motivation

Motivation

Joanna W. Ng[1], Mark Chignell[2], James R. Cordy[3], and Yelena Yesha[4]

[1] IBM Canada
jwng@ca.ibm.com
[2] Universtiy of Toronto
chignell@utoronto.ca
[3] Queen's University
cordy@cs.queensu.ca
[4] University of Maryland
yeyesha@umbc.edu

Abstract. Key architectural elements of the web, namely, HTTP, URL and HTML enable a very simple *user model of the web* based on hyperlinks. While this model allows browser-based access to a wide array of online content and resources, the limitations in user experience provided in this interaction model are increasingly apparent. Two decades after the birth of the web, new technologies such as Rich Internet Application, AJAX, and Web 2.0 seek to improve web user interfaces, but in general their main benefit is to individual server sites. Little advancement has been made to advance the *user model of the web* at a macro level where the interaction is driven not by the server but by the user. This paper reviews the problems of the current internet in order to motivate the discussion of the smart internet that will occur in later chapters of this book.

1 Introduction

In 1989, Tim Berners-Lee invented the web and began the modern internet era. The internet is viewed as an 'irreversible innovation' of enhanced digital connectivity [1]. From its inception to the present, the Uniform Resource Locator (URL) has been used as the address of the specific web server from which users obtain resources and content. In this now classic model, the browser on the client device first makes a *connection* with the corresponding web server. The corresponding web server then processes the *request* sent in HTTP transfer protocol from the browser of the client. The web server directs and/or performs the requested units of functions or fetches the requested resources and sends the *response* back to the browser of the client also in *HTTP* transfer protocol as an *HTML* format response page. When the connection between the user's browser and the corresponding web server is no longer needed, the connection is *closed*. These connect-request-response-close interactions between a user's browser and a web server provide a simple usage model for the web. In spite of its simplicity, users have benefited greatly from having ready access to this massive, distributed, and loosely coupled network of information. However, as time has passed the

M. Chignell et al. (Eds.): The Smart Internet, LNCS 6400, pp. 3–8, 2010.

server-centric model of the internet has become a barrier that stands in the way of more fulfilling user-centric interactions that can handle the complex data sets and tasks that are increasingly prevalent.

2 Technological Advances

Advancement in the first decade of the Web era (the 1990s) focused on overcoming practical issues of web application development and deployment imposed by the web architecture. These issues included: security; scalability; performance; transactions and others. In the second decade of the Web (around 2000) technologies related to improvement of web user experience began to emerge. For example, Rich Internet Applications (RIA) aimed at "combining the media-rich power of the traditional desktop with the deployment and content rich nature of web applications" [2] in order to provide better user experience. The Web 2.0 initiative sought to enhance user experience by adding social computing tools, and by allowing users and other less technical participants to publish, as well as consume, content through lightweight programming models [3] and tools such as blogging. Ankolekar et al [4] suggested combining semantic Web [5] and Web 2.0 technologies. They provided a scenario of how this can be done so that it is beneficial, and argued that the tasks of creation, exchange, and reuse have to be solved. They emphasized the importance of an approach that is centered more on users and communities. AJAX combined asynchronous data retrieval using the XMLHttpRequest object and data interchange in XML, with DOM and other standards-based presentation like XHTML and cascade style sheets (CSS) all bound together in JavaScript. The intent was to offer a web application user experience comparable to the desktop, but through the browser [6].

3 The Problems of the Server-Centric Approach

The server-centric *(users for the web)* model of Web interaction has prevailed over the last two decades. While powerful, it is in need of replacement as its shortcomings become increasingly clear. The problem of how to move Web interaction to a user-centric approach, where services and content are aggregated across multiple sites according to user needs, has yet to be addressed.

In this section we consider the deficiencies of the server-centric model in more detail. These deficiencies have led to a server-centric model that is onerous for users. In order to accomplish a particular task or purpose, users are typically forced first to access information from various sites, and then to manually customize the information acquired from these sites. User patience with such inconvenience is starting to wear thin [7].

The inconvenience of the current model for users stems from five major shortcomings.

1. The lack of *integration from the user's perspective,* to aggregate resources and content from multiple web servers centering on the user, her tasks and the context. Technologies like *portals* and *mashups* provide partial solutions to this problem, but both lack an aggregation model and framework to drive service

composition from the user's perspective that can be handled and controlled by users themselves.

2. The lack of *individualization* is increasingly becoming an issue as users push for a user model for the web that is aware and adaptive to the user's real time context and situation. Today's personalization technologies use approaches like user categorization, configuration and customization but do not fully support real time, individualized requirements.
3. The absence of *server-initiated connections* such as asynchronous connections and service level batch processing is another handicap in today's primitive user model of the web. The user has to initiate and track tasks, and is provided with little, if any, support both in terms of aiding prospective memory (remembering what has to be done in the future) and in terms of carrying out complex tasks.
4. The lack of any notion of *service level collaboration*, the idea that multiple users may collaborate on a service instance, is another limitation that makes it difficult for people to work collaboratively when interacting with the Web.
5. Finally, *user control* over web pages is very limited and is primarily controlled by server side software programmers.

Research work in context-aware computing [8] the Semantic Web [9] and personalization [10] has made advances with respect to some of these shortcomings. However, without a cohesive and advanced *user model of the interaction* at a macro level (not just at the individual site level), and without a *web model* to capture the conceptual structure of Web content and services, these types of incremental advances will not lead to significant change.

In the following section we will further motivate the need for a form of interaction that better accommodates the needs of users.

4 Human Factors

Perhaps the most damaging consequence of the service-centric type of interaction is the amount of unnecessary cognitive effort that users have to expend in integrating material from multiple server sessions. This violates the strong psychological need to have tasks that are well-integrated and that do not require switching between activities. In this section we will consider the human factors of Web interaction, pointing out the need to change fundamentally the way that Web interaction occurs. A related motivation for improving Web interaction is the concept of calm computing advocated by Weiser [11].

Switching between activities is time consuming and effortful, and people often don't do it particularly well. Task switching can occur over both short and long time intervals. In short-term task switching, such as might occur when attempting to integrate information from multiple Web pages, a high load is placed on human working memory. Working memory is a limited temporary store of information used during cognitive processes. It acts as a temporary store for episodic long term memory (LTM), feeding information into and retrieving information from the LTM [12]. There is also a related central executive function that is responsible for storing information regarding the current active goals, the intermediate results of cognitive processes, and expected inputs from sequential actions. This executive function may be characterized as a supervisory process that controls other cognitive processes. This working memory system has limited capacity and is easily overloaded. Simply put, people are not good at remembering multiple things at once.

Task switching over longer time intervals creates a load on prospective memory. Marsh et al [13] defined prospective memory as "memory for one's intentions". Within this broad definition prospective memory tasks may be defined with different levels of stringency. For instance, a task may involve having to do a particular thing at a particular time. Alternatively, the timing of the future task may be uncertain depending on external circumstances. Prospective memory tasks are particularly difficult when timing of the future task depends on external contexts that do not involve explicit triggers. In such cases people may have to remember to check the status of the system in order to determine when the conditions are right (e.g. in a healthcare context, lab test results becoming available without the knowledge of the supervising physician) for performing the intended task. People frequently [14] use email messages as task reminders and may even send themselves email messages as additional reminders. These types of ad hoc reminders are used because remembering to remember (prospective memory) is a difficult task that people are frequently faced with.

Multi-session environments create problems for prospective memory and working memory, because they interfere with other tasks that need to be performed while the to-be-remembered task is being held in memory [15]. This may be a particular problem in Web interaction, which typically does not have the reminders and constraints that tend to exist in the physical world (e.g., papers on desks or sticky notes placed on refrigerator doors).

Searching and browsing represent two aspects of Web interaction that are currently poorly integrated. As Morris et al. [16] noted, "Considering search and browse actions in isolation results in impoverished user interfaces that do not adequately assist users with common scenarios such as re-finding previously encountered Web pages, resuming an activity after an interruption, or conducting complex, multi-session investigations." They cited research that a substantial number of Web page accesses are in fact re-visits, and they developed a system intended to support multi-session investigations by assisting with task context resumption and information refinding. However, rather than develop bandaid solutions to these problems it would seem to be more efficient to fix the problem of server-centric sessions that generate a burden on users.

It is often the case that people underestimate the importance of human factors in task performance. When people learn to do something a particular way it eventually seems natural, even if without extensive training it is very un-natural (e.g. typing on a QWERTY keyboard). In addition, when people are busy performing tasks they may not have awareness of how well or efficiently they are performing the tasks. Thus in using the internet they may feel subjectively that they are doing well in handling multiple sessions and constantly switching between tasks, even when their performance is in fact suffering. An example of this lack of awareness of impaired performance can occur with drinking and driving, and also occurred with cell phones and driving. Many people felt that they could talk on the phone without it affecting their driving even as the accident statistics showed that cell phone use increased the accident risk more than four times. Counter-intuitively, the main problem was not with the hands and eyes, since the accident risk remained high even when hands-free units were used. Thus it appears that the cognitive processing of the conversation is interfering with the driving. The driver may "see" the road, but not the implications of hazards that could be interfered from the scene if more cognitive processing were applied to it.

Attending to things requires effort. Attention controls the significance of stimuli that people perceive [17]. Neisser [18] used the analogy of picking a sandwich from a plate of sandwiches to characterize the selective aspect of attention. Selective attention involves choosing one thing to process to the exclusion of others. In contrast, divided attention arises in a multi-tasking situation where more than one stimulus is of interest at the same time. Divided attention is effortful, and people have difficulty rapidly switching attention between tasks. The modern desktop computer, with multiple screens of information open at the same time, represents a situation that people are poorly equipped to handle.

Roda and Thomas [19] reviewed research relating to attention with the aim of identifying research directions for developing systems that could support human attentional mechanisms effectively. Based on a review of relevant research literature they identified the following properties of attention switching and distraction:

"*(1) There is always a cost associated in switching attention from a task to another one.*
(2) Higher task complexity implies higher costs for attention switch.
(3) The cost of switching attention from one task to another can be reduced if cues are provided about the task to be performed next (at least in situations of task alternation).
(4) Increasing the time between attention switches does not reduce the cost of the switch unless this time is constant (i.e. attention switches happen regularly), or at least predictable.
(5) Stimuli related to familiar (and recent) tasks are more likely to act as distractors for current tasks."

5 Roadmap of Part 1

The current internet is designed for the convenience of the server rather than the user. With its server-centric architecture and multi-session user interactions, the current internet places an unnecessary cognitive processing burden on users, overloading attentional and memory functions. The need for smart internet functionality can be seen in examples of flawed interaction that occur in many different domains. In Part 1 of this book the need for the smart internet is motivated with examples and discussions relating to healthcare. The chapter by Yu et al. looks at the challenges facing emergency department physicians as they interact with information technology while performing their work. Weber-Jahnke and Williams then look more broadly at the domain of healthcare, discussing the relationship between the smart internet and healthcare reform. In the final chapter of part 1 by Ng et al., an overview of the smart internet is provided which sets the stage for the more detailed material presented in parts 2 and 3 of the book. The chapter by Ng et al. presents the smart internet vision in terms of three broad guiding principles:

- A User-Centric Model for Instinctive Interaction
- Session for Users and their Matters of Concern
- Collaborative and Collective Web Interactions

That vision is then pursued in the remaining parts of this book, with Part 2 dealing with smart interactions, and Part 3 dealing with smart services.

References

1. Hoffman, D.L., Novak, T.P., Venkatesh, A.: Has the Internet become indispensable? Comm. ACM 47(7), 37–42 (2004)
2. Allaire, J.: Macromedia Flash MX: A Next Generation Rich Client. Macromedia White Paper (2002)
3. O'Reilly, T.: What is Web 2.0? Design Patterns and Business Models for the Next Generation of Software. O'Reilly Media, Inc., Sebastopol (2005)
4. Ankolekar, A., Krotzsch, M., Tran, T., Vrandecic, D.: The two cultures: mashing up Web 2.0 and the semantic Web. In: Proceedings of the 16th International Conference on World Wide Web, WWW 2007, pp. 825–834. ACM, New York (2007)
5. Berners-Lee, T., Hendler, J., Lassila, O.: The Semantic Web. Scientific American 284, 34–43 (2001)
6. Garrett, J.J.: Ajax: A New Approach to Web Applications. Adaptive Path Inc., White Paper (2005)
7. Raman, T.V.: Toward 2^w. Beyond Web 2.0. Comm. ACM 52(2), 52–59 (2009)
8. Dey, A.K.: Understanding and Using Context. Personal and Ubiquitous Computing 5(1), 4–7 (2001)
9. Berners-Lee, T., et al.: A Framework for Web Science. Foundations and Trends in Web Science 1(1), 1–134 (2006)
10. Baldoni, M., Baroglio, C., Henze, N.: Personalization for the Semantic Web. In: Proc. Reasoning Web, pp. 173–212 (2005)
11. Weiser, M., Brown, J.S.: The Coming Age of Calm Technology. Xerox PARC (October 1996)
12. Baddeley, A.D.: Is working memory still working? American Psychologist 56, 851–864 (2001)
13. Marsh, R.L., Cook, G.I., Hicks, J.L.: An analysis of prospective memory. In: Medin, D.L. (ed.) The Psychology of Learning and Motivation. Elsevier, Amsterdam (2006)
14. Whittaker, S., Sidner, C.: Email overload: exploring personal information management of email. In: Proceedings of ACM SIGCHI, pp. 276–283 (1996)
15. Hicks, J.L., Marsh, R.L., Cook, G.I.: Task interference in time-based, event-based, and dual intention prospective memory conditions. Journal of Memory and Language 53, 430–444 (2005)
16. Morris, D., Ringel Morris, M., Venolia, G.: SearchBar: a search-centric web history for task resumption and information re-finding. In: Proceeding of the Twenty-Sixth Annual SIGCHI Conference on Human Factors in Computing Systems, CHI 2008, Florence, Italy, April 05-10, pp. 1207–1216. ACM, New York (2008)
17. Kahneman, D.: Attention and Effort, p. 246. Prentice Hall, Englewood Cliffs (1973)
18. Neisser, U.: Selective Reading: A method for the study of visual attention. In: Nineteenth International Congress of Psychology, London (1969)
19. Roda, C., Thomas, J.: Attention aware systems: theory, application, and research agenda. Comp. Hum. Behav. 22(4), 557–587 (2006)

Smarter Healthcare: An Emergency Physician View of the Problem

Erin Yu[1], Ryan Kealey[1], Mark Chignell[1], Joanna Ng[2], and Jimmy Lo[2]

[1] Interactive Media Lab, Department of Mechanical and Industrial Engineering, University of Toronto
[2] IBM Centre for Advanced Studies
erin.yu@utoronto.ca, ryan.kealey@utoronto.ca, chignell@mie.utoronto.ca, jwng@ca.ibm.com, jimmylo@ca.ibm.com

Abstract. This chapter motivates the need for smarter interaction with a case study in healthcare that demonstrate the current state of interaction. The special challenges of practicing emergency medicine are reviewed, and a scenario is constructed to illustrate problems with current methods based on an observations study carried out at a hospital. A further scenario is then constructed showing how the problems that were observed may be avoided with smarter interaction. While the demonstrations of flawed interaction in this chapter only apply to emergency medicine, we believe that similar problems may be found in a broad range of domains.

Keywords: Healthcare; emergency rooms; flawed interaction; user interface design.

1 Introduction

This chapter begins with the observation that current emergency department (ED) technologies may not support the specific needs of ED physicians. Healthcare is mission-critical, real-time, and is a complex socio-technical system that requires consideration, communication, collaboration, and coordination. In this chapter we examine current interactions in Emergency Medicine and propose improvements based on the idea of smart interactions. The organization of this chapter is as follows. First there is an introduction to the characteristics of healthcare. This is followed by discussion of interaction in emergency medicine. The emergency medicine case study begins with a description of the methodologies used and why they were used. These methodologies are comprised of ethnography, contextual inquiry, and interviews. This description is followed by a summary of the results obtained. The results of the observations are categorized and presented. A current scenario of interaction is used to provide a holistic understanding of the observational data and the issues that are apparent in the ED. Smart interactions are proposed in order to address the issues determined from observation, and an idealized future scenario, demonstrating the value of the new style of interaction that is proposed. The chapter then concludes by discussing the overall properties of the interactions observed and the benefits that would accrue from improved forms of interaction.

M. Chignell et al. (Eds.): The Smart Internet, LNCS 6400, pp. 9–26, 2010

2 Healthcare Domain

Clinical work in hospitals exhibit many characteristics that make deployment of technology challenging yet highly beneficial. These characteristics highlight the unique qualities of healthcare work that demonstrate a need for a stronger understanding of the interactions that take place within healthcare environments. Our study attempted to determine what challenges these characteristics pose to the storing, managing and exchanging of information.

- *None-routine:* Emergencies, exceptions, and interruptions occur frequently in hospitals [1] which makes pre-scheduling of activities difficult. In the Emergency Department, patient volume, conditions, and arrival times vary greatly day to day, and the physicians are expected to adapt to the situation and process as many patients through the system as possible.
- *Mobile:* Physicians are constantly moving between patients, medical facilities, and other clinicians in order to enter or retrieve information. The nature of physicians' work is highly mobile, and "information is located where it's most used [2]. This demonstrates the need for accessing critical, time-sensitive information where it is needed most.
- *Context-driven:* Physicians are frequently switching from one patient to another, one device to another [4], and one software application to another. As a result, their activities are constantly paused and resumed, which requires constant readjustment and processing of contextual information.
- *Highly collaborative:* Multiple clinicians provide care for each patient [2, 3, 5]. Therefore information needs to be communicated between people in different roles, shifts, and location.
- *Multi-tasking:* Each clinician provides care for multiple patients in parallel. Physicians are expected to keep track of each patient's condition, progress, and location in their head.
- *Time-critical:* There is a need to complete certain tasks in a temporal sequence to process patients through the flow; in other words, tasks often need to be performed in certain order. Also, patients' conditions change with time which in turn affects the physician's work.
- *Information-rich:* Physicians are faced with constant need for interpreting rich data, as they deal with heavy information loads of various kinds that change with time. For example, in order to diagnose a patient with an abdominal pain, a physician is required to process blood test results, sonogram results, medical history, etc., In addition, their individual knowledge from previous experience often influences the decision making process.

These characteristics of clinical work illustrate the need for ubiquitous, context-aware, personalized technology; therefore, the healthcare domain is a fertile area for technological interventions. However further study is needed in order to determine how interactions play out in the emergency department and whether current systems and methods for communication sufficiently address the requirements of healthcare work.

3 Case Study: Data Collection and Analysis

A case study was conducted as the method of data collection to observe the overall workflow and communication practices at the Emergency Department at a large academic teaching hospital in Toronto. As part of the case study, contextual inquiries and semi-structured interviews were performed; subsequently, field notes and pictures were collected.

3.1 Data Collection: Observation

Emergency physicians were shadowed as they performed their work. Observations were made by two observers over two shifts, each of approximately six hours in duration. In the first shift one physician was shadowed while she worked with critical cases. In the second shift, the same physician was observed in a non-critical zone where the patients had minor injuries or sickness. During the second shift, one senior attending physician, one senior resident, and two medical students were shadowed.

During the observation period extensive notes were taken, with particular emphasis on process, communication practices, and critical incidents that occurred. Consistent with the requirements of the ethics protocol approved for this study, recordings were not made and no identifying information concerning patients was documented. Photos were taken of the work area in order to capture the type of information systems and the layout of the work area; however, patients did not appear in any of the pictures.

3.2 Data Collection: Interviews

The emergency physicians were interviewed after the completion of their shifts. Follow-up questions were asked based on examples of flawed interaction that were observed on their shift. In addition, open-ended questions were asked about problems that they experienced in using information systems to perform the tasks that they were concerned with. Thus our goal was to capture a broad range of examples of flawed interaction, relying not only on physician memory and accumulated experience, but also real-time observation of problems as they happened.

3.3 Data Collection: Interviews

We constructed a scenario from the data gathered in order to communicate the detailed aspects of the case, particularly the current workflow and context in the ED. The following scenario (scenario A) describes how the personas perform the tasks of diagnosing and treating multiple patients as their day progresses.

Scenario 1

It was a regular December day in Toronto. A fifth year (senior) resident Dr. Morgan was just starting his shift in the emergency department. The waiting room was full and there were patients aplenty. Dr. Morgan checks the patient management system to see the list of all patients in the Green zone, and assigns a hand-off patient from the previous resident to himself. Dr. Morgan then goes back to the screen with the list of patients and sorts the list by EP (responsible emergency physician) column to see who else is under his care. Mr. Singh, the hand-off patient, is a 77 year old male in room 26 with complaints of terrible chest pain. Dr. Morgan retorts to his attending Dr. Chow "well this one is a hand-off, you know how they are. I'll probably have to redo all the examinations myself!" The previous resident had ordered a CT scan, and Dr. Morgan was waiting for the results.

While waiting he goes to the patient to introduce himself and ask some of his own questions. After a brief interview with the patient, Dr. Morgan comes back to his work station to check the digital whiteboard to determine whether the CT result has come in. The green flag beside Mr. Singh's name indicates that the CT results came in over 10 minutes ago, but Dr. Morgan had not been notified of the new results. After checking the alert he logs into the separate imaging computer and pulls up the scan. After some inspection, Dr. Morgan cannot immediately determine the issue and goes to check the patient's chart and medical history for any clues. When he gets to the chart bins, he cannot find Mr. Singh's chart in the bin for room 26, even after considerable effort. After some exploration he eventually asks a passing nurse for that unit what had happened to the chart. She informs him that Mr. Singh had to be moved to room 14; sure enough the chart for this patient is found in bin 14. After finally locating and looking through the chart Dr. Morgan cannot determine the issue as the chart is incomplete and only has limited information. He decides to continue questioning Mr. Singh about specific details regarding the pain and his medical history. After speaking with the patient and gaining a bit more insight, such as the fact that Mr. Singh has a history of heart problems, Dr. Morgan is about to consult with his attending Dr. Chow when he is interrupted in his duties by an emergency page for him in the orange zone (ICU).

When he arrives he is informed of a young 20-year-old woman (Ms. Smith) who has come in complaining of very intense pain and whose heart rate had dropped well below safe levels (the reason for the emergency page). After a brief discussion with the patient, Dr. Morgan goes back to his desk to pull up any history for this patient from the database, but is interrupted by the friends of the patient. One of the friends is an oncologist and believes that the patient is suffering from colorectal cancer. After some more deliberation between the oncologist, Dr. Morgan and other physicians it is deemed that the patient should be directly admitted to oncology. Dr. Morgan resumes his duties in the blue zone of the emergency department. He finds Dr. Chow and proceeds to detail Mr. Singh's situation; his findings (the scans) and conclusions. Since it is a teaching hospital Dr. Chow has a few students under her wing; Dr. Morgan is her senior resident and she is also in charge of the two medical students (2nd and 3rd year respectively). Dr. Chow goes over the case with them and discusses her opinions on the matter. They pull up any information the hospital has and the 'trends' for this patient (how things have changed since his arrival and any previous trends he had) this leads to more than eight open windows on the computer screen and a messy chart board. Ultimately the group decides that based on previous charts, the patient's history of heart problems, the current level of pain and the patient's age that it would be better to be safe than sorry and refer Mr. Singh to general medicine. In order for Dr. Morgan to complete the referral he must get in touch with the GM senior resident. He calls the department in order to determine who the senior resident is and to try and locate that person. He leaves a message and waits for the call back to his mobile phone. When he does receive the call back (a little while later) he finds out that the senior resident for general medicine has been in the very next room just a few steps away from him. Dr. Morgan and the GM resident discuss the situation and after going over all the details Dr. Morgan hands the patient off to general medicine. He then continues with the scores of other patients waiting in the ED.

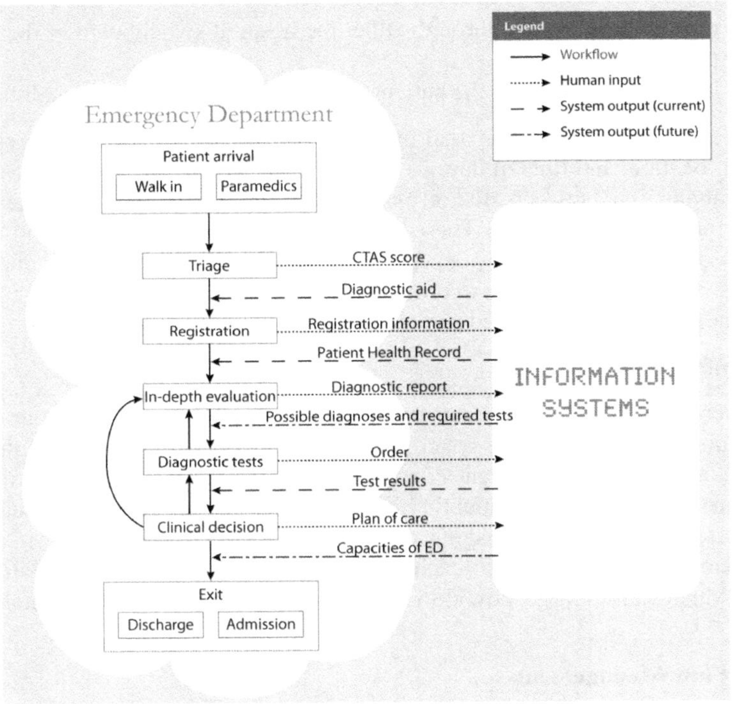

Fig. 1. Information Flow Summary

Figure 1 depicts the flow of information between the user and the information system used in the ED. In this figure both recording and retrieval of information are done manually, and can lead to large disruptions in physician workflow. As an example, even though the test results are output by the system, no indications are provided to alert the user therefore the physician must continually check the system.

3.4 Data Analysis: Categorical Aggregation

Affinity diagramming technique was used to aggregate, synthesize, and categorize the data. Raw notes taken during the observation and interviews were first interpreted and transcribed, then parsed into broad categories of issues, or "themes". Such categories included Communication, Use of Information Systems, Patient Flow Management,

Interruptions, Notification and Alerts. In addition, the affinity diagrams helped discover the relationships between the entities and systems observed.

Communication

We observed a number of barriers in regards to communication at the ED. To request a consultation, the physician went to through a number steps including:

- determining what the process is for that particular type of consultation,
- finding out who is on shift,
- finding the contact information,
- paging the specialist through either the hospital switchboard or the online paging system,
- leaving a message on the patient condition, and waiting for a call back.

The current system lacks contextual information around the user, such as staff schedule, their location, and time of day.

Communication between doctors and nurses are typically done face-to-face or through paper order forms. These manual forms of communication are well-established but limited in many aspects. The nurses are unaware of the doctor's other priorities, and therefore unable to provide needed information in a timely manner. The paper charts are often misplaced and are prone to illegibility and error.

Use of Information Systems

Issues were mainly due to the fact that the Emergency Department of our case study uses a number of independent systems to manage patient information in the ED. For example, an overview of patient conditions and statuses is provided in the (patient management system); each patient's historical health records and lab results are kept in a different system; their imaging test results are stored in yet another. The physicians were required to log into each of these systems to gather information on one patient, which caused large slow-downs in efficiency not to mention mental strain and fatigue.

Patient Flow Management

One large area of concern that we observed was in regards to the flow of patients and the management of these patients in the ED. There is very little support for determining the status of each patient and their position in the sequence. Some questions that may arise as a physician manages the ED include: how many patients are in each zone? How many in the waiting room? How many empty beds are available? How many patients are in a bed but have been referred to other services? Who is waiting for what test result? Who can/should be processed next? The issue is that entry time, consultation times, departure time and length of stay (LOS) are not currently tracked; thus these questions remain largely unanswered. Understanding the impacts their tasks have on the overall patient flow would aid the physicians in making better judgment calls on what tasks or patients to take on next.

Notifications & Alerts

We observed that notifications on abrupt patient condition change or arrival of new patient were delivered by a nurse in person or through a page. For new information on patients under their care, the physicians were continually checking the systems to see whether new information has arrived. In the patient management system, there were indicators for new lab or radiology results; however these were of little help, because the system was not aware of who the current user is and was not able to suggest whether or not the new information is actually 'new' to the user.

Interruptions

We also observed that the physicians experience constant interruptions, each of which required a decision to select a task to attend to immediately. Examples of interruptions include page calls, phone calls, consult requests, patients demanding prompt care, arrival of sicker patients, and test results. The doctors are required to manage these interruptions and multiple tasks in their head, which is a burden on their working memory and is prone to human error.

3.5 Verification of Data

Once the current issues were identified, Scenario B was constructed to show the use of Smarter Interaction methods in the context of the ED.

A one-hour "Friday morning rounds" meeting was set up with 15 or so ED physicians at the hospital, to present the summarized data and the derived scenarios for feedback and validation. This meeting functioned as an ad-hoc focus group with the participants providing a considerable amount of feedback and advice.

We presented and discussed our thematic analysis and scenarios in order to better understand the physician viewpoint and to determine what barriers existed (if any) to deployment of technologies designed to solve the observed issues. The physicians were enthusiastic and excited about the deployment of mobile technology; however they were skeptical about the integration of the systems as it had been attempted in the past without success. After determining the requirements for the system it was time to plot the path toward a solution.

4 Impediments of Current System

The emergency department is a unique work environment and in order to properly support the currently flawed interactions that were observed, we must improve aspects of the work through technological interventions. The recurring issues that we found seem to echo the problems identified in the preceding introduction to Part 1 of this book. In that paper the authors describe the problems in the current iteration of the internet and the need to move to a smarter internet. The shortcomings of the current internet which are also relevant to information technology in emergency medicine are:

- A lack of integration from the user's perspective
- A lack of individualization & context-awareness
- Lack of server-initiated connections
- Lack of service-level collaboration
- Limited user control

We found that aspects of our problem categories mimic the issues in the current iteration of the internet and thus fit well into this need for smarter systems. Consequently we propose a solution that naturally parallels the concept of the smart internet, as introduced in Chapter 3 of this book. If we can make the interactions smarter, the workplace can support the clinicians and provide better care for patients. In order to reach this goal, however, we must identify how our observations are linked to the identified impediments to smart internet described previously in the introduction to Part 1. The following sections delve deeper into each specific impediment of the current internet relating it both to the literature and to specific issues that were observed in our case study.

4.1 Lack of Integration from the User's Perspective

An emergency department is a dynamic working environment, continually shifting resources to meet the changing needs of the patient. As such it is important to have systems in place that allow for quick access to information from areas within and outside the ED [6]. In 1998 an Emergency Medicine workgroup identified that the integration of information systems in healthcare is one of 4 major strategies that needed to be implemented to bring medicine into the future [7] and in 2004, another workgroup reiterated this same need for integration in emergency medicine [8]. Also the Institute of Medicine's 1999 report indicates that many medical errors can be linked to incomplete or incorrect information, especially those dealing with drug dosages, interactions, and patient histories, and that the situation can be improved by better information systems that "make drug and patient information readily accessible at the time it is needed" [9]. It is important to overcome the "fragmentation of information" by integrating systems to provide more complete and correct data to allow physicians to make better, more informed decisions [10], [11] ,[12]. Cook & Woods [13] found that when the physicians must constantly shift their attention (due to distraction and interruptions) and mentally integrate data from disparate sources, they may not form a "complete and coherent mental picture of the current state of the system" (as cited in [14], p.417). Therefore it is important that systems be designed to support, and not interrupt or distract the workflow of the clinician, through integration of information from disparate sources.

In our observations we found a lack of integration in the emergency department systems. Over 8 independent systems are used daily in the ED: an electronic whiteboard for patient management, a medical imaging system, a web-based internal portal, a drug distribution system, a discharge preparation system, and electronic medical records. Each system requires a separate log-in and the systems do not communicate with one another. In Scenario 1, the disconnect between the systems is apparent when Dr. Morgan attempts to piece together Mr. Singh's ailment; the information regarding one patient is spread across multiple systems requiring multiple log-ins. This translates to increased time dedicated to simply getting onto the systems and finding the appropriate information. Something as simple as 'log-ins' can "shift the focus" of the clinician and interrupt an otherwise quick and simple process, not to mention the fact that one must remember the username and password for each system, which can cause unnecessary cognitive burden on the user [15]. The lack of integration also means that

Fig. 2. Disparate information systems accessed through multiple workstations

information is not kept together and that doctors must check multiple systems to find patient history, order lab/imaging tests, and check imaging scans (observational data). When information is disparate and disconnected, it burdens users by requiring them to organize and aggregate the information themselves instead of providing processed information. Observational and interview data demonstrate the frustration users felt when interacting with the ED systems (see Table 1). The current lack of system integration creates pain points in the physicians' workflow, increases their cognitive burden, and increases the time to complete vital tasks.

4.2 Lack of Individualization and Context Awareness

Current ED systems have not been designed properly for the unique nature of work in the emergency department and the needs of the physicians who work there and sometimes this can lead to errors in order entry and documentation causing orders on the wrong patient, medication mix-ups and more [16]. Previous studies have found that failing to meet user needs in the medical domain can lead to unwanted consequences such as wasted time & poor quality of care [17],[18], and medication errors [19]. How can we provide better support? For one thing, we can implement systems that have an awareness of the users and their context. Kjeldskov & Skov [20] define context-aware computing as "an application's ability to adapt to changing circumstances and respond according to the context of use" (as cited in [21], p.5). Context in the emergency department will therefore include aspects of scheduling, patient lists, patient histories, departmental procedures, personnel, etc. that are associated & linked with the current user. A context-aware application will have the ability to interpret these contextual variables and adapt behaviour to better suit the situation [21]. If the application can present contextually sensitive information in a way that is consistent with the user mental models and their preferences for information display then this has the potential to reduce cognitive load and improve clinical performance [22], (as cited in [14], p.418).

The system in the ED that we observed has neither an awareness of the users who are interacting with it, nor what their current needs are; therefore, it fails to provide individualized support. For example, the electronic whiteboard application is accessed by all ED physicians on shared workstations using a common login (Dr. Jacques Lee, personal communication, 2009). Therefore the system has no way of presenting relevant information specifically for the current user. Scenario 1 mentions the EDIS interface that is shared amongst all ED physicians. This screen displays one long list of all physicians who are in the ED and the waiting area without the support for viewing an individualized list for a particular user. If systems can implement contextual support, it can help reduce the cognitive burden placed on physicians with personalized order sets for specific conditions and reduce search time by more effectively organizing and preparing information based on which patients are currently being taken care of [23], [18]. In the Smart Internet the system should provide the right information to the right individual at the right time, using its awareness of users, their context, and their goals.

4.3 Absence of Server-Initiated Connections

Work in the Emergency Department is very mobile, in many EDs doctors comment that much of their work happens on the go, moving from one area to the next [24]. Furthermore, this type of work is fast-paced, non-routine, time-critical and highly uncertain [25],[1]. Thus there is a desire amongst clinicians for systems that provide timely and 'mission-critical' information "on the go" (Dr., Mike Feldman, personal communication, 2009; [26]). A lack of relevant information at point of care is a major cause of medical error [9], [27],[28],[29] and so providing this information is important for patient safety and for clinical performance.

In their review of the literature on handheld computing applications in healthcare, Lu, Xiao, Sears & Jacko [30] found that when up-to-date information is provided to the clinician via handheld applications, it can aid clinicians in their ability to make better educated decisions regarding patient illness at the point of care. Therefore it is imperative that we develop technologies that allow for server-initiated connections; such that information can be pushed to users instead of the user having to pull it from the system, freeing up valuable time & cognitive resources [31], [32]. Freeing up cognitive resources can have a strong effect on clinical performance since much of the current workflow of emergency department clinicians is subject to many interruptions [33],[34]. This, coupled with the multitasking nature of the ED can lead to errors through the disruption of memory processes [33]. Emergency department clinicians are already burdened with increased cognitive load simply due to the nature of their work [23], thus anything that can be done to either reduce cognitive load or keep from adding more will have beneficial results. If the system is aware of the users who interact with it, their current matter of concern, and their current situation (context), then the system would also be able to initiate tasks on behalf of the user (such as providing timely notifications) to alleviate prospective memory issues and to save the clinician time by reducing the need to keep checking the 'inbox'. Server-initiated connections can also aid in the completion of lengthy administrative procedures that have to be completed in order to accomplish certain goals (ordering tests, consultations, discharging, etc):

> *We have different processes for ordering different tests. I have to remember what the process is and who to speak to depending on the time of day. It would be nice if it told me it's before 4, so you need to speak to X (Dr. Jacques Lee, personal communication, Dec. 4, 2009).*

Fig. 3. Order box for manual test orders

These processes are time consuming to complete and a cognitive burden to keep in memory. The proposed ED system is able to initiate tasks, track progress, and aid in their completion without the user having to direct every action. Currently in the ED the user-system interaction only occurs when the physician actively seeks information using the system, typically at the workstation (e.g. manually checking for lab/imaging results). This is especially frustrating for physicians, because the system requires them to frequently visit a fixed desktop workstation to check for updates, interrupting their workflow and taking them away from patients (study observations). Feedback from users suggests that deployment of mobile notifications is desired (Dr. Jacques Lee, personal communication); Dr. Mike Feldman, personal communication). The envisaged system would not only have knowledge of the users, their schedules, patients under their care, and their progress but also provide timely notifications to users on the go, making server requests on their behalf.

4.4 Lack of Any Notion of Service Level Collaboration

The clinical environment is a frenzy of communication patterns that can challenge the cognitive systems of the users to exhaustion. This is mainly due to the fact that medical work, especially in an ED is highly collaborative [33],[34],[35]. The treatment of any one patient is distributed across multiple 'team' members including physicians, nurses, technicians, and clerks and all of these individual members need to communication and collaborate, often in different locations within the hospital [24],[36]. There seems to be a preference among physicians for synchronous communication (face to face, phone) over asynchronous (messages, pages, whiteboards), and of the synchronous events the majority that occurred were face-to-face with a small percentage on the phone [36],[35]. This preference for synchronous communication was replicated in the data we collected, with physicians indicating that there is no substitute for synchronous communication for certain procedures (consults, hand offs). Due to this we determined that trying to replace a synchronous communication instance with asynchronous would be met with strong resistance from the users; however we felt that a significant improvement can be made to asynchronous communication instances.

Many of these communication procedures and events are different depending on the departments involved; consultation practice specifically, varies widely between departments within hospitals, plus informal, convenience-based "curbside" consultations are common [37]. We found evidence that ED physicians require access to communication structures that aid their ability to perform consultations and collaborative events their duties can reduce cognitive burdens. There is a need for communication structures that can effectively support service-level collaboration such as consultations. Consultations represent an integral communication event since they are explicitly linked to patient care; in that most consultations represent discussion of a particular case either during shift or between shifts [23].

The system should support collaboration, allowing for multiple users to share a 'matter of concern' such as 'diagnosis of patient A' or 'interpretation of lab results for patient A'. In the hospital that we observed the current system does not allow for these kinds of collaborations instead they occur through multiple modalities (e.g. the user must first determine who the responsible and available resident is, then they must page said resident and leave a message for call back about the case, they wait for the callback and eventual get to speak to the resident on the phone discussing the case). A new system could support and initiate these collaborations by aiding in the process of determining who to call and how to call them. The users should only have to indicate that they would like a surgery consult and the system should then do the rest.

4.5 Lack of User Control

Currently physicians have no control over when and how they are reached, what information is displayed in the interface, and how it is displayed. The emergency department is a unique, fast-paced, dynamic working environment and anything but predictable. ED physicians work in a "complex and highly pressured system" and in order to successfully perform their job they need adequate personalizable support [36]. ED physicians are unique people; different types of physicians have different needs and preferences for things like evidence-based resources and handheld devices [38]. Also in implementing any kind of new system in the ED, one must realize that physician adoption is slow; physicians will resist anything that impedes or fails to enhance their job [39].

Studies by Hu and colleagues [40], [41],[42] have also shown that physician adoption can be linked to "their specialized training, autonomous practice and professional work arrangements" (as cited in, [43], p.206). Therefore it is important to design with efficiency in mind as well as the unique needs and pressures of the emergency department clinician. Studies on mobile computing have shown that doctors who do use handheld computers in clinical practice report diverse patterns of use; a one-size fits all approach to design would not be sufficient [26].

Finally research in medical expertise and decision-making have shown that physicians of differing levels of experience may have different levels of decision support needs due to changing memory & decision-making processes; these requirements and user needs would not be addressed in 'one-size fits all' decision support system [44],[45],[46]. Additionally ED physicians are obviously very busy people who try to maximize their time with patients; however they also have to deal with many interruptions (between one every 8.5 minutes to every 10 minutes) regarding items of various levels of criticality [34]. Unfortunately there is often little context to support the reason for the interruption leading to increased uncertainty as to the nature of the interruption. This can have profound effects on physician's workflow; a physician may leave important duties to attend to pages that could have been deferred until a later time [47].

Currently users have little ability to control how they interact with the systems; for example when and how notifications on new test results are received, how the user sees the list of patients under their care, and what device is used to request consultation. Each physician has slightly different preferences and work practices, and these differences need to be accounted for in a smarter interaction system. In addition to these personal preferences, clinical workflows also factor into the usefulness of alerts. The importance of test results often depends on other test results (i.e. some are for primary diagnosis, others for secondary diagnosis - if the result for the primary comes back with a specific result then the secondary tests would become more critical, however first the primary test results would need to be consulted). It is thus important to consider that different physicians may have different user preferences and desire different levels of control; furthermore, one physician's preference may vary depending on the situation. If we allow a measure of control, a way for users to denote how, when, and in what contexts they are notified we may be able to provide them with a system that is tailored to their individual needs and personalized clinical workflow.

5 Case Study: Scenario

Another scenario was created to illustrate the potential application of Smart Internet in the ED. This scenario was used as a basis for creating a storyboard depicting a sequence of events that the user and the system go through to achieve a task [48]. Visual representations of the personas (physicians), environment (the ED), and the system interfaces were created.

The storyboard was presented to the ED physicians to communicate our vision for Smart Internet and garner feedback. It triggered an active discussion concerning 1) whether the context illustrated in the scenario was correct or not, 2) whether the components of the proposed system would be feasible and useful, and 3) whether the technology discussed has been studied or implemented elsewhere.

Scenario 2

Dr. Morgan checks his mobile device in his commute to the hospital to see the list of patients who are currently being treated in the Green zone, where his shift is in. Via secure connection, he reads up on each of the patients' triage reports and medical records. By the time he gets into the hospital, he is aware of the statuses of the hand-off patients'. He meets with Dr. McPhee, who was in charge of the Green zone in the previous shift, to briefly discuss each patient under his care. Dr. Morgan then proceeds to Room 26 to meet Mr. Singh, one of the hand-off patients. As Dr. Morgan walks into the room, the system recognizes that he is at Mr. Singh's bedside and brings up Mr. Singh's medical record on the mobile device. From the record, he learns that the patient has a history of heart conditions and that a CT scan has been ordered by Dr. McPhee. Moments later, the screen refreshes to indicate Mr. Singh's CT scan result is back. After reading the summary report on his mobile device, Dr. Morgan walks back to the workstation to examine the images. No apparent abnormality is observed. Dr. Morgan puts in a request for Dr. Chow to review Mr. Singh's CT scans at her convenience.

Dr. Morgan is interrupted by an emergency page for him in the Orange zone (ICU) through his mobile device. As he walks over, he is able to bring up the patient record and get a brief background on the case. By the time he arrives at the patient's room, he is informed that the patient is a 20 years old female with a very low heart rate, complaining of very intense pain in the lower abdomen. Dr. Morgan examines the patient and orders ultrasound and CT scans from a checklist on his mobile device. Two friends of the patient, one of whom is an oncologist at the hospital, approach Dr. Morgan. The oncologist believes that Ms. Smith is suffering from colorectal cancer. Following some deliberation with the oncologist, Dr. Morgan decides to transfer Ms. Smith directly to oncology. When Dr. Morgan indicates that this transfer is desired on his mobile phone, the system finds an oncology resident on shift and makes a call. Dr. Morgan describes the case and the need for a direct admission to oncology. The occurrence of this consultation gets automatically noted in Ms. Smith's record.

Dr. Morgan goes back to the Green zone and resumes his duties. He finds Dr. Chow and proceeds to detail the situation with Mr. Singh, particularly regarding the unremarkable scans. Dr. Chow sits with Dr. Morgan at the computer and pulls up the historical trends for this patient via a quick link from the patient record. After discussion, the physicians decide that Mr. Singh needs to be referred to general medicine. With a few clicks on his mobile device, Dr. Morgan is able to locate and call an available GM resident directly. Dr. Morgan and the GM resident discuss Mr. Singh's case over the phone; this call is also logged as part of Mr. Singh's patient record for housekeeping purposes. Dr. Morgan opens the updated list of tests queue to see which lab and imaging results are back, then he quickly checks the list of patients in the Green zone on his mobile phone to decide which patient needs his attention next.

The previous scenario 2 describes a proposal for a smarter emergency department including context-aware applications and push notifications. This new system is an ideal future, and similar to the ideal vision of the smart internet, in order for this reality to fully take form, work needs to be done on new technological interventions that can support the clinician tasks and all the requirements that were identified in our observations.

6 Conclusion

While one can imagine many important applications for applying smarter interactions in medicine, we believe that it is necessary to make detailed observations in hospitals to identify clear requirements and opportunities for developing how healthcare applications and software systems. This study exemplifies this approach with a detailed requirements gathering effort followed by technology development to support new applications that address the requirements.

Requirements analysis was carried out based on ethnographic observation. In this study we looked at the current situation in the Emergency Department of a large scale academic teaching hospital in Toronto, Canada. We used contextual inquiry to collect data; we followed an ED physician, 1 senior resident, 2 medical students and one registration clerk in 2 separate 6 hour observations.

In contextual inquiry questions are posed during the observation to the participants in order to obtain more context for their actions and to build a much more representative understanding of the situation. We also held two semi-structured interviews to provide further insight as to the nature of problems in the ED. The data gathered were summarized into relevant major categories using Affinity Diagramming. The current problems we observed fell into 5 major categories: communications, integration, notifications, patient tracking, and individualization. From these categories we developed scenarios to inform the design process by holistically describe the problem areas, use cases, and workflow in the ED.

A future scenario was developed to illustrate the improvements we hope will flow from a Smart Internet approach that can aid clinicians in performing their duties, in order to decrease wait time and increase patient safety in the ED. The scenarios, problems identified, along with potential solutions, were presented to a group of Emergency Physicians in a focus group to validate our findings and gather their feedback. Future work includes iterations of design, development, and evaluation of varying levels of prototypes to support the scenarios.

7 Limitations

The authors recognize that while a qualitative approach was appropriate for this study, it did lead to some limitations. Since this was a voluntary participation study, and only a few physicians were available for observation, our ability to generalize to the larger population is diminished. Also since the study was undertaken at only one location the findings should not be generalized to other cases (other hospitals). The format of the focus group, which included a presentation then a group discussion, while facilitating feedback through peer interaction, may have stifled responses from individuals who were less outgoing or may have discouraged those with different perspectives from speaking up.

Acknowledgements

We would like to thank Drs. Ivy Cheng, Mike Feldman, and Jaques Lee for sharing their knowledge of emergency medicine with us. This research was supported by an IBM CAS Fellowship held by Erin Yu and by an IBM Faculty Award provided to Mark Chignell, and by funding from NSERC.

References

1. Xiao, Y.: Artifacts and Collaborative Work in Healthcare: Methodological, Theoretical, and Technological Implications of the Tangible. Journal of Biomedical Informatics 38(1), 26–33 (2005)
2. Bardram, J.E., Bossen, C.: Mobility Work: The Spatial Dimension of Collaboration at a Hospital. In: CSCW (2005)
3. Activity-based Computing, http://www.activity-based-computing.org/
4. Muñoz, M.A., Rodríguez, M., Favela, J., Martinez-Garcia, A.I., González, V.M.: Context-Aware Mobile Communication in Hospitals. IEEE Xplore, 38–46 (2003)
5. Bossen, C.: The Parameters of Common Information Spaces: the Heterogeneity of Cooperative Work at a Hospital Ward. In: CSCW (2002)
6. Aronsky, D., Jones, I., Lanaghan, K., Slovis, C.M.: Supporting Patient Care in the Emergency Department with a Computerized Whiteboard System. Journal of the American Medical Informatics Association 15(2), 184–194 (2008)
7. Cordell, W.H., Overhage, J.M., Waeckerle, J.F.: For the Information Management Work Group, Strategies for improving information management in emergency medicine to meet clinical, research, and administrative needs. Ann. Emerg. Med. 31, 172–178 (1998)
8. Barthell, E.N., Coonan, K., Finnell, J., Pollock, D., Cochrane, D.: Disparate systems, disparate data: integration, interfaces, and standards in emergency medicine information technology. Acad. Emerg. Med. 11, 1142–1148 (2004)
9. Kohn, L.T., Corrigan, J.M., Donaldson, M.S.: To Err Is Human: Building a Safer Health Care System. National Academy Press, Washington (1999)
10. Coonan, K.M.: Medical informatics standards applicable to emergency department information systems: making sense of the jumble. Academic Emergency Medicine 11(11), 1198–1205 (2004)
11. Feied, C.F., Handler, J.A., Smith, M.S., Gillam, M., Kanhouwa, M., Rothenhaus, T., Conover, K., Shannon, T.: Clinical information systems: instant ubiquitous clinical data for error reduction and improved clinical outcomes. Academic Emergency Medicine 11(11), 1162–1169 (2004)
12. Stead, W.: Rethinking electronic health records to better achieve quality and safety goals. Annual Review of Medicine 58, 35–47 (2007)
13. Cook, R.I., Woods, D.D.: Operating at the 'sharp end': the complexity of human error. In: Bogner, S. (ed.) Human error in medicine, pp. 255–310. Erlbaum, Mahwah (1994)
14. Patel, V.L., Zhang, J., Yoskowitz, N.A., Green, R., Sayan, O.R.: Translational cognition for decision support in critical care environments: a review. Journal of Biomedical Informatics 41(3), 413–431 (2008)
15. Bardram, J.E.: Hospitals of the future–ubiquitous computing support for medical work in hospitals. In: Proceedings of UbiHealth 2003 the 2nd International Workshop on Ubiquitous Computing for Pervasive Healthcare Applications (2003)

16. Ash, J.S., Berg, M., Coiera, E.: Some unintended consequences of information technology in health care: the nature of patient care information system-related errors. Journal of the American Medical Informatics Association 11(2), 104–112 (2004)
17. Holzman, T.G., Griffith, A., Hunter, W.G., Allen, T., Simpson Jr, R.J.: Computer-Assisted trauma care prototype. Medinfo 8(2), 1685 (1995)
18. Little, B., Johnson, D., Tingle, J., Stanfill, M., Roy, M.: Project NEED: New Efficiency in an Emergency Department in Transforming Health Care Through Information: Case Studies. In: Einbinder, L., Lorenzi, N.M., Ash, J.S., Gadd, C.S. (eds.) , New York, pp. 167–177 (2010)
19. Kushniruk, A.W., Triola, M.M., Borycki, E.M., Stein, B., Kannry, J.L.: Technology induced error and usability: the relationship between usability problems and prescription errors when using a handheld application. International Journal of Medical Informatics 74(7-8), 519–526 (2005)
20. Kjeldskov, J., Skov, M.: Supporting work activities in healthcare by mobile electronic patient records. In: Masoodian, M., Jones, S., Rogers, B. (eds.) APCHI 2004. LNCS, vol. 3101, pp. 191–200. Springer, Heidelberg (2004)
21. Bricon-Souf, N., Newman, C.R.: Context awareness in health care: A review. International Journal of Medical Informatics 76(1), 2–12 (2007)
22. Wachter, S.B., Agutter, J., Syroid, N., Drew, F., Weinger, M.B., Westenskow, D.: The employment of an iterative design process to develop a pulmonary graphical display. J. Am. Med. Inform. Assoc. 10, 363–372 (2003)
23. Laxmisan, A., Hakimzada, F., Sayan, O.R., Green, R.A., Zhang, J., Patel, V.L.: The multitasking clinician: decision-making and cognitive demand during and after team handoffs in emergency care. International Journal of Medical Informatics 76(11-12), 801–811 (2007)
24. Bardram, J.E., Christensen, H.B.: Pervasive computing support for hospitals: An overview of the activity-based computing project. IEEE Pervasive Computing, 44–51 (2007)
25. Laskowski, M., McLeod, R.D., Friesen, M.R., Podaima, B.W., Alfa, A.S.: Models of Emergency Departments for Reducing Patient Waiting Times. PLoS One 4(7) (2009)
26. McAlearney, A.S., Schweikhart, S.B., Medow, M.A.: Doctors' experience with handheld computers in clinical practice: qualitative study. British Medical Journal 328(7449), 1162 (2004)
27. Leape, L.L.: The preventability of medical injury. Human Error in Medicine, 13–25 (1994)
28. Leape, L.L., Bates, D.W., Cullen, D.J., Cooper, J., Demonaco, H.J., Gallivan, T., Hallisey, R., et al.: Systems analysis of adverse drug events. Journal of the American Medical Association 274(1), 35 (1995)
29. Lottridge, D.: Emotional response as a measure of human performance. In: CHI 2008 Extended Abstracts on Human Factors in Computing Systems, pp. 2617–2620 (2008)
30. Lu, Y.C., Xiao, Y., Sears, A., Jacko, J.A.: A review and a framework of handheld computer adoption in healthcare. International Journal of Medical Informatics 74(5), 409–422 (2005)
31. Leman, P., Guthrie, D., Simpson, R., Little, F.: Improving access to diagnostics: an evaluation of a satellite laboratory service in the emergency department. Emergency Medicine Journal 21(4), 452 (2004)
32. Kilpatrick, E.S., Holding, S.: Use of computer terminals on wards to access emergency test results: a retrospective audit. British Medical Journal 322(7294), 1101 (2001)
33. Coeira, E., Jayasuria, R.A., Hardy, J., Bannan, A., Thorpe, M.E.: Communication loads on clinical staff in the emergency department. MJA 176(9), 415–418 (2002)
34. Fairbanks, R.J., Bisantz, A.M., Sunm, M.: Emergency department communication links and patterns. Annals of Emergency Medicine 50(4), 396–406 (2007)

35. Woloshynowych, M., Davis, R., Brown, R., Vincent, C.: Communication patterns in a UK emergency department. Annals of Emergency Medicine 50(4), 407–413 (2007)
36. Spencer, R., Logan, P., Coiera, E.: Socio-technical Factors Surrounding Practices Related to Telephone, Paging and Information System Use in an Emergency Department. In: Coiera, E., Chu, S., Simpson, C. (eds.) Health Informatics Society of Australia (HISA), Royal Australian College of General Practitioners, RACGP (2003) (combined conference) (August 2003)
37. Schuur, J., Moreau, J., Bohan, J., Fauchet, G., Lobon, L., Lyn, E., Nathanson, L., Stack, A., Temin, E., Tibbles, C.: 16: Emergency Department Consultation Practices and Documentation Vary Widely Across Hospitals. Annals of Emergency Medicine 54(3-1) (2009)
38. Lottridge, D., Chignell, M., Danicic-Mizdrak, R., Pavlovic, N.J., Kushniruk, A., Straus, S.E.: Group differences in physician responses to handheld presentation of clinical evidence: a verbal protocol analysis. BMC Medical Informatics and Decision Making 7(1), 22 (2007)
39. Lowenhaupt, M.: Justify before You Buy. Healthcare Informatics 21, 36–37 (2004)
40. Hu, P.J., Chau, P.Y.K., Sheng, O.R.: Adoption of telemedicine technology by health care organizations: an exploratory study. Journal of Organizational Computing and Electronic Commerce 12(3) (2002)
41. Hu, P.J., Chau, P.Y.K., Sheng, O.R., Tam, K.Y.: Examining the technology acceptance model using physician acceptance of telemedicine technology. Journal of Management Information Systems 16(2), 91–112 (1999)
42. Sheng, O.R., Hu, P.J., Wei, C.P., Higa, K., Au, G.: Adoption and diffusion of telemedicine technology in health care organizations: a comparative case study in Hong Kong. Journal of Organizational Computing and Electronic Commerce 8(4), 247–275 (1998)
43. Walter, Z., Lopez, M.S.: Physician acceptance of information technologies: Role of perceived threat to professional autonomy. Decision Support Systems 46(1), 206–215 (2008)
44. Norman, G.R., Brooks, L.R.: The non-analytical basis of clinical reasoning. Advances in Health Sciences Education 2(2), 173–184 (1997)
45. Norman, G.R., Young, M., Brooks, L.R.: Non-analytical models of clinical reasoning: the role of experience. Medical Education 41(12), 1140–1145 (2007)
46. Young, M., Brooks, L.R., Norman, G.R.: Found in translation: the impact of familiar symptom descriptions on diagnosis in novices. Medical Education 41(12), 1146–1151 (2007)
47. Friedman, S.M., Elinson, R., Arenovich, T.A.: A study of emergency physician work and communication: a human factors approach. Israeli J. Emerg. Med. 5, 35–42 (2005)
48. Preece, J., Rogers, Y., Sharp, H.: Interaction Design: Beyond Human Computer Interaction. John Wiley & Sons, New York (2002)

The Smart Internet as a Catalyst for Health Care Reform

Jens H. Weber-Jahnke[1] and James Williams[2]

[1] Department of Computer Science, University of Victoria
jens@acm.org
[2] Ontario Telemedicine Network
jamesbw@uvic.ca

Abstract. Health care systems around the world are under pressure to lower costs and improve outcomes. Over the last decade, the Internet has begun to impact the traditional consumer-provider relationship in the health care sector. Patients are now commonly known to search the Internet for information and services relevant to their condition in addition to consulting with their providers. The Smart Internet has been envisioned as a major step in evolving the Internet into a more user-centric, pro-active and intelligent medium. In this chapter, we discuss the opportunities of Smart Internet technologies in context of health care applications. We characterize the current state of Internet-based health applications and summarize important challenges to be addressed in order to be able to use the Smart Internet for reforming health care systems.

Keywords: Smart Internet, health care, consumer health informatics, medicine 2.0, eHealth.

1 Introduction

Health care systems around the world are in desperate need of reform, facing rapidly increasing service costs and aging patient demographics. In order to improve the sustainability of their health care systems, many jurisdictions have invested significant resources in the implementation of Information and Communication Technologies (ICTs) in support of health care. Such so-called *eHealth* technologies include electronic health records, clinical decision support systems, and tele-medicine applications.

Although there are many benefits to the use of ICTs in a health care setting, many experts believe that long-term sustainable health care reform requires a paradigm shift more fundamental than simply migrating paper-based health data to a computer-supported information systems. They postulate that patient empowerment is a pivotal factor for success. Traditional approaches to health care delivery have involved asymmetries of power and information, relegating patients to a mostly passive role. Caregivers have not only exercised control over the nature and frequency of treatments, but they have also acted as the primary source of knowledge.

From an abstract vantage point, the shift in health care towards patient empowerment has been foreshadowed by changing service models in other industries. For example, the situation in health care can be compared with the telecommunication industry before the introduction of direct dialing technology, or with the financial

M. Chignell et al. (Eds.): The Smart Internet, LNCS 6400, pp. 27–48, 2010

industry prior to the adoption of automated teller machines (ATMs) and Internet banking. In both cases, new technologies have acted as catalysts for reforming industries that were expected to become unsustainable in the future. Furthermore, these technologies were explicitly intended to afford users the means to manage interactions directly, thereby eliminating asymmetries of information.

Analogously, there is evidence indicating that Smart Internet technology may act as a catalyst for sustainable reform of the health care industry, by empowering patients to become active and equal partners in matters of their health. While the first generation of Internet-based health services consisted of health portals that catalogue information, a new breed of smart applications has reached the market, utlizing this information in context of concrete health services. "Healthcare 2.0" has been defined as the use of social software and its ability to promote collaboration between patients, caregivers and medical professionals. In this chapter, we describe how the emerging vision of the Smart Internet applies to the health care industry, including its unique opportunities, current solutions and future challenges. Due to the sensitive nature of health care, we will also emphasis issues pertaining to information security and privacy, as well as governance.

2 ICT and Our Health Care Systems Today

Health care is an information-intensive domain, involving a diverse set of collaborating service providers who need to access and exchange patient-related data. Many of the inefficiencies and cost overruns experienced in health care systems around the globe today are associated with a lack of access to relevant information. Common examples of inefficiencies include: unnecessary duplication of laboratory work; cancellation of scheduled treatments (e.g., surgery) because of missing data or prerequisites; prescription of unnecessary or adverse drugs; low adherence to preventative care guidelines, because the data is not available to generate alerts and reminders; erroneous prioritization in waiting lists due to missing data; adverse events because of missing counter-indications.

While ICT has played an important role in supporting financial and administrative ("outside") functions for the health care industry, these technologies have only recently been introduced to support "inside" functions at the point of care. A recent survey of the US Centre for Disease Control found that less than half of physicians are using some form of electronic medical record (EMR) in 2009 (43.9%). With 20.5% using EMRs with basic functionality and only 6.3% using a fully functional EMR [1]. Similar numbers are reported from Canada [2], while other industrialized nations such as Australia, Denmark and the UK have significantly higher adoption rates (78%-98%). Even in jurisdictions with high EMR adoption, systems are often used as data silos, and data exchange over the Internet is lacking [3].

One of the major obstacles to Internet-based data exchange has been the difficulty in defining shared health information interoperability standards, as well as the inertia involved in marshalling political support to adopt cross-jurisdictional interoperability infrastructures. Although investments in eHealth initiatives are growing, the benefits to patient outcomes are not always apparent, if not clearly in doubt [4]. An increasing number of industry observers are advocating that eHealth initiatives shift to become more consumer (patient) oriented. Some of these commentators have noted how Internet services are profoundly changing evidence-based health care and contributing to patient empowerment [5]. Neftel points to several recent studies showing that patients are increasingly using the Internet as a tool for diagnosis, medical decision support, preventative care and chronic disease management [6]. Siempos et al. have shown that laypersons may reach correct diagnoses by using general Internet tools such as Google [7], and Tang and Ng demonstrated that even professional physicians can significantly improve their decision-making by using such services [8].

The Internet makes high-quality health care information accessible to patients and care providers in an unprecedented way. However, it also contains a vast and rapidly increasing amount of extraneous information. Using the Internet in the absence of smart methods to customize the right information for a particular context has been compared to drinking from a fire hydrant [5]. Alternatively, coming from the medical domain, Neftel compares the current Internet with an individual who manifests the savant syndrome – a condition that combines a narrow area of expertise or brilliance in otherwise intellectually limited and often autistic persons [6]. He states that "*the savant syndrome of the Internet presents both doctors and patients with the same problem, namely inflationary dilution by infinite abundance*" and concludes that medical expertise will continue to be needed to address this problem. Smart Internet technologies enable us to codify and automate some of this expertise and, thus, provide more effective uses of the Internet for health care services.

3 Smart Internet Technologies

Like the term Internet, the Smart Internet lacks a succinct, intensional definition. Instead, it is typically defined extensionally, by describing properties and examples of its services and components. In addition to its emphasis on task completion, [9] a defining property of the Smart Internet is its user-centered focus and its awareness of the context in which it is used. In their keynote paper, Ng et al. state that "*the Smart Internet supports an instinctive user model of the web, one in which the discovery, aggregation and delivery of services and resources results in rendered content that is optimal for each user or group's situation*" [10]. Since a usage context may involve several individuals, Smart Internet applications should support multi-user collaboration. The authors note that the traditional Internet has five major weaknesses, with respect to these aims: (1) it does not sufficiently integrate resources from a user's perspective, (2) it lacks mechanisms for individualization, (3) it does not support automatic, server-initiated connections, leaving the user to initiate all interactions, (4) it does not permit multiple users to collaborate on a service instance, (5) it gives users very limited control over resources. The goal of the Smart Internet paradigm is to move beyond these limitations by introducing frameworks that allow resources and services to be discovered, aggregated and delivered in a manner that respects a user's goals, tasks and concerns.

In order to achieve these goals, Smart Internet architectures require a better awareness of the *context* in which users operate. According to Dey, "*context is any information that can be used to characterize the situation of an entity. An entity is a person, place, or object that is considered relevant to the interaction between a user and an application, including the user and the applications themselves.*" [11]. Given the breadth of this definition, it is natural to ask how contextual information can be made available for automatic consumption by the Smart Internet. Over the last decades, several research topics in computer science and software engineering have furnished partial replies to this question. In this section, we will specifically address research results in the domain of ubiquitous computing, the semantic web, social computing and cloud computing. We will summarize the contributions of these research domains in the rest of this chapter.

3.1 Ubiquitous Computing

In his seminal work about the computer for the twenty-first century, Weiser stated that "*the most profound technologies are those that disappear. They weave themselves into the fabric of everyday life until they're indistinguishable from it*" [12]. Weiser coined the term Ubiquitous Computing (ubicomp) to describe a new era of computing that he expected would be achievable within twenty years. Today, Weiser's vision appears almost as utopian as it did twenty years ago. Nevertheless, important progress has been made and several enabling technologies have been developed during this period. Davies and Gellerson suggested that software engineering issues lie at the heart of the remaining challenges [13]. They point out that, while computer and networking hardware have advanced as predicted, ubicomp lacks middleware to allow "*us [to] combine components to form applications unforeseen at the time of their deployment*". Want and Pering point out that the limitations on ubicomp progress have moved to the higher levels of abstraction, primarily into the software area [14]. They argue that software capabilities have not advanced at a pace that can take full advantage of the hardware and networking infrastructure.

Significant advances have been made when it comes to incorporating spatial information into user context models. User positioning services based on satellite data, cell phone tower triangulation or wireless access point localization have become broadly available in consumer devices, and are actively used in Internet services, e.g., Google Latitude, and location-ware advertising. Mobile software applications are increasingly utlizing contextual information about their user's location in order to lighten cognitive burdens, e.g., the personal task manager OmniFocus associates tasks with user locations (omnigroup.com).

Other types of contextual information have also found their way into current Internet applications, including information about the *device* being used (e.g., smartphone vs. laptop), the *identity/role* of the user, as well as temporal details. Contextual information pertaining to processes or goal-directed sequences of actions performed by users are less commonly used in current Internet applications, except for very specific domains, such as navigation systems and e-learning applications.

Researchers have investigated general approaches to integrating context-awareness into the Web Engineering process. Kaltz and Ziegler have proposed a *context system* as pluggable module that can be added as a *filter* or *lens* to general Web software [15], while Jahnke et al. have developed a context system as an extension to general Web portal software [16].

Current research challenges in ubiquitous computing can be partitioned into two categories: (1) challenges with *perceiving implicit human input,* and (2) challenges in *actuating system behaviour*. Schmidt defines implicit human computer interaction as "*an action performed by the user that is not primarily aimed to interact with a computerized system but which such a system understands as input*" [17]. Researchers have warned that the dynamic and fluid nature of human context is extremely difficult to model in computer based systems; they have advised that any context-aware system using such information should be engineered under the assumption of a high likelihood of "getting things wrong". Consequently, these systems should act conservatively, clearly indicate actions taken and leave risky actions up to the user [18]. These considerations indicate that an augmented ability to model and reason about human context is a pivotal prerequisite for advancing the vision of ubicomp and the Smart Internet.

3.2 Semantic Web

Research and development efforts concerning the Semantic Web are aimed at making Web-based resources accessible for automated interpretation – that is, allowing computers to "understand" the meaning of Web content [19]. The concept of intelligent agents that are tasked to aid humans in utilizing the Internet is obviously an important building block for the Smart Internet, given its emphasis on proactivity and aids for human comprehension. A large amount of effort has been dedicated to the development of semantic markup languages that allow users to publish Web content, along with codified metadata about the meaning of the content. Examples of such languages are the Ontology Web Language (OWL), the Resource Description Format (RDF) and XML-based extensions of HTML (XHTML). Query languages have been created on top of these markup languages for retrieval of Semantic Web content, e.g., the SPARQL Protocol and RDF Query Language [20]. Logic-based reasoning, inference and proof systems for semantic web content are the subject of active development, with a set of challenges that include scalability, uncertainty, vagueness, inconsistency and deceit [21].

At the heart of the Semantic Web is the notion of creating shared ontologies – formal models of relevant concepts and relationships in a particular domain. Several success stories exist about defining and adopting such ontologies for particular domains, e.g., the Goodrelations ontology for eCommerce [22] and the 'Friend Of A Friend' (FOAF) ontology that is used to describe social networks [23]. Ontologies with successful adoption on the Semantic Web typically share the trait of brevity, containing up to a few hundred concepts. Unfortunately, ontologies for health care are significantly larger due to the complexity of the information in this domain. For example, the 'Systematized Nomenclature of Medicine – Clinical Terms' (SNOMED CT) has approximately 370,000 "pre-coordinated" (predefined) concepts and allows users to define additional "post-coordinated" concepts [24]. Moreover, as clinical knowledge evolves, SNOMED CT is being changed with new releases every six months. Another challenge is the avoidance and elimination of redundancy, as no efficient algorithm has yet been found to identify duplicate concepts in ontologies of this scale. As a result of this additional complexity, more research is needed on assessing and improving the scalability of Semantic Web technology for health care applications [25].

3.3 Social Computing

Social computing applications constitute a relatively recent development in application design. Although not restricted to the Internet, most social computing platforms are web-enabled applications that focus on online social networking and collaboration. The term 'Web 2.0' was introduced to denote Internet architectures that permit content to be easily generated and published by users. Although the original World Wide Web (WWW) was intended to support collaboration through the use of email, hyperlinks and bulletin boards, the first generation of Internet applications (Web 1.0) tended to contain static content. Content generally flowed in one direction – from the site author to the user.

In contrast to the first generation of websites, Web 2.0 applications offer increased levels of participation. Users are enabled to act both as readers and writers, generating content and creating a visible history of their activities [26]. Social computing applications focus explicitly on the networking aspect, providing facilities for users to create virtual communities through the use of various collaboration and connection mechanisms. Users of a social networking application such as Facebook begin their usage scenario by creating a profile that contains personal information. Once complete, the user can begin the process of constructing a virtual network through the mutual initiation of relationships with other users. In contrast to bulletin boards and Web 1.0 technologies, these relationships are tracked in an explicit (and often visible) manner.

Although social computing applications have been available for several years, social networking applications have only recently entered the health marketplace. The most important offerings consist of the various Personal Health Record (PHR) systems, such as Microsoft HealthVault and Google Health [28]. Intended to support the creation of comprehensive records of personal health information, these applications support data sharing with medical professionals and family members through the use of explicit access instructions.

Social computing is of value for the Smart Internet for a number of reasons. First, it provides a form of communication that can facilitate collaboration and information sharing. Second, social computing architectures also support a type of asynchronous interactions, whereby services can operate on profile or network data while the user is offline. Third, social computing can provide a method for harnessing collective intelligence. Fourth, the network created by friendship connections, (as well as the user's profile data), can provide information for applications that deliver customized services, thereby facilitating a type of context awareness. These benefits do, however, come with a cost: the dynamic nature of social computing applications also gives rise to significant challenges in the areas of privacy and security [27].

3.4 Cloud Computing

The term 'cloud computing' describes the use of the Internet as a computing platform for providing services that have traditionally been provided in-house by desktops workstations and servers [28]. Cloud services are generally partitioned into: 1) 'software as a service', in which third parties provide applications, 2) 'infrastructure as a service', in which third parties make networks and storage space available, and 3) 'platform as a service', where third parties provide frameworks for application development. Unlike traditional outsourcing relationships, data in a cloud application is typically distributed across multiple data centres; in the absence of explicit restrictions on geographical location, data may be stored in multiple legal jurisdictions.

Cloud computing has received significant attention due to popular applications by Google and other companies. A well-known example is Google Docs, which provides a cloud-based alternative to locally installed office software programs such as Microsoft Office. Enterprise computing applications have similarly been offered in the cloud, such as the customer relationship management services offered by Salesforce.com. In addition, an increasing number of cloud computing service providers are offering virtual server infrastructure to their clients. Amazon's Elastic Computing Cloud (EC2), IBM's Blue Cloud and Google's App Engine are among the most popular offerings out of a rapidly growing number of cloud computing services. One of the drivers for organizations switching to cloud computing concerns cost-savings, since obtaining services from a third party may reduce the need for expertise, infrastructure and maintenance. In addition, cloud computing offers organizations the ability to maintain variable levels of capacity, as cloud computing approaches are capable of dynamically configuring resources to meet a client's needs.

The development of cloud computing was an important step towards realizing the vision of the Smart Internet. Not only does cloud computing support automated service delivery and dynamic configuration, but it also provides a model for the integration of services based on multiple servers. From an individual user's perspective, it extends the use of the Internet beyond the scope of Web pages and data repositories into the realm of full-featured, process-aware applications providing complex services. By implementing this shift, the Internet becomes increasingly aware of aspects of human-computer-interaction (HCI) that had formerly been dealt with only at the level of the local personal computer (PC). For example, a scientific author using a cloud-based word processor together with an Internet search engine to retrieve related work could be provided with more intelligent recommendations of search results based on an automated analysis of the text authored so far. Analogously, physicians entering patient data in cloud-based EMR applications could be supported by having the applications offer the newest practice guidelines and research results on a particular patient case. The shift to cloud-based services allows service providers to collect more information about users for the purpose of creating more accurate user profiles, which can be used to anticipate user needs and individualize Internet offerings. Clearly, this movement has also generated new questions pertaining to individual information privacy and trust [29].

4 Smart Technologies in Health Care

With health care becoming an increasingly-important concern due to the aging demographics of industrialized nations, and with the Internet becoming increasingly available to the public in developing nations, there has been much activity on the development of Internet-based health care applications. The term *Medicine 2.0* has been coined to refer to applications of Web 2.0 technologies [26] to health care. Eysenbach defines 'Medicine 2.0' applications as "Web-based services for health care consumers, caregivers, patients, health professionals, and biomedical researchers, that use Web 2.0 technologies as well as semantic web and virtual reality tools, to enable and facilitate specifically *social networking, participation, apomediation, collaboration*, and *openness* within and between these user groups" [30].

Social networking has been introduced earlier in this chapter. The term *participation* in the above definition refers primarily to the empowerment of patients through the Smart Internet to more actively participate and take control of aspects of their health care. It also refers to the aspect of translational medicine, which increases the ability of patients and health professionals to participate in scientific studies [31]. Traditionally, such studies have been impeded by difficulties in soliciting informed consent of patients, caregivers and other stakeholders required to participate.

Apomediation has been introduced as a new term to refer to a "middle way" in which users can retrieve trusted and high-quality information and services relevant to their health. Apomediation refers to a combination of the traditional *mediation* approach to information delivery (i.e., professional experts who provide information and services to consumers) and the opposite *dismediation* approach, in which consumers bypass "middlemen" completely in order to search information and services on their own. Apomediation employs computer or human agents for the purpose of "guiding" consumers in their self-directed activities.

The concept of *collaboration* emphasizes the fact that health care is a highly team-oriented endeavour, while the term *openness* refers to the objective of having transparent and mobile health information available to all stakeholders who should rightfully be able to access it.

Many of today's emerging Medicine 2.0 applications are relevant to the notion of the Smart Internet, since they implement partially the principles that, according to Ng et al. set the Smart Internet apart from the traditional Internet [10], namely an *instinctive user model, sessions for users and their matter of concerns*, and *collective and collaborative web interactions.*

In the rest of this section, we will describe some of the emerging technologies available in the health care space. Although the Smart Internet is currently a distant goal, some of the existing applications in the health care space are clearly steps in this direction. Since there are many kinds of applications using diverse technological paradigms, we will structure our discussion firstly by the types of the primary users (i.e., consumers and providers) and secondly by the supported function (i.e., social networking, participation, apomediation, collaboration, and openness).

4.1 Health Consumer Services

Design and use of emerging health consumer services is constrained by a number of factors relating to human behaviour and motivation. The following factors are particularly important, and are each discussed in the following subsections: participation; collaboration; social networking; apomediation; openness.

4.1.1 Participation

Personal health record (PHR) services clearly provide a means by which patients may actively participate in their health care. Several Internet-based PHR services have emerged over the last several years. Prominent examples are Google Health,

Microsoft Health Vault, Dossia and myPHR [32]. PHRs allow consumers to share their health records with other users, including professional care providers, family and friends. They also offer individualized services related to individual consumer health profiles, such as health decision support, guidelines, and drug recommendations. PHR services often have public application programming interfaces (APIs), and consumers can choose to add third-party Web services to their health profile, including telemedicine services that enable remote consultation via audio/video, drug registries that automatically notify consumers when there is a recall, and search engines to find clinical trials that consumers may participate in. The latter feature allows consumers to participate in clinical research without the traditional health care professional as an intermediary.

Personalized medical decision support engines like MEDgle.com provide a growing variety of services to engage health care consumers as active participants in their health. Services include "automated nurses" that answer questions about health (eNurse), a *what-if* tool to estimate the long-term impact on health conditions on life expectancy and disease development, the construction of social support networks, and educational games using Facebook and other platforms.

4.1.2 Collaboration

Existing web-based forums and tools allow health consumers to participate in collaborative health management for purposes of managing addictions, dietary issues, obesity, and other conditions. Web Assisted Tobacco Interventions (WATI) sites have used this approach; for example, StopSmokingCenter.net provides peer-to-peer support and computational tools (e.g., money savings, life expectancy statistics) to help consumers quit smoking. Van Mierlo et al. found that peer-to-peer responses were rapid (25% of forum messages were responded to within 12 minutes) and conclude that achieving similar responsiveness with professional consultants would be significantly more expensive [32].

4.1.3 Social Networking

First generation PHR products on the market provide limited support for social networks. While many of these sites allow users to share portions of their health record, the mechanisms are typically primitive. However, there are an increasing number of second generation products and prototypes adding social networking features for patients as well as their caregivers, e.g., family and friends. PatientsLikeMe is a prominent example of an Internet service that invites consumers (patients and caregivers) to share health profiles and compare them with patients in similar situations. Participating consumers are motivated by the desire to find answers to the questions "*given my current health status, what is the best possible outcome and how can I collaborate with others to achieve this outcome?*" Qualitative studies of the discussions between members of a particular community (patients diagnosed with amyotrophic lateral sclerosis) indicate that the application supports consumers in finding and offering health advice and promotes self-management [33].

Dedicated social networks have been created for particular types of health conditions, such as CaringVoices, a network for cancer survivors and their caregivers [33]. Other ad-hoc social networks emerge based on the desire to communicate and control emerging threats in a timely manner. For instance, the UN/WHO and the CDC made significant use of Twitter, Facebook, YouTube and a variety of other Web 2.0 platforms in the 2009 H1N1 pandemic [34].

4.1.4 Apomediation

The use of apomediation to guide patients in their self-directed activities is becoming increasingly common in health care. The guidance may be performed by professionals as well as experienced laypersons, e.g., patients and caregivers who have been in a similar situation. Proudfoot carried out a qualitative study with 26 patients that have recently been diagnosed with bipolar disorder and found that expert patients can act as effective apomediaries [33]. Apomediation may also be performed by computer-based agents and wizards who acquire information about the consumer's health profile and then point out relevant information and services. An example for such a computer-based agent is the "eNurse" at MEDgle.com.

Another form of apomediation concerns the trustworthiness of Internet-based content and services. The Health on the Net (HON) foundation has been founded as a not-for-profit organization to issue certificates to Internet sites that comply with an eight-point "HONcode" to assure ethical and trustworthy Web content (www.hon.ch). The HON foundation provides browser plugins and other search tools, which guide consumers to Internet resources that are HONcode certified, effectively acting as an apomediary on content quality.

4.1.5 Openness

In the context of consumer-focused health applications, openness has several connotations, including the visibility of provider-managed health records to consumers, the sharing of health data among consumers and other stakeholders, and the freedom to migrate health information between service providers. We briefly discuss these issues below.

While many jurisdictions have policies to allow consumers to request information on their health records stored at health service provider organizations, the administrative hurdles that must be surmounted in order to retrieve this information are often formidable. Even where requests have been granted, laypersons may have difficulties making sense of the data produced. Some provider organizations have begun to offer Internet-based services to allow patients to access data stored about them. The benefits of such PHR services pertain not only to improved data quality (patients adding / correcting data) but also to improvements concerning auditing of service billing and record access privacy. This type of service avoids the traditional "audit paradox", in which third party auditors (non clinicians) check access to confidential health data to verify that it was retrieved exclusively on a clinical "need-to-know" basis, and, in doing so, violate the same principle they are seeking to uphold.

Other Medicine 2.0 sites are based on the premise that progress in health care is held back by "locking up" relevant data and applying restrictive policies that prevent broad sharing of medical evidence. The "Openness Philosophy" of PatiensLikeMe.com[1], for example, makes a plea for its users to openly share their medical data for the benefit of everyone.

---

[1] http://www.patientslikeme.com/about/openness

At a time where Internet-based computing is shifting our notion of software as a product to software as a service (SaaS), the "Open Data" and "Open Knowledge" movements have gained importance on par (or even surpassing) that of the "Open Source" movement[2]. Of particular relevance to PHR data is the threat of a potential vendor lock-in that would prevent consumers from sharing their data freely with other services or from migrating to a competitive service provider altogether [35]. Many current consumer health applications have published open APIs in response to these concerns. However, less onerous migration services are required to truly empower consumers to freely control their data.

4.2 Health Provider Services

4.2.1 Participation

Governments, health authorities, hospitals and individual clinics have been implementing practice management software for providers for several decades. The focus for the majority of these systems has been on professional users (providers) working for a particular organization. Patients normally lack direct access to these systems and even providers working for different health care organizations would often be blocked from participating in the same systems. Price conducted an empirical study in the context of Canadian healthcare that demonstrated how disruptive the use of such single-tenant architectures could be for the continuity of care for palliative patients [36]. Palliative care is a particularly relevant medical domain, as it requires the participation of different types of professional and informal caregivers in an in-patient and out-patient setting.

Some of the most promising applications to emerge in this area take inspiration from cloud-computing, using a multi-tenant architecture that avoids problems with traditional organizational boundaries. Since these applications are Internet-based, they can provide seamless services to care providers and consumers alike. Doctations.com is an example of a cloud-based service provider offering subscription services to providers and consumers. Its *DocPatients network* provides an online community to facilitate participation of patients in provider ehealth processes.

4.2.2 Collaboration

Multi-tenant applications can also serve to bridge the gaps between organizational boundaries. Systems like Doctations.com provide a whole range of inter-practice collaboration services, including multi-media messaging, scheduling, workflow management, and document management. Other systems leverage group intelligence by facilitating peer-to-peer consultation, research on rare diseases, terminology standardization etc. For example, MedTing.com is an application that enables physicians to share medical images and videos, get advice from peers, discuss cases, rate and recommend cases, and retrieve relevant professional publications from sources such as Pubmed. Bortolon et al. report on an application of wiki technology for the group-based translation of large medical nomenclatures into other languages [33].

---

[2] http://en.wikipedia.org/wiki/Open_Data

Other sites (e.g., MyHealthInnovation.com) are specifically created to use "crowd intelligence" to incubate new ideas and give credit to individuals contributing to the community.

4.2.3 Social Networking

Associations for professional health care providers have started to use social networking technologies to facilitate information exchange among their members. Access is typically restricted to members of the association. One example is the Asklepios system of the Canadian Medical Association, which provides physicians, residents and medical students with a social networking platform [33].

Providers can also benefit from access to consumer social networks, which often provide services for performing research and aggregating data. The consumer network service PatientsLikeMe provides information on the symptoms reported on rare diseases, the effectiveness of experimental drugs on participating patients, and side effects.

4.2.4 Apomediation

Smart Internet technologies have enabled health care providers to become active apomediaries in support of Internet-savvy patients and their relatives. Providers write blogs, answer questions, and develop guidelines in support of the consumer community. They may do this on a voluntary basis, or they may receive payments for their contributions. The joint HealthCentral.com / Wellsphere.com networks have a combination of blogs, tools, knowledge bases and advice services driven by knowledgeable apomediaries, serving a claimed user community of over 10 million health consumers.

Some existing applications also support inter-provider apomediation in the context of Continuing Medical Education (CME) and professional development. The Open Educational Resource[3] (OER) and Knowledge for Health (K4Health)[4] are two sites that offer online learning content. Even Internet-based virtual worlds such as SecondLife have been used for medical education [34].

4.2.5 Openness

Given the workloads imposed by overloaded health care systems, staying up to date with respect to the latest research has been a traditional challenge for health care providers [37]. Web 2.0 technologies like RSS feeds, social bookmarking, blogs and mash-ups allow providers to stay informed about new research results being published in their various fields of practice. In addition, consumer health networks such as PatientsLikeMe.com allow providers to correlate their experience with data from a much larger patient population in order to provide more evidence-based decisions.

5 Evolving Smart Internet Technologies for Health Care

Our brief tour of existing applications in health care has revealed the presence of several mechanisms relevant to the concept of Smart Internet systems. First, the use of

---

[3] openeducation.zunia.org

[4] k4health.org

cloud computing in applications such as Doctations has provided a method for integrating the efforts of multiple servers. Second, apomediation techniques using human or software agents may partially facilitate the Smart Internet goal of reduce the cognitive burden on users. In particular, the use of software agents such as the aforementioned eNurse can provide patients with a familiar domain-oriented metaphor, as opposed to general Internet search engines. In addition, the multi-tenancy supported by some of the cloud computing architectures could help address the problems identified by Price [36] concerning the disruptive effects of single-tenant services on health care delivery.

Despite these advances, it is clear that current Web-based health applications fall short of achieving the goals set out in the Smart Internet vision. Many of the current problems are technical, but significant challenges also exist in the political, legal and social domains. Furthermore, there are complex interactions between the issues in these different areas; future progress towards evolving the Smart Internet for health care will depend on our ability to effectively recognize and reconcile these dependencies. The situation therefore calls for substantial interdisciplinary efforts. In the sections to follow, we will analyze some of the existing challenges from a variety of perspectives.

5.1 Context

Perhaps the most difficult challenge is that of context-aware computing. The Smart Internet should recognize and store information about the context of its users, and should act on this data by adapting its services automatically as required. Current approaches to context information modeling and retrieval are still immature and have tended to fail even in simple applications [18]. In general, health care requires extremely complex, temporal context information with high assurance of accuracy, as illustrated in the scenario presented in Chapter 1 of this book. Health care is also an inherently "risky" domain. Given the progress made in the two decades after publication of Weiser's ubicomp vision, it is doubtful that the technical challenges of successfully modeling, retrieving and reliably acting on complex health-care related context information will be overcome within at least a decade of this writing.

Of course, this does not mean that particular context-aware functions may not be used to build a smarter Health Internet in the short term. Existing Intranet context models and standards that have been developed in the health domain may realistically be adapted to broad-scale Internet use. One example would be the standards of HL7's Clinical Context Object Workgroup (CCOW), which deal with the synchronization of different health information systems in respect to particular subjects (i.e., patients) [38]. In this approach, the patient identity is the single point of focus (context information) shared by all the applications used by the provider.

The challenges moving such simple contextual function from Intranet to Internet scale are mainly political, rather than technical. As with other forms of Internet-scale identity management (e.g., single sign on of user identities), controversies may arise with respect to control and governance of a shared subject identity context manager.

More significant advances in context-based computing for Internet-based health care applications may be possible by following a "learning" rather than a "modeling" approach to context enactment. Several promising theories have been developed in the field of Computational Intelligence, including Case based reasoning (CBR), a technique that has found successful applications in health care (e.g., clinical decision support) as well as other business domains (e.g., recommender systems) [39]. From a technical point of view, CBR approaches may well be in reach; for example, be companies like Google and Microsoft may be capable of providing smart search and dashboard Internet functions based on context data learned from patient cases in Google Health or Microsoft Health Vault, respectively. However, the political, legal and sociological issues arising with entrusting profit-driven organizations with highly confidential, personal data and relying on their services may be insurmountable in the short run. The development of open standards to store and enact context-information in a decentralized fashion at organizations trusted by users may overcome some of these socio-legal-political hurdles. Initiatives for such standards exist in related areas, e.g., the Liberty Alliance for decentralized identity and trust management (www.projectliberty.org).

5.2 Dynamic Social Binding

Social networking has provided a foundation from which to support collaboration. However, current approaches to social networking do not go far enough. Health care episodes often involve teams of practitioners that coalesce around a patient for a limited period of time. At present, social networking tools do not support dynamic social binding – the capability to select other users dynamically to share interactions at a given level of detail. Current social networking applications allow the formation of networks through fairly cumbersome means. They are also not geared towards tracking temporal information about the network, such as the duration for which two users were joined. In order to provide dynamic social binding, new tools and techniques are required for both the data structures, and the user interfaces.

In addition, a key requirement of Smart Internet systems concerns the ability to maintain the user's tasks, goals and matters of concern as persistent states, in order to track progress. Social networks provide a type of persistent state, in the form of a user's network and profile details. Websites like PatientsLikeMe encourage users to update various metrics daily, which provides a persistent data store of personal health information. However, the services available to PatientsLikeMe users are still largely invoked by the user, who bears the burden of remembering her various tasks and sub-tasks. Consequently, such sites are frequented primarily by patients with major existing health conditions (chronic, acute or palliative), while healthy consumers lack motivation to keep reporting their data. Thus, these sites are less effective for preventative care.

5.3 Server-Initiated Interactions, Automatic Service Discovery and Delivery

The Smart Internet is meant to interact with users proactively, discovering and delivering services automatically in anticipation of user needs. Internet-based health care applications available today provide only limited support for these kinds of interactions. Servers may push messages with embedded Web links to users under certain circumstances. For example, the preventative care and health improvement site Healthierme.com sends email dialogues to users who have not logged in for a while, asking them about their activity level and weight loss goals. The benefit of using email as a vehicle of server-initiated interactions is that it is broadly available to users. The disadvantage of using such a general medium is its unreliability; autogenerated emails may get filtered by spam processors or users may get overwhelmed by high volumes of incoming messages.

Automatic service discovery may be based on explicit queries (e.g., a patient registering their interest in diabetes chronic disease management) or a machine-learning approach using data about previous interactions (e.g., a recommender system that uses knowledge about services used in the past). From a user's point of view, a service discovery/delivery mechanism should be unobtrusive and select only those services with a high fit to the user needs. In reality, however, business interests play a major role in current Internet service discovery and delivery. Service providers are able to pay for preferential ranking of their services in recommender systems and search engines. While this economic bias is commonly accepted in general commerce, health consumers and providers tend to be more concerned about its influence.

As the use of mobile, Internet-enabled devices has become more prevalent in the general population, there has been a rapid increase in health related mobile services. Many current consumer services are life-style changing applications (weight loss, activity tracking, addiction prevention etc.). Still, an increasing number of diagnostic, chronic and acute care services are becoming available. What is needed in order to make health services automatically discoverable and deliverable is a shared semantic description of their properties. Such a description could be compared to generic drug names vs. brand name drugs. Semantic Web (services) technologies combined with a shared registration approach may enable this vision [40].

5.4 Integrated User Perspective

Current Internet-based health care applications are typically built in silos with little integration among them. Users interacting with multiple Internet resources at the same time (e.g., multiple Web sites) should ideally be able to browse new resources "in context" with other, currently open sessions. The only current (as of this writing) commonly available solution for such shared context currently pertains to matters of identity management: Liberty Alliance standards or Microsoft's Passport provide cross-session user identity management solutions, while HL7's CCOW standards can be used to browse multiple Web sites in context of the same subject (patient).

Web portal technology may be used as an interface layer between independently developed Internet resources and users [41]. Resource synchronization and context-awareness can be handled in the Web portal in order to present an integrated "dashboard" view of relevant Web resources. The problem with this approach is that it requires a significant amount of set up and customization. Evolving Web portal technology into simple-to-use end-user services may play an important role in enabling integrated user perspectives. As Jahnke et al. have demonstrated, domain-specificity (e.g., health care) effectively constrains the problem and makes solutions more attainable [41].

5.5 Collective Intelligence

There have been several high-profile successes of Internet-based health care applications harnessing collective intelligence in order to solve difficult problems, e.g., finding treatments for incurable diseases. One highly publicized example is the patient-driven clinical trial on the effectiveness of Lithium for patients with Amyotrophic Lateral Sclerosis (ALS) [42]. It demonstrates how quickly Internet-enabled health care consumers can make the transition from being knowledge seekers to knowledge producers. In this case, users of the health social networking site PatientsLikeMe.com found a Web-based report about preliminary research from an Italian team, indicating potential benefits of Lithium for ALS patients. These users started a growing World-wide "self-trial" movement even before the Italian research was officially published in a peer-reviewed journal. Preliminary results from the Lithium/ALS self-trial on PatientsLikeMe were available even before planning for a controlled clinical experiment was finalized. In light of the results, which did not indicate significant benefits of Lithium for ALS patients, some researchers argued that running a formal clinical trial was a waste of resources and would put unjustified hardship on patients, due to the side effects of taking Lithium. Others argued that the PatientsLikeMe study lacked the necessary rigour of randomized controlled trials and therefore generated unreliable data [43].

The above example clearly shows the potential power of Internet-based collective intelligence for health care (fast knowledge generation, large subject population, less expensive). However, it also indicates the current challenges that have to be overcome with respect to producing credible results, which hold up established data quality and research standards. With fast-progressing diseases like ALS, the collective intelligence generated through Internet applications like PatientsLikeMe has been received as timely and helpful to consumers. However, more research is needed on how to translate the rigour of established traditional biomedical research methods into the paradigm of Internet-based collective intelligence.

5.6 Security, Privacy and Governance

Despite the benefits promised by the Smart Internet, there are several challenges that arise with respect to privacy, security and data governance. In this section we will briefly detail some of the most important issues involved in bringing this next generation of online services to the health care sector.

5.6.1 Service Composition

The emphasis of the Smart Internet on the dynamic discovery and composition of services from multiple servers invites a certain amount of logistical complexity. Similar to cloud computing approaches, the servers involved in a Smart Internet transaction may be managed by more than one entity; data may be duplicated and dispersed among a variety of geographical areas and legal jurisdictions. Smart Internet service providers can potentially outsource their data and network management functions to subcontractors, who may subcontract or assign those functions to others in turn. The complexity that arises from this state of affairs creates a number of problems for the organization using the services.

First, the organization may have no idea where its information is being stored, and by whom. Given that jurisdictions differ in their approach to regulation, this feature introduces uncertainty regarding the risks to which the information in question is subjected [44]. The potential layering of subcontractors also makes it difficult for organizations to use the traditional risk mitigation strategies of contracts and service level agreements. If a service provider outsources to a third party, the legal jurisdiction in which the data resides may change[5]; the user of the service may also be vulnerable if the original service provider did not pass on the various privacy and security obligations to the third party. Although the use of geospecific services may provide partial answers to some of these issues, further work is needed to clarify and mitigate the residual risks.

Second, the organization may not know what safeguards are being used to protect data at a given point in time. The fact that data can reside on multiple servers provided by unknown third parties provides some challenges for the confidentiality, integrity and availability of health information. As Scheier noted one can link a server to an insecure network merely by assigning a new network card to it [45]. It is extremely difficult to provide safeguards in this setting.

The problem for health care organizations is that the use of adequate security measures is often mandated by law. For instance, statutes like the *Health Insurance Portability and Accountability Act*, and the Ontario *Personal Health Information Protection Act* require health care organizations to implement safeguards for personal health information. It is unlikely that courts in either the United States or Canada would allow organizations to delegate this responsibility to a Smart Internet service provider. On the other hand, it is also quite difficult for an organization to perform due diligence activities surrounding the security of a Smart Internet application, due to the distributed and dynamic architecture.

The use of protocols for negotiating transactions between servers is a current area of research that is worth investigating. As well, the proprietary nature of most security software can be addressed through standardization. For instance, the National Institute of Standards and Technology's 'Security Content Automation Protocol' (SCAP) is intended to specify and organize security-related information in standardized ways. SCAP includes specifications for software flaws and configuration issues [46]. In addition, the use of tamper-proof coprocessors is being urged as a mechanism for affording protection in distributed environments [47].

Third, the requirement for servers to be automatically configured and dynamically allocated to a user's needs may invite the use of multi-tenant architectures. While advantageous from a usability standpoint, multi-tenancy creates a problem for auditing. In addition, if the hardware hosting another user's data is seized in response to a court action or government request [48], the data of other users may be exposed.

While the use of virtualization technology may provide some optimism for maintaining security in situations involving multi-tenancy, researchers have noted that current virtualization-based security techniques are unsuitable for highly dynamic environments [49]. Drawing from the cloud computing literature, other researchers have suggested that server security measures for multi-user, distributed and dynamically configured systems should include the use of encryption, strong access controls,

[5] This can create problems for companies in European Union member states, which are prohibited from sending personal information to jurisdictions without adequate privacy protection.

and frequent backups [46]. However, encryption in the cloud computing context is not straightforward [50]. Until the state of the art advances, it seems clear that health care providers should think carefully before storing their information in environments that permit multi-tenancy.

Fourth, Smart Internet services using distributed and dynamic architectures may cause difficulties for health care providers with respect to the traditional notions of custody and control. Given that many regulatory instruments are drafted with these concepts in mind, Smart Internet architectures that do not permit organizations to identify who has custody of their data are likely unsuitable for use in health care. In addition to further architectural work on the infrastructure for Smart Internet services, possible solutions to this issue include tracing tools that allow real-time visualization of where data is located, and automated policy negotiation architectures.

5.6.2 Collaboration

As we have seen, the Smart Internet encourages collaboration in the course of web interactions. Building on traditional approaches to collaboration, (e.g., in Web 2.0 technologies), the Smart Internet envisions applications that support dynamic social binding – the capability to select other users dynamically to share interactions at a given level of detail. The resulting complexity means that Smart Internet services may face privacy challenges that are a superset of those affecting current social computing applications. Users of Smart Internet services need to be provided with intuitive, yet powerful, mechanisms for controlling how other users may access their personal information.

Privacy issues with social computing systems are particularly acute in health care, due to the highly sensitive nature of personal health information. In some cases, providers of social computing platforms encourage users to share this type of information. As an example, users of PatientsLikeMe almost invariably publish information classified as confidential by the HIPAA, e.g. 75% publish full face photos. (see Study of the ePatient as a provider of health content in the Internet [33]).

In contrast to vendors of social networking products, health care providers are subject to legal obligations with respect to ensuring the confidentiality of health information. As summarized by Williams [27], there are a number of privacy issues affecting online collaboration tools in the health care domain. As a first example, certain difficulties arise from the complex nature of the interactions envisioned by both social computing and Smart Internet applications. If users partially base their willingness to disclose personal information on an expectation of how data flows through a system or process, then higher levels of complexity will make the process much more difficult to assess [51]. Second, users must have some level of trust that other users are genuine, and acting in good faith. Some of the current systems do not provide much comfort on this front; for instance, medting allows almost anyone to sign up for a physician account. In order to alleviate these concerns, Smart Internet services for health care should provide mechanisms for fostering trust, including authentication for health care providers, and detection mechanisms for fraudulent user accounts and suspicious user activity. In addition, architects and designers of Smart Internet applications should have metrics for assessing the efficacy of their trust-enhancing mechanisms. Although first steps in this direction are provided in [52], more work is required on this front.

5.7 Governance and Quality

As part of their information governance activities, health care providers often maintain programs that examine the quality of their software systems. As a result, approaches to testing and certifying Smart Internet services will be a critical area of research for the health care sector. As Healey points out, it is difficult to test systems that are highly distributed, dynamically configured, and managed by more than one organization [53]. Given that health care providers are typically subject to an obligation to provide data integrity, the testing and certification of Smart Internet services is an important topic for future research.

6 Conclusions

Health spending in OECD countries increased from 4½ percent of the GDP in 1960 to 12½ of GDP in 2007 and is expected to continue to grow faster than the GDP. Lowering costs and improving outcomes have been described as the "health care imperative" by the Institute of Medicine of National Academies, with consumer-focused strategies as an important enabler [54]. The Internet has become a common tool for actors involved in the health care business, including consumers, professionals, and researchers. Emerging Internet-based health care applications exhibit some of the characteristics defined for the Smart Internet. However, important challenges remain to be tackled for a more profound paradigm shift towards smart interactions and services. These challenges will require a significant evolution in the standards, architecture and governance of the Internet. Implementing these changes will require a collective political will, motivated by a joint "killer application". Health care has the potential to become such a killer application. Even now, the Internet has noticeably begun to shift powers from health care providers to consumers. This shift of power has associated risks in terms of data quality and privacy. However, proper technological and political development can mitigate these risks and the systemic benefits of empowering health care consumers to become more self-sufficient far outweigh residual risk factors for individuals.

Canada has recently launched several voluntary certification programs and mandatory licensing regulations for health care-related software and services, including consumer health products and any type of software used for patient management. Other jurisdictions have implemented or are in the process of planning similar initiatives. These certification regimes will have a major impact on the health care software ecosystem and the potential future development of the Smart Internet in this domain. Further interdisciplinary research is required to explore the relationship of regulatory regimes and technology development and adoption.

Acknowledgment

The authors would like to acknowledge and thank the IBM Centre for Advanced Studies and the Natural Science and Engineering Research Council of Canada for supporting this research.

References

1. Hsiao, C.J., Beatty, P.C., Hing, E.S., Woodwell, D.A.: Electronic medical record/electronic health record use by office-based physicians: United States, 2008 and preliminary 2009, NCHS Health E-Stat. Centre for Disease Control and Prevention (2009)
2. Fast Facts - Current and expected use of EMRs. Can Fam Physician 56 (2010)
3. Meyer, I., Husing, T., Dobrev, A., Korte, W., Artmann, J., Stroetmann, K.: Availability and usage of ICT applications among European primary care physicians. Studies in health technology and informatics, 142–143 (2009)
4. Lynas, K.: Spending scandal batters Ontario agency responsible for creating EHR system. Canadian Pharmacists Journal 142, 173–173 (2009)
5. Eysenbach, G., Diepgen, T.L.: The role of e-health and consumer health informatics for evidence-based patient choice in the 21st century. Clinics in Dermatology 19, 11–17 (2001)
6. Neftel, K.: Patient empowerment through the internet. Swiss Medical Weekly: Official Journal of the Swiss Society of Infectious Diseases, the Swiss Society of Internal Medicine, the Swiss Society of Pneumology 138, 728 (2008)
7. Siempos, I., Spanos, A., Issaris, E., Rafailidis, P., Falagas, M.: Non-physicians may reach correct diagnoses by using Google: a pilot study. Swiss Med. Wkly 138, 741–745 (2008)
8. Tang, H., Ng, J.H.: Googling for a diagnosis–use of Google as a diagnostic aid: internet based study. BMJ 333, 1143–1145 (2006)
9. Chignell, M.: Modeling the User in Smart Interactions. In: Pre-proceedings of SITCON: The CAS / NSERC Strategic Workshop in Smart Internet Technologies (2009)
10. Ng, J., Chignell, M., Cordy, J.: The Smart Internet: Transforming the Web to Fit User Needs. In: Pre-proceedings of SITCON: The CAS / NSERC Strategic Workshop in Smart Internet Technologies (2009)
11. Dey, A.K.: Understanding and using context. Personal and Ubiquitous Computing 5, 4–7 (2001)
12. Weiser, M.: The computer for the twenty-first century. Scientific American 265, 94–104 (1991)
13. Davies, N., Gellersen, H.W.: Beyond prototypes: Challenges in deploying ubiquitous systems. IEEE Pervasive Computing, 26-35 (2002)
14. Want, R., Pering, T.: System challenges for ubiquitous & pervasive computing. In: ICSE 2005: Proceedings of the 27th International Conference on Software Engineering, pp. 9–14 (2005)
15. Kaltz, J.W., Ziegler, J., Lohmann, S.: Context-aware Web engineering: Modeling and applications. Revue d'intelligence artificielle 19, 439–458 (2005)
16. Jahnke, J.H., Bychkov, Y., Dahlem, D., Kawasme, L.: Context-Aware Information Delivery in Health Care. Revue d'intelligence artificielle 19 (2005)
17. Schmidt, A.: Implicit human computer interaction through context. Personal and Ubiquitous Computing 4, 191–199 (2000)
18. Greenberg, S.: Context as a dynamic construct. Human-Computer Interaction 16, 257–268 (2001)
19. Bemers-Lee, T., Hendler, J., Lassila, O.: The semantic web. Scientific American 284, 34–43 (2001)
20. Prud'Hommeaux, E., Seaborne, A., & others.: SPARQL query language for RDF. W3C working draft 4, World Wide Web Consortium (2006)

21. Lukasiewicz, T., Straccia, U.: Managing uncertainty and vagueness in description logics for the Semantic Web. In: Web Semantics: Science, Services and Agents on the World Wide Web, vol. 6, pp. 291–308 (2008)
22. Hepp, M.: GoodRelations: An ontology for describing products and services offers on the web. In: Gangemi, A., Euzenat, J. (eds.) EKAW 2008. LNCS (LNAI), vol. 5268, pp. 332–347. Springer, Heidelberg (2008)
23. Ding, L., Zhou, L., Finin, T., Joshi, A.: How the Semantic Web is Being Used: An Analysis of FOAF Documents. In: Hawaii International Conference on System Sciences, vol. 4, p. 113 (2005)
24. Price, C., Spackman, K.: SNOMED clinical terms. BJHC&IM-British Journal of Healthcare Computing & Information Management 17, 27–31 (2000)
25. Wroe, C.: Is Semantic Web technology ready for Healthcare? In: Sure, Y., Domingue, J. (eds.) ESWC 2006. LNCS, vol. 4011. Springer, Heidelberg (2006)
26. Murugesan, S.: Understanding Web 2.0. IT Professional 9, 34–41 (2007)
27. Williams, J.: Social Networking Applications in Health Care: Threats to the Privacy and Security of Health Information. In: Proc. of 2nd Intl. ICSE Workshop on Software Engineering in Health Care (SEHC). ACM, New York (2010)
28. Hayes, B.: Cloud computing. Communications of the ACM 57(7) (2008)
29. Cachin, C., Keidar, I., Shraer, A.: Trusting the cloud. ACM SIGACT News 40 (2009)
30. Eysenbach, G.: Medicine 2.0: social networking, collaboration, participation, apomediation, and openness. Journal of Medical Internet Research 10(3) (2008)
31. Ding, L., Zhou, L., Finin, T., Joshi, A.: How the Semantic Web is Being Used: An Analysis of FOAF Documents. In: Hawaii International Conference on System Sciences, vol. 4, p. 113c (2005)
32. Steinbrook, R.: Personally Controlled Online Health Data–The Next Big Thing in Medical Care? New England Journal of Medicine 358, 1653 (2008)
33. Medicine 2.0 Proceedings. J. Med. Internet Res. 10(3) (2008)
34. Medicine 2.0 Proceeding, vol. 2 (2009), `http://www.medicine20congress.com`
35. Kienle, H.M., Lober, A., Muller, H.A.: Policy and Legal Challenges of VirtualWorlds and Social Network Sites. In: RELAW 2008: Proceedings of the 2008 Requirements Engineering and Law, pp. 21–25 (2008)
36. Price, M.: Circle of Care Modeling: Improving Continuity of Care for End of Life Patients. PhD thesis, University of Victoria, School of Health Information Science, Canada (2010)
37. Grimshaw, J.M., Thomas, R.E., MacLennan, G., Fraser, C., Ramsay, C.R., Vale, L., Whitty, P., Eccles, M.P., Matowe, L., Shirran, L., Wensing, M., Dijkstra, R., Donaldson, C.: Effectiveness and efficiency of guideline dissemination and implementation strategies. Health Technol. Assess 8, iii-iv, 1–72 (2004)
38. Marietti, C.: The eyes have it. CCOW (Clinical Context Object Workgroup) brings both cooperation and competition together to tackle visual integration. Healthcare Informatics: The Business Magazine for Information and Communication Systems 15, 39 (1998)
39. Aha, D.W., Marling, C., Watson, I.: Case-based reasoning commentaries: introduction. The Knowledge Engineering Review 20 (2005)
40. Payne, T., Lassila, O.: Semantic web services. IEEE Intelligent Systems 19, 14–15 (2004)
41. Jahnke-Weber, J.H., Bychkov, Y., Dahlem, D., Kawasme, L.: Semantic support in composing Web Portal pages. In: Clarke, S. (ed.) End User Computing Challenges and Technologies: Emerging Tools and Applications. IGI Global (2007)
42. Frost, J.H., Massagli, M.P., Wicks, P., Heywood, J.: How the Social Web Supports Patient Experimentation with a New Therapy: The demand for patient-controlled and patient-centered informatics. In: AMIA Annual Symposium Proceedings, p. 217 (2008)

43. Wohlsen, M.: Patient-Led Drug Trials Defy Medical Establishment. The Associated Press (2008)
44. Schwartz, E.: The Dangers of Cloud Computing. InfoWorld (2008)
45. Scheier, R.L.: Busting the nine myths of cloud computing. InfoWorld (2009)
46. Kaufman, L.M.: Data security in the world of cloud computing. IEEE Security and Privacy 7, 61–64 (2009)
47. Itani, W., Kayssi, A., Chehab, A.: Privacy as a Service: Privacy-Aware Data Storage and Processing in Cloud Computing Architectures. In: IEEE International Conference on Dependable, Autonomic and Secure Computing, pp. 711–716 (2009)
48. Larkin, E.: Will Cloud Computing Kill Privacy? PC World (2010)
49. Christodorescu, M., Sailer, R., Schales, D.L., Sgandurra, D., Zamboni, D.: Cloud security is not (just) virtualization security: a short paper. In: Proceedings of the 2009 ACM Workshop on Cloud Computing Security, pp. 97–102 (2009)
50. Wang, C., Wang, Q., Ren, K., Lou, W.: Ensuring data storage security in cloud computing. In: Proc. of IWQoS, vol. 9 (2009)
51. Gross, R., Acquisti, A., Heinz III, H.J.: Information revelation and privacy in online social networks. In: ACM Workshop on Privacy in the Electronic Society, p. 80 (2005)
52. Moturu, S.T., Liu, H., Johnson, W.G.: Trust evaluation in health information on the World Wide Web. IEEE Engineering in Medicine and Biology Society, 1525–1528 (2008)
53. Healey, M.: 8 Questions To Ask Before Going Live in the Cloud. Information Week (2009)
54. Yong, P.L., Olsen, L.: The Healthcare Imperative: Lowering Costs and Improving Outcomes. The National Academies Press, Washington (2010)

Overview of the Smart Internet

Joanna W. Ng[1], Mark Chignell[2], James R. Cordy[3], and Yelena Yesha[4]

[1] IBM Canada
jwng@ca.ibm.com
[2] Universtiy of Toronto
chignell@utoronto.ca
[3] Queen's University
cordy@cs.queensu.ca
[4] University of Maryland
yeyesha@umbc.edu

Abstract. The aim of this chapter is to introduce the key characteristics of the Smart Internet, envisaged as addressing the current problems reviewed in the introduction to Part 1 of this book. After introducing the key principles of the smart internet, a distinction is made between smart interactions, and smart services, each of which are then dealt with in Parts 2 and 3 of the book.

Keywords: Smart internet, interactions, user models, web.

1 Introduction

Research work in context-aware computing [1] the Semantic Web [2] and personalization [3] has made advances with respect to some of the shortcomings of the Internet identified earlier in this book. However, without a cohesive and advanced *user model* at a macro level (not just at the individual site level), and without a *web model* to capture the conceptual structure of Web content and services, these types of incremental advances will not lead to significant change.

This chapter proposes an extension to the web, referred to as the *smart internet,* which includes a new user model of the web, *smart interactions*, that is centered on the perspective of the user instead of the server. This advanced user model is enabled by a new web model, referred to as *smart services*, that provides the integrated web infrastructure necessary to support the technical requirements of the smart interaction user model.

The notion of a smart internet requires a transformation in our understanding of the web and its architecture – a complete change of perspective, from a server-centric understanding to a user-centric one. This change will be much like the Copernican revolution, where the presumed structure of the solar system changed from an Earth-centric one to a Sol-centric one.

Three major extensions are called for in this transformation. First, a new "Copernican" *user model for the web* is needed that is centered on the users' concerns and cognition. Second, a new kind of *session concept* is required that centers on the user's perspective and her situation rather than the server's perspective of user interactions. Thirdly, the *concept of dynamic social binding of web interactions*, to

M. Chignell et al. (Eds.): The Smart Internet, LNCS 6400, pp. 49–56, 2010

turn what is currently a single user web interaction model into multi-users' collaborative web interactions under the user's control, is also needed.

In essence, the *smart internet* supports an instinctive *user model of the web*, one in which the discovery, aggregation and delivery of services and resources results in rendered content that is optimal for each user or group's situation.

Formulating a user model could potentially benefit from empirical studies of web browsing. Beauvisage [4] includes a survey of many such studies, and his own study, based on his approach of "web territories". These "territories" includes three dimensions related to browsing behavior: navigation dynamics, user dynamics, and content dynamics. He used statistical classification for the purpose of describing those dimensions.

This chapter presents our vision for the *smart internet,* and outlines some of the research challenges posed by the two complementary aspects, *smart interactions* and *smart services*. The making of this vision into a reality will require many kinds of expertise and technical solutions. It is our hope that this book will encourage researchers to address these challenges.

2 The Smart Internet Vision

The smart internet will be an evolving extension of the internet in which online services and resources are discovered, aggregated and delivered dynamically, automatically and interactively in response to a user's or group's evolving concerns and situations, which may involve real time or proactive performance of tasks that address users' goals.

All aspects of this interaction must be conducted with awareness of, and adaptation to, the user's personal and group context, task requirements and characteristics. The resulting aggregation of resources and content will be delivered in a manner appropriate to the user's current concerns or situation, and as a unified entity abstracting relevant content and services from a single site, or from multiple sites and organizations.

To be practical, the smart internet must be an evolution and extension of the current internet, building on the existing basic architectural elements of HTML, URLs and HTTP, while hiding these techno-centric elements behind objects and interactions that are more appropriate and intuitive, tailored to the end user's current domain, goals and concerns. Rather than the user initiating interactions to accomplish tasks themselves, the smart internet should allow the user's current concerns to drive the implicit discovery and aggregation of services and resources to serve the user and support the user's cognition and action.

This section highlights the three distinct principles of smart internet that set it apart from the internet today: an *instinctive user model, sessions for users and their matter of concerns,* and *collective and collaborative web interactions.*

Each of these principles is described below.

2.1 Principle 1: A User-Centric Model for Instinctive Interaction

The term "user model" has been used in a number of different ways in the literature on human-computer interaction [5]. Norman [6] distinguished between three different conceptual models relating to use of interactive systems: the user model; the design model; the system image. While the latter terms represent the designer's model of the system and how the system presents itself to the user, the term "user model" can refer not only to the user's model, but also to a model of the user (closer to Norman's concept of design model). In the present discussion, user model refers to the model of the user and her tasks that is assumed in designing systems, methods of interaction, and in guiding specific interactions.

Identifying and applying appropriate user models is essential, in keeping with the requirements of user-centered design (e.g., [6]). Instead of being user-centered, the user model of the internet today is by and large techno-centric, exposing the fundamental components of the web architecture, resulting in a "one HTML page at a time" interactive model convenient for the server. The widespread use of the Internet should not be taken as proof that the techno-centric user model is sufficient. Users adapt to fit what the web has to offer, and in order to use valued content and services, they are willing to connect to myriad web sites, filtering the relevant information for their own context in order to address the task at hand. But this causes a great deal of inconvenience and wasted effort. What we seek instead is an alternative user-centric model that leads to interactions that are instinctive for the user, rather than being fitted to the server and awkward for the user.

There are three critical implications of the principle of instinctive user model for the web.

1. *Metaphors as Cues for Instinctive Response*

The system image of the smart internet should use metaphors based on objects and operations from real world analogies that are familiar and appropriate to users and map well to the user's current domain of concern. Well-chosen metaphors hide the techno-centric elements of the system, while promoting a good mapping between the concerns of the user and the functionality of the system.

Meaningful user interactions are driven by goals that are then reflected in the things that matter to the user when interacting with the system. These "matters of concern" ("*moc*") should drive the design of interactions, so that users no longer deal directly with URLs and logon forms for secured sites, not because they are not needed but because they are handled for them behind the scenes, just as people can drive cars without having to worry about all the details of how the engine is working.

Google maps "points of interest" are an example that illustrates the type of interaction envisaged, where the prime metaphor for user interaction is based on objects and operations like "Interest Category" and "Find Direction" that are in the user's domain.

2. *Web Page Content and Control by and for Users*

Another implication of instinctive interaction is the transfer of control of the rendered HTML page to end users so that individualized content is dynamically and adaptively aggregated for effective interaction with the user's *mocs*. Content and services could then be placed in individualized contexts based on the current collection of *mocs* applicable to the current persona (e.g., a user may have different personas depending on whether she is at home, at work, or mobile).

a. *Aggregative Content*
Currently online users have to deal with the one page per response per domain server request-response model of web interaction. The principle of instinctive interaction requires a completely different method of interaction.

In the smart internet, the rendered response is *aggregated for the purpose of the user* as a whole person with multiple current matters of concern. Transforming from *the users for the web* to *the web for the users* means providing *moc*-relevant resources and content extracted and abstracted from one or more servers and tailored to the concerns of the individual.

b. Adaptive to system of interactions
Instinctive interaction should be tailored not to a device or situation, but to a lifestyle and *the user's systems of interaction and other elements of context that are part of that lifestyle.* Adaptation to user's multiple systems of interaction is not just in form factor (e.g., different devices) but also in function. Traditionally, mobile devices provide a squeezed miniature of their desktop counterpart, resulting in inferior user interfaces. Instinctive interaction requires a different approach where subset units of functions that are optimal for the device of interaction; persona in context and other factors of context are adapted for the user's *moc.*

3. *Control*
The control of the HTML page as rendered response is transferred from the server to the user. Web application development for the smart internet enables users to control the form and content of web pages so as to suit their own purposes and context. For example, users can specify different preferences, rules and policies for aggregation for their various personas (personal, professional etc.) and *mocs*. These pre-set user rules and conditions then control how pages are put together.

4. *Calm, Instinctive, Cognitively Compatible*
Not only should the metaphors and entities of smart internet interactions match key features in the user's problem domain, but the methods and style of interaction should be compatible with *the user's cognition.* This is in sharp contrast to existing internet interaction, which requires its users to initiate and drive interactions with the web to accomplish their tasks. Such interactions are synchronous in nature, and users bear all the cognitive burden of initiating actions and remembering where related information is located.

In contrast, smart interaction, while still leveraging the web as a platform, provides better support for the user's cognition, reducing the amount of information that has to be held in prospective memory, reducing the complexity of tasks to be performed by the user, and so on.

The concept of *calmness* has emerged as a key aspect of ubiquitous computing which relates to how users' attention is engaged. Human attention has a number of key properties (e.g., [7]), including limited capacity, and differences in types of attentional resource (with a key distinction being between verbal and visuo-spatial attentional resources). In order to be calm, interactions should engage both the center and the periphery of the user's attention moving back and forth between the two. Peripheral attention does not require the executive processing of focal attention but allows a person to maintain awareness of information in the environment. The periphery at a given moment may be the center of attention in the next and smart interaction should exploit the properties of cognition to provide information and options in a way that it easy for people to perceive and assimilate while going about other activities. By loading more processing in to the periphery, smart interaction informs without overburdening, freeing users' cognitive capacity to handle more things [8] while making tasks calmer and less disruptive.

Calmness in the smart internet may be achieved in many different ways, such as by adding asynchronous interfaces to allow *mocs to move* back and forth between the periphery and the center of attention depending on user specified rules, and aggregating and adapting based on the user's changing personas and context.

2.2 Principle 2: Session for Users and Their Matters of Concern

Today, the notion of session keeps track of the user and their interactions from the perspective of the server. The session ends when the user stops interacting with the site. Traditionally, a user session is defined as "a series of requests issued by a user to a web site in a single visit to the site" [9]. Technically, user sessions are HTTP sessions used to preserve the conversational state between a given server site and connection with a browser instance of a client device. Important session information such as user account and password are preserved and associated with the corresponding client, avoiding the need to ask for the same required information in a given request-response dialogue, resulting in better user experience. The existing concept of session, (i) is associated with one particular server, and (ii) is bounded by user's real time synchronous interactions.

When the web's center of gravity is re-focused on the user, the concept of session must be extended beyond the server site view of user initiated real time synchronous interaction. In the smart internet, sessions are oriented to the perspective of users and their matters of concern, rather than simply being states that the server site wants to keep track of. Two major implications follow from this shift of emphasis.

1. *Interactions need not be synchronous*

Sessions centered on the user and her matters of concern should not be exclusively real time synchronous interactions initiated by the user. To sufficiently support the user's matter of concerns, smart interaction needs to add, (i) asynchronous interaction patterns, such as events and asynchronous conversations. Examples might include setting up of monitors; reminders or alerts based on certain conditions (triggers) or the setting up of prospective memory related tasks of *mocs* such as scheduled tasks, and (ii) batch processing where sequences of service interactions within or across several server sites are remembered and repeated automatically.

2. *Session as a Cohesive Continuum across multiple systems of interaction*

Web applications in the smart internet see users, their concerns and tasks as a continuum of ubiquitous access across one or more systems of interaction. This revised concept of session has the following implications: (i) Smart internet sessions maintain *mocs* as persistent states in order to keep track of progress towards the user's goals and sub-goals and the need for user's attention for each *moc*. Smart internet sessions will involve semantic integration of a relevant set of composite services and server site sessions to deduce and maintain (persist) overall state and progress of *mocs*. (ii) This persistence means that users will not lose or change their state or the state of their matters of concern when switching system of interactions. Thus users will always be able to continue where they last left off. (iii) This means that switching personas or context does not throw the user into a new logon session. When re-authentication is required, it will be done on the user's behalf (without requiring the user's involvement). This also means that the user's multiple systems of interaction can function as a cohesive unit, forming a continuum for the users and their *mocs*. This is very different from today, when each change of system of interaction leads to a new session that is treated as if unrelated to previous sessions.

2.3 Principle 3: Collaborative and Collective Web Interactions

The third principle of the smart internet that distinguishes it from the current internet is that it explicitly supports close collaborate between users to resolve shared matters of concern. This principle has the following implications.

1. Dynamic Social Binding

Dynamic social binding is defined as the capability to select other users dynamically to share interaction elements for different levels of interactions associated with *mocs*. Shared interactions will occur at different levels of intensity, ranging from sharing of views as read-only, to co-execution or delegation of tasks and sub-tasks of mocs, thereby turning web interactions from solitary undertakings to multi-user collaboration. Online shopping can be used to demonstrate the application of this principle. Suppose a user, A, has started a matter of concern relating to online Christmas shopping for his children. He places multiple items from the catalog into the shopping cart. Using dynamic social binding, user A selects his wife, user B, to co-execute different elements of interaction for the online Christmas shopping task as a moc. Now user B is enabled to participate and collaborate in operations of user A's *moc* such as adding items to the shopping cart. Once the collaborative work has been completed, User A can transfer the session to user B or end the dynamic social binding session and continue to checkout himself.

2. Collective Intelligence

In Smart interaction, matters of concern become the major drivers of activity, explicitly centering the processing on user needs and interests. In keeping with this focus on mocs, text and semantic search in the smart internet should return search results in units of *mocs* as a (pre-set; or ready-to-use as-is or with minor modification) purpose-built composite collection of related services and resources instead of being simply a list of unrelated single hyperlinks as in today's internet. We envision a new kind of search interface that enables users to locate, customize, consume, rate and review. Tools should also be available for users to personalize their own search interfaces based on their mocs. Queries such as "what do people with similar profiles to mine do in similar matters of concern (*moc*)?" should also be answered by the collective intelligence provided by other users with similar mocs. This functionality can be provided by harvesting statistical data concerning historical behavior, user ratings, user reviews and feedback presented to users. Proactive analysis on such collective intelligence can be done as batch processing so that it is readily available at runtime to support new user interactions.

3 The Research Agenda

Web science studies the web as an empirical science as well as a science of synthetic formalism and algorithms, with the goals being (i) to derive hypotheses that predict and explain the web and (ii) to formalize the engineering of the web. It is intended to be a multidisciplinary science of the web [10]. Research on the smart internet fits within the scope of web science. With respect to the Web science of the *smart internet*, two major research activities are identified, namely: (i) formalizing an advanced ***user model*** of the web (for *smart interactions*) that centers around users and their matters of concern and (ii) formalizing a ***web model*** (for *smart services*) including formalizing the algorithms required to orchestrate the web as a cohesive platform that enables the advanced user models required for smart interaction. These two major research activities are addressed, respectively, in the following two parts of this book.

4 Conclusion

To be practical, the smart internet must be an evolution and extension of the current internet, building on the existing basic architectural elements of HTML, URLs and HTTP, while hiding these techno-centric elements behind objects and interactions that are more appropriate and intuitive, tailored to the end user's current domain, goals and concerns.

The research agenda for transition to a *smart internet* can be seen as falling within the scope of web science; extending the internet towards the goal of developing a new web model we call *smart services* that views web services at the macro level to support users as individuals, and the smart interactions that they require.

There are three major principles that distinguish the smart internet from the web in its current form, namely: (i) an instinctive user model; (ii) a session model focusing on the user's concerns, not just a single server site; and (iii) collective and collaborative web interactions. It is our belief that the research agenda in the smart internet will take us on a journey of transformation in re-engineering the web to focus on users rather than servers.

References

1. Dey, A.K.: Understanding and Using Context. Personal and Ubiquitous Computing 5(1), 4–7 (2001)
2. Berners-Lee, T., Hendler, J., Lassila, O.: The Semantic Web. Scientific American 284, 34–43 (2001)
3. Baldoni, M., Baroglio, C., Henze, N.: Personalization for the Semantic Web. In: Proc. Reasoning Web, pp. 173–212 (2005)

4. Beauvisage, T.: The Dynamics of Personal Territories on the Web. In: Proceedings of the 20th ACM Conference on Hypertext and Hypermedia, HT 2009, pp. 25–34. ACM, New York (2009)
5. Booth, P.A.: Introduction to Human-Computer Interaction. Erlbaum, Hillsdale (1989)
6. Norman, D.: The Design of Everyday Things. Basic Books, New York (1990)
7. Wickens, C.D., Hollands, J.G.: Engineering psychology and human performance, 3rd edn. Prentice-Hall, Englewood Cliffs (2000)
8. Weiser, M., Brown, J.S.: The Coming Age of Calm Technology. Xerox PARC (October 1996)
9. Kleinberg, J.: Authoritative sources in hyperlinked environment. J. ACM 46(5), 604–632 (1999)
10. Berners-Lee, T., et al.: A Framework for Web Science. Foundations and Trends in Web Science 1(1), 1–134 (2006)

Part II
Smart Interactions

Smart Interactions

Joanna W. Ng[1], Mark Chignell[2], James R. Cordy[3], and Yelena Yesha[4]

[1] IBM Canada
jwng@ca.ibm.com
[2] Universtiy of Toronto
chignell@utoronto.ca
[3] Queen's University
cordy@cs.queensu.ca
[4] University of Maryland, Baltimore County
yeyesha@umbc.edu

Abstract. As discussed in Chapter 3, the Smart Internet consists of both smart interactions and smart services. Part 2 of this book covers smart interactions, which are briefly introduced here. Since the requirements for user interaction are driven by human needs and the properties of human cognition, we will also consider research requirements relating to smart interaction in this introduction, and a brief roadmap of the remaining chapters in this section will also be provided.

Keywords: Smart interactions, smart internet, user models, web.

1 Introduction

The smart internet needs to be much more user-centric and responsive to user needs for web interactions to address user's matters of concerns than is the current internet. The goal of the smart internet with respect to user modeling is not to have a deep psychological understanding of each user, but rather, to develop normative models that represent their broad characteristics and is optimal for the purpose of why user uses the web. At the same time, such models have to be flexible and adjustable (such as by filling in the details and parameterization of a normative user model) to suit particular contexts. In general, the user model will contain *metaphors; concepts; objects; operations and relationships among them* [1]. The baseline user model of the current web uses hypermedia as the uniform interface. It provides resource identification from the perspective of the server side with great simplicity [2]. In order to move from this baseline model to smart interactions, we propose a research agenda aimed at formulating this normative *user model of the web* that encapsulates the key elements of all three principles of the smart internet, focusing on the user. One key assumption in this formation is that user modeling should occur at a macro level across the web instead of occurring only at a micro level (i.e. bringing improvement to individual server sites).

M. Chignell et al. (Eds.): The Smart Internet, LNCS 6400, pp. 59–64, 2010.

2 Developing the Smart Internet User Model

Empirical research is needed to determine how users would want to use the web at a macro level as a platform of services and resources to support them in achieving their goals and addressing their matters of concern. Research relating to *smart interactions* (that is, the ***user model for the smart internet***) should address the following issues.

Metaphors that elicit instinctive response to goals and concerns

Appropriate metaphors allow people to more easily transfer existing knowledge and skills to new situations. Metaphors can exist at different levels of abstraction and detail. For example, the bookmark is a widely adopted metaphor of the current internet that hides the techno-centric architectural element of the web, namely the URL. The shopping cart is another widely used metaphor.

One key research issues in smart interactions is to identify metaphors for this new *user model of the web,* that are exemplars of all three smart internet principles, in order to best elicit instinctive user responses towards her goals and concerns, leveraging services and resources from the internet as her supporting platform.

As an overall metaphor, we propose the *"matter of concern" (moc)* as a way of connecting user needs and interests to content; resources and services of the web. The metaphor of matters of concern may entail concepts such as *to-do list* as a collection of all mental *tasks* related to resolve the concern of the matter. Such collection is structured as a flexible meta-model that is compatible with user's thinking and remembering things that have to be done. A person's matters of concern may drift in and out of focus, and change in their priorities, depending on the context. One of the challenges for smart interactions is to translate metaphors of such intrinsic dynamics into cohesively integrated artifacts of user interfaces as *system images* [3]. Another challenge is to build, manage and maintain, for the user, appropriate process models, state-transition diagrams, and the like to support detailed task interactions and completion of a given *moc*. Areas for future research may include formulating the definition of additional objects and operations of the *moc* metaphor, and translating them into user interaction artifacts, that effectively elicit user responses that are appropriate for moving towards goals or addressing concerns. For example, how to define these objects and operations, so that they can function as effective *perceptual substitution* [4] such that the assessment of the states and progress of a *moc* (which can become very complex) will be transformed into fast operations for the user in order to elicit instinctive responses appropriate to the status of the *moc*.

Additional research in the web science of *smart interactions* may also lead to additional metaphors to be defined and identified towards the goals of the *smart internet.*

Another key research question is to find out what are the objects and operations in the current internet that users would rather not be made aware of (even though they are necessary or even critical to the web as a system) so that they can be better focused on objects and operations directly relevant to their goals; tasks and concerns. The follow on question is to ask how to make them invisible. Objects and operations such as logon forms, or input form data for personalized data that is constant may exist in many *to-dos* (which may involve multiple secured server sites) of a given *moc.* These result in operations that are complex and cognitively challenging (e.g. remembering multiple account numbers and passwords or having to look them up before keying in) operations, resulting in distraction of the user from her goal of resolving the matters of concern. A good metaphor for the normative user model of *smart interactions* will make these distracting operations invisible.

A Model that enables Task Simplification

The advanced user model required for smart interaction includes the aspect of transforming difficult tasks into simple ones. Tasks are simplified by making them more *narrow* and *shallow* in shape [3]. For instance, a given matter of concern (such as booking a vacation) typically involves multiple bookmarks (such as car rental reservation link; hotel reservation link; air ticketing link; points of interest links etc.), where each maps to different tasks related to booking a vacation. Instead of the user mentally keeping track of all necessary to-dos regarding booking vacation by manually managing these hyperlinks for that concern, they can be collapsed into a *moc.* The user benefits not only by the cognitive offloading, but she can keep using this *moc* over again in the future; or share it with a friend, or have it rated or commented, and so on. In general, task simplification will lead to reduced cognitive effort and an increase in cognitive compatibility. Task simplification requires a re-engineering of the web, so that no compromises in efficiency or effectiveness are made in order to create a simpler view of the task for users.

Research is needed to determine when and how tasks may be simplified. Since this is an engineered solution that has to work across a wide range of Web interactions, user testing cannot be used to determine what works and what doesn't on an ad hoc basis. Instead, predictive models of task simplification are needed, along with rules for linking simplified views of tasks in the user interface with more detailed views of the task at the back end. When this process works well the user becomes a *supervisory controller* (cf. [5]) specifying what needs to be achieved and monitoring the outcomes without worrying about the details. Task simplification for smart interaction is like the analogy of autopilot, but applied to the scope of the web: the plane is flown in autopilot mode (telling it where to go and making sure that it gets there) rather than the manual mode, with all the effort and expertise that requires. In the travel booking example, a supervisory control type of interaction would allow the user to simply activate the 'booking travel' *moc* whereupon all recommended transactions would be presented to the user for confirmation or modification, with the web working behind the scene to carry out the details implied by the user selections.

Service level batch processing, while still very new, will play a significant role in the engineering of the web to fulfill the *smart interactions* requirement of the user as supervisory controller.

Possible future research may involve mapping task taxonomies identified in human factors and human-computer interaction research into patterns of smart interactions where users can exercise supervisory control over a simplified view of the task.

A Model that provides Cognitive Support

Cognitive support may be loosely defined as the *assistance offered by an artifact* for a user to think about and solve problems relating to his concern. Theories of applied cognition offer insight into why some abstracted class of artifacts (and their uses) lead to more effective cognition [4,6] and reduce or completely eliminate the possibility for error. User models of smart interaction exemplify the principle of: "knowledge in the world, not in the head" [3]. The less a person needs to know about a task she is concerned about, without compromising the system's (which is the web as a platform) ability to complete the task in a way the user would want, the better. A key strategy in smart interaction is to let the system keep track of how things stand with regard to ongoing mocs. If keeping track of the states of the matter of concerns is offloaded to the system, then the user may be informed about task status on a "need to know basis" through *alerts* or *reminders*. By moving *mocs* in and out of the user's awareness based on the user's need to know, the interface can be made more calm and the task memory load of the user can be reduced but with increased processing capacity for the user.

Such a metaphor with the dimension of providing good cognitive support to users will drive new definition of *session* that go beyond that of today's session which tracks only user initiated interaction and only one server site at a time. Additional research is required to define sessions that support smart interactions requirements such as maintaining and managing states for *mocs* per user often involving multiple server sites. One area of research in this regard is the role of personal agents as a means of creating persistent sessions that address matters of concern for users.

In addition, integrative research between human-computer interfaces and web architecture at a macro level for batch processing (in terms of task completion behind the scene without user involvement) and asynchronous services (in terms of system-initiated connections and interactions, but user-initiated) will be critical to enable real world implementation of an advanced user model that provides cognitive support to its users.

Falconer and Storey [7] recognized the importance of cognitive support to the user, and discussed cognitive load reduction by introducing cognitive support to tools. They discussed the difficulty of working through a large amount of data by the user. They also provided a cognitive support theoretical framework, and used it to design a cognitive support tool.

Relevant future research on cognitively compatible user models might include the integration of the various cognitive support methods that have been proposed into a system for reducing cognitive complexity in smart interaction. Another area of research would involve how interruptions should occur. An early example of this type of research is the work on attentional user interfaces by Horvitz et al. [8]. How errors are prevented is also another key research area.

A Model that enables Adaptive Aggregation

The user model for smart interaction should adapt dynamically to the user's context. Context can be defined as any information that can be used to characterize the situation of an entity (a person, place or object) to bring the most relevant content to the user [9]. Adaptation can be applied to the presentation layer, and/or the service execution layer. The goal is to bring most relevant server side resources from multiple sources to the user as an individual. Relevant research on this topic would include what aspects of the user model to adapt and when to adapt them. One goal of such research might be to define a meta-model; rules and framework to guide aggregation of content enabled by technologies such as mash ups.

The Concept of Dynamic Collaboration

"Connect-request-response-close" is the basic interaction cycle between a browser client and a given server site for a single user today. One dimension of the user model of the smart internet is the capability for the user to dynamically bind to another user who can i) share views ii) share execution iii) transfer execution.

Dynamic binding for collaborative server side services is a fairly new research area. It sees collaboration not as an application in itself but as a service that can be integrated into a larger context of operations. Dynamic collaborative services (as in Service Oriented Architecture) will be a key research area for enabling this functionality. Possible research issues include adding objects and operations to start and stop dynamic collaborations within a *moc;* the design of appropriate collaborative interfaces for smart interaction; interruption patterns in dynamic collaboration; access control and policy enforcement; security and privacy control and others.

3 Roadmap of This Section

Smart interaction is a complex topic that includes many research issues. The following chapters address a number of these issues.

McGrenere et al address the problem of when and how to interrupt users. Although their work focuses on collaboration amongst software developers as a case study, the problem applies broadly across many multi-tasking contexts particularly where tasks have asynchronous components and where coordination and communication are required as part of collaboration. The Chapter provides an example of iterative requirements analysis and design to create better notification and interruption features. It is likely that these methods, and perhaps some of the findings, should also apply to other forms of collaboration.

Spence and Marziali deal with the problem of group interaction in their Chapter, focusing on applications involving healthcare and the elderly. They raise the issue of how to make Web interactions more inclusive. They describe how the issues of acceptance, usability and trust need to be dealt with in online group interactions.

In their chapter, Martin et al., address the issue of predictive analytics. In keeping with the smart interaction approach, they address the issue of how to provide enhanced information and guidance in the context of decision-making tasks. Their approach is to use predictive analytics to provide cognitive support. After reviewing available methods for implementing predictive analytics they then show how predictive analytics capability can be added to smart interaction as a mediator between online services and back-end data warehousing and data mining capabilities.

Personalization is a major part of the smart interaction vision, but the challenge is how to provide users with powerful personalization tools without requiring them to become programmers (or even to be aware that they are doing a form of programming). Xiao et al describe methods for allowing end-users to dynamically compose and personalize services to meet their own needs. They use a goal-driven method where users specify their goals in terms of keywords, from which a task list is generated. They use historical usage data in composing the task list based on user keywords. The feasibility of this approach is then demonstrated in a proof of concept prototype.

Storey and Grammel also tackle the problem of personalization but they do it from the perspective of mashups. Their chapter surveys six mashup development environments from an End User Development (EUD) perspective. The environments are explored, summarized and compared in terms of their features across six different themes (Levels of Abstraction, Learning Support, Community Support, Discoverability, UI Design and Software Engineering Techniques).

Storey and her colleagues examine the interplay between smart interactions and smart services through the lens of smart media. After reviewing past use of media in HCI they then propose a role for smart media within the smart internet framework, motivating that role through some sample high level scenarios. They also outline some of the challenges that need to be faced in creating and applying smart media objects.

4 Conclusion

Smart interactions represent a radical departure from existing Web interaction. While this new form of interaction should be highly beneficial to researchers, it also entails many research challenges. In this chapter we have motivated the need for smart interaction in terms of a user model that provides cognitive support to the user. The chapters in the remainder of this section address various aspects of the multi-faceted construct that is smart interaction.

References

1. Johnson, J., Henderson, A.: Conceptual Models: Begin by Designing What to Design. Interactions 9(1), 25–32 (2002)
2. Fielding, R.T., Taylor, R.N.: Principle design of the modern Web architecture. ACM Transactions on Internet Technology 2(2), 115–150 (2002)
3. Norman, D.: The Design of Everyday Things. Basic Books, New York (1990)
4. Walenstein, A.: Cognitive Support in Software Engineering Tools: A Distributed Cognition Framework, PhD thesis, Simon Fraser University, Vancouver, BC (2002)
5. Sheridan, T.B.: Humans and automation: System design and research issues. Wiley and Sons, New York (2002)
6. Walenstein, A.: Theory-based Analysis of Cognitive Support in Software Comprehension Tools. In: Proc. Intl. Workshop on Program Comprehension, pp. 75–84 (2002)
7. Falconer, S.M., Storey, M.-A.: A Cognitive Support Framework for Ontology Mapping. In: Aberer, K., Choi, K.-S., Noy, N., Allemang, D., Lee, K.-I., Nixon, L.J.B., Golbeck, J., Mika, P., Maynard, D., Mizoguchi, R., Schreiber, G., Cudré-Mauroux, P. (eds.) ASWC 2007 and ISWC 2007. LNCS, vol. 4825, pp. 114–127. Springer, Heidelberg (2007)
8. Horvitz, E., Kadie, C., Paek, T., Hovel, D.: Models of attention in computing and communication: from principles to applications. Comm.. ACM 46(3), 52–59 (2003)
9. Dey, A.K.: Understanding and Using Context. Personal and Ubiquitous Computing 5(1), 4–7 (2001)

Designing Effective Notifications for Collaborative Development Environments

Joanna McGrenere[1], Jin Li[2], Jimmy Lo[2], and Elena Litani[2]

[1] Department of Computer Science, University of British Columbia
joanna@cs.ubc.ca
[2] IBM Canada Toronto Lab
{jinli,jimmylo,elitani}@ca.ibm.com

Abstract. We describe research conducted to improve the design and management of notifications in the Jazz collaborative development environment. Scenario-based design was used in conjunction with focus groups that included eight representative Jazz users. The end result of this research is presented as a proof of concept prototype implementing a new notification architecture.

Keywords: user-centered design, scenario-based design, notifications, interruptions, focus group, prototype, collaborative-development environment, software development.

1 Introduction

As noted in the preceding introduction to Part 2, defining how interruptions should occur is an area of research that is relevant to smart interaction. This chapter examines the problem of how to design interruptions in the context of software development. Software development is a complex, labour intensive process. Software projects of all sizes are commonly developed by teams of people working together, reacting and responding to each other, to get software delivered in a timely fashion. Integrated development environments (IDEs), such as Eclipse, have been the industry standard development tool [1]; they focus primarily on supporting an individual software developer. Jazz [2], by contrast, is a collaborative development environment (CDE) which has been designed by IBM to transform software delivery, making it more collaborative, productive and transparent for development teams using the agile development process [3]. This is consistent with Principle 3 of the Smart Internet (Chapter 3), namely that the smart internet should support collaboration between users to resolve shared matters of concern. A CDE is designed specifically to enhance team process and interaction; the assumption is that this support will result in an increase in team productivity [4].

An analogy to a CDE, distinct from the software development domain, is Google Docs [5], which offers a collaborative document authoring environment, enabling multiple users to synchronously and asynchronously edit documents online. The tool tracks who made changes to a document and when, and can roll back to any version. Jazz is a collaborative development environment that helps developers to collaboratively develop application code.

M. Chignell et al. (Eds.): The Smart Internet, LNCS 6400, pp. 65–87, 2010.

The agile development process is more adaptive to constant change than traditional software development methods such as the Spiral Method [6]. It requires notifications as a means of maintaining awareness of the constant and rapid changes happening on the team. By notification, we simply mean that the user receives an indicator of an event; email, instant messages, events listings are common forms of notifications. Jazz supports notifications of events that are fired based on user activities (e.g. marking a defect as resolved) as well as system activities (e.g. the outcome of a build). However, these notifications often interrupt and overwhelm Jazz developers, making it hard for them to focus on getting their work done. The goals of the research reported in this chapter were to explore and validate this problem, to generate design solutions to the problem, and to create a preliminary proof-of-concept prototype instantiating the solutions.

We posit that Jazz presents a unique environment in which to investigate notification management. Jazz has built-in system knowledge of development teams, their internal structure, and the artifacts being developed, which greatly simplifies the access and monitoring of team-related activities, and has the potential to enable smart interaction without traditional artificial intelligence techniques [7]. This is directly related to Principle 2 of the Smart Internet (Chapter 3), which points to the need for the *system* to keep track of users' ongoing matters of concern. For matters that cannot be completed within a single session (which is rarely possible in software development), the system will need to keep users informed about task status.

To address our research goals, we took a multi-phase approach, using scenario based design [8] as our primary methodology. We conducted a series of three focus groups with eight representative Jazz users to collect user input on two scenarios as well as a number of other dimensions. Based on that input, we designed and implemented a prototype that partially addresses the notification problems that we validated. Each of these phases is described in detail in this chapter.

The main contributions of our work are threefold: (1) We validated and prioritized the pain points (difficulties) experienced by developers and other team members with respect to notifications and awareness of team activity; (2) We generated design requirements for the high priority pain points we identified; and (3) We created a preliminary design for the "Inbox" UI widget, and implemented a proof of concept prototype. Secondary contributions include the development of two detailed scenarios which bring to life notification issues in Jazz, as well as a preliminary taxonomy of notification types in Jazz.

2 Related Work

The literature related to the work presented in this chapter includes research on interruption management, on the design and evaluation of IDEs and CDEs, including studies of collaboration among software developers.

2.1 Interruption Management

In recent years, there has been considerable attention paid to the topic of managing interruptions in the Human-Computer Interaction and related research communities [5].

Interrupting users with many non-critical events, for example, has been shown to lower productivity and cause stress and frustration [9]. In this chapter we use the more neutral term "notification" to mean the same thing as a system delivered "interruption." The two main components to interruption management that have been studied, albeit largely independently, are: (1) *timing* of interruption delivery based on user context [10]; and (2) *presentation format* of the interruption based on user context [11, 12]. In a pure timing-based model, notifications are queued up until it is a "good time" to interrupt the user, and all of the queued notifications are delivered at once. In a pure presentation-format based model, notifications are always delivered right away, but the way that the notification is presented, in particular the degree of intrusiveness (which also has been referred to as the degree of attentional draw [13]), is adjusted based on context.

A user's context generally refers to what the user is doing at a given moment, and at its highest level reflects whether the user is busy or not. The two primary ways to determine context are: (1) Automatically (or system determined), where the system attempts to detect when users are interruptible or not [7, 14], and (2) Manually (or user determined), where users declare their preferences, generally through a clickable dialog, as to when they can be interrupted, and the system interrupts users accordingly. The latter is currently how Jazz works, as do many other interruption-based communication applications, such as Lotus Sametime [15].

Context is more involved than simply the degree to which the user is busy doing an activity. Knowing when to interrupt should depend on the *importance* of the interruption content. This is sometimes referred to as the interruption's *relevance* or *utility*. (Each term has subtly different meanings which we ignore here.) Research has shown that matching the intrusiveness of a notification signal to the importance of the notification content improves productivity, over having a single notification style, regardless of content [13]. That work varied the presentation dimension, but not the time dimension of notifications.

In a collaborative development environment such as Jazz, the system can determine user's context more accurately than a general collaborative environment such as Google Docs [5]. This makes Jazz a unique environment on which to study notification management. For example, given the project team information, the system knows the roles and hierarchical structure of the team. Given the current project plan and schedule, the system knows which artifacts are most relevant and important, and the temporal importance of certain events/milestones.

Ideally, a system would be designed to vary both of the time and presentation dimensions based on context.

2.2 IDE and CDE Design and Evaluation

Similar to the topic of interruption management, there has been considerable work reported in the literature on user-centered approaches to the design and evaluation of IDEs [16, 17]. None of the literature on IDEs, however, focuses on designing for interruptions. There is also a well-established literature on developer collaboration [18, 19] and a burgeoning literature on the design of CDEs that support this collaboration [20, 21, 22]. Similar to the IDE literature, however, this literature largely ignores the issue of interruptions. Two exceptions are given next.

A recent study of collocated software developers showed that maintaining awareness is one of seven key information needs of these developers [23]. And more specifically, tracking the state of resources that developers depend on as well as tracking what their co-workers are doing are two of developers' highest information needs. This work noted that some awareness information comes through instant messaging clients and alert tools, as well as check-in emails, and that developers are often interrupted. But the paper does not seek to address the issue of interruption specifically. By contrast, Chong and Siino [24] do focus directly on the topic of interruptions in their ethnographic study comparing two software development teams, one of which used a paired-programming style and the other whose team members worked predominantly alone. Interestingly, they found that there were differences in terms of the length, content, type, time, context of occurrence, and strategies for handling work interruptions between the two distinct team structures. The authors report a number of implications for design, including the need to ease awareness of multiple tasks and that interruptees should be given greater control over interruption duration and conclusion; both of these implications point to the need for developers to better manage interruptions. The work reported in this chapter is consistent with that need.

3 Description of Jazz

The Jazz platform is an IBM initiative and Rational Team Concert (RTC) is the first product that is built on Jazz. Version 1.0 of RTC was released in June 2008, and version 2.0 was released in June 2009. RTC has an Eclipse-based client interface, a Microsoft Visual Studio client interface, and a Web interface (Web UI). Currently, developers primarily use the Eclipse-based client interface to build and deliver artifacts. The Web UI does not yet support the full functionality of the Eclipse-based client. Throughout this chapter we largely use Jazz and RTC interchangeably.

Jazz supports rapid peer-to-peer informal communication and lightweight awareness through events and feeds. Jazz provides three auto-generated feeds, designed with the expectation that they will keep developers informed of all the changes relevant and important to them: 1) build events from a developer's team areas; 2) team events for all of the team areas that a developer belongs to within the connected project areas; 3) work item events for all changes to a developer's work items. Developers can create system queries and use those queries as sources of events and feeds. The events are queued temporally, as shown in the Event Log section of the Team Central view shown on the left in Figure 1, and developers primarily use this view in the Eclipse-based client interface to sift through the events list to make sense of what is happening on the team.

Events in the Team Central view are automatically refreshed on a predefined time interval, and are displayed in temporal order. The icons shown in the first two columns in the Event Log section provide developers information about an event's type or importance at a quick glance. For example, for a given developer's instance of the client, the "@" image overlay in the first column indicates that that developer's name has been called out in the comments of the work item and needs his/her immediate attention. The binocular image in the second column indicates that the developer is simply watching the work item, but is not the creator or owner (thus, usually isn't responsible to act on the work item).

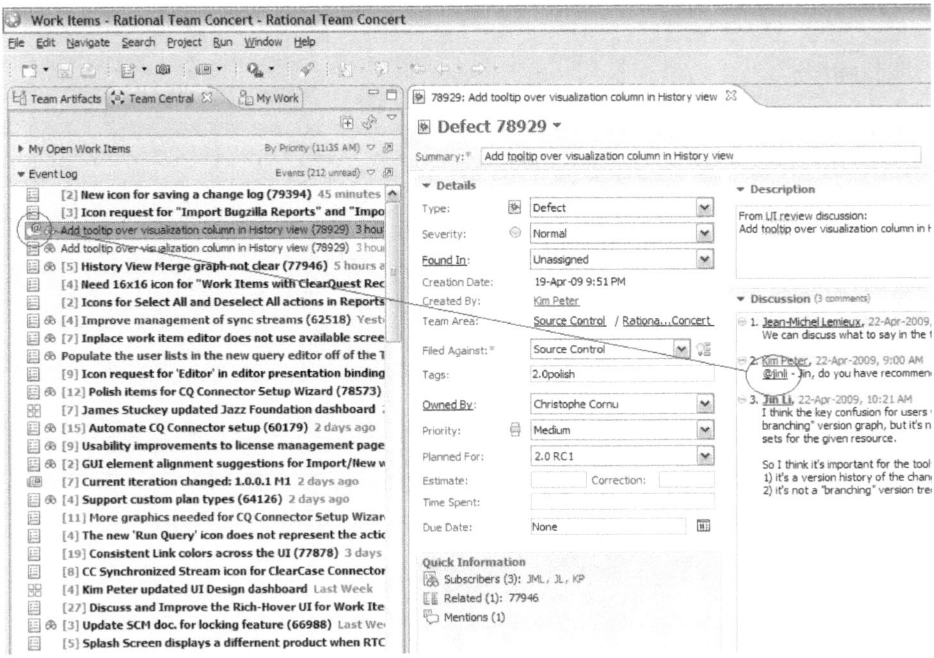

Fig. 1. Rational Team Concert. Team Central pane shown on the left, with the Event Log open. The editor on the right shows the content for Defect 78929, and the two red circles connected by a line markup show how the @userid tagged message in the comments for Defect 78929 is displayed in the Event Log section to raise the intended user's attention.

Jazz delivers events through an integrated feed architecture. There are a large number of event types to which developers can subscribe; for example, approvals on work items, build results, delivery of source code changes, team process changes, and news from subscribed feeds.

When developers are working on multiple projects, they can end up subscribed to many feeds, to the point of being overwhelmed by events and having difficulty distinguishing the important events from the less important ones. Furthermore, events have implicit levels of importance. For example, events that require an immediate reply or action from developers (such as work item approvals), events that may require a reply from developers (such as work item changes), events that indicate a problem with a project build (such as build errors), events of a team on which the developer is a member (such as a new work item assignment for a team member). We speculate that developers could be more effective if they could easily determine the importance of events. In Jazz, there is rudimentary interface support for events separation and filtering. Developers can create separate sections in the Team Central view to show different event types or events of different importance. As illustrated in Figure 2, developers can use filters to limit the types of events shown in the Team Central view.

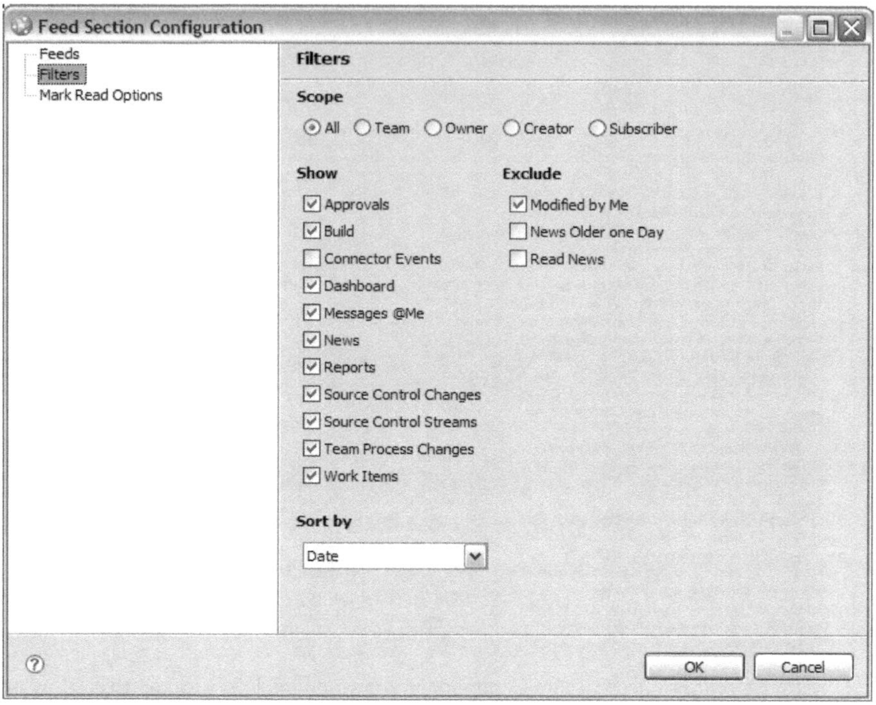

Fig. 2. Events filter configuration dialog box in Rational Team Concert.

The importance of events can also be set explicitly. As previously mentioned, Jazz allows users to tag messages with "@userid" in order to draw the attention of a particular developer (see the connected red circles in Figure 1). For example, Developer A may add "@developerB" to the text of his status update on a given work item, knowing that the update will cause an event to fire, and this will help ensure that Developer B actually reads the update note.

The My Work view in Figure 3 is another mechanism to help developers focus on certain events / activities in the Jazz system. The My Work view is developers' personal view of all the work items they have been assigned, and in principle is supposed to allow developers to plan, estimate, and track their daily work. The problem is that events related to these work items are not shown in the My Work view. Developers must switch to the Team Central view to scan for related events and switch back to My Work view to mentally connect events with work items, which significantly reduces the usefulness of the My Work view.

In Jazz, developers also rely heavily on other communication channels such as email and instant messaging. Currently, developers must rely on separate views and mechanisms to monitor and triage all the various events, and to prioritize their work.

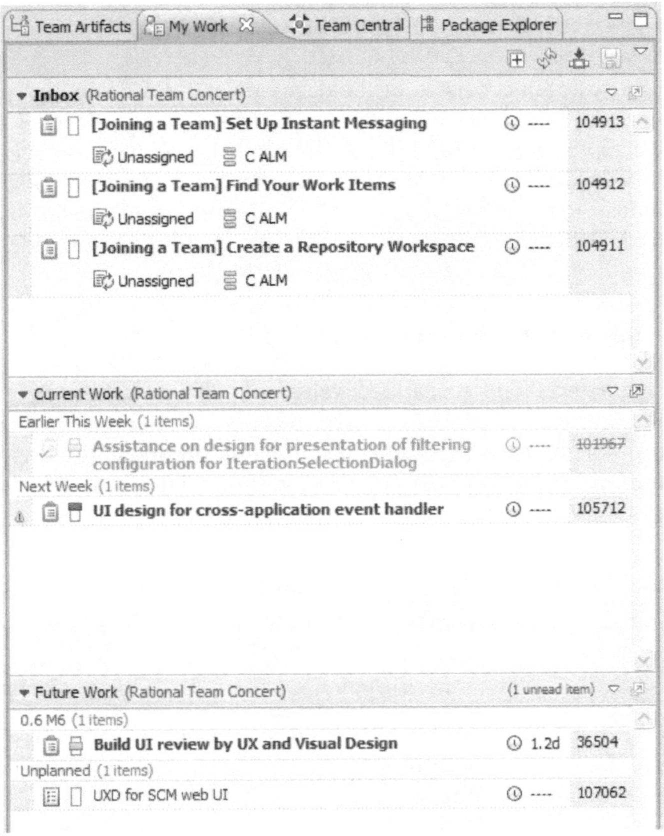

Fig. 3. My Work view in Rational Team Concert showing three newly assigned work items that haven't been processed, two current work items, and two future work items.

4 Overview of Research Methodology

We took a multi-phase approach, using scenario based design [8] as our primary methodology. In Phase I, we created a preliminary taxonomy of existing notification types in Jazz and, in parallel, we drafted an As-Is user scenario to encapsulate the problems resulting from those notifications and poor awareness. Secondly, we built an envisioned To-Be user scenario to illustrate potential design solutions that address those notification problems. In Phase II, we conducted a series of two focus group sessions with eight Jazz users: (1) to validate the As-Is scenario and to clarify notification pain points experienced, and (2) to prioritize those pain points and validate the To-Be envisioned scenario with its improved notification and awareness structures. In Phase III, we brainstormed and created low-fidelity prototypes for interface design ideas to support the new structures, and then conducted a third and final focus group session with the same Jazz users to explore design requirements and solutions. Finally, in Phase IV, we created a medium-fidelity prototype of an "Inbox" UI widget that aims to partially address the notification problems we validated.

5 Phase I – Taxonomy and Scenario Development

Phase I of our research consisted of the development of a taxonomy and two scenarios. A scenario is a concrete narrative description of a specific interaction which is chosen to be representative of real use. In our research we used scenarios to show event notifications in context. The taxonomy and scenario development brought the academic-industry research team together, clarifying our own understanding of event notifications and interruptions in Jazz, and was designed to provide an anchor for discussions with our focus group participants in Phase II.

5.1 Taxonomy of Notifications in Jazz

In parallel with the As-Is scenario development, the research team identified and classified the notification types in a CDE such as Jazz. This helped us to frame the notification problem space as well as our research questions for later phases of this research. We enumerated all possible notifications in Jazz, from which we developed the taxonomy for the notifications in Jazz that is shown in Table 1.

Table 1. Taxonomy of Jazz notifications, showing event initiator and directness

How an event is initiated	Who initiates an event	
	Individual	*Group*
Direct	Intentionally notifies others	n/a
Indirect	Unintentionally generates notification(s)	Unique for a CDE; Team process improvement

We use two dimensions to classify the notification types in Jazz. The first dimension reflects who initiates the notification, either an individual or a group of people. The second dimension reflects how the notification is initiated, either directly or indirectly. The labels inside the two-by-two table cells are high-level descriptors for the class of activities that fit within each cell. We provide some selected examples for each category next.

5.1.1 Individual-Direct: Individual Intentionally Notifies Others

- An individual starts a phone call, or sends an instant message or email to another person.
- An individual sends an announcement to a team.

Each of these results in the recipient(s) receiving a notification.

5.1.2 Individual-Indirect: Individual Does Something Which Unintentionally Generates Notification(s)

- A developer initiates a build which generates a notification to all team members that a build has just started; some time later, the team is notified that the build has either passed or failed.

- A developer commits code into the source control repository, and team members are notified about the code commit event.
- A developer adds a new comment or changes the status of a bug report in the defect tracking system, and other developers who have dependency on the bug are notified about the changes.

5.1.3 Group-Indirect: Team Process Improvement

We believe there is a unique notification opportunity in a CDE such as Jazz, whereby group activities could be monitored over a longer period of time and then used for analytics and pattern discovery to improve team process. When interesting findings emerge, notifications would be generated. These analytics and resulting notifications are not in place today, but envisioned examples include:

- The team use of the default optimistic locking during coding iterations leads to significant coding conflicts and lengthy resolution. When the system recognizes this issue it notifies the team lead, ideally with metrics and pattern visualizations. This may prompt the team to adopt a pessimistic locking mechanism for certain sub-system development to improve team productivity.
- When assigning developers to work on a piece of code, project managers or team leads are notified that certain teams or individuals might be more suitable for the task based on past team velocity, on-time delivery, and other metrics of a similar nature.
- The team lead pre-sets specific metric thresholds and is notified by the system when they are reached. For example, more than 100 bugs reported against a component indicates potential trouble. More generally, the team lead could be notified about inefficiencies in the team.

This third category of notifications, unique for CDEs, provides interesting future notification research opportunities.

5.2 As-Is Scenario

One of the researchers on the team (Li) is a member of the Jazz development team. The core content of the As-Is scenario largely emerged from his over-one-year immersion with Jazz developers using Jazz itself to develop Jazz, and the Jazz development scenario [25]. The academic-industry research team iterated on the As-Is scenario draft over several weeks to clarify task flow, terminology, and event notifications. The final As-Is scenario consisted of 10 paragraphs (768 words), covered 12 event types in all three Jazz notification taxonomy categories, involved 6 personas, and spanned a two-week period. The following is a one paragraph excerpt of the As-Is scenario:

Patricia (Project Manager) and Marco (Team Lead) are working together to plan the next iteration and need to verify the availability of all the developers for the next week. Marco tries to instant message Deirdre (Component Developer) to confirm that she will be off this Friday as usual, as that will impact the scheduled planning. Deirdre has blocked all IMs, so that she can focus on her work, and as a result Marco is forced to use email instead. Deirdre does not notice Marco's email request until sometime later.

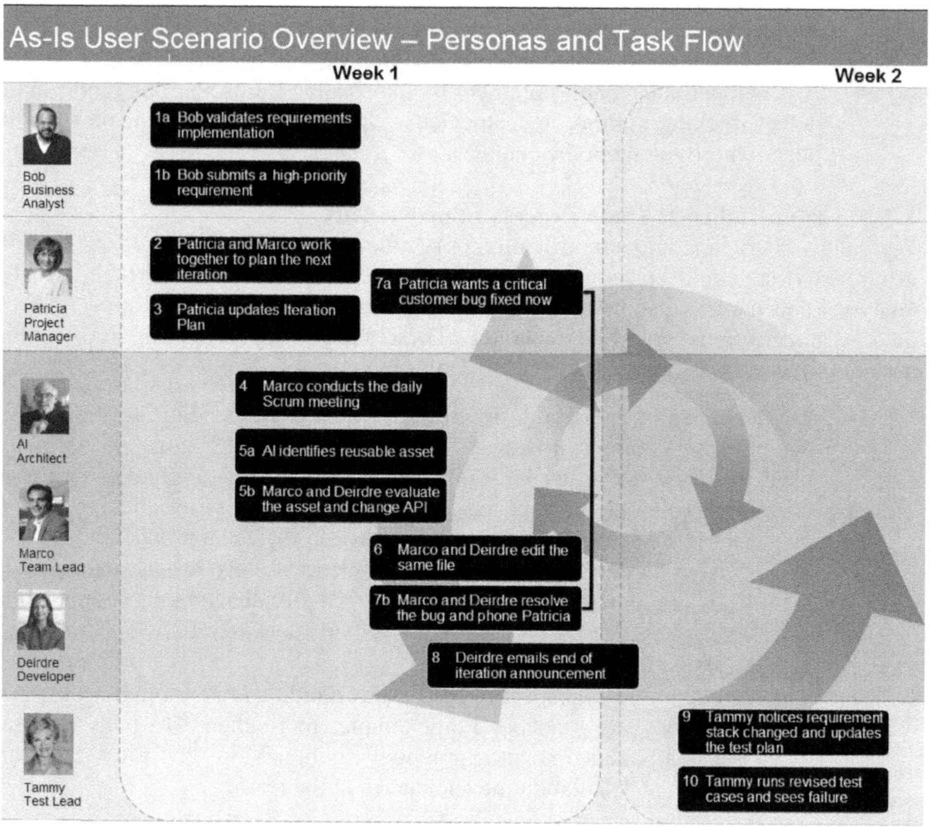

Fig. 4. As-Is scenario overview, including personas, timeline and task flow.

Figure 4 provides a visual overview of the As-Is scenario. This was shown to the participants in the focus group (Phase II), prior to reading through the full scenario, so that they could easily absorb the scenario and get a big picture view of the personas, timeline, and task flow (the black boxes) involved.

5.3 To-Be Scenario

After completing the As-Is scenario and the taxonomy of notifications in Jazz, the research team created a parallel To-Be scenario. For each notification problem highlighted in the As-Is scenario, the To-Be scenario included an envisioned specific design solution. Figure 5 provides a visual overview of the To-Be scenario.

The sample excerpt of the To-Be scenario that parallels that given for the As-Is scenario (in Section 5.1) is as follows:

Patricia (Project Manager) and Marco (Team Lead) are working together to plan the next iteration and need to verify the availability of all the developers for the next week. Marco instant messages Deirdre (Component Developer) to confirm that she has completed an assigned feature, as that will impact the scheduled planning.

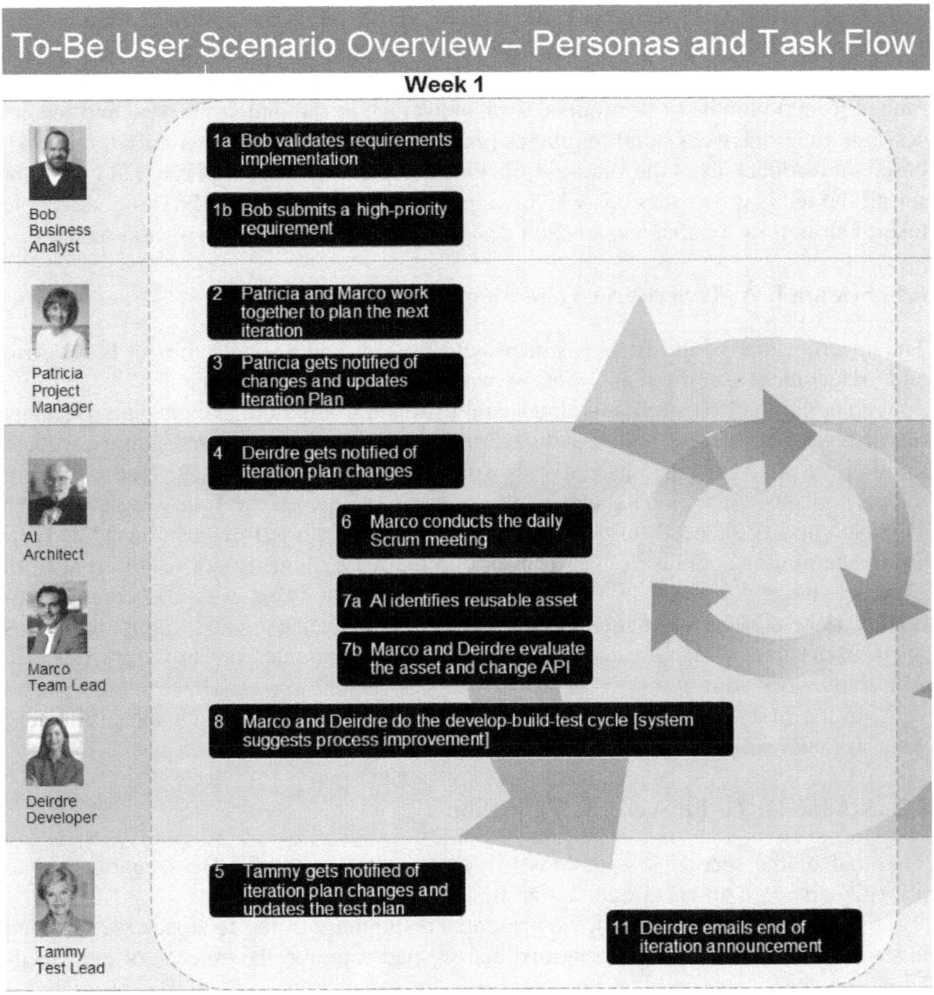

Fig. 5. To-Be scenario overview, including personas, timeline and task flow.

Deirdre has blocked all IMs, so that she can focus on her work; however, as her boss, Marco's IM gets through and she replies immediately.

This excerpt shows that an understanding of both the internal team personnel structure and Marco's current task allows Jazz to raise the priority of the IM event, and unblocks the IM channel for iteration planning purpose.

6 Phase II – User Scenario Validation and Findings

Phase II of our research was scenario validation. We conducted two focus group sessions, each session lasting 1.5 hours, with eight representative participants, all IBMers who use Jazz. We used a screener to recruit participants from the project management, team lead, coding and testing domains, with a requirement of at least three months Jazz experience. Of the eight participants, we had two project managers, two team leads, three developers and one tester. All participants were male and their Jazz experience ranged from 3 months to 12 months, with an average of 6 months. The first and second sessions were one week apart to give us time to modify the To-Be scenario, if required, based on feedback from the first session. One of the researchers was the lead facilitator for all the focus group sessions which were audio taped, and we had a designated note taker. Our high-level goal was to elicit design requirements based on a valid scenario.

6.1 Session I: As-Is Scenario Validation

The specific goal of the first session was to present and validate the As-Is scenario and to document specific pain points experienced by our participants.

We started the first session with a round of self-introduction. We gave an overview of our research, timeline and objectives for the focus group sessions. Then we walked through the As-Is scenario narrative one paragraph at a time to gather feedback from the participants. At various stages of the scenario, we asked the following questions: 1) Have you experienced this issue (e.g., critical bug reported by customer)? 2) How did the communication/awareness transpire in that case? Is it similar or different from what we have described in the scenario? 3) In what ways was the communication/awareness effective or ineffective? At the end of scenario walkthrough, there was open discussion on specific pain points that our participants currently experience in their daily work with Jazz.

After the first session we modified the To-Be scenario, with the changes reflecting what we had learned.

6.2 Session II: To-Be Scenario Validation

The goal of the second session was to validate the revised To-Be scenario, and to prioritize the pain points elicited in the first session.

To begin the second session, we presented a summary of the feedback we received in the first session. Participants agreed that we had captured the essence of their feedback and there was nothing important missing or misrepresented. We presented a summary of the pain points gathered in the first session and asked participants to rank them. One comment from the first session was that the As-Is scenario didn't universally apply across all team structures. We reflected on our scenario development, and told the participants that it was impossible for one scenario to adequately cover all team structures. We clarified that the To-Be scenario favoured an agile team structure, recognizing that it would not be a perfect fit for all structures. Participants acknowledged our decision, and then we walked through our revised To-Be scenario narrative one paragraph at a time. At the end of the scenario discussion, we put up a list of high-level notification issues and had an open discussion, to solicit design requirements for the problems.

6.3 Scenario Validation Findings

Overall, we learned that the scenarios were valid. Participants told us that they are indeed overwhelmed by the volume and multiple sources of notifications, such as email, instant messaging, phone, and event notifications in Jazz. There needs to be a balance between keeping developers informed / aware of their team members' activities and protecting developers' work time / space so that they can perform their primary tasks effectively. This feedback confirms the notification problems that our scenarios were designed to bring out. However, there were two main concerns raised from the validation sessions which we discuss here.

First, participants felt that the timescale (our scenarios spanned a two-week period as described in Section 5) used in the scenarios was too compressed, which could have an impact on the severity or importance of notifications and awareness. We acknowledge this limitation, but believe the timescale may be less of a factor than one would initially assume. For example, the content of a missed email from several weeks ago can all of the sudden become urgent, even though there were a number of weeks when the matter could have been dealt with in a non-urgent manner. We did, however, make some minor adjustments to the timescale to address the concern.

Second, the scenarios did not universally apply across all team structures, but elements in the scenarios did apply to everyone. For example, change of priority for a work item applies to different team structures. As noted above, the scenarios resonated better with an agile team structure. That makes sense since the scenarios were used for guiding the development of Jazz which is a CDE for agile teams.

Table 2 below summarizes the pain points that emerged in the first session, and how the participants rated them in the second session. Participants were given a sheet of paper that showed the list of seven pain points in the first column of Table 1, and asked to rank order the list, from one to seven, with one being the most problematic.

As shown in the table, "awareness of changes by others that affect my current work" and "prioritizing all incoming communication related to my current work" were rated as most problematic since they had the lowest mean ranks (representing the most problematic pain points). We focus our design efforts in Phase III predominantly on these two pain points.

Table 2. Seven notification pain points and their severity rankings (from 1=highest severity to 7=lowest severity) in Phase II. Column "1st" reflects the number of participants who gave the pain point in a given row a first order ranking, and so on. The last column shows the mean rank across the eight participants, which was used to identify the most problematic pain points.

Notification Pain Points	**Ranks**							**Mean**
	1st	2nd	3^{r}	4th	5th	6th	7th	
Blocked communication path to others	2	1		1	2	1	1	3.9
Blocking communication path to others			1		2		5	6.0
Awareness of changes by others that affect my current work	1	5		1	1			2.5
Notifying others who are (may be) affected by changes in my work	1		5		1	1		3.4
Locating important communication related to my current work	1	1	1		2	1	2	4.5
Prioritizing all incoming communication related to my current work	3	1	1	2		1		2.8
Identifying process improvement opportunities				4		4		5.0

Our main findings can be categorized into four themes, each of which we address in turn.

6.3.1 Theme #1: Individual Needs Come First, Team Needs Second

As stated in this chapter's introduction, a general belief is that when moving from an IDE to a CDE, the team benefits first and foremost, and as a result team productivity increases. Our participants reported differently. Despite the intention behind a CDE to support and benefit a team, the team is not the first priority for developers. For example, a build notification is supposed to be useful to the entire team, but rather we found that developers generally only want to be notified of build failures, and further, only failures that are caused by *their* code. Another example is work items notification. Currently developers who subscribe to a work item are notified of any changes to that item, serving the team's awareness needs. However, there's no notion of priority of a change, thus developers are overwhelmed by all changes, even at the low-level of spelling corrections and adding, removing, and then re-adding the same file attachment.

Design should focus on benefits to the individual (for example, better awareness of all things that would affect one's work), with the expectation that improved notification and awareness for the individual will in turn lead to a productivity improvement for the team. This is reflected by the highly rated paint point of prioritizing all incoming communication related to one's current work. Participants concurred that notifications in a CDE should be targeted to help the individual developer first, rather than targeting the team as a whole.

6.3.2 Theme #2: Notification Customization Presents Unique Opportunities and Challenges

There is no one size fits all solution. Jazz developers wanted to be able to customize to remove irrelevant notifications, but when presented with the possibility of blocking notifications based on their type, there was universal concern. Specifically we were told that blocking all notifications of a certain type was problematic because some of those notifications might be important.

With built-in system knowledge of team structure and associated artifacts in Jazz, there is a lot of opportunity to design an effective notification mechanism. For example, if Jazz knows that a developer is working on a particular work item right now, any events related to that work item could be made more salient to grab the developer's attention. This is significantly different from other collaborative systems such as Google Docs [5] (e.g. it's difficult to guess what business users might be writing at a given time). Furthermore, research on context modeling and management (such as that described in [26]) could be leveraged to include more sophisticated context-awareness in the design. For example, knowing that a developer is working on a particular work item right now may not be enough; knowing, in addition, whether or not the developer is alone in his office versus talking with another colleague could impact the form of notification delivery.

One of our research assumptions had been that notification filtering and customization were relatively static, in that developers would update their filters once, or at best very infrequently. We discovered, by contrast, that developer needs for notifications actually evolve throughout the development cycle, rendering static customization inappropriate. For example, we heard that build failure notifications might not be important and needed during the early phases of a development iteration, but would become increasingly important later on. Related to this point, we note that one insight from our research is that in order to keep the signal to noise ratio low, clearly identifying events that should not generate notifications (e.g. early build failures) is as important as identifying those that should generate notifications.

6.3.3 Theme #3: Notification UI Should Not Block Users: Control Must Remain with the User

Consistent with other human-computer interaction research, our participants were leery of the system taking over too much control [27]. For example, developers might get notified that one or more work items they are currently working on are being pushed to the next development iteration. By no means should that notification also try to assist these developers by automatically pushing the work item(s) into future work on their behalf. Developers may want to finish a conceptual piece of the work item before shelving it. Developers don't want to feel that technology is controlling and enforcing how their time is spent.

6.3.4 Theme #4: Don't Want Technology "Watching You"

Related to the above points, developers don't want to feel like they are being watched. Notifications can serve different purposes for different roles. Project managers may like to see many notifications; this gives a sense of activity and progress. On the other hand, some developers choose not to follow team process (e.g. deliberately do not change the status of work items to "in progress") because this often generates many notifications that only help others to track their progress, and have no benefits to the developers themselves.

7 Phase III – Exploration of Design Requirements

The main goal of Phase III was to identify and prioritize design requirements and to explore design ideas that met those requirements. We accomplished this by conducting brainstorming sessions within our research team to itemize design requirements based on the previous two focus group sessions, by generating design sketches, and then by soliciting input on the prioritization of those requirements and sketches in the third and final focus group session. Seven of the original eight participants attended this session.

Table 3 lists the requirements that were generated by our team as well as the average rating each requirement received from the participants during the third focus group session. Participants were given a sheet of paper that showed the exact table given in Table 3, except the last column was left blank for participants to enter their rating according to the following scheme: A – Must have, B – Nice to have, and C – Not important. The average was calculated by assigning values of 3, 2, and 1 to A, B, and C respectively. We note that all requirements were rated as A or B by the seven participants; C did not appear on any response sheet.

Table 3. Design requirements rated in Session 3 by the participants. Scale is 1 to 3, where higher numbers represent a more important requirement. ($N = 7$).

#	Requirement Description	Mean rating
1	Central place to view and prioritize work items and events that are scoped in 3 ways: for me, my team and the world.	2.4
2	My View Requirements:	
2.1	Ability to easily see and manage work items/events that require my immediate attention or action (inbox idea)	3
2.2	Ability to do fine grain subscriptions/watches (e.g., subscribe to the work item vs. work item changes by a particular person; pre-filtering on events arriving in inbox)	2.6
2.3	Ability to separate items that need immediate attention/action, from current work, from future work (todo)	2.9
3	Ability to see all events in a newly designed Team Central like view	2.4
3.1	Ability to show work items/events in various timelines: today, this week, next week, this iteration , next iteration, entire release, etc.	2.3
3.2	Ability to filter and sort contents by work item	2.7
3.3	Ability to filter and sort contents by event types	2.6
3.4	Ability to filter and sort contents by priority	2.9
3.5	Ability to filter and sort contents by timeline	2.1
3.6	Ability to filter and sort contents by team member	2.3
4	Ability to present view in 3 formats: full, docked, and mini	2.6

Given the high mean ratings across almost all of the requirements, it was apparent that all the requirements put forward were deemed to be important. In addition, participants deemed requirements that allowed them to deal with priority notifications to be the most important (requirements: 2.1, 2.3, and 3.4).

Next we listed the event types that we envisioned being supported by the system, which include: builds (auto-generated, user generated, etc.), source control, work items (changes to attributes such as comments), dependent work items, plan changes, instant messages / chats, email, RSS feeds. We asked if there were any missing. The participants requested phone calls and meeting invites to be included.

Finally, we showed the participants our most promising preliminary sketch, shown in Figure 6, which captures many of the requirements given in Table 3. We walked through the design elements and solicited free form input from the participants.

The UI sketch includes four distinct components for managing notifications:

- **Inbox** for *important* incoming notifications
- **All My Events** for the *full set* of incoming notifications
- **Current ToDo** and **Future ToDo**, which represent active tasks and future tasks and all their associated notifications.

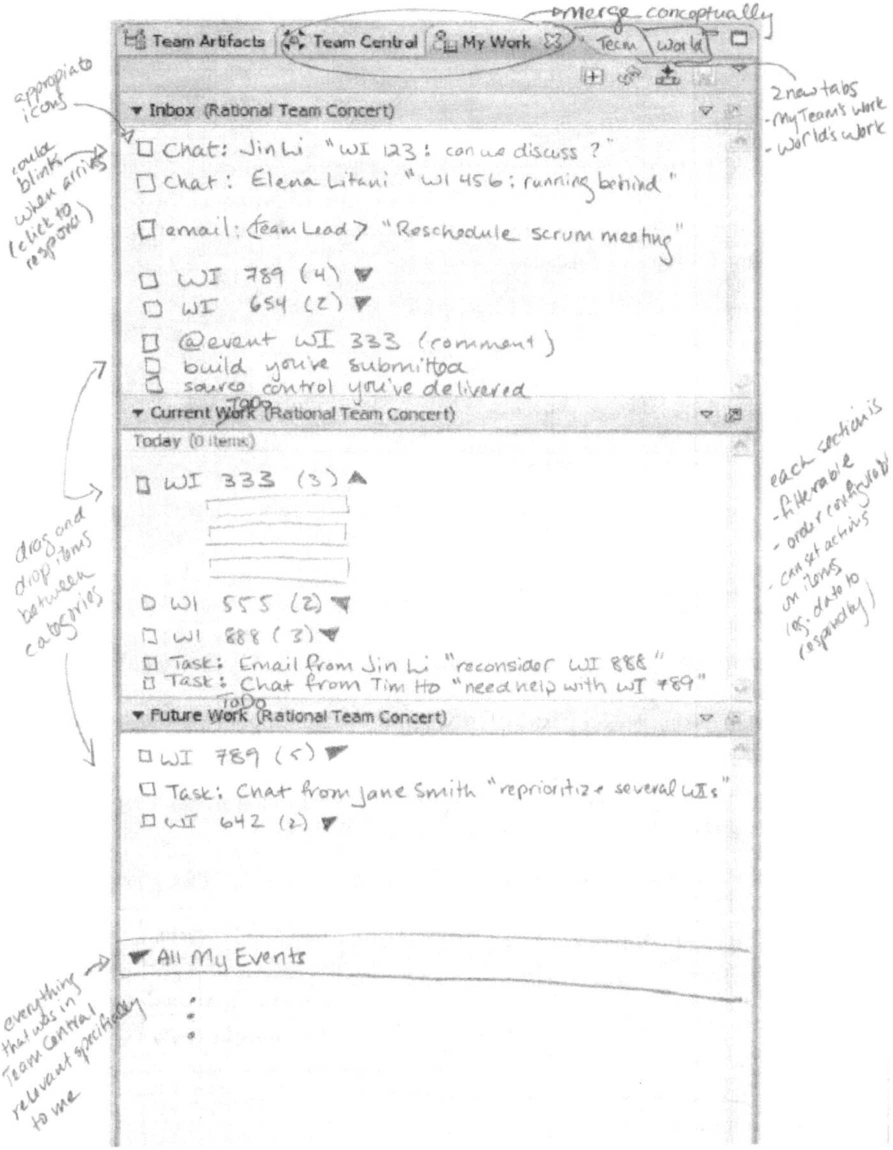

Fig. 6. Preliminary sketch of the "Inbox" UI widget to manage notifications

Each of these four distinct components can be shown relative to the individual user, the user's team(s), or "the world" (i.e., other teams within the organization), which increases the scope of what is displayed. The core design elements are summarized as follows.

Unification of all notifications important to the user, through a notification "Inbox"

All high-priority, user-relevant notifications for all event types arrive in a single place, by default in temporal order. The full set of events ("All My Events") is still available to the user so there is no loss of information.

User control over notification management

The user can delete notifications from the Inbox or move them individually through drag-and-drop interaction to Current ToDo or Future ToDo areas. Moving a notification to one of these areas creates a work item or task, if the notification doesn't naturally fit into an existing one already.

Notifications are automatically grouped

All events relating to a particular work item, for example, appear together, enabling the user to easily digest the current activities related to a particular work item. Additional filtering/sorting is available.

Small amount of automated assistance is provided

For example, when an instant message appears in the inbox, the user can choose to move it directly to one of the ToDo areas without responding, and an automated response is sent to the sender indicating that the recipient has queued the chat request.

Visual design supports the user

Link highlighting between the events in the Inbox and All My Events allows the user to see where in the stream of full events his/her specific events are found. Colour coding of events by type supports easy scanning. Blinking instant messages makes time critical request more visually salient.

As we displayed the UI sketch, the participants freely commented on the various design elements. The most salient feedback was as follows:

- The "Inbox" component of the design should be renamed, although no clearly better name emerged during the discussion. Using "Inbox" is confusing given that in desktop computing it already refers exclusively to email events. Here, it is referring to many types of events. For the balance of this chapter, we continue to use the term "Inbox" for consistency, but are in the process of identifying a better term.
- There was some concern about how large the inbox would grow and how it could be managed so that it wouldn't become overwhelming. We noted that the design idea is to have a relatively small set of items in the inbox; for example, only urgent notifications and those generated from specific persons are identified. Clearing the inbox every day automatically was discussed as a possibility. The research team acknowledges that this will be a key design issue.
- In terms of persistence and visibility, the "Inbox" component should always be *visible* in some capacity and the overall UI widget should always be *available*, regardless of what the user is doing. Thus, users can always go to one central place to review all notifications, and they will always be aware of incoming notifications.
- The design should allow the grouping of items. This will allow users to chunk notifications in a user-determined appropriate way. Events related to a particular

work item should, by default, be sub-tasks under that work item. The system could also allow items to be tagged by the user and then grouped according to tags.
- In terms of the Team View, users should be able to select from a set of teams, and view only the data for those teams.
- Privacy was raised as an issue, but there was no consensus on how to manage privacy in the end. In particular, there was a lot of discussion about privacy when viewing others' task spaces (specifically Current and Future ToDos). Some participants explicitly noted that they see the Inbox and ToDos sections as a "personal organizer" that they do not by default want to share. One possibility is to have tasks as private by default, but allow them to be marked public. Tasks marked "active" could possibly be made public automatically.

Overall, participants were excited by and supportive of our design direction. The majority of their feedback reflected relatively minor things that would be straightforward to incorporate into the design. They did, however, raise two issues that will require considerable more thought, namely, the ability to keep the "Inbox" a reasonable size and the need to manage privacy appropriately.

8 Phase IV – Medium Fidelity Prototyping

After prioritizing the design requirements and gathering feedback on our UI sketch in Phase III, we gained confidence in our design direction and explored possible implementations. We decided to prototype the "Inbox" UI widget directly in Jazz so that we could see it in action, and more importantly, it would enable us to eventually perform controlled experiments and gather user feedback. The "Inbox" UI widget prototype is implemented as a Web UI using AJAX, and it presents developers a central place to view and prioritize their work and relevant events. It implements the design requirements that address the two pain points that were rated most problematic by participants in our research (see Table 2 in Section 6). This is a first step in creating a new notification architecture framework in Jazz Web UI.

This prototype, shown in Figure 7, is based on the viewlet widget in Jazz Web UI, with extensions to implement the functions and user interactions identified in Phase III of our research.

Every 15 seconds, the notification viewlet parses all the incoming events from the feeds developers have configured and performs categorization based on event type. For example, as shown in Figure 7, Jin's real-time instant message request is automatically put into the Inbox section and prefixed with "Chat:" to facilitate easy identification. Other event types that would require immediate user attention, such as build events and hot defects, are also placed automatically into the Inbox section of the notification viewlet. The ability to configure the types of events that could appear in the Inbox section has not yet been implemented.

The notification viewlet provides indicators to help users quickly identify some pertinent attributes, such as the type, state, priority and severity, of the event. An event prefixed with an "*" indicates that it is an un-read event. A red time stamp indicates that it is an urgent event (from the sender's point of view). A blinking chat event indicates immediate response is expected. The event number is shown inside a pair of brackets after the event message. Icons are used for different event types in the

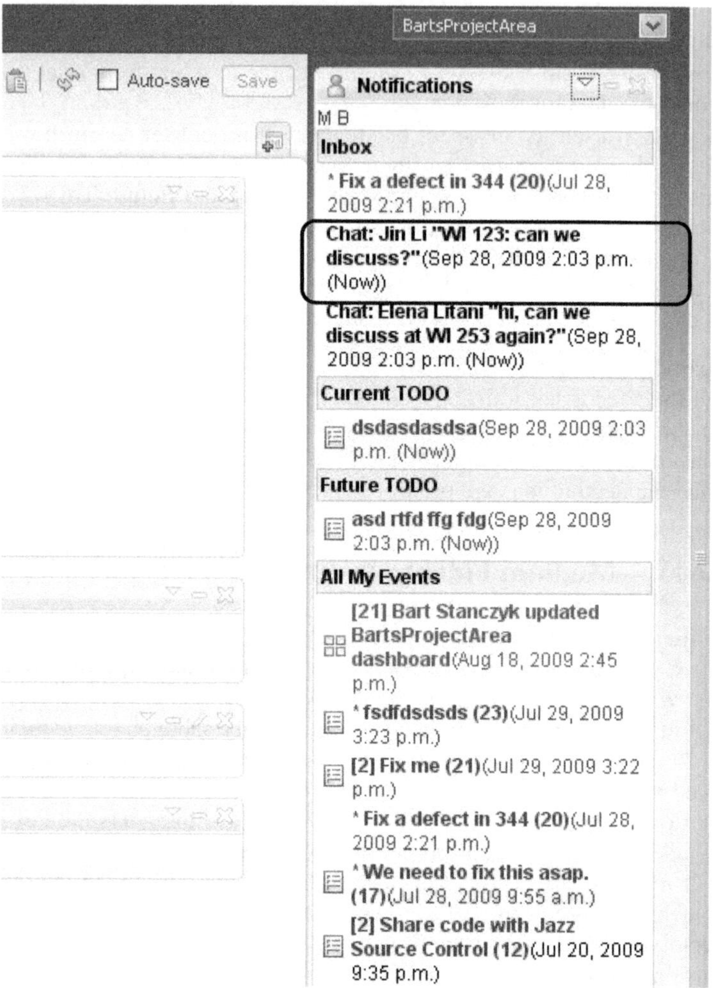

Fig. 7. Extended Jazz Web UI viewlet implementing the "Inbox" UI widget. Callout box (not part of the prototype) highlights an incoming chat from Jin Li.

notification viewlet to allow easy identification. For example, four-square-blocks icon indicates a Dashboard update event; bullet-list icon indicates an external event.

Users can move an event between the sections of the notification viewlet. Figure 8 shows the user moving an urgent event from the All My Events section into the Future ToDo section of the notification viewlet. While the user is dragging the event object, a floating text box is created with a green title bar and a copy of the event message. The floating text box follows the mouse cursor movement until it is dropped to a section in the notification viewlet. Users can perform drag-and-drop between the four sections of the notification viewlet, allowing users to further categorize the events according to their work priority.

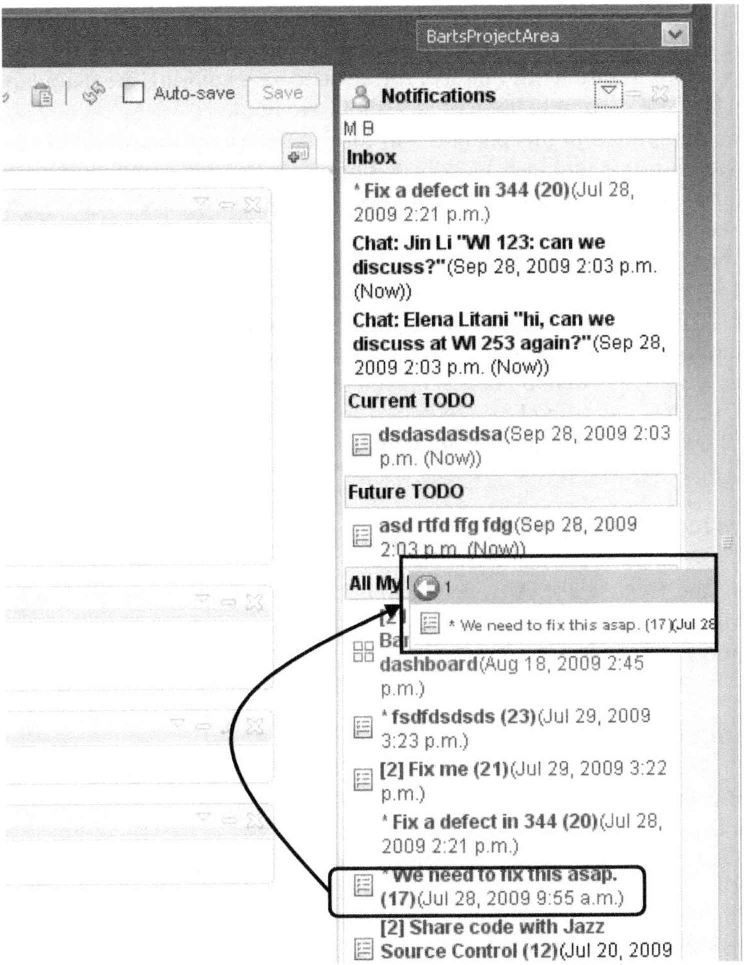

Fig. 8. Drag and Drop support for events in the "Inbox" UI widget. While dragging, a floating text box is created to provide feedback on the event being moved and where it is being moved to. Callout boxes are not part of the prototype.

This Web UI prototype has been demonstrated to various product and research teams in IBM and well received. We are preparing to evaluate its effectiveness, initially through field trials, and eventually through controlled experiments.

9 Conclusions

Through scenario-based design and the participation of eight representative users, we have validated the top notification pain points in the Jazz CDE, and identified design requirements for high priority pain points. Our "Inbox" UI widget prototype represents a first step in creating a new notification architecture for the Jazz CDE. Next steps involve evaluating our prototype with additional representative users. We expect to iterate on the design, before deploying it in the next release of the Jazz WebUI. Farther reaching future work on this project includes exploring the unique notification category for CDEs, namely team process improvement.

The work reported in this chapter will inform the Smart Internet initiative in that it will provide insights into user models that reduce cognitive complexity in smart interaction. First, Principle 2 of the Smart Internet points to the need for the *system* to keep track of users' ongoing matters of concern, rather than leaving this to the *user*. For matters that cannot be completed within a single session, the system will need to keep users informed about task status. One way to do this is through notifications. Second, Principle 3 of the Smart Internet points to the need to support collaborative and collective interactions. Again, the need to keep others (such as collaborators) informed about one's activities may be best achieved through effectively designed notifications. Our research has identified key design requirements to these Smart Internet Principles and has shown how they could be implemented via a UI prototype.

Acknowledgments

We thank the Centers for Advanced Studies (CAS) Canada and IBM Rational division for their generous support of this research. We would also like to thank all the participants in our focus group sessions.

References

1. Eclipse, http://www.eclipse.org
2. Jazz, http://www-01.ibm.com/software/rational/jazz/
3. Manifesto for agile software development, http://agilemanifesto.org/
4. Booch, G., Brown, A.W.: Collaborative Development Environments (2002), http://www.booch.com/architecture/blog/artifacts/CDE.pdf (retrieved 10/15/2009)
5. Google Docs, http://docs.google.com
6. Boehm, B.: A Spiral Model of Software Development and Enhancement. ACM SIGSOFT Software Engineering Notes 11(4), 14–24 (1986)
7. Horvitz, E., Apacible, J.: Learning and reasoning about interruption. In: Proceedings of ACM ICMI 2003, pp. 20–27 (2003)
8. Carroll, J.M. (ed.): Scenario-based design. John Wiley, New York (1995)
9. Mark. G., Gudith, D., Klocke U.: The cost of interrupted work: more speed and stress. In: Proceedings of ACM CHI 2008, pp. 107–110 (2008)
10. Chen, D., Vertegaal, R.: Using mental load for managing interruptions in physiologically attentive user interfaces. In: Extended Abstracts ACM CHI 2004, pp. 1513–1516 (2004)
11. Avrahami, D., Hudson, S.E.: QnA: Augmenting an instant messaging client to balance user responsiveness and performance. In: Proceedings of ACM CSCW 2004, pp. 515–518 (2004)
12. Oberg, B., Notkin, D.: Error reporting with graduated color. IEEE Software 9(6), 33–38 (1992)
13. Gluck, J., Bunt, A., McGrenere, J.: Matching attentional draw with utility in interruption. In: Proceedings of ACM CHI 2007, pp. 41–50 (2007)

14. Van Dantzich, M., Robbins, D., Horvitz, E., Czerwinski, M.: Scope: Providing awareness of multiple notifications at a glance. In: Proceedings of AVI (2002)
15. IBM Lotus Sametime, http://www.ibm.com/lotus/sametime
16. Kline, R.B., Seffah, A.: Evaluation of integrated software development environments: Challenges and results from three empirical studies. International Journal of Human-Computer Studies 63(6), 607–627 (2005)
17. Storey, M., Damian, D., Michaud, J., Myers, D., Mindel, M., German, D., Sanseverino, M., Hargreaves, E.: Improving the usability of Eclipse for novice programmers. In: Proceedings of the 2003 OOPSLA Workshop on Eclipse Technology Exchange, eclipse 2003, pp. 35–39 (2003)
18. Bird, C., Nagappan, N., Devanbu, P., Gall, H., Murphy, B.: Does distributed development affect software quality? An empirical case study of Windows Vista. In: Proceedings of IEEE ICSE 2003, pp. 518–528 (2003)
19. Chong, J., Hurlbutt, T.: The social dynamics of pair programming. In: Proceedings of IEEE ICSE 2007, pp. 354–363 (2007)
20. Čubranić, D., Storey, M.A.: Collaboration support for novice team programming. In: Proceedings of ACM GROUP 2005, pp. 136–139 (2005)
21. de Faria, E., Yamanaka, K., do Amaral Tavares, J., Henrique Lacerda Pinto G., Henrique Sudrio de Melo, L.: AIDDES - Distributed intelligent pair-software development environment. In: Proceedings of IEEE International Computer Software and Applications Conference, pp. 494–495 (2008)
22. Ho, C., Raha, S., Gehringer, E., Williams, L.: Sangam: A distributed pair programming plug-in for Eclipse. In: Proceedings of the 2004 OOPSLA Workshop on Eclipse Technology Exchange, eclipse 2004, pp. 73–77 (2004)
23. Ko, A.J., DeLine, R., Venolia, G.: Information needs in collocated software development teams. In: Proceedings of IEEE ICSE 2007, pp. 344–353 (2007)
24. Chong, J., Siino, R.: Interruptions on software teams: a comparison of paired and solo programmers. In: Proceedings ACM CSCW 2006, pp. 29–38 (2006)
25. Jazz user scenario, https://jazz.net/wiki/bin/view/Main/CALMScrumScenario
26. Villegas, N., Muller, H.: Managing Dynamic Context to Optimize Smart Interactions and Services, SITCON (2010)
27. McGrenere, J., Moore, G.: Are we all in the same "bloat"? In: Proceedings of Graphics Interface 2000, pp. 1870–196 (2000)

Smart Group Interactions

Ian Spence[1] and Elsa Marziali[2]

[1] Department of Psychology, University of Toronto,
[2] The Kunin-Lunenfeld Applied Research Unit, Baycrest
{ian.spence,elsa.marziali}@utoronto.ca

Abstract. The use of groups has had great success in medical and psychiatric contexts for over a century. Group interactions provide the critical social and emotional support that is frequently necessary for change and clinical improvement. In recent years, information technology has been used to enhance and extend traditional face-to-face group approaches. We describe three recent projects that use online group approaches and we discuss some of the opportunities and challenges that are part of this approach. Many medical conditions involve seniors, who are often computer novices, and so issues of usability, acceptance, and trust must be carefully and fully addressed by researchers and clinicians who wish to use online group approaches as part of their treatment model.

Keywords: Online groups; Emotional benefit; Caregivers; Chronic disease; Aging at-risk drivers.

1 Introduction

This chapter, like Chapters 1 and 2 of this book, looks at the need for smarter interaction from a healthcare perspective. In this case it is with respect to group interactions among elderly patients. The discussion below highlights some of the properties of group interaction that make them inherently "smart" and also reports on a study that evaluated the impact of meditational technology on group interactions of elderly patients.

The American physician Joseph Pratt was the first to use a formal group method as the central component of a medical intervention just over a century ago [1]. He formed groups (calling them "classes") of fifteen to twenty patients with tuberculosis who had been rejected for sanatorium treatment. Pratt's patients were poor as well as tubercular and Pratt considered poverty to be a major factor in impeding recovery. The patients in his classes had to agree to an educational model which required substantial changes in lifestyle (hygiene, nutrition, outdoor activity) which were recorded statistically. The classes met weekly to update the statistical record and compare notes; those who gained weight and showed other clinical improvements acted as models for the others. One of the most important and unanticipated benefits was the positive emotional effects that participation had on the group members.

Pratt's success inspired others to make groups the focal point of their therapy with a variety of other medical conditions. Since these early beginnings, group approaches have helped patients with a wide range of problems, both medical and psychiatric, including rheumatoid arthritis, post-myocardial infarction, schizophrenia, obesity,

M. Chignell et al. (Eds.): The Smart Internet, LNCS 6400, pp. 88–102, 2010.

addiction, substance abuse, problem gambling, Parkinsonism, and cystic fibrosis [2, 3, 4, 5, 6, 7, 8, 9, 10].

1.1 The Power of Groups

Why do groups work in so many different clinical contexts? They work principally because individuals are comforted by the realization that they are not alone and that others are similarly afflicted. A climate of trust develops and group members feel free to care about and help each other. Under the direction of a trained moderator, the group provides support, makes available information, offers options, and challenges erroneous thinking. Difficulties can be resolved, new behaviors learned, and more effective methods of self-discovery and relating to others are developed.

The emotional benefits of group interactions are considerable and indeed are critical to success [11, 12]. In cases of medical illness, there is evidence that group therapies help people to cope better with their problems, enhance quality of life and, in some cases, even extend life [13]. Feelings of isolation, depression, and anxiety are involved in many clinical and personal problems. Group interactions can help to deal with these major barriers to recovery.

1.2 Disadvantages of the Traditional Approach

There are barriers to the implementation of the group approach. Not the least of these is the geographical barrier. It is usually necessary to bring the participants together to a single location at a set time and repeat this collective gathering on multiple occasions. Even under optimal circumstances, this entails a certain amount of inconvenience to individuals. Unfortunately, however, inconvenience is only a few steps away from impossibility.

In many situations it may be very difficult, or even impossible, to assemble the group at regular intervals. For example, if a potential participant lives in a remote location, the cost and inconvenience of travel (and possibly parking) may present an insurmountable hurdle. In addition, many potential group members may find it difficult to take the time to travel and to attend group sessions because of family or work responsibilities. Furthermore, if a potential participant suffers from a relatively uncommon ailment and lives in a small community, the critical mass necessary for the formation of a local group may be unattainable. Thus, for a variety of reasons, the practical barriers to attendance may be so discouraging that, for all practical purposes, the group approach is not a feasible option for many individuals.

Another difficult situation involves family members who care for relatives with dementias. These individuals are usually housebound with virtually no opportunity to take an extended leave from the duties of caregiving. Likewise, individuals who are afflicted by a chronic disease that hinders their mobility are also prevented from benefiting from the group approach.

Modern information technologies may be able to offer solutions to these barriers to participation and, in addition, offer new possibilities and approaches that are not available with the traditional face-to-face group interaction model.

1.3 Smart Interactions

Health care costs are skyrocketing and innovative approaches are needed to help control expenditures. With more health care information available to the consumer via the internet than ever before, there has been an increase in approaches to treatment that encourage managed wellness and patient-centric health care. The availability of new technologies has set in motion a transformation of the delivery of traditional health care and technology and will play an increasingly important role in coming years. As part of this revolution, enhanced online group processes will augment, and may largely replace, traditional face-to-face groups. However, attempting to replicate clinical face-to-face interactions in a distributed virtual environment brings new challenges as well as new opportunities.

When the group members connect online, new resources for enhancing and extending the basic group model become available. Traditional face-to-face group interactions have the potential to become "smarter" when they occur online. According to Ng, Chignell, and Cordy [14], "smart interaction" is user-centric and is achieved when "online services and resources are discovered, aggregated and delivered dynamically, automatically and interactively in response to user or group's evolving concerns and situations". Of course, traditional face-to-face groups already embody a certain measure of "smartness," since the utility and power of the group process depends upon the evolution and improvement of interactions among the group members over multiple sessions, in response to the concerns of individual members. Nonetheless, translating the traditional group process to the online environment has the potential to make face-to-face group processes even "smarter." Smart interactions hold the promise of improved outcomes, while also making better use of resources and offering a significant reduction in costs. The notion of "smartness" implies that services in the online environment are tailored to the needs of the individual and that these services will adapt smoothly to the current task context. Although, at present, this vision of the Smart Internet is a work in progress and the research described in this paper is consistent with these general goals.

In this paper, we describe some novel projects that use a smart group approach and our initial efforts to address some of the challenges. One project,"Caregivers," has been active for more than five years. A more recent project,"Chronic Disease," builds on the pioneering work with caregivers by developing a generalized approach to tackle a variety of chronic diseases (chronic obstructive pulmonary disease, HIV/AIDS, arthritis, diabetes, etc.). The third project,"Seniors in Accidents," which has just launched, proposes a smart group solution to a significant societal problem that will become increasingly important as aging boomers become seniors.

2 Caregivers

This pioneering project (begun six years ago) used information technology to provide group support to caregivers of individuals suffering from dementias [15, 16, 17]. The caregiver is typically a family member who provides care for a very dependent individual. The duty of care is demanding and also profoundly isolating since the caregiver is rarely able to leave the home. The caregiver experiences a reduced quality of life and becomes susceptible to illness and depression, with negative consequences for the caregiver and patient. Usually, but not always, the caregiver is the spouse and is normally close to the same age as the individual with the dementia. Hence, the typical caregiver is also a senior who has little or no experience with computers or the internet.

2.1 The Caring for Others© Website

The password-protected website, Caring for Others©, was specially designed for seniors (icons, large text, simple navigation, etc.). A variety of services was available (see Fig. 1), including email, a discussion forum, and moderated video meetings.

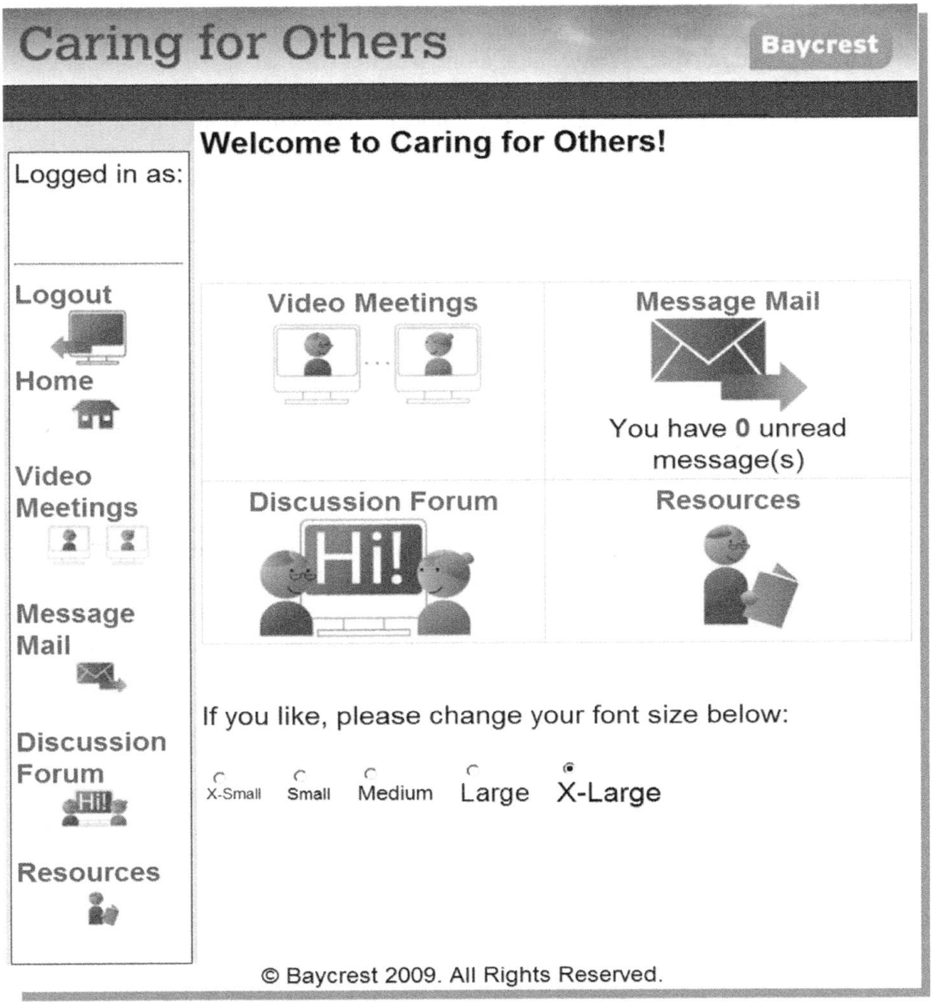

Fig. 1. The Caring for Others© website. Large, self-explanatory icons minimized keyboard use and made navigation easy to the four principal areas of the site. Font size could easily be changed to a comfortable level. The integrated email functionality and discussion forum made learning other software unnecessary.

Older caregivers with no prior experience of computers readily adopted the technology, and benefited in terms of improvements in their physical and mental health [15, 16, 17]. Although the number of seniors using technology to access information is growing rapidly, they need hardware and software designed in ways that make access and navigation simple and intuitive.

There are many challenges to the design, development, and implementation of internet-based health care interventions. Knowing the needs and abilities of the users is essential. Older adults approach the internet with motivations, knowledge, and skills that differ from younger adults and adolescents. Seniors in their seventies and eighties may not have used computers before and may be resistant to acquiring new skills late in life. The major barriers here are psychological, social, and cultural. While attention to factors such as font size, ease of navigation, minimizing keyboard use, etc., is essential, attending to these alone will not solve all usability problems.

On the other hand, older adults are among the fastest growing group of novices. They are using the internet in increasing numbers, largely to communicate with family, to obtain health-related information and for travel planning. In response, software developers have begun to address the common characteristics of aging that frequently impede the effective use of technology. Failing eyesight, problems with muscle coordination, lags in learning, difficulties in acquiring new behaviors and in retaining new concepts, all contribute to seniors' difficulties with the user interface. While significant efforts have been made to accommodate the limitations of persons with physical disabilities [18, 19, 20], these enhancements alone do not ensure a successful experience for most seniors. Merely dealing with physical constraints that are a function of aging is not enough; psychological and social barriers to using technology also have to be addressed. An online environment that replicates, as much as possible, the typical clinic-based, face-to-face encounter between a professional care provider and a patient, would be preferable.

The Caring for Others© website was intended to replicate the typical clinic-based support group programs that are sometimes available to caregivers. The website adhered to common usability guidelines for older adults [21, 22]. For example, the site used uncluttered pages with subtle color contrasts and users made their choices by clicking on large, self-explanatory icons. Use of the keyboard was minimized since very few participants had experience with typing. Although the site provided several services, such as information handbooks, a discussion forum, and email, the most innovative aspects—at the time, six years ago—were video conferencing for one-on-one communication and video conferencing for group interactions.

Microsoft ASP.NET, an Access/SQL Server database, and Macromedia Flash Communication Server, managed the video streams. No client desktop software was required other than the free Macromedia plug-in. Although as many as nine viewing streams were available, the conference facilitator allowed only one outgoing stream at any one time to prevent participants talking over each other. The outgoing stream was passed by the facilitator to a single speaker as individual participants requested the floor. The video stream was saved and subsequently burned to optical disk; a custom built tool allowed the researchers to review and code the recorded interactions at a later time [23].

Since usability was critical to the success of the project, it was important to get user feedback during and after the group sessions. Participants were interviewed and asked to respond to a series of questions about specific web site features and their ease of use. Overall, the participants found the large icons, color contrasts, and uncluttered pages easy to follow. Also, large "GO" buttons helped to ensure that they could move forward and backwards without getting "lost" [24]. Based on this feedback, the site was modified to eliminate problems.

3 Chronic Disease

In developed countries about 80% of seniors have a chronic disease, and of these, 30% have three or more chronic conditions. Sixty percent of all hospitalizations and visits to hospital emergency departments are due to exacerbations of chronic illnesses. Thus, it is not surprising that 60% to 80% of general medical costs are related to the care of persons with chronic disease [25]. Of concern is the fact that persons with chronic disease show less than 50% adherence rates to prescribed medical regimes [26]. Factors that affect adherence include: socioeconomic status, personality and cognitive issues, depression, anxiety, medication frequency, complexity and side effects.

Increasingly, patients are expected to assume responsibility for managing their own chronic conditions. Disease-specific educational support groups moderated by health professionals or trained lay persons are being implemented by health care systems nationally and internationally to cope with the enormous demands for health care services. A Chronic Disease Self-Management Program (CDSMP) is being evaluated in large-scale trials in the USA and internationally (UK Expert Patient Program) [27]. However, typically information technology is not being used to provide a platform for the group support programs.

We recently conducted a feasibility study with three support groups on a new website, Caring for Me©, modeled on the earlier Caring for Others© website. Patients with chronic disease benefited in terms of improved self care and reduction in social isolation [27]. The average age of the group members was 60.8 years and most were women (83%). Approximately half lived alone and the remainder lived with family. The chronic disease categories included: lupus, spinal cord tumors, poliomyelitis, multiple sclerosis, heart disease, hypertension, and diabetes.

More than half of the participants had never used computers. All were willing to have computers and webcams installed in their homes and were very receptive to the training sessions provided by the project technician. A simplified training manual that focused primarily on negotiating the Caring for Me© website was used.

A qualitative analysis of the archived videoconferencing sessions and the follow-up interviews used trained raters who employed a detailed coding system to capture the different stages of group development [16, 28]. We observed a high degree of group bonding and cohesiveness in all three groups. Group members bonded, identified with each other, and provided empathic support. Further analyses of the data yielded four salient themes:

(1) Loss of Ability, Identity, and Independence. Sample comments included, "Worst thing about being disabled is that you can't do the things you did before"; "I haven't been out in 6 years except for doctors appointments"; and "I have a new walker and that may help me to get out more." Participants identified issues associated with their chronic disease, such as needing to retire early with the concomitant financial difficulties. Others complained that they had to rely on public transportation because they could no longer drive.

(2) Anger and Frustration. An overarching theme was the demeaning way in which they were viewed by others. The following statements convey their frustrations. "I used to work as a nurse–now I'm on welfare"; "It's so frustrating arranging Wheel-Trans" (door-to-door accessible transit service for persons with physical disabilities); and "The disabled are treated like second-class citizens."

(3) Acceptance and Adjustment. One difficult challenge was learning to live with the disability without the prospect of returning to full health. Many found it difficult to acknowledge that they needed help; most painful of all, was coping with negative attitudes toward the disabled. Typical comments included, "At times I feel resentful, and I guess angry; frustrated, but I have to live with it"; "I don't like asking for help"; "A major problem is not adjusting to disability, but adjusting to people's attitudes."

(4) Social Support. Surprisingly, the group members rarely discussed the people that they counted on when in need. On the contrary, they frequently expressed the wish not to be a burden to others. They saw the group as a vital source of social support: "At least we have each other," and 'These meetings are the highlight of my week."

Feedback on usability was largely positive. Most accessed the site weekly to attend the videoconferencing meetings. Participants commented: "To be able to see a person I was talking to - that was very helpful"; "To put a face to a voice - that made a tremendous difference"; "It was a great experience and I did not have to use Wheel-Trans"; and "Great opportunity to learn about technology." Seventy-eight percent said that the Web site was easy to use and 95% felt that using computers to meet online was very positive or moderately positive.

Attendance at the weekly meetings varied. One group had good attendance throughout the facilitated and mutual self-help sessions. In the other two groups, a core group attended regularly, while the remaining members attended less frequently. However, despite variations in attendance, most thought they had benefited from their involvement in the project. Sample comments were: "People in the group are trying to help each other and nobody is there to laugh at you or judge you," "We are all in the same boat," "Sharing information was very instructive," "We don't feel alone, [loneliness] is the worst thing," "I think it was wonderful, it was great. I have never missed a meeting," and, "This was a new and very positive experience for me."When asked to compare the online support group to a clinic-based face-to-face support group, the responses included: "It is better for people who have a hard time opening up to other people because you do it in your own living room," "You would not be able to go into such a depth in a face-to-face conversation and in a large group," and, "It's better because you are not distracted by anything, it is better than [a clinic group]."

4 Seniors in Accidents

Driving is more than a means of mobility for more than three million Canadian seniors; it is also a symbol of independence and freedom. Most seniors drive without incident, but crashes do occur. The financial cost to the Canadian taxpayer is around one billion dollars per year. The personal and social costs, both physical and mental, are also substantial. The situation is similar in most other developed countries.

Changes in the cognitive abilities of aging drivers affect the safety of all road users and continued driving by those who are no longer safe represents a public health challenge [29]. On the other hand, premature restriction threatens personal mobility and independence [30]. Restriction and cessation of driving have been associated with a variety of social and health problems [31, 32] often triggering depression, feelings of loneliness, and loss of confidence [33, 34, 35]. Addressing the problem of premature restrictions is important not only for continued mobility in seniors, but also for independence, quality of life and well-being [36].

The intervention that we are currently developing will offer a unique blend of: (1) social networking to enable communication and information sharing among drivers and their families; (2) support for the promotion of well-being and enhancement of mobility; and (3) diagnostic and remedial tools for cognitive skills. Experience gained by one of our collaborators from community-based Driving Cessation Support Groups (DCSG) [30] will be used in the development of online support for those who have restricted or suspended driving. Compared to participants attending traditional support groups, the DSCG participants exhibited significant improvements in depression scores, increases in quality of life scores, and decreases in memory and behavioral disturbances from baseline to completion of the support group sessions. In addition, compared to baseline, participants attending the DCSG were happier, and were less angry and surprised at the loss of their license at the end of the support group sessions compared to traditional support group participants.

We plan to use and extend this approach [30] in the online environment for older drivers. Negative outcomes (e.g., reductions in quality of life, decreased mobility, feelings of loss, increased dependence) often are associated with both voluntary and involuntary driving cessation. We expect that the use of support groups, in an online environment, will assist aging drivers to prepare for the day when they no longer drive.

An important function of the moderated groups will be to encourage participation in the cognitive testing and training programs that will be offered. Playing action videogames improves visual selective attention, AVF, visual acuity, contrast sensitivity, and speed of processing [37, 38]. These are all perceptual-cognitive functions that deteriorate as a normal consequence of aging. Each is critically important to safe driving. We have developed computerized tests that may be administered online for seniors to self-assess their performance in these areas. We will also explore the use of videogames with older drivers who have reduced AVF, contrast sensitivity, and speed of responding. Not all seniors are interested in the action videogames that engage younger players, and we are developing non-violent videogames that use a simple controller on the Nintendo Wii. These games may be more suited to seniors. However, we will continue to use first-person shooter games to train those seniors who are accepting of the genre. Generally, little encouragement is needed to maintain videogame-based training (the games are usually found to be enjoyable and addictive) in contrast to many other approaches to cognitive training [38].

We are developing and testing methods for communication and social support that will be novel in this context. We are implementing features commonly found on widely used social networking services (e.g., MySpace, Facebook, Twitter) to facilitate the growth of social relations among participants through their shared interests.

Participants will be able to add individuals from the pool of other participants to their social network. The system will support features like "walls", "profiles", "friends", etc. These features will facilitate and encourage the formation and growth of networks.

Since loss of license is associated with a loss of independence, it is generally a traumatic event for seniors. Consequently, we must be extremely careful regarding what information is presented, how it is presented, and how we protect the information provided by the users of the site (see Challenges, below). Some of the precautions that we are implementing include the following: participants are informed at registration that the site does not offer medical services or medical advice; they are cautioned that the results of tests are for information only and that no prescription for action is offered or implied; they are advised that the cognitive training programs are experimental and that positive results are not guaranteed. Participants are strongly encouraged to seek face-to-face professional or medical help if they have any concerns regarding the results of any test or their reading of any evidence-based information on the site.

5 Challenges

Many contexts in which groups can be helpful involve seniors since that demographic is more likely to experience problems that require medical or psychiatric attention. By 2050, the world population over the age of 60 will triple [40]. And, coupled with an increase in life expectancy, this means that the number of older people that will make use of healthcare systems will increase dramatically. Online smart group approaches can help improve the quality of care and reduce costs. However, there are a number of usability, ethical, security, privacy, and data analysis challenges that confront researchers who wish to use online groups for clinical practice or research.

5.1 Usability

Most web sites are built by young people whose knowledge and skills differ markedly from those of older generations. These differences are not restricted to computer and internet use. The life experiences of the two groups are about as different as can be imagined. While the challenges of designing websites for younger adults are formidable enough, they are magnified in an older population. Moreover, some important aspects of interaction are quite different and some of the prescriptive advice that works well for younger users may be inappropriate for seniors [41,42].

The usual way of managing usability issues is by conducting usability testing sessions before releasing new software for general use. Unfortunately, this is of limited value with older populations [43]. The principal problem is heterogeneity. There is no commonly accepted definition of "old," and designing websites for populations that can range in age from the fifties to the nineties poses many challenges.

While designing to accommodate wide variations in physical and cognitive skills is difficult, acceptance may be an even trickier problem. If the user is anxious, apprehensive, suspicious, or lacking in confidence, this can be a recipe for failure, even if the individual is perfectly capable of negotiating the site in other respects [44, 45, 46, 47]. Previous experience, cultural factors, aptitudes and attitudes all come into play in determining whether or not the online approach will be accepted. There is probably no general solution for dealing with these barriers, except to stress the importance of sympathetic personal contact with prospective group members. A compassionate and caring recruiter can often allay fears and suspicions.

Flexibility in the early stages of site implementation is essential. User opinions should be actively solicited and modifications made to the site as soon as problem areas are identified [15, 16].

5.2 Evidence-Based Information and Services

With the rapid development of web applications supporting the exchange of health information and the delivery of remedial programs, disease-specific information and standard therapies will increasingly be delivered online. In order to ensure the accuracy of the information and its interpretation by consumers, clinicians and researchers must evaluate the quality of the information for accuracy and clarity of presentation. As far as possible, only evidence-based information and therapies should be offered.

Consumers have the right to know that the services they receive in a technology-based environment meet the highest professional standards of health care. Currently there is no regulating system for monitoring the credentials of the providers, and whether evidence-based models of therapy are used. Ultimately, an e-health regulatory body to which health professionals can be held accountable will be required to protect consumers, especially older adults who may be more vulnerable. These issues can be addressed only through research initiatives focused on demonstrating that high quality health care information can be provided when technology is used to deliver health care services.

5.3 Security and Privacy

Users must have a high degree of confidence that their personal data will not be misused. They must be assured that measures are in place to prevent the inadvertent exposure of their data. There are at least three classes of individuals that require different approaches with regard to security and privacy: (1) other web users; (2) other registered users of the site; and (3) privileged users, such as the site administrator, the group moderators, and the researchers themselves.

Site Access. In many cases, it will be desirable to restrict access to the site, or at least to parts of the site. Entry to restricted areas should require registration and subsequent login with password protection (with the usual strength-of-password checks [48]). Within the web site there should be at least three levels of security: (1) naturally, the site administrator must have access to all links and user groups; (2) the professional facilitators should have access only to the members within the groups that they facilitate; and (3) the participants should have direct access only to other members within their own group.

All e-mail messages, threaded discussion text, and video conference sessions should be encrypted and stored on the server only for as long as necessary. Subsequently, all information should be copied to external media which should be stored in a secured area unless needed for statistical analyses. Data on the server will generally be deleted at this stage. All electronic data should be destroyed after a fixed period, generally about five years.

Participants may be required to use an alias rather than their own name on the site. The site should suggest a unique alias if a participant is unable to generate one. This simple device will help to prevent other users becoming aware of individual identities (e.g., via the discussion board, social networking facilities, or videoconferencing). On the other hand, knowing the true identities of other group members can be an important element in the development of trust and so good judgment must be used in balancing the potential benefits against the risks. Participants should be made aware of the possible risks and benefits so that they may make an informed decision.

Social Communication. Researchers will be able to study the effects of computer-mediated communication on the development of trust among the group members in ways that were previously impossible [49, 50, 51, 52]. Using social networking and discussion board data, it will be possible to chart the development and maintenance of the online social networks. Statistical data mining of the text interactions (e.g., discussion board, instant messaging, and social networking) will allow the identification of concerns and challenges discussed by the group participants. Qualitative analysis of these interactions will likely reveal opportunities for the introduction of new approaches to treatment.

However, a major privacy problem is shielding participants' identities from other participants. If identities are not protected, it may be possible for one participant to associate another's private information with a name. If this were to happen, private information could be at risk. It is relatively simple to ensure anonymity on discussion boards, instant messaging, or social networking facilities—the use of aliases should make it unlikely that individual identities will be exposed. Obviously, individuals may choose to reveal their identities, but they must accept the potential consequences of doing so. This should be made clear to participants in online groups when they give their signed - informed consent.

Ensuring privacy in videoconferencing groups is more difficult (just as it is in ordinary face-to-face groups). Our solution is to offer participants the option of using an avatar. An avatar is an object (usually a depiction in caricature) on the computer screen that represents the user. In our applications it is a cartoon-like image that is appropriate to the group context (e.g., an aging driver). It is necessary to make a selection of avatars available to participants if they choose this option to help protect their privacy.

Another source of potential disclosure occurs during data analysis. The data collected from analyzing discussion board, instant messaging, social networking, and videoconferencing interactions will often be coded [53,54,55] by trained researchers, graduate students, and research assistants. As far as possible the data should be anonymised and encrypted (see below) and subsets of the database made available to researchers in proportion to their data analytic needs.

5.4 Smart Internet

The studies that we have described in this paper have taken advantage of existing internet technology. Although this has resulted in a number of advantages relative to the traditional group method, there is much more that can be done within the framework of the Smart Internet [14]. However, further significant progress will probably only occur when real improvements in technologies like voice recognition are made.

When practical, accurate, real-time conversion of speech to text is available, there is the potential to assist the moderator of the group to guide the group process. Real-time data mining of the stream of discourse will help to identify important themes at both the group and individual levels. While skilled moderators perform this function in both traditional and online groups—and do so remarkably well—they are sometimes subject to lapses of memory and failures to detect patterns of interaction that could help move the therapeutic process forward, if they had been recognized early enough.

In addition to assisting the moderator to guide the live group process, the development of a database would allow the development of personalized sources of information for individual group members. When individual matters of concern are identified, the creation of a customized online library of information relative to the individual's issues becomes possible. This library could be adjusted to accommodate the educational level of the group member as well as providing up-to-date evidence-based information relevant to the matters of concern. Group members in any clinical situation will have different capabilities, concerns, and histories; it is important to recognize these idiosyncratic variations if effective change is to result.

Finally, the ability to create a database of discourse and interaction would open up new possibilities for further analysis and evaluation. At present, recording and coding group interactions is a time consuming and expensive activity. Nonetheless, it is an essential part of research in this area. Without such analysis it would be impossible to judge the effectiveness of the group process and the lack of an objective record would make devising future improvements much more difficult.

6 Conclusions

The power of groups to promote and assist remediation in many clinical areas is beyond dispute. The opportunities offered by new information technologies can enhance the traditional face-to-face group method in many ways. However, we must be careful to anticipate difficulties and challenges during the implementation of group methods that are consistent with the defining principles of the Smart Internet [14]. This is not merely a case of developing new and smarter software that we can adjust and modify at leisure. It will be important to anticipate and avoid problems before the widespread introduction of new and increasingly automatic methods. We must constantly be aware of the possibility of creating an online environment that may do harm to individuals.

Acknowledgments

This research was supported by the *Canadian Institutes of Health Research (CIHR)* and by Bell Canada through its *Bell University Laboratories (BUL)* R&D program.

References

1. Pratt, J.H.: The Organization of Tuberculosis Classes. Medical Communications of the Massachusetts Medical Society 20, 475–492 (1907)
2. Rutchick, I.E.: Research on Practice with Groups in Health-Care Settings. Social Work in Health Care 15, 97–114 (1990)

3. Strauss, G.D., Spiegel, J.S., Daniels, M., Spiegel, T., Landsverk, J., Roybyrne, P., Edelstein, C., Ehlhardt, J., Falke, R., Hindin, L., Zackler, L.: Group Therapies for Rheumatoid-Arthritis - A Controlled-Study of 2 Approaches. Arthritis and Rheumatism 29, 1203–1209 (1986)
4. Stern, M.J., Plionis, E., Kaslow, L.: Group-Process Expectations and Outcome with Post-Myocardial Infarction Patients. General Hospital Psychiatry 6, 101–108 (1984)
5. Fenn, H.H., Dinaburg, D.: Didactic Group-Psychotherapy with Chronic-Schizophrenics. International Journal of Group Psychotherapy 31, 443–452 (1981)
6. Strauss, G.D., Pedersen, S., Dudovitz, D.: Psychosocial Support for Adults with Cystic-Fibrosis - Group-Approach. American Journal of Diseases of Children 133, 301–305 (1979)
7. Kotkov, B.: Experiences in Group Psychotherapy with the Obese. Psychosomatic Medicine 15, 243–251 (1953)
8. Chafetz, M.E., Bernstein, N., Sharpe, W., Schwab, R.S.: Short-Term Group Therapy of Patients with Parkinsons Disease. New England Journal of Medicine 253, 961–964 (1955)
9. Levin, A.: What Makes Group Therapy Work for Substance Abusers? Psychiatric News 40, 34 (2005)
10. Coman, G.J., Evans, B.J., Burrows, G.D.: Group counselling for problem gambling. British Journal of Guidance & Counselling 30, 145–158 (2002)
11. Yalom, I.D., Leszcz, M.: The Theory and Practice of Group Psychotherapy. Basic Books, New York (2005)
12. Saiger, G.M.: Group Psychotherapy with Older Adults. Psychiatry-Interpersonal and Biological Processes 64, 132–145 (2001)
13. van Dijk, M., Janssen, W.: Psychosocial Support for Cancer Patients: A Review of the Literature. Psychologie & Gezondheid 37, 5–14 (2009)
14. Ng, J.W., Chignell, M., Cordy, J.R.: The Smart Internet: Transforming the Web for the User. In: Martin, P., Kark, A.W., Stewart, D. (eds.) Proceedings of the 2009 Conference of the Centres for Advanced Studies on Collaborative Research, CASCON 2009, Ontario, Canada, November 02-05, pp. 285–296. ACM, New York (2009)
15. Marziali, E., Dergal, J., McCleary, L.: A Systematic Review of Practice Standards and Research Ethics in Technology-Based Home Health Care Intervention Programs for Older Adults. Journal of Aging and Health 17, 679–696 (2005)
16. Marziali, E., Donahue, P.: Caring for Others: Internet Video-Conferencing Group Intervention for Family Caregivers of Older Adults with Neurodegenerative Disease. The Gerontologist 46, 398–403 (2006)
17. Marziali, E., Damianakis, T., Donahue, P.: Internet-Based Clinical Services Virtual Support Groups for Family Caregivers. Journal of Technology in Human Services 24, 39–54 (2006)
18. Microsoft Accessibility, `http://www.microsoft.com/enable/`
19. Apple Accessibility, `http://www.apple.com/accessibility/`
20. IBM Accessibility, `http://www-03.ibm.com/able/`
21. Web Content Accessibility Guidelines 1.0, `http://www.w3.org/TR/1999/WAI-WEBCONTENT-19990505`
22. Web Accessibility Initiative (WAI), `http://www.w3.org/WAI`
23. SAVI Viewer developed by MeLogic, `http://www.savisys.com`
24. Gwizdka, J., Spence, I.: Implicit Measures of Lostness and Success in Web Navigation. Interacting with Computers 19, 357–369 (2007)
25. WHO: Chronic Diseases and Health Promotion, `http://www.who.int/chp/en/.2007`

26. Dunbar-Jacob, J., Mortimer-Stephens, M.K.: Treatment Adherence in Chronic Disease. Journal of Clinical Epidemiology 54S, 57–60 (2001)
27. Lorig, K.R., Ritter, P., Stewart, A.L., Sobel, D.S., Brown, B.W., Bandura, A., González, V.M., Laurent, D.D., Holman, H.R.: Chronic Disease Self-Management Program: 2-Year Health Status and Health Care Utilization Outcomes. Medical Care 39, 1217–1223 (2001)
28. Marziali, E.: E-Health Program for Patients with Chronic Disease. Telemedicine and e-Health 15, 176–181 (2009)
29. Dobbs, B.M.: Medical Conditions and Driving: A Review of the Literature (1960-2000) DOTHS 809 690. U.S. Department of Transportation, Washington, DC (2005)
30. Dobbs, B.M., Harper, L., Wood, A.: Transitioning from Driving to Driving Cessation: The Role of Specialized Driving Cessation Support Groups for Individuals with Dementia. Topics in Geriatric Rehabilitation 25, 74–87 (2009)
31. Marottoli, R., Mendes de Leon, C., Glass, T., Willams, C., Cooney, L., Berkman, L.: Consequences of Driving Cessation: Decreased Out-Of-Home Activity Levels. Journals of Gerontology, Series B, Psychological Sciences & Social Sciences 55, S334–S340 (2000)
32. Marottoli, R., Mendes de Leon, C., Glass, T., Williams, C., Cooney, L., Berkman, L., Tinetti, M.: Driving Cessation and Increases Depressive Symptoms: Prospective Evidence from the New Haven EPESE. Journal of the American Geriatrics Society 45, 202–206 (1997)
33. Fonda, S., Wallace, R., Herzog, A.: Changes in Driving Patterns and Worsening Depressive Symptoms among Older Adults. Journals of Gerontology, Series B: Psychological Sciences & Social Sciences 56, S343–S351 (2001)
34. Ragland, D., Satariano, W., MacLeod, K.: Driving Cessation and Increased Depressive Symptoms. The Gerontological Society of America 60A, 399–403 (2005)
35. Yassuda, M., Wilson, J., von Mering, O.: Driving Cessation: The Perspective of Senior Drivers. Educational Gerontology 23, 525–538 (1997)
36. Carp, F.: Significance of Mobility for the Well-Being of the Elderly. In: Transportation in an Aging Society: Improving Mobility And Safety For Older Persons, vol. 2, pp. 1–21. Transportation Research Board/National Research Council, Washington, DC (1988)
37. Feng, J., Spence, I.: Effects of Cognitive Training on Individual Differences in Attention. In: Harris, D. (ed.) HCII 2007 and EPCE 2007. LNCS (LNAI), vol. 4562, pp. 279–287. Springer, Heidelberg (2007)
38. Feng, J., Spence, I., Pratt, J.: Playing an Action Video Game Reduces Gender Differences in Spatial Cognition. Psychological Science 18, 850–855 (2007)
39. Spence, I., Feng, J.: Videogames and Spatial Cognition. Review of General Psychology (June 2010) (in press)
40. United Nations, Population Division. Population Ageing and Development (2009), `http://www.un.org/esa/population/publications/ageing/ageing2009.htm`
41. Chisnell, D.E., Redish, J.C., Lee, A.: New Heuristics for Understanding Older Adults as Web Users. Technical Communication 53, 39–59 (2006)
42. Czaja, S.J., Lee, C.C.: Designing Computer Systems for Older Adults. In: Jacko, J.A., Sears, A. (eds.) The Human-Computer Interaction Handbook. Erlbaum, Mahwah (2003)
43. Wilson, C.E.: Triangulation: The Explicit Use of Multiple Methods, Measures, and Approaches for Determining Core Issues in Product Development. Interactions 13, 46–63 (2006)
44. Smither, J., Braun, C.: Technology and Older Adults: Factors Affecting the Adoption of Automatic Teller Machines. The Journal of General Psychology 121, 381–389 (1994)

45. Zeithmal, V., Gilly, M.: Characteristics Affecting the Acceptance of Retailing Technologies: A Comparison of Elderly and Nonelderly Consumers. Journal of Retailing 63, 49–68 (1987)
46. Dyck, J.L., Smither, J.A.: Older Adults' Acquisition of Word Processing: The Contribution of Cognitive Abilities and Computer Anxiety. Computers in Human Behavior 12, 107–119 (1996)
47. Mathur, A.: Adoption of Technological Innovations by the Elderly: A Consumer Socialization Perspective. Journal of Marketing Management 9, 21–35 (1999)
48. Microsoft Online Safety, https://www.microsoft.com/protect/fraud/passwords/checker.aspx
49. Olson, G.M., Olson, J.S.: Distance Matters. Human-Computer Interaction 15, 139–178 (2000)
50. Olson, G.M., Olson, J.S., Venolia, G.: What Still Matters about Distance. In: Proceedings of HCIC 2009 Human-Computer Interaction Consortium (2009)
51. van der Kleij, R., Schraagen, J.M., Werkhoven, P., De Dreu, C.K.W.: How Conversations Change over Time in Face-to-Face and Video-Mediated Communication. Small Group Research 40, 355–381 (2009)
52. Wilson, J.M., Straus, S.G., McEvily, B.: All in Due Time: The Development of Trust in Computer-Mediated and Face-To-Face Teams. Organizational Behavior and Human Decision Processes 99, 16–33 (2006)
53. Berg, B.L.: Qualitative Research Methods for the Social Sciences. Allyn & Bacon, Boston (2005)
54. Neuman, L.: Social Research Methods: Qualitative and Quantitative Approaches. Allyn & Bacon, Boston (1997)
55. NVivo, http://www.qsrinternational.com/

Supporting Smart Interactions with Predictive Analytics

Patrick Martin[1,*], Marie Matheson[1], Jimmy Lo[2], Joanna Ng[2], Daisy Tan[2], and Brian Thomson[2]

[1] School of Computing, Queen's University
{martin,matheson}@cs.queensu.ca
[2] IBM Canada Toronto Laboratory
{jimmylo,jwng,tand,thomson}@ca.ibm.com

Abstract. Smart interactions, where web services are configured and integrated across multiple servers in order to better address the needs of the user, will be much more user-centric and responsive to user needs than current interactions. However, Smart interactions associated with decision-making tasks will specifically have to provide enhanced information or guidance linked to that task. In this paper we examine how predictive analytics can be used to provide cognitive support for smart interactions and outline a method consistent with the smart internet user model to facilitate the creation of predictive analytics components or services to support smart interactions for decision-making tasks.

Keywords: Smart internet, predictive analytics, data warehouse.

1 Introduction

The concept of the *Smart Internet* proposes to invert the traditional hyperlink-based model of the Web where interactions are driven by the server and instead provide a model in which web services are configured and integrated across multiple servers in order to better address the needs of the user [1]. This new interaction paradigm is referred to as *smart interactions*.

Smart interactions will be much more user-centric and responsive to user needs than current interactions. They will therefore need to provide a number of features including task simplification, cognitive support, context awareness, adaptive aggregation and dynamic collaboration [1].

Cognitive support, in particular, helps a user to think about, and to solve, their problems. It follows the principle that the less a person needs to know about a task they need to accomplish the better. In other words, the more knowledge the system can provide about a task, the less the user needs to know in order to successfully accomplish it.

Predictive analytics, which has grown out of Business Intelligence (BI), is a potentially useful method for providing cognitive support for smart interactions in decision-making tasks. Predictive analytics is used to analyze large amounts of data with a large number of variables to predict or recommend future actions. It can use a variety

* This research is supported by the Centre for Advanced Studies, IBM, Canada Ltd.

M. Chignell et al. (Eds.): The Smart Internet, LNCS 6400, pp. 103–114, 2010.

of techniques including clustering, classification, decision trees, neural nets, regression modeling and hypothesis testing. The core element of predictive analytics is the predictor, which is a variable that can be measured for an entity to predict future behaviour. For example, a credit card company could consider age, income, credit history and other demographics as predictors for a card applicant's risk factor. Multiple predictors are combined into a predictive model that, when subjected to analysis, can be used to forecast future probabilities with an acceptable level of reliability. Predictive analytics differs from BI in that BI focuses on past performance and the discovery of trends while predictive analytics forecasts behavior and results in order to guide specific decisions [2].

In this paper we consider the role predictive analytics can play in supporting smart interactions for decision-making tasks and describe a method for incorporating predictive analytics into these smart interactions. We illustrate the use of the method with an example scenario.

The remainder of the paper is organized as follows. Section 2 explains the concept of smart interactions and gives several use cases to illustrate decision-making tasks where predictive analytics would be useful in supporting smart interactions. Section 3 presents background on predictive analytics. Section 4 describes our method for incorporating predictive analytics into smart interactions and Section 5 discusses an example scenario. Section 6 summarizes the paper.

2 Smart Interactions

As outlined in Chapter 3 of this book (and earlier, in [1]), the vision of the Smart Internet differs from our current Internet in three main ways [1]. The first difference is a more user-centric model of interactions. As opposed to the current server-controlled page-at-a-time interactions the new model will support goal, or task, oriented interactions that can aggregate content from multiple servers while remaining under the user's control. The second difference is a notion of session that is focused on users and their tasks. Currently, sessions are server-oriented and consist of a series of requests by a user to a server in a single visit. In the Smart Internet, sessions will be defined in terms of user tasks and may involve both synchronous and asynchronous interactions with multiple servers. The third difference is that the Smart Internet will support collaborative and collective interactions as opposed to just interactions between one user and one server.

We can see that the interactions involved in the Smart Internet, which are called smart interactions, will need to be user-centric and involve increased support for users. Smart interactions, for example, could automatically enhance a system's responses to a user's requests by exploiting data about the user, their context or their past experiences with the system. Smart interactions could also add value by providing additional information or guidance tailored to the user and the task at hand.

In this paper, we are particularly interested in decision-making tasks where predictive analytics would be useful in supporting smart interactions. Examples of decision-making tasks where smart interactions could enhance the user's experience include the following:

Emergency room patient risk assessment: When a patient arrives at a busy hospital emergency room, the staff must quickly assess the seriousness of the patient's problem. The patient management system could be linked to a risk assessment service employing predictive analytics to automatically provide guidance in assigning a priority. When a staff member interacts with the patient management system to input an initial profile of the patient the system could provide this profile to the risk assessment service that combines the input with other data such as patient history, the recent history of visits to the emergency room and results of previous visits with similar profiles in order to give staff guidance concerning the urgency or priority of the patient.

Selecting an investment: Financial institutions typically provide a wide variety of investment products, which means that customers may have to examine a large amount of information before purchasing a product online. Interactions with an on-line financial system could be enhanced with a recommendation service using predictive analytics to select appropriate investment options by comparing the user's profile with other similar profiles and the successful options selected by those users.

Personalizing on-line shopping: Smart interactions with an electronic commerce system will often involve personalization of the interaction to the particular user. As a user explores a company's web site and makes purchases the system could collect data about the customer's purchases and the products they examine while browsing. This information could be passed to a recommendation service that uses predictive analytics to recommend products and services that are likely to be most attractive to a customer given their interaction history, personal profile and current behavior on the site.

3 Background

Predictive analytics use data-mining techniques in order to make predictions about future events, and make recommendations based on these predictions. This should not be confused with business analytics. Similar to predictive analytics, business analytics use data mining techniques, but rather than modeling or predicting future behaviors, trends in past data are found and used to anticipate what might happen in the future [2]. The focus is on finding patterns and tendencies that have occurred in the past and linearly projecting them into the future. The trends are simply extended in order to make a prediction, with the assumption that the system will continue to behave exactly as it has in the past.

Predictive analytics perform many of the same tasks as business analytics, and are often built upon business analytic systems. It can be said that predictive analytics are prescriptive, rather than descriptive [3]. For example, if a model is able to predict errors based on a correlation of variables then it should be able to do an analysis and recommend a solution. Additionally, predictive analytics is able to not only deal with continuous changes, but discontinuous changes as well.

Section 3.1 describes recommendation systems, and how they may be used as a predictive tool for Smart Interactions. The subsequent sections focus on common techniques for predictive analytics including: segmentation-based modeling, cost-sensitive learning, reinforcement learning and collaborative filtering.

3.1 Recommendation Systems

A growing issue of computational systems is the problem of information overload [4]. This is when there is an overwhelming amount of data that is made available to users, making it difficult for them to identify and locate the particular information that is relevant to them. Recommendation systems provide a form of information filtering that removes extraneous data and presents to the user only the small subset of available information that is considered to be most applicable to the current user task.

Recommendation systems use some form of predictive analytics. By predicting what information is most valuable to a user, recommendation systems help decide which data to display and how to present it is a useful way. Recommendation or information filtering will be essential in many Smart Internet applications.

In order to make recommendations, the system can make use of available statistical data about the user and other users with similar preferences, their profile and demographic information, and the current context of the application environment in order to decide which data is most relevant to the specific user and situation.

Recommendation systems are particularly prominent in applications involving electronic commerce. Electronic commerce, or E-commerce, consists of the buying and selling of products or services over a computer network, most commonly, the Internet. Personalized recommendations are utilized in these applications to enhance responsiveness of customers and relationship marketing [5]. Principally, statistical and knowledge discovery techniques are used to make product recommendations in real-time customer interactions in online shopping environments [6].

Personalized recommendations system approaches can be classified as either content-based or preference-based [5]. In the content-based approach, techniques such as associative rule mining are applied to a customer's purchase history in order to offer product recommendations to them. In the preference-based approach, product recommendations are made based on other customers who have similar interests and historical data, using techniques such as collaborative filtering.

Using predictive analytic techniques to perform recommendations, rather than the traditional method of having users navigate the database by performing searches, allows for a much more user-centric environment.

3.2 Segmentation-Based Modeling

Segmentation-based modeling is an approach in which data records are partitioned into segments, and separate predictive models are applied individually to each segment. For consumer-based predictive models, the segments correspond to subpopulations of the customers in the database.

The process of segmentation modeling is traditionally a sequential process. The segmentation of the data records is first performed using a process such as conventional decision tree algorithms, unsupervised clustering algorithms, domain expertise or intuition [7]. After these segments have been defined, predictive models are developed individually for each segment.

A drawback of the sequential segmentation model is that it ignores the strong influence that segmentation exerts on the predictive accuracies of the models within each segment. Some segmentation-based models apply the segmentation and develop the predictive models for each segment simultaneously, avoiding the negative influence present in the sequential approach.

ProbE [7] is a data-mining engine developed for the enhancement of predictive modeling systems. The models produced by ProbE have been shown to consistently be of higher quality than ones produced using the sequential process. Additionally, ProbE produces its models completely autonomously, avoiding the need for system users to have some form of data mining expertise in order to manually tune the modeling systems parameters.

The segmentation scheme that is produced depends heavily on the predictive models that are generated for use in each segment. For example, if a stepwise linear regression is used, then the resulting segmentation will contain segments corresponding to regions of the response surface that are locally linear, while the boundaries between segments will correspond to detected non-linearities. However, if a joint Poisson/log-normal modeling process is used, the resulting segments will correspond to distinct risk groups whose loss characteristics are estimated in accordance with standard actuarial practices.

ATM-SE (Advanced Targeted Marketing for Single Events) is a predictive modeling application built on top of the ProbE data-mining engine, developed by IBM. ATM-SE is used to mine high-dimensional customer interaction and promotional histories for modeling customer profitability and response likelihood for retail industries [7, 8].

3.3 Cost-Sensitive Learning

Learning classifiers attempt to create a policy that can make a decision based on environmental data, which will theoretically result in the best outcome. In classical machine learning and data mining applications, the assumption is made that all possible errors made by the classifier are equal. This is often not the case. For example, in medical diagnosis applications, if an error is made that mistakenly diagnoses a healthy patient to be ill then it may have less dire consequences than diagnosing a sick patient as healthy. Cost-sensitive learning strategies account for variations in cost consequent from erroneous decisions made by the policy [9, 10].

Boosting learning algorithms are a family of techniques that begin by learning a prediction model through the combination of weak classification learning rules and then using a sample re-weighting mechanism to emphasize points that are difficult to classify. These can be extended to be cost-sensitive learners by modifying the boosting's loss function so that the two following conditions are met: 1) the expected boosting loss is minimized by the optimal cost-sensitive decision rule and 2) the empirical loss minimization emphasizes a neighbourhood of the target cost-sensitive boundary [10].

3.4 Reinforcement Learning

Reinforcement learning is an approach often applied to predictive analytics. The learning environment consists of a discrete set of states and actions, and a set of transitions between them. At each step of the learning algorithm, the environment takes one of several viable actions, receives some positive or negative finite reward and transitions to the corresponding state. The goal is to maximize the total reward accrued over time by finding a policy that will choose the optimal action for any state of the environment. By making observations of the system during experimental actions, the learner attempts to infer this optimal policy.

There are three categories of methods for reinforcement learning: indirect, direct and semi-direct [9]. This categorization depends on how the environment is modeled and how the system learns.

Indirect, or "simulation-based", learning methods attempt to create a model of the environment. These models are then used by the learner to experiment with and observe in order to learn and make decisions. Abe et al [9] present an approach for indirect reinforcement learning in which a Markov decision model (MDP) is built through estimations of transition probabilities and the associated immediate rewards. Using the data generated by this model, the system learns and updates the policy based on current estimates of the value function. By using an estimated optimal policy, rather than a function approximation, it is possible to introduce new data types as the system learns.

Direct, or "Batch", learning methods directly estimate the values of possible actions at any given state, rather than trying to create a dependable model of the environment. Often, a value-iteration based supervised learning scheme is used in order to estimate a value function which will be used as the policy in future decision-making. Direct methods include adaptive heuristic critic, temporal difference and Q-learning [11].

Temporal-difference prediction methods belong to a class of prediction methods called incremental learning procedures. The difference between temporally successive predictions is used to update the learner's policies, rather than the conventional method of using only the difference between an initial prediction and actual outcomes [12]. At each step in the algorithm, the prediction of a future event is updated to reflect changes or differences in the environment since the last step.

The Adaptive Heuristic Critic is an adaptive policy iteration algorithm [13] in which the value function is computed using the temporal difference method. Rather than maximizing an immediate reward, the learning attempts to maximize a heuristic value.

Q-Learning [14, 15] is a technique that uses an expected reward function that, given the state of the system, gives the expected value of taking an action and follows a fixed policy thereafter. The Sarsa (State-Action-Reward-State-Action) learning algorithm is an on-policy Q-learning algorithm that interacts with the environment and updates its policy based on an expected immediate reward function, by using supervised learning on characterizing features. In the first iteration, a value function is obtained based on the expected reward, and is updated in subsequent iterations to reflect the change in policy.

The third category of reinforcement learning, semi-direct learning, combines the strategies of both the direct and indirect methods. Essentially, it is a direct method, but mirrors some indirect aspects such as data-sampling and reward estimations. Abe et al [9] propose an algorithm in which a selective sampling of data is performed. Only states that conform to the following condition -- that the action taken in the next step is the best action with respect to the current estimate of the value function -- are used. In learning the reward that is estimated by the function is used, rather than the rewards that are actually observed.

3.5 Collaborative Filtering

Collaborative filtering [16] is a class of predictive analytics that focuses on finding resemblances between entities, and uses close relationships to make predictions about them. In practice and in research, collaborative filtering is often used successfully in recommender systems [6].

A customer who has a history or demographic that significantly resembles another's is likely to make similar purchases. Thus, a service can recommend a product to a customer based on the fact that a very similar customer has purchased it, or a similar product, in the past. Similarly, web pages visited by one customer may be recommended to the other customers.

The item set recommendation problem, a type of recommendation problem that is often studied, concerns the decision of which items should be recommended to a consumer given a set of items that have been added to a virtual shopping cart. A set of items purchased in a single transaction is called a market basket. Before a transaction has been completed, the set of items in a market basket are called a partial basket, and might not be the final basket that is purchased. Hong et al. [17] have proposed a statistical modeling technique as a possible solution to this problem. Memory-based approaches identify similarities between users based on their ratings of a set of items [12].

Most memory-based collaborative filtering systems use a nearest-neighbours approach, which consists of three phases [18]. First, the users of the system rate items or services that they have previously experienced. Then, the filtering system matches the user for whom they are trying to create a predictive model with other participants who have similar rating patterns. These relations can be obtained through simple statistical correlations. The closest matches are selected as neighbours of the user, and become the user's *neighbourhood*. Finally, items that the neighbours have rated highly that the user has not yet experienced are recommended to the user.

A common problem in recommendation systems that use collaborative filtering is their inability to scale, due to space and calculation complexities. Clustering is a method that can be used to improve the scalability of item recommendation using item-based collaborative filtering. Clustering refers to an unsupervised process through which data items are classified into disjoint groups (clusters) based on similarities between them [19].

Huang [20] presents such an item-based clustering scheme for collaborative filtering. The k means algorithm is a basic clustering algorithm that uses an input value, k, to decide how many clusters to create. The first k items encountered by the system are used as the centers of the clusters, and each remaining item is compared to the closest cluster. The centers are re-computed in each subsequent pass of the algorithm, based on the comparisons of the added items. It is found that the number of neighbours has a significant effect on the quality of predictions made by the system. Thus, since this algorithm allows control of this value, better prediction models are possible than with traditional collaborative filtering methods.

Conner et al. [18] expand the k-means algorithm for clustering to support range attributes, allowing the user to make preferences along multiple dimensions. Furthermore, this allows more efficient manipulation of very large data sets in predictive models.

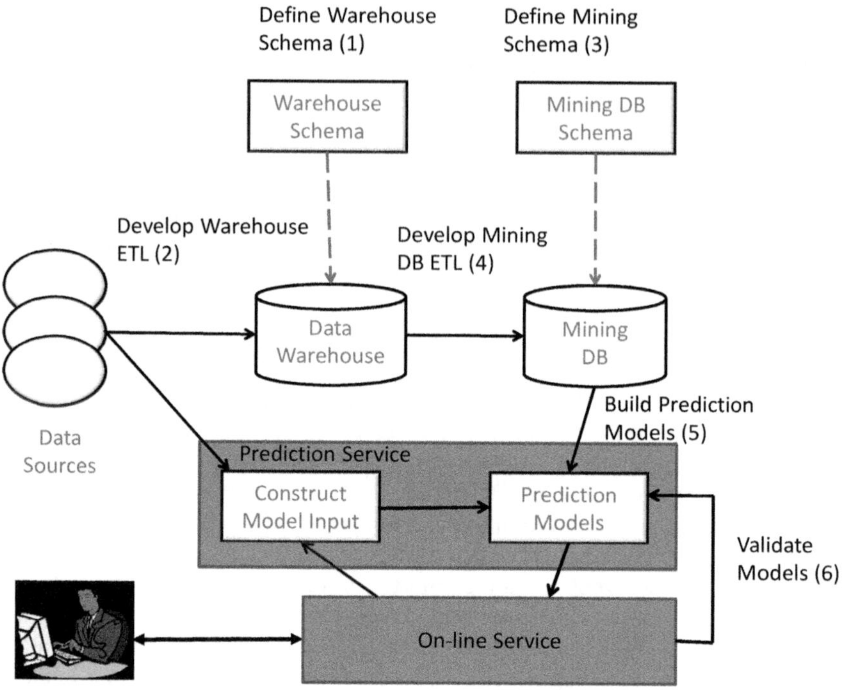

Fig. 1. Adding predictive analytics to smart interactions.

4 Integration Method

We propose the method shown in Figure 1 to integrate predictive analytics into smart interactions for decision-making tasks embodied by some on-line service. Our method is similar to the CRM Analytics Framework by Bigus et al [3], which is an end-to-end framework for developing and deploying pre-packaged predictive modeling solutions. We differ from their framework in that our method is intended to support real-time interactions and uses real-time data from the interaction to set the context for each specific analysis.

Our method contains both on-line and off-line steps. We build the prediction models off-line from data collected by the system in various data sources (steps 1 – 5). The models are incorporated into a Prediction Service that can be accessed in real-time by the target on-line service to enhance the users' interactions with that service.

Our method consists of the following steps:

1. **Define data warehouse schema.** The data sources relevant to the decision-making task are selected and the set of attributes needed to build the prediction models is identified. The data sources may include operational databases and log sets. An appropriate star schema for the warehouse must be defined. The data is extracted into a data warehouse to allow for efficient analysis without interfering with the operation of the data sources.

2. **Develop data warehouse Extract-Transform-Load (ETL) routines.** The relevant data from the data sources must be retrieved, transformed to meet the star schema and then loaded into the data warehouse. These routines can be run periodically to keep the warehouse relatively consistent with the data sources.
3. **Define mining database schema.** Depending on the decision-making task, we may choose to use one or more of the predictive modeling approaches discussed earlier in the paper. A number of prediction modeling algorithms work on a single table so that the mining schema will join the fact and dimension tables into a single table. The analysis may also be at a different level of aggregation than the data in the warehouse so all necessary aggregations will be performed. The mining schema contains both extracted and predicted attributes so that reporting can be performed on the results of the prediction models.
4. **Design mining database ETL routines.** The relevant data from the data warehouse must be retrieved, transformed to conform to the mining database schema and then loaded into the mining database. These routines can be run periodically or on demand.
5. **Build prediction models.** We develop one or more prediction models from the data in the mining database in order to produce the results desired for the interaction. For a given interaction, the input data is collected from the interaction and fed into the models to produce the results for the interaction.
6. **Validate and update prediction models.** We perform a closed loop analysis to validate the models by measuring the success of the interaction output. If the degree of success is not sufficient then the models are updated.

Once built, the prediction models, as shown in Figure 1, can be incorporated into a prediction service that can be accessed by the target on-line service. The prediction service can be consulted in real-time as part of the smart interaction between a user and the target on-line service. The prediction service would first construct an input vector to the prediction model based on data about the current interaction and other necessary historical data from the data sources. The input would be given to the prediction model that would provide a prediction that is returned to the on-line system. The results of the prediction on the user interaction can be fed back to the prediction system to validate the models (step 6).

5 Example Scenario

The area of e-commerce and personalized marketing is one where smart interactions can be applied. For instance, customer interactions with an e-commerce system can be enhanced with real time personalized suggestions for all stages of every purchase. As an example, we specifically consider the scenario in which space on web pages such as the category page and shopping cart page visited by a customer must be filled with an offer for the "best" products, that is, the most appealing products to the specific customer tailored to the buying stage during their interaction with the system.

In applying our method for integrating predictive analytics into smart interactions to this scenario we first define a schema for a warehouse to hold data relevant to the analysis. We can identify three sets of useful feature attributes for the scenario:

1. **Customer profile attributes**, which can be used to cluster customer purchases based on similarities in customer demographics. These attributes would be extracted from databases holding customer information and purchase histories.
2. **Product purchase profiles**, which can be used to identify combinations of products that tend to be purchased together and average order sizes. These data would be extracted from the e-Commerce transactional database.
3. **Interaction behavior**, which can be used to characterize the current session and find similarities with other sessions and with previous successful marketing offer placements. These attributes may consist of clickstream data such as which pages were examined; properties of the content occupying these pages; what links were followed and in what order; search terms used by the customer, and the contents of the customer's shopping cart. Other possible attributes include the referral site that brought the customer to the web site, the time the customer spends on specific types on content such as looking at certain pages, hovering on pop-ups, and details like "immediate undos".

We can define a warehouse schema with three fact tables, one for each of the customer profiles, product purchases and interaction behavior. The fact tables would be linked through common dimension tables. The customer profile and product purchases could be extracted from operational databases for the system. The interaction behavior could be obtained from transaction and Web logs for the system.

The mining schema defined for this smart interaction could consist of three tables. These tables could contain the joins of the corresponding fact tables with their dimension tables. We can develop three predictive models, based on each of the different attribute sets, using reinforcement learning or collaborative filtering. The information about the current interaction and customer can then be input to the models to obtain individual recommendations. The recommendations from the three models can then be assigned weights and combined to provide a final recommendation for the best use of the advertising space.

We can measure the effectiveness of the recommendations from predictive analytics by running a split A/B test [21] with predetermined static recommendations as control, and measure the success via the click-through rate of the offer, the number of orders and order size.

6 Summary

The Smart Internet proposes to shift the focus of the Web applications and servers onto the user in order to better meet users` needs. Smart interactions are the new user-centric interactions that are part of this vision. They differ from traditional Web interactions primarily because of the potential involvement of multiple servers and the increased user-control. The smart interaction paradigm, which focuses on providing more complete support for complex user tasks that can span multiple services, is ideally suited to the variety of decision-making tasks currently by users. Predictive analytics, which mine data to help predict beneficial future actions, are a powerful tool for decision-making.

In this paper we consider how predictive analytics can be integrated into smart interactions for enhanced guidance and support for decision-making tasks. We present an integration method that involves both off-line and on-line components. Given a particular decision-making task, we first build a data warehouse that combines data from the set of relevant data sources. We next select predictor attributes from the warehouse and extract this data into a mining database that is analyzed with the prediction algorithms to construct prediction models. The prediction models are incorporated into a prediction service that is used in real-time as part of a smart interaction with the target on-line system.

We initially plan to explore using our method to support smart interactions with e-commerce systems. Our first experiment with the method will implement the web page advertising scenario discussed in the paper. We also plan to research issues related to deploying prediction models in the e-commerce environment. One issue is to examine ways to dynamically refine models as more data becomes available. A second issue is how to provide increased user control such as a method for users to select a desired outcome of the analysis and a way for users to provide input in terms of the type of model to be used.

Acknowledgments

The authors thank IBM's Centre for Advanced Studies and MITACS for their support of this research.

References

1. Ng, J.W., Chignell, M., Cordy, J.R.: The Smart Internet: Transforming the Web for the User. In: Martin, P., Kark, A.W., Stewart, D. (eds.) Proceedings of the 2009 Conference of the Centres for Advanced Studies on Collaborative Research, CASCON 2009, Ontario, Canada, November 02-05, pp. 285–296. ACM, New York (2009)
2. Agosta, L.: The Future of Data Mining – Predictive Analytics. DM Review (2004)
3. Bigus, J., Chitnis, U., Deshpande, P., Kannan, R., Mohania, M., Negi, S., Deepak, P., Pednault, E., Soni, S., Telkar, B., White, B.: CRM Analytics Framework. In: Proc. of 15th Int. Conf. on Management of Data (COMAD 2009), Mysore, India (2009)
4. Tung, L., Xu, Y.: A framework for e-commerce oriented recommendation systems, Active Media Technology. In: Proceedings of the International Conference on AMT 2005, May 19-21, pp. 309–314 (2005)
5. Chuang, H., Wang, L., Pan, C.: A Study on the Comparison between Content-Based and Preference-Based Recommendation Systems, Semantics, Knowledge and Grid. In: Fourth International Conference on SKG 2008, December 3-5, pp. 477–480 (2008)
6. Sarwar, B., Karypis, G., Konstan, J., Riedl, J.: Analysis of recommendation algorithms for e-commerce. In: Proceedings of the 2nd ACM Conference on Electronic Commerce, EC 2000, Minneapolis, Minnesota, United States, October 17-20, pp. 158–167. ACM, New York (2000)

7. Apte, C., Bibelnieks, E., Natarajan, R., Pednault, E., Tipu, F., Campbell, D., Nelson, B.: Segmentation-based modeling for advanced targeted marketing. In: Proceedings of the Seventh ACM SIGKDD International Conference on Knowledge Discovery and Data Mining, San Francisco, California, pp. 408–413 (2001)
8. Apte, C.V., Hong, S.J., Natarajan, R., Pednault, E.P., Tipu, F.A., Weiss, S.M.: Data-intensive analytics for predictive modeling. IBM J. Res. Dev. 47(1), 17–23 (2003)
9. Abe, N., Pednault, E., Wang, H., Zadrozny, B., Fan, W., Apte, C.: Empirical Comparison of Various Reinforcement Learning Strategies for Sequential Targeted Marketing. In: Proceedings of the 2002 IEEE international Conference on Data Mining. IEEE Computer Society, Washington (2002)
10. Masnadi-Shirazi, H., Vasconcelos, N.: Cost-sensitive boosting. IEEE Transactions on PP Pattern Analysis and Machine Intelligence 99, 1 (2010)
11. Kaelbling, L.P.: Reinforcement learning: A survey. Journal of artificial intelligence research 4, 237–285 (1996)
12. Sutton, R.S.: Learning to predict by the method of temporal differences. Machine Learning 3(1), 9–44 (1988)
13. Barto, A.G., Sutton, R.S., Anderson, C.W.: Neuron-like adaptive elements that can solve difficult learning control problems. IEEE Transactions on Systems, Man, and Cybernetics, SMC 13(5), 834–846 (1983)
14. Watkins, C.J.C.H.: Learning from Delayed Rewards. Ph.D. thesis, King's College, Cambridge, UK (1989)
15. Watkins, C.J.C.H., Dayan, P.: Q-learning. Machine Learning 8(3), 279–292 (1992)
16. Goldberg, D., Nichols, D., Oki, B.M., Terry, D.: Using collaborative filtering to weave an information tapestry. Comm. ACM 35(12), 61–70 (1992)
17. Hong, S.J., Natarajan, R., Belitskaya, I.: A New Approach for Item Choice Recommendations. In: Kambayashi, Y., Winiwarter, W., Arikawa, M. (eds.) DaWaK 2001. LNCS, vol. 2114, pp. 131–140. Springer, Heidelberg (2001)
18. Connor, M., Herlocker, J.: Clustering items for collaborative filtering. In: Proc. of the SIGIR Workshop on Recommender Systems, Berkeley CA (1999)
19. Papamichail, G.P., Papamichail, D.P.: The k-means range algorithm for personalized data clustering in e-commerce. European Journal of Operational Research 177(3), 1400–1408 (2007)
20. Huang, Y.: An item based collaborative filtering using item clustering prediction. In: ISECS International Colloquium on Computing, Communication, Control, and Management, CCCM 2009, vol. 4, pp. 54–56 (2009)
21. Marketing Research: A/B Split Testing (2010), `http://www.marketingexperiments.com/improving-website-conversion/ab-split-testing.html`

A Framework for Automatically Supporting End-Users in Service Composition

Hua Xiao[1], Ying Zou[2], Ran Tang[2], Joanna Ng[3], and Leho Nigul[3]

[1] School of Computing, Queen's University
huaxiao@cs.queensu.ca
[2] Dept. Of Electrical and Computer Engineering, Queen's University
{ying.zou,ran.tang}@queensu.ca
[3] IBM Toronto Lab
{jwng,lnigul}@ca.ibm.com

Abstract. In Service Oriented Architecture (SOA), service composition integrates existing services to fulfill specific tasks using a set of standards and tools. However, current service composition techniques and tools are mainly designed for SOA professionals. It becomes challenging for end-users without sufficient service composition skills to compose services. In this paper, we propose a framework that supports end-users to dynamically compose and personalize services to meet their own context. Instead of requiring end-users to specify detailed steps in the composition, our framework only requires end-users to specify the goals of their desired activities using a few keywords to generate a task list. To organize the task list, we analyze the historical usage data and recover the control flows among the tasks in the task list. We also mine the task usage pattern from the historical usage data to recommend new services. A prototype is designed and developed as a proof of concept to demonstrate that our approach enables end-users to discover and compose services easily.

Keywords: Personalized Service Composition, Context-awareness, Mining Historical Usage Data, Service Oriented Architecture.

1 Introduction

Web services are considered as self-contained, self-describing, modular applications that can be published, located, and invoked across the Web. The Service-Oriented Architecture (SOA) uses loosely coupled Web services as basic constructs to build more complex systems in a flexible and rapid way. However, a single service generally cannot fulfill the functionality required by end-users. Service composition based on end-user context and inputs is required to enable the Smart Internet functionality espoused in this book.

A significant amount of effort from industry and academics intends to provide infrastructure, languages and tools to compose the services using well-defined business processes to streamline business operations. Such SOA systems tackle complex business requirements across organizations. However, little attention has been paid to allowing end-users to compose services to fulfill their daily activities that can be

M. Chignell et al. (Eds.): The Smart Internet, LNCS 6400, pp. 115–136, 2010.

represented as ad-hoc processes. For example, planning a trip is an ad-hoc process for many end-users. It involves several tasks, such as searching for transportation, booking accommodation, and checking restaurants. These tasks can be performed dynamically to achieve the goal of trip planning.

In today's on-line experience, an end-user, who is not familiar with Web service standards and tools, frequently re-visits websites and uses on-line services to perform daily activities, such as planning a trip. The end-user potentially composes an ad-hoc process to fulfill his or her needs. Such an ad-hoc process is characterized by a set of tasks performed by end-users without a strict pre-defined plan. Consider a scenario that a person plans a trip to Vancouver in two contexts: (1) John, a business man, lives in Toronto and travels to Vancouver for a business meeting. He would like to take Air Canada, as a reliable transportation vehicle, to stay in the Marriott since he is a valued member of Marriott, and to find a formal seafood restaurant for an important business dinner. (2) Emily, who is a student at the University of Calgary, wants to take a vacation in Vancouver. She chooses to plan her trip at the lowest cost. She will take Greyhound bus, search for a motel in Vancouver and look for fast food chains, such as Wendy's and MacDonald's. In both contexts, each end-user has to manually browse different services offered by Websites and Web services to gather information for performing the same tasks in trip planning. It is often challenging for end-users to know all the relevant Web services or websites that can assist them to make a decision.

Specialized service mediators, such as expedia.com [1], can be used to search for accommodation, flight and train information. However, they cannot automatically provide services that are personalized to a particular end-user (e.g., traveler with luxury plans, or traveler on a small budget). Moreover, the services provided by the service mediators are pre-defined and limited. For example, the end-user has to visit other websites to check the reviews about a hotel or a restaurant and check if the airline suggested by expedia.com is in part of the alliance in which they collect their frequent flyer points. The end-user has to repeat the same step when planning the next trip. It would be ideal if an end-user can compose a travel planning service using the SOA techniques. Then the composed service automatically gathers the needed information and presents it to the end-user based on his or her preference.

In the current state of practice, composing services requires a large number of professionals (e.g., business analyst, system integrator and service developer) with strong SOA background. The development process involves various technical tools and languages to specify, compose, and deploy services. To produce a composed service, the professionals in different roles and tools must interact in harmony. Unfortunately, non-expert end-users do not possess knowledge of most of these tools and lack the knowledge of SOA standards. In short, involving end-users in service composition involves the following two challenges:

- **Complexity in service description and discovery.** The Web Service Description Language (WSDL) [2] is commonly used to define the programming interface of a service, such as the operations offered by a service and the format of messages sent and received between services. However, WSDL is too complex for non-expert end-users. WSDL is primarily intended for SOA experts to understand the interface and parameters of a Web service and to correctly invoke a service. It creates difficulty for end-users to understand the functionality of a service as they seek to discover an appropriate service.

- **Limited support for composing services on the fly.** A system integrator can specify BPEL (Business Process Execution Language) [3] processes to compose Web services using tools, such as IBM WID (WebSphere Integration Developer) [4]. After deployment of a Web service, the composition logic is difficult to customize to accommodate changes to consumer's requirements, as this involves a long lifecycle from design, development and testing to deployment. An ad-hoc process involves the dynamic integration of various services (e.g., Web services, and websites) on-the-fly. Moreover, it is also infeasible to expect an end-user to specify the details of each task and orchestrate a well-defined process in BPEL.

These challenges represent barriers for integrating SOA into an end-user's activities for improved quality of life and productivity. To address these challenges, our work focuses on the following two aspects:

1) **Context aware service discovery.** We design and develop techniques that automatically capture an end-user's context which denotes changes in an end-user's environment (i.e., operational and physical environment), and use the context to assist in service discovery. This avoids the need for end-users to understand the WSDL description of a Web service. It should also reduce the amount of information required from end-users in order to specify well-defined criteria for service discovery.
2) **Dynamic service composition.** We devise techniques that dynamically search and compose services on-the-fly to assist an end-user in fulfilling their desired goals (such as planning a trip). We aim to provide an approach to shelter the end-user from complex programming issues.

The remainder of this paper is organized as follows. Section 2 discusses the requirements and potential techniques for enabling end-user friendly service composition. Section 3 presents our framework that automatically composes services on the fly and personalizes composition results for end-users. Section 4 describes a proof of concept prototype that implements the proposed framework. Section 5 gives an overview of related work. Finally, section 6 concludes the paper and presents the future work.

2 Requirements and Techniques for Building End-User Friendly Service Composition Environments

It is challenging for end-users without deep understanding of SOA knowledge and standards to integrate SOA technology in their daily on-line experience. In this section, we discuss the requirements crucial for the involvement of end-users in the service composition process. Then we introduce the enabling techniques that support the achievement of the requirements.

2.1 Requirements for End-User Friendly Service Composition Environments

Generally, end-users are most concerned with the ease of use of service composition tools. The tools are expected to be intuitive to use without a steep learning curve, be quickly mastered, and simplify their daily tasks. The technology details (e.g., how the services are developed, deployed and delivered) is not the end-user's concern. To meet the end-user's expectation, we envision that the following requirements are important to acquire in the service composition environment.

(1) Automatic Generation of Ad-Hoc Processes
In the current state of practice, SOA practitioners manually describe the details of each task and the interactions among tasks using BPEL. In an end-user environment, most of the activities or goals (e.g., plan a trip) are spontaneously prompted from an end-user. An end-user may not have a clear plan for achieving a goal. To guide an end-user to achieve her goal, our aim is to reduce the amount of inputs required from end-users. Instead of specifying the complete tasks to achieve their goal, an end-user is required to describe a high level goal using keywords. For example, for planning a trip, an end-user can specify the keywords, such as travel, Vancouver and student. To understand the semantic meaning of an end-user's goal, ontologies provide rich and machine-understandable semantic meanings for a given goal. We use ontologies to expand the semantic meanings of the keywords and automatically infer the possible tasks that need to be performed by an end-user. To assist end-users to walk through the task list, we track the usage of tasks by the end-users of the same goal. We identify the possible execution orders among tasks performed by the majority of the end-users to guide end-users to complete the tasks in the list in a particular order. An ad-hoc process contains a list of tasks and the suggested execution orders among the tasks.

(2) Context aware service discovery
Effective service discovery requires the ability to detect an end-user's context at the run-time environment. This context characterizes the operational conditions for an end-user to fulfill a goal, such as server workloads, end-user's profiles, computation resources, scheduled tasks, and end-user's preferences. The context of the run-time environment should also capture the functional and non-functional capabilities of deployed services. For example, non-functional requirements, such as processing time, end-user's ranking and provider reputation, can be taken into account during the discovery of deployed services. We develop techniques for automatically capturing and using the context to assist in generating searching criteria and providing personalized service discovery. This would reduce the amount of information required from end-users in order to specify well-defined criteria for searching Web services.

(3) Accurate service recommendation
A major challenge when composing services is to predicate the needed services. Current SOA runtime environment, service explorer tools allow a system integrator to search for services from the service repository. However, the results returned by the explorer are usually context insensitive. To improve the accuracy in recommending services, we trace the execution of the already generated task list and recover the usage patterns among tasks. Each task is associated with a set of already discovered services. We recommend a desired service by retrieving the task usage patterns of historical task lists that have the similar context as the desired service. For example, if an end-user is developing a service for a bookstore and other end-users already have a task list to produce a service for a video store deployed, then we can use the task list for the video store which contains services such as the inventory management, account management, credit card authorization to improve the search results. The

end-user who is developing the bookstore may have already performed tasks such as picking an inventory management and selecting account management service, so we can recommend a credit card authorization task based on the knowledge learned from other task lists.

Using data mining techniques (such as frequent item set mining), we can estimate the accuracy of our recommendation in the same manner that online bookstores such as amazon.com give for their book recommendation. For example, we can recommend a credit card authorization service and indicate that the recommended service is used by 90% of the services which have an inventory management service and account management service. Recommending services would reduce the complexity of composing services and would help an end-user pick the most popular (and ideally most widely deployed and tested) services to build their new services. This work would in turn permit the creation of high-quality well-tested services.

(4) Customizable composition results
The generated ad-hoc process guides end-users to invoke Web services and achieve their goal. However, a Web service in the generated ad-hoc process may not provide all the functionality that an end-user needs. For the example of the trip planning, an end-user may visit a trip advisor website (a HTML based website) before making decision. The Web services need to interoperate with other Web resources. A Mashup is a Web page or application that remixes data or functionalities from two or more external sources to create a new service. In our work, Mashup provides a light-weight user-friendly graphic environment for an end-user to customize the composed services as well as integrate various Web resources and Web services.

2.2 Enabling Techniques

In this section we review techniques for allowing end-users to compose services. The techniques covered in this brief review are ontologies, contexts and context-aware systems, and mashups.

2.2.1 Structure of Ontologies

An ontology expresses common concepts (e.g., people, travel and weather), and the relations among the concepts. Fig. 1 illustrates an example ontology that defines the concept "travel". The semantic of a high level concept (e.g., "travel") can be further expanded into four sub-concepts: "Transportation", "Accommodation", "Tourist Attraction" and "Car Rental".

Ontologies are manually described using different ontology specification languages, such as Web Ontology Language (OWL) [5] and Resource Definition Framework (RDF) [6]. To capture the general structure and concepts of ontologies specified in various languages, we summarize the common entities and relations in different ontologies as follows.

- *Class*: is an abstract description of a group of resources with similar characteristics. For example, "LuxuryHotel" is a *class* which describes the common characteristics of different hotels. *Class* is also called "concept", "type", "category" and "kind" in various ontology languages.
- *Individual*: is an instance of a *class*. For example, "Hilton Hotel" is an *instance* of *class* "Hotel", i.e., "Hilton Hotel" is an *individual*.

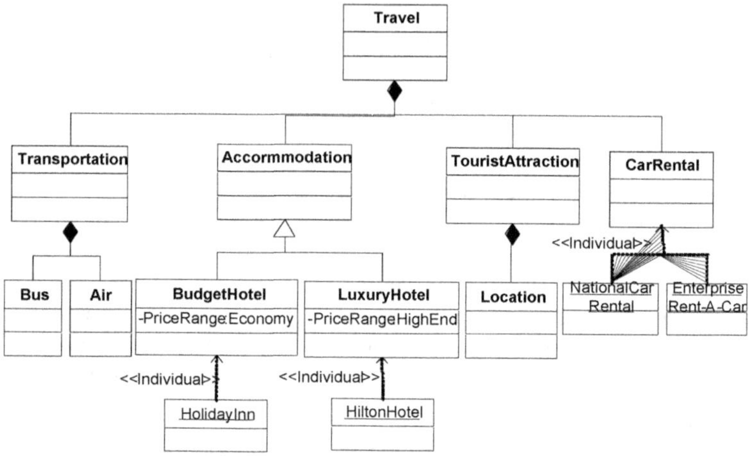

Fig. 1. An example ontology.

- *Relation*: defines ways in which *classes* and *individuals* can be related to one another. Typical *relations* include *subclass*, *partOf*, *complement*, *intersection* and *equivalent*. *Subclass* extends a *class* to convey more concrete knowledge. *PartOf* relation indicates that a class is a part of another class. *Complement* selects all members (classes or individuals) from the domain of the ontology that do not belong to a certain class. *Intersection* describes a class which contains the members shared by all the classes in the given class list. *Equivalent* expresses that two classes contains exactly the same set of individuals.
- *Attribute*: describes a property of a *class* (and an *individual*). *Attribute* is also called "aspect", "property", "feature" or "characteristic" in various ontology specification languages. For example, "PriceRange" is an *attribute* of *class* "LuxuryHotel".

2.2.2 Contexts and Context-Aware Systems

A context involves several pairs of context types and context values. Specifically, a context type describes a characteristic of the context. A context type is associated with a specific context value which may vary over time with the changing environment. For example, the context types for an end-user could include location, identity, and time. The context type "location" may be assigned with a value, such as "New York". A context scenario is the combination of different context types with specific context values to reflect an end-user's situation. A context model is used to specify the relations and storage structure of various context types and values.

A context-aware system is designed to adapt the operations of systems to an end-user's context without explicit intervention from the user [7]. A context aware system generally consists of two parts: (1) sensing and managing contexts; and (2) adapting the system to the changing contexts. Context sensors are used to retrieve context values from different resources. The Global Positioning System (GPS) receiver is an example context sensor to detect location. To adapt the behaviors based on different context scenarios, the most common approach for context-aware systems is to manually construct mapping rules between the context scenarios and the corresponding reactions. For example, IF-THEN rules are commonly used as mapping rules. More specially, the IF sentence describes the context scenario; and the THEN sentence represents the corresponding reactions. For example, if a person is in a meeting and receiving a phone call, then his/her cell phone is automatically switched from the ringing mode to silence or vibrate mode.

2.2.3 Mashups

A Mashup is a lightweight Web application that integrates multiple data or functions into one application to create a new service. Mashups are generally browser-based applications. End-users can easily access the Mashup applications using Web browsers (e.g., Internet Explorer and Firefox) without installing any software on the client side. Several products, such as Microsoft Popfly[8], Yahoo! Pipe [9] and IBM Mashup center [10], provide user friendly environment for end-users to manually connect Web resources into one Web page. Such environments are easier for non-expert end-users to learn and to manually compose services. For example, an end-user can integrate email client, Google calendar and weather report into a single Web page by connecting data flows among Web resources and dropping a new Web resource into an existing page. For further discussion of Mashups see the next Chapter (Grammel and Storey) of this book.

3 An Overview of Our Framework

Fig. 2 provides an overview of our proposed framework for generating and personalizing ad-hoc processes. The framework is built using a client/server architecture. On the client side, end-users interact with the service composition environment through a composition user interface (UI) which is built using Mashup pages. The composition UI provides an end-user interface to enable end-users to specify the goal, navigate through the generated ad-hoc process, edit the process, and select services. To capture an end-user's context, context sensors are developed to monitor the end-user's activities in their computing environment. We deploy context sensors as plug-ins into various applications, such as Web browsers and on-line calendars.

The server contains three major components that process the contextual information gathered from the client, generate an ad-hoc process and analyze historic usage data to recommend services. The components are described as follows:

The **Composition engine** receives the goal of service composition from end-users and automatically composes a personalized ad-hoc process. The composition engine uses the goal description (i.e., keywords) to find a matching ontology. In an ontology, the semantics of a high-level goal is expanded into more concrete concepts. The composition engine uses the concepts as keywords to search services from service repositories. The service repository allows service providers to advertise their services and provide interfaces for automatic service discovery. To facilitate the execution and selection of the services, we abstract the discovered services into tasks and use historical usage data to identify the control structures among tasks. The resulting ad-hoc process can be stored and shared among multiple end-users. To enable end-users and composition tools to understand the properties of Web services, we describe services using descriptive tags (i.e., keywords). The detailed information of the tag-based service description schema is described in our earlier publication [11].

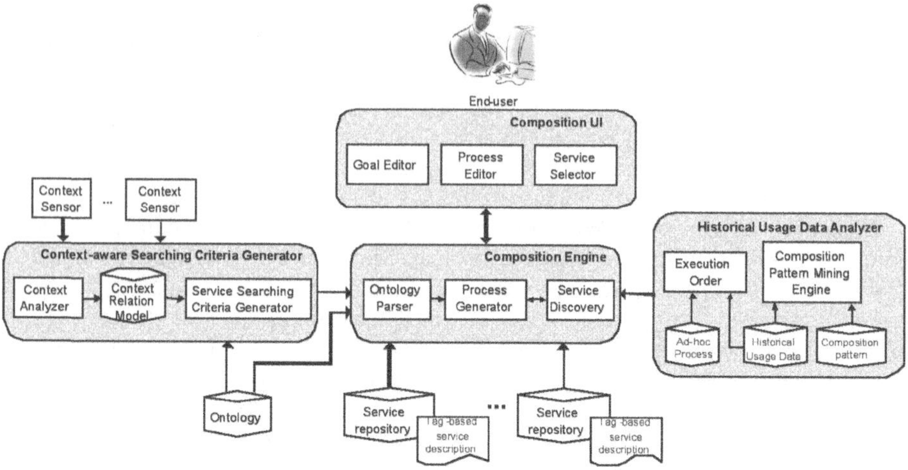

Fig. 2. An overview of our framework.

Context-aware searching criteria generator captures and analyzes the changing context scenarios of an end-user. This component automatically formulates searching criteria to discover the desired services in the service repositories. To formulate searching criteria to meet contextual requirements, existing approaches pre-define an end-user's context using context models in various forms [12]. Rules are generally specified to connect the context types to the possible end-user's preferences and generate searching criteria for service discovery. However, the context types may vary considerably between end-users. It is challenging to anticipate a complete set of context types to satisfy all the possible end-users. Fixed rules are not flexible enough to accommodate the changing environment and various personal interests. In contrast to existing approaches which require end-users manually specify the relations among context types, we seek an automatic approach to recognizing the relations without overwhelming end-users. For example, luxury hotel and limited budget are two context types in conflict. Therefore, the services for booking luxury hotels are automatically filtered out when an end-user has very limited budget. We expect that such relations can be used to express more accurate searching criteria to reflect an end-user's context.

Historical usage data analyzer analyses the historical usage data to mine execution order among the tasks in the task list. Moreover, the historical usage data analyzer identifies frequent task usage patterns from historical usage data. To obtain the historical usage data, we track end-users' interaction with the server, such as the selected tasks, the invoked services and the time of the invocation. When an end-user executes a task list, the executed tasks are recorded as an execution instance. In each execution instance, the tasks are placed in the order in which they are executed. When many end-users have executed a task list, a large amount of execution instances are collected. These execution instances can be used to mine execution order of the underlying task list. The historical usage data are generally analyzed periodically to recognize task usage patterns and store them in a database. When a task list is composed, a new task can be recommended by matching the task list with the stored patterns. Each task is associated with a set of already discovered services. Consequently the associated services are recommended to the end-user.

In the following sub-sections, we present the details of the three major components: service composition engine, context-aware searching criteria generator, and historical usage data analyzer.

3.1 Ontology-Based Ad-Hoc Process Generation

Once an end-user specifies the goal using keywords, we find the relevant ontology to extend the semantic meanings of those keywords. The concept (i.e., classes, individuals, and attributes) defined in the ontology could be used to search for relevant services. However, a large number of services could be returned and mixed together. It is a tedious job for end-users to manually organize and select their desired services. To guide the execution of services, we propose to sort the functionally similar services under one task and identify the execution order of tasks based on historical usage data. Specifically, we use the relations between concepts in the ontology to identify a list of unique tasks which are associated with one or more functionally similar returned services. Then, we mine the task execution order using historical usage data. Finally, we can generate an ad-hoc process which contains a set of tasks with suggested execution order.

To identify tasks, we decompose the goal using the ontology to locate a subset of concepts used for service discovery. We use a depth first traversal to find the most concrete class or individual in the search criteria. A terminal node, such as "*location*", "*BudgetHotel*" and "*LuxuryHotel*" shown in Fig. 1, is a terminal node in the ontology graph which does not have child classes or individuals. The attributes of classes or individuals are included as a part of the node in the ontology graph. Terminal nodes represent the most detailed knowledge about the root class which is the goal specified by end-users. Therefore, we visit the terminal node which has the longest path from the root concept. Simply using a terminal node in the search criteria may prevent us from discovering some services since a single keyword from the terminal node provides limited knowledge. Similar to some search engines, which use the expanded query to search for the relevant documents [13], we extend the search keywords by including the parent node, the attributes of the terminal node, and the sibling terminal nodes as the keywords to search for services in service repositories. For example, as shown in Fig. 3, *"Holiday Inn"* is a terminal node with the longest paths from the root "*Travel*". Its parent, *"BudgetHotel"* and attribute, *"PriceRange: Economy"*, are collected as keywords to search for services (i.e., *keywords(Budget Hotel)={Budget Hotel, Holiday Inn, Price Range, economy}*). Once a service is identified from the group of classes, individuals and attributes, these concepts are marked as a task, shown in Fig. 3. We derive the task name from the name of the parent class. For the example shown in Fig. 3, the task corresponding to individual *"Holiday Inn"* and class *"Budget Hotel"* is named after the parent, *"Budget Hotel"*. If no relevant Web services are retrieved from the path, we remove the failed nodes (i.e., the parent along the children) from the ontology graph. We recursively identify the next terminal node with the longest path from the root and repeat the same procedure, until all the terminal nodes are visited. Finally, we get a list of tasks, and each task maps to several services with similar functionality.

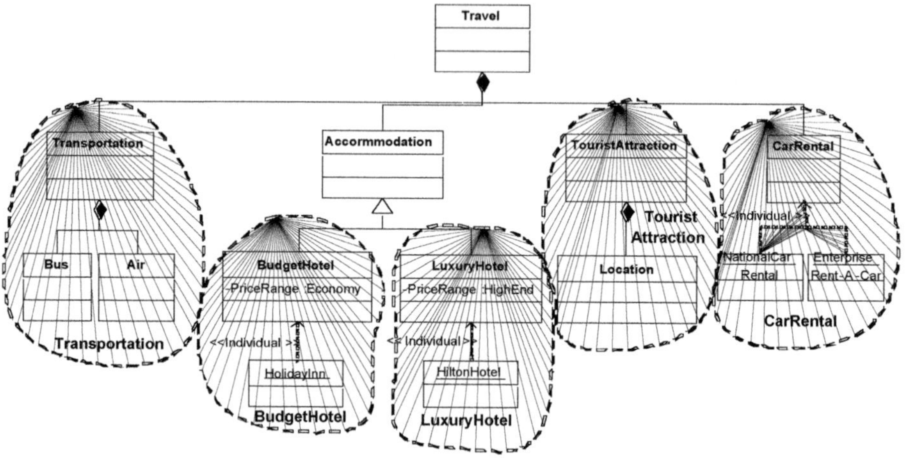

Fig. 3. An example of generating a task list.

To help end-users navigate and execute the tasks, we mine the task execution order using historical usage data. A task list contains many tasks. The execution order between the tasks may be found in the historical usage data. Historical usage data consists of execution instances. Each execution instance may contain execution order of some tasks in the task list. Suppose we have a task list {A, B, C, D, E}. It is possible that one execution instance in the historical usage data has executed tasks A and B, and another execution instance has executed tasks C, D and E. Thus, the execution order between tasks A and B can be found in one execution instance and the execution order among tasks C, D and E can be found in another execution instance. By aggregating all execution instances, we can obtain the overall execution order among the task list {A, B, C, D, E}. Specifically, we identify the execution order using the following steps:

1) Find the execution instances that record the execution of more than one task in the task list in the historical usage data.
2) Identify the execution flow among each execution instance which is a graph where the nodes are tasks and the edges represent execution order between tasks. The edges are determined using the ordering of tasks in the execution instance. If task A immediately precedes task B in the execution instance, we create a direct edge from A to B in the execution flow. Loops can exist in the execution flow if some tasks are repeated in the execution instance.
3) Combine the execution flow of each execution instance to obtain an overall execution flow of the task list. The overall execution flow contains all tasks in the task list as nodes. The edges from execution instances are merged in the overall execution flow.
4) Recognize different control flow structures (e.g., sequence, alternative, parallel and loop) to describe the task execution order in the task list. A sequence structure organizes tasks in a sequential order. Parallel structure and alternative structure contain multiple execution paths. In a parallel structure, all paths need to be executed. In an alternative structure, only one path can be executed.

A loop structure contains tasks that can be repeated several times in one execution instance. To identify the control flow structures, we check all the execution instances to locate a starting task (i.e., the first task to be executed) and traverse the overall execution graph from the starting task. If a loop edge is encountered during the traversal, we mark the repeated tasks in a loop structure. When several paths branch out from one task and the tasks on the different paths are all executed without a particular order, we treat such paths as a parallel structure. If several paths branch out from one task and the tasks on the different paths cannot be executed in the same execution instance, we define such paths as an alternative structure.

As an example shown in Fig. 4, we identify the execution order of the task list generated from the ontology shown in Fig. 3 to form an ad-hoc process which connects a set of tasks with control flow constructs. However, the historical usage data may not always available. When there is no historical usage data available, we use the knowledge from the ontology to identify some simple relations (i.e., alternative and parallel relations) among tasks. The detailed approach of identifying relations among tasks using ontologies are described in our earlier publication [14].

3.2 Generating Context Aware Searching Criteria

In an end-user's context, context types can be dynamically added and removed due to the changing environment. The value of a context type also evolves over time as an end-user's computing environment changes. We need a flexible context model to dynamically adjust the context relations to accommodate the updated context types and their values. Context values capture more accurate characteristics of an end-user's context than a context type. For example, location is a context type. When the location changes, the GPS device can identify and update the location with a concrete context value, such as "Los Angeles". To correctly model an end-user's context, we focus on capturing the relations among context values instead of the high-level relations among context types. Moreover, we analyze the relations among context values to derive the searching criteria for the desired services that match the context.

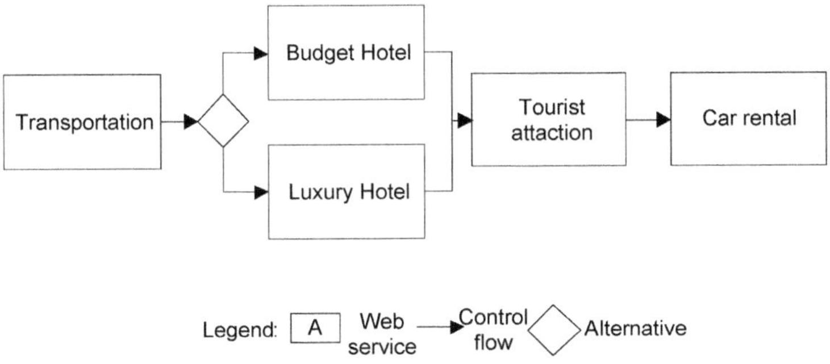

Fig. 4. An example ad-hoc process after the execution order is identified.

Identify relations among context values. To correctly model the relations among context values, it is critical to understand the semantic meanings of each context value. Ontologies capture the relevant information related to a particular concept using expert knowledge. To gain a better understanding of a context value, we search for existing ontologies that describe the meaning of a context value. To derive the relations among multiple context values, we can check the overlaps of concepts in the corresponding ontologies.

We identify three types of relations among two context values: intersection, complement and equivalence. Intersection relation refers to the case that the ontologies of two context values contain common entities (e.g., classes or individuals). Fig. 5 illustrates examples of intersection relations. In Fig. 5, the context values "*travel*" (i.e., the context type is "activity") and "*Los Angeles*" (i.e., the context type is "location") contain the common class "*Tourist Attraction*". Context values "*Los Angeles*" and "*NBA*" contain the same class "*Los Angeles Lakers*". When the ontologies of two context values have no overlaps and these two context values together represent all the information in the given domain, we say that such context values complement each other. For example, "*Budget Hotel*" and "*Luxury Hotel*" are in a complement relation. The equivalent relation means that the ontologies of two context values are the same. Equivalent relations are usually explicitly specified in the ontologies of the context values. The relations between two context values are inherited from the relations between their corresponding ontologies. Furthermore, we combine the relations between two context values to construct a relation graph that describes the relations among all context values. The context values with the equivalent relations are merged into one in the relation graph. An example of the relation graph is shown in Fig. 5(3).

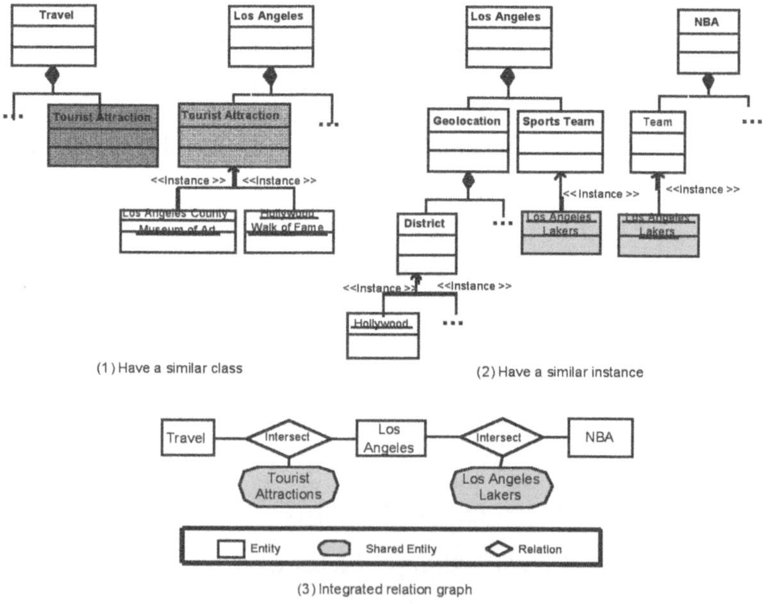

Fig. 5. Example of relations between two context values.

As a result, the intersection and complement relations among context values are captured in a relation graph.

Generate service searching criteria. Service searching criteria are a set of keywords which describe the potential services that an end-user is interested in a given context scenario. In our approach, service searching criteria are generated from the entities in the intersection of the ontologies of the context values. For the example shown in Fig. 5, an end-user travels to "*Los Angeles*", and likes NBA games. The ontologies of "*Los Angeles*" and "*NBA*" illustrate an intersection relation between "*Los Angeles*" and "*NBA*" (i.e., the common entity is "*Los Angeles Lakers*"). It is likely that the end-user would be interested in a game played by "*Los Angeles Lakers*". To generate searching criteria, we analyze the intersection of ontologies to extract the name, the attributes and instances of the entities in the intersection. The entities in an intersection relations are expressed as AND relations in the searching criteria. The complement relations among context values reflect the conflicting context values. We use the complement relations to determine the alternative expressions (i.e., OR) in the generated searching criteria. For example, an end-user prefers "*Budget Hotel*" as specified in the end-user profile. However, the end-user always takes "*Luxury Hotel*" by analyzing historical usage data. Both "*Budget Hotel*" and "*Luxury Hotel*" have an intersection relation with the context value "*Travel*". Generally, the "*Budget Hotel*" and "*Luxury Hotel*" cannot be reserved in the same time due to the complement relation between "*Budget Hotel*" and "*Luxury Hotel*". In the searching criteria, "*Budget Hotel*" and "*Luxury Hotel*" are expressed as an alternative relation.

If services can be discovered using the generated searching criteria, a new task is updated in the task list to be recommended to the end-user. The returned services are treated as the associated services to the new task in the task list. If the recommended task exists in an ad-hoc process, we update the associated services with the task. The approach for context aware service recommendation is discussed in details in [14].

3.3 Mining Task Usage Patterns

We employ the Apriori algorithm [15] to identify task usage patterns from historical usage data in two steps: (1) detect the most frequently used sets of tasks (i.e., task sets); and (2) recognize task usage patterns from the frequent task sets.

Detect frequent task sets. We analyze the execution of tasks recorded in the execution instance and enumerate possible combinations of tasks of varying sizes to form candidate task sets. We start with generating initial candidate task sets of size 1, then size 2 and so on. A task that appears in at least one execution instance becomes a candidate task set of size 1. Given the candidate task sets of size n, we generate larger candidate task sets of size n+1 in the following steps:

1) Group the candidate task sets of size n, such that all task sets in each group have n-1 tasks in common and each task set in the group has one different task. Suppose we have 5 candidate task sets of size 2 (i.e., n=2), namely, {A, B}, {A, C}, {A, D}, {B, C} and {B, D}. We divide them into 2 groups: groupA [{A, B}, {A, C}, {A, D}] and groupB [{B, C}, {B, D}]. All task sets of size 2 in each group have 1 (i.e., n-1) task in common.

2) Expand the candidate task sets in each group obtained in step 1) from size n to size n+1. As mentioned earlier, the task sets of size n in a group contain n-1 common tasks and 1 different task. We maintain the n-1 common tasks in each task set. To expand the task sets to size n+1, we generate the pair-wise combinations among the different tasks and merge a combination with the common tasks to form a task set. For example, groupA contains three task sets: {A, B}, {A, C} and {A, D}. The task sets have one common task A. Each task set in groupA contains a different task (i.e., B, C and D). The pair-wise combinations among the different tasks are {B, C}, {B, D} and {C, D}. The task sets of size 3 are generated by merging {A} with each combination. The resulting task sets of size 3 is {A, B, C}, {A, B, D} and {A, C, D}.

3) Calculate the frequency of a newly generated candidate task set appearing in all execution instances. Specifically, a support is defined as the number of execution instances that contain the candidate task set. For example, if a task set, {A, B, C} occurs in 16 execution instances, its support is 16. We filter out infrequent candidate task sets using a support threshold.

4) Repeatedly generate larger candidate task sets until no larger candidate task sets can be achieved. We rank all candidate task sets by their supports and select the ones with the highest support as a frequent task set.

Generate task usage patterns. We recognize task usage patterns as rules which can be represented as a context and an effect. The context and effect specify different sets of tasks correspondingly. When a context is satisfied, the effect will also take place. For example, if the task set {"car rental", "check map"} is executed, it is likely that the task set {"check weather"} will be executed. A task usage pattern describes the associations between a context and an effect. We represent task usage patterns in the format of "context→effect" (e.g., context task set {$task_2$, $task_3$... $task_N$}→ effect task set {$task_1$}). In the previous example, we represent the pattern as "{car rental, check map} →{check weather}". We recommend new tasks by matching the existing task list with the context task set of a pattern. If an existing task list matches the context task set of a pattern, we recommend the tasks in the effect task set of the pattern to extend the task list.

The strength of the task usage pattern is measured by the following equation.

$$strength = \frac{support\ of\ (context\ taskset \cup effect\ taskset)}{support\ of\ context\ taskset}$$

Essentially, the equation evaluates the frequency that the context task set and the effect task set are executed together. The strength is in the range of 0 to 1. The higher the strength is, the more frequently the task usage pattern is exhibited in that context. For example, strength of 50% indicates that when the context task set is executed, there is 50% probability that the effect task set will be executed. Using a threshold value, we can ensure that only the strongly supported patterns are used to recommend tasks to end-users.

4 Implementation

To evaluate the feasibility of our proposed approach, we built a prototype to help end-users generate ad-hoc processes. The prototype is developed in Java. We use IBM Mashup Center [10] as the service Mashup platform. IBM WebSphere Service Registry and Repository (WSRR) [16] are adopted by our prototype to register and manage services. In our current implementation of the prototype, the ontologies are manually searched using Swoogle [17] and Freebase [18], and imported into our ontology database. We implemented a generic ontology description model as the internal ontology representation. The generic ontology description model captures the information needed by our framework regardless the ontology languages. An ontology parser is implemented using OWL API [19] to read the ontologies described by OWL and RDF then convert the ontologies into the generic ontology description model. The current version of our prototype has four features: context detection, task list generation, new task recommendation and task execution order detection.

***Context detection*:** To demonstrate the functionality of our context-aware service recommendation, we design and develop a Firefox extension to capture the contextual data when an end-user uses the browser. The annotated screenshot is shown in Fig. 6. The Firefox extension can detect the contextual data from the Windows operating system; track the visited websites, bookmarks and Google online Calendar. Our context-aware recommendation approach can dynamically process different context types and values. Therefore, we can easily add new context sensors to detect contextual data from the applications and devices other than the browser.

***Task list generation*:** To automatically generate a task list, we use the goal description (i.e., keywords) to find the matching ontology and decompose the goal into a set of tasks as described in section 3.1. Fig. 7 is an annotated screenshot for

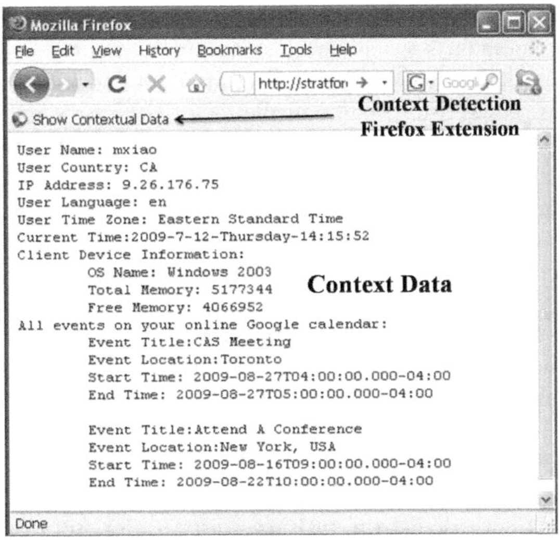

Fig. 6. Annotated Screenshot for Context Detection.

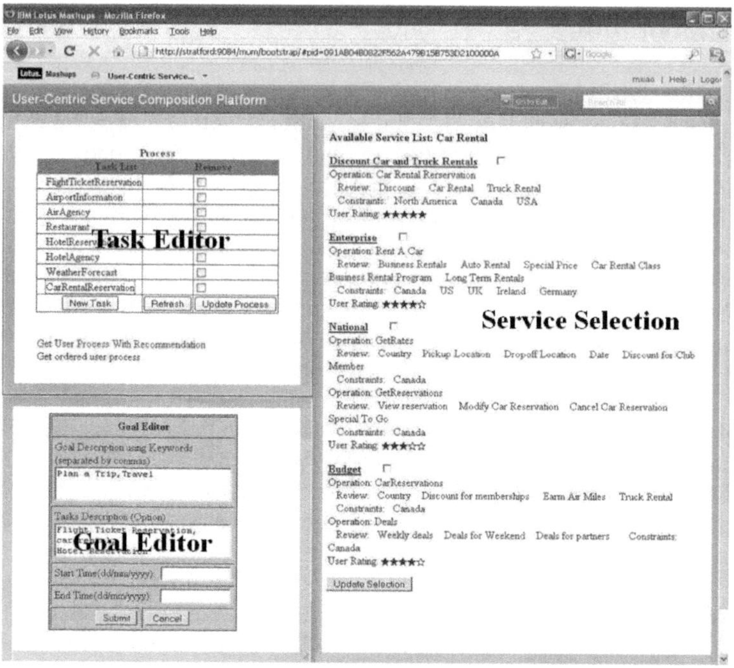

Fig. 7. Annotated Screenshot for Service Composer Panel.

composition UI. An end-user can specify her goal (e.g., plan a trip to New York) in the *Goal Editor*. A task list relevant to the goal is automatically generated and presented in the *Task Editor*. A task in the task list can be associated with one or more services. As shown in Fig. 7, once an end-user selects the "*Car Rental*" task in the *Task Editor*, the associated services are automatically displayed in the *Composition UI* on the right side of the markup page. We allow an end-user to select and invoke the desired services. An end-user can edit the task list in the *Task Editor.* For example, an end-user can remove a task if it is not needed by selecting the "*Remove*" check box. An end-user can also add a new task by specifying keywords for searching for services. We record the modifications as the end-user's preferences. When an end-user specifies the same goal, our prototype provides the previously refined task list.

New service recommendation: Due to the diversified requirements of different end-users, the tasks generated from ontologies may not contain all the desired services. We need to recommend new tasks to refine the task list. In our prototype, we use two different ways to recommend new services: (1) we mine the historical usage data to identify task usage patterns to recommend new tasks and the associated services as described in Section 3.3; (2) we analyze an end-user's context to recommend services with the response to an end-user's context.

Task execution order detection: To guide end-users to navigate through the task list to fulfill the goal, we detect the task execution order from historical usage data and generate the control flow among tasks. Fig. 8 is a screenshot of the suggested execution order of tasks in the ad-hoc process.

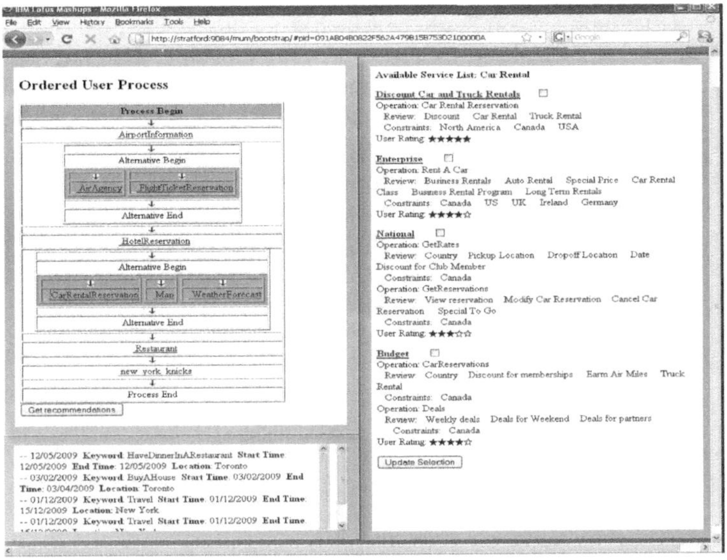

Fig. 8. Suggested execution order among tasks by analyzing historical usage data.

5 Related Work

Automatic service composition. In current research, two major approaches provide automatic service composition: model driven service composition and goal driven service composition. In the model driven approach, the design document, such as UML (Unified Modeling Language) diagrams, workflows, and abstract business process, are transformed to executable business processes. For example, Pistore et al. [20][21] propose an approach to automatically generate an executable BPEL process from abstract BPEL process. In the goal driven approach, a goal for the service composition is expressed using either formal or informal languages. Process models are created on the fly to realize the goal. Most approaches in this category treat service composition as an Artificial Intelligence (AI) planning problem [22][23]. The goal of AI planning is to find a set of actions which can transit from the initial state to the target state. The initial state of AI planning is the current state of the world; the target state is an end-user's goal; and the actions are available services. The approach proposed by Wu et al. [24] is an example of the goal driven approach. Wu et al. use an AI planning called SHOP2 to automatically compose DAML-S Web services. SHOP2 decomposes the goal into smaller and smaller sub-goals, until a Web service is found to fulfill the sub-goal. However, most of existing approaches require formal semantic description of abstract business processes or services, such as the pre and post conditions for each service. Therefore these approaches have limited support for dynamic services composition. Especially, WSDL services do not have formal semantic descriptions. Our approach reflects the changing context of an end-user without the predefined processes or tasks. In the goal driven approach, the goal could be described based on the input and output of services. For example, Hu et al. [25] describe the goal as the desired input and output of the composite service. The process of service composition is to find a set of services which can convert the input into the desired output. To handle large-scale distributed service composition, Hu et al. use the publish/subscribe model to describe the input and output of services. In the publish/subscribe model, publishers produce data in the form of advertisements, and subscribers register their interests by issuing subscriptions. Hu et al. map service inputs to subscriptions, and service outputs to advertisements. Using the existing distributed publish/subscribe network, they can compose services in a distributed environment. Yan et al. [26] and Li et al. [27] extend the publish/subscribe model in service composition to support dynamic service discovery (e.g., discovery of Web services whose attributes can change) and execute the business processes in distributed environments. However, simply matching the interfaces of Web services cannot guarantee the correctness of functionality for the composite process. A Web services with the same input and output may have totally different functionality. Our approach aims to compose services based on the functionality of services. We enable end-users to select services while there is more than one service having the same functionality. Similar to our approach, ontologies are used in service discovery and service composition [28][29]. In [28], the services are classified using ontology to guide end-users to search for services. The approach in [29] uses ontology to semi-automatically compose services by matching the interface of individual services. Different from the aforementioned approaches, our approach identifies the required tasks from ontologies.

Supporting End-users in Service Composition. Mashups supports a manually but user friendly way to compose services without following the formal definition of business processes. Carlson et al. [30] provide an approach to progressively compose services based on the interface matching. Given a service, Carlson et al. use the output description of the service to match the inputs of existing services in the repository. This approach can recommend the next potential services through matching the input and output descriptions. By recommending the next potential services, an end-user can compose an executable business process. Liu et al. [31][32][33] propose a Mashup architecture which extends the SOA model with Mashups to facilitate service composition. Similar to the work of Carlson et al. [30], Liu et al. match the input with output to help end-users compose services. They also use tags and Quality of Service (QoS) to select services. Our work enhances service Mashups by providing guidance to end-users as they create their Mashups through the automatic composition of services. The aforementioned approaches gradually compose services using the matches between the input and output of service interfaces. End-users cannot preview the composition results. Our approach allows end-users to specify goals and generate the overview of the processes before services are executed.

In addition to Service Mashups, there are some other approaches which provide support for end-users to compose services. The project UbiCompForAll (Ubiquitous service composition for all users) [34][35] provides support for non-IT professionals to compose services. UbiCompForAll did an initial experiment on evaluating a service composition tool for creating mobile tourist services by end-users. UbiCompForAll uses different case scenarios relevant to the city guide to develop and validate the user interfaces of the service composition tool. However, no concrete results on providing support for end-users have been revealed by UbiCompForAll. Obrenovic et al. [36] provide a spreadsheet-based tool to help end-user compose services. A spreadsheet (e.g., Microsoft Excel) is a software application that uses rectangular tables to display information. In a spreadsheet, the content is put in cells of the table, and the relations among cells are defined by formulas. Obrenovic et al. extend the spreadsheet to enable it to exchange messages with services and support different composition patterns. However, it is challenging for those end-users who are not familiar with the spreadsheet to understand and manipulate the data in spreadsheet, especially to use formulas to control data. Our approach is built up on Mashup pages. Mashups are very similar to regular Web pages and provide a relatively easy way for non-expert end-users to manually compose services.

Context-aware service discovery and composition. Context-aware techniques have been generally used to discover and recommend services. Yang et al. [37][38] design an event-driven rule based system to recommend services according to people's context changes. Balke and Wagner [39] propose an algorithm to select Web services based on user preferences. The algorithm starts with a general query. If there are too many results, it expands the service query with constraints using user preferences. By adding constraints step by step, the algorithm narrows the number of returned services to a small value. To select and recommend services, those approaches need to predefine the reaction to a specific context using rules. In our work, we automatically extend the semantics of the context value using ontologies, and use the semantics to recommend services.

Mining historical usage data. Liang et al. [40] mine service association rules from service transactional data. Agrawal et al. [41] propose a technique for mining workflows from execution logs. Cook and Wolf [42] develop an approach to recover business processes from event logs. Schimm [43] recovers hierarchically structured business processes. The aforementioned approaches focus on recovering a pre-defined workflow or business process. In our work, we discover the execution order of a list of task when there is no pre-defined workflow.

6 Conclusions and Future Work

In this paper, we present a framework that dynamically generates an ad-hoc process and personalizes the process to fit it with the context of end-users. Our approach hides the complexity of SOA standards from end-users and helps an end-user fulfill their daily activities. By discovering the semantic relations among context values using ontologies, our approach can identify an end-user's needs hidden in the context values and recommend the desired services. To refine the generated ad-hoc process, we identify task usage patterns by mining the historical usage data to recommend new tasks. We also recover the execution orders among the tasks in the ad-hoc process by analyzing historical task execution data. A prototype is developed as a proof of concept to demonstrate that our approach enables end-users to discover and compose services easily.

In our current approach, end-users need to manually provide the input data to invoke services. In the future, we plan to develop an approach to automatically generate service input data by analyzing user's context, historical execution data and the output of other services. In addition, we found that the quality of generated ad-hoc processes highly depends on the quality of the ontology relevant to the goal. However, there is no existing approach to help us select the appropriate ontologies for ad-hoc process generation. In the future, we plan to improve our approach to search for relevant ontologies. To address issue of low quality ontologies, we plan to investigate the possibility of using information from other resources (e.g., online Web pages) to refine the generated ad-hoc process.

Acknowledgements

This work is financially supported by the IBM Toronto Centre for Advanced Studies and NSERC.

References

1. Expedia, `http://www.expedia.com/` (last accessed on March 10, 2010)
2. Chinnici, R., Mreau, J.J., Ryman, A., Weerawarana, S.: Web Services Description Language (WSDL) Version 2.0. W3C Recommendation, June 26 (2007), `http://www.w3.org/TR/wsdl20/` (last accessed on March 10, 2010)
3. Web Services Business Process Execution Language Version 2.0, `http://docs.oasis-open.org/wsbpel/2.0/OS/wsbpel-v2.0-OS.html` (last accessed on March 10, 2010)
4. IBM WebSphere Integration Developer (WID), `http://www-01.ibm.com/software/integration/wid` (last access on March 15, 2010)
5. Smith, M.K., Welty, C., McGuinness, D.L.: OWL Web Ontology Language Guide. W3C Recommendation (2004), `http://www.w3.org/TR/owl-guide/` (last accessed on March 10, 2010)
6. Beckett, D., McBride, B.: RDF/XML Syntax Specification (Revised). W3C Recommendation (2004), `http://www.w3.org/TR/rdf-syntax-grammar/` (last accessed on March 10, 2010)
7. Baldauf, M., Dustdar, S., Rosenberg, F.: A Survey on Context-aware Systems. International Journal of Ad Hoc and Ubiquitous Computing 2(4), 263–277 (2007)
8. Montgomery, J.: Microsoft Popfly: Building Games without a CS Degree, `http://expression.microsoft.com/en-us/cc963994.aspx` (last accessed on April 3, 2010)
9. Yahoo! Pipes, `http://pipes.yahoo.com/pipes/` (last accessed on March 10, 2010)
10. IBM Mashup Center, `http://www-01.ibm.com/software/info/Mashup-center/` (last accessed on March 10, 2010)
11. Xiao, H., Zou, Y., Tang, R., Ng, J., Nigul, L.: An Automatic Approach for Ontology-Driven Service Composition. In: IEEE Intl. Conference on Service-Oriented Computing and Applications 2009, Taipei, Taiwan, pp. 17–24 (December 2009)
12. Strang, T., Linnhoff-Popien, C.: A context modeling survey. In: The First International Workshop on Advanced Context Modelling, Reasoning and Management, Nottingham, England (September 2004)
13. Bhogal, J., Macfarlane, A., Smith, P.: A Review of Ontology based Query Expansion. Informaltion Processing and Management 43(4), 866–886 (2007)

14. Xiao, H., Zou, Y., Ng, J., Nigul, L.: An Approach for Context-aware Service Discovery and Recommendation. In: Proc. The 8th International Conference on Web Services (ICWS 2010), Miami, Florida, USA, July 5-10 (2010)
15. Agrawal, R., Imielinski, T., Swami, A.N.: Mining Association Rules between Sets of Services in Large Databases. In: 1993 ACM SIGMOD International Conference on Management of Data, Washington, D.C., United States, May 26-28, pp. 207–216 (1993)
16. IBM WebSphere Service Registry and Repository, `http://www-01.ibm.com/software/integration/wsrr/` (last accessed on March 10, 2010)
17. Swoogle, `http://swoogle.umbc.edu/` (last accessed on March 10, 2010)
18. Freebase, `http://www.freebase.com/` (last accessed on March 10, 2010)
19. OWL API, `http://owlapi.sourceforge.net/` (last accessed on March 24, 2010)
20. Pistore, M., Marconi, A., Bertoli, P., Traverso, P.: Automated Composition of Web Services by Planning at the Knowledge Level. In: International Joint Conference on Artificial Intelligence (IJCAI), Pasadena, California, USA, pp. 1252–1259 (2005)
21. Pistore, M., Traverso, P., Bertoli, P., Marconi, A.: Automated Synthesis of Composite BPEL4WS Web Services. In: International Conference on Web Services (ICWS) 2005, Orlando, Florida, USA, July 11-15, pp. 293–301 (2005)
22. Küster, U., Stern, M., König-Ries, B.: A Classification of Issues and Approaches in Service Composition. In: International Workshop on Engineering Service Compositions (2005)
23. Rao, J., Su, X.: A Survey of Automated Web Service Composition Methods. In: First International Workshop on Semantic Web Services and Web Process Composition, San Diego, CA, USA, pp. 43–54 (July 2004)
24. Wu, D., Parsia, B., Sirin, E., Hendler, J., Nau, D.: Automating DAML-S Web Services Composition Using SHOP2. In: Fensel, D., Sycara, K., Mylopoulos, J. (eds.) ISWC 2003. LNCS, vol. 2870, pp. 195–210. Springer, Heidelberg (2003)
25. Hu, S., Muthusamy, V., Li, G., Jacobsen, H.: Distributed Automatic Service Composition in Large-Scale Systems. In: Distributed Event-Based Systems Conference (DEBS), Rome, Italy, July 1-4, pp. 233–244 (2008)
26. Yan, W., Hu, S., Muthusamy, V., Jacobsen, H., Zha, L.: Efficient Event-based Resource Discovery. In: ACM Distributed Event-based Systems Conference (DEBS) 2009, Nashville, TN, USA, July 6-9 (2009)
27. Li, G., Muthusamy, V., Jacobsen, H.: A Distributed Service Oriented Architecture for Business Process Execution. ACM Transaction on the Web 4(1) (January 2010); Article 2 (33 pages)
28. Arabshian, K., Dickmann, C., Schulzrinne, H.: Ontology-Based Service Discovery Front-End Interface for GloServ. In: Aroyo, L., Traverso, P., Ciravegna, F., Cimiano, P., Heath, T., Hyvönen, E., Mizoguchi, R., Oren, E., Sabou, M., Simperl, E. (eds.) ESWC 2009. LNCS, vol. 5554, pp. 684–696. Springer, Heidelberg (2009)
29. Arpinar, I.B., Aleman-Meza, B., Zhang, R., Maduko, A.: Ontology-Driven Web Services Composition Platform. In: IEEE International Conference on E-Commerce Technology, San Diego, California, July 6-9, pp. 146–152 (2004)
30. Carlson, M.P., Ngu, A.H.H., Podorozhny, R.M., Zeng, L.: Automatic Mash Up of Composite Applications. In: Bouguettaya, A., Krueger, I., Margaria, T. (eds.) ICSOC 2008. LNCS, vol. 5364, pp. 317–330R. Springer, Heidelberg (2008); Agrawal, R., Gunopulos, D., Leymann, F.: Mining Process Models from Workflow Logs. In: Sixth International Conference on Extending Database Technology, pp. 469–483 (1998)

31. Liu, X., Huang, G., Mei, H.: Towards End User Service Composition. In: 31st Annual International Computer Software and Applications Conference, Beijing, China, pp. 667–678 (2007)
32. Liu, X., Huang, G., Mei, H.: A User-Oriented Approach to Automated Service Composition. In: 2008 IEEE International Conference on Web Services (ICWS), Short paper, Beijing, China, September 23-26, pp. 773–776 (2008)
33. Liu, X., Hui, Y., Sun, W., Liang, H.: Towards Service Composition Based on Mashup. IEEE Congress on Services (2007)
34. Floch, J., Stav, E., Blakstad, E.: Compose Your Own City Guide. VERDIKT Conference, Oslo, Norway, Novermber 3-4 (2009), `http://www.sintef.no/project/UbiCompForAll/UbiCompForAll%20City%20Guide%20-%20verdikt_conf_abstract.pdf` (last accessed on June 17, 2010)
35. UbiCompForAll - Ubiquitous service composition for all users, `http://www.sintef.no/Projectweb/UbiCompForAll/Home/` (last accessed on June 17, 2010)
36. Obrenovic, Z., Gasevic, D.: End-User Service Composition: Spreadsheets as a Service Composition Tool. IEEE Transactions on Service Computing 1(4) (October-December 2008)
37. Chen, I.Y.L., Yang, S.J.H., Jiang, J.: Ubiquitous provision of context aware Web services. In: IEEE International Conference on Services Computing (SCC) 2006, Chicago, USA, September 18-22, pp. 60–68 (2006)
38. Yang, S.J.H., Zhang, J., Chen, I.Y.L.: A JESS-enabled context elicitation system for providing context-aware Web services. Export Systems with Applications 34(4), 2254–2266 (2008)
39. Balke, W.T., Wagner, M.: Towards Personalized Selection of Web Services. In: Proceedings of the International World Wide Web Conference (WWW 2003), Budapest, Hungary, pp. 725–733 (2003)
40. Liang, Q., Chung, J., Miller, S., Ouyang, Y.: Service Pattern Discovery of Web Service Mining in Web Service Registry-Repository. In: IEEE International Conference on E-Business Engineering, Shanghai, China, October 24-26, pp. 286–293 (2006)
41. Agrawal, R., Gunopulos, D., Leymann, F.: Mining Process Models from Workflow Logs. In: Sixth International Conference on Extending Database Technology, pp. 469–483 (1998)
42. Cook, J.E., Wolf, A.L.: Event-based detection of concurrency. In: Sixth International Symposium on the Foundations of Software Engineering, Lake Buena Vista, Florida, USA, November 3-5, pp. 35–45 (1998)
43. Schimm, G.: Generic linear business process modeling. In: Mayr, H.C., Liddle, S.W., Thalheim, B. (eds.) ER Workshops 2000. LNCS, vol. 1921, pp. 31–39. Springer, Heidelberg (2000)

A Survey of Mashup Development Environments

Lars Grammel and Margaret-Anne Storey

Department of Computer Science, University of Victoria
lars.grammel@gmail.com, mstorey@uvic.ca

Abstract. This chapter presents a survey of six mashup development environments and looks at how mashups fit into the vision of the smart internet. The fast-paced expansion of mashup development environments has resulted in a wealth of features and approaches. To provide an overview of End User Development support in current mashup development environments, we explore, summarize and compare their features across six different themes (Levels of Abstraction, Learning Support, Community Support, Discoverability, User Interface Design and Software Engineering Techniques). We found that the mashup development environments provide many features to support end users, but there is still much room for further improvement, especially in relation to the smart internet. We believe that by connecting matters of concern to mashups, mashup development environments can become an essential part of the smart internet. Such a connection would enable mining of mashup elements, which could facilitate automatic mashup creation and customization.

Keywords: Smart Internet, smart interactions, mashup, mashup development environment, Microsoft Popfly, Yahoo! Pipes, IBM Mashup Center, Serena Business Mashups, Google Mashup Editor, Intel MashMaker, survey, end user development, end user programming, web 2.0.

1 Introduction

The vision of the smart internet calls for user- and context-centric information aggregation and presentation [1]. Mashup development environments allow the users to specify the aggregation and presentation themselves. This could be an important part of the smart internet, because it puts the users in control to tailor information processing and display towards their own needs.

Mashups are applications that reuse and combine data and services available on the web. They are developed in a rapid, ad-hoc manner to automate processes and remix information. This enables the users to explore information in new ways and can save valuable time that may have been lost in laborious routine tasks.

Mashup development is a promising End User Development (EUD) application area for several reasons. As the underlying platform, the web provides access to a growing number of publicly available services. By using such services, the development effort shifts from traditional programming towards finding high-level services [2], gluing these services together [2] and creating User Interfaces (UIs). These activities involve

M. Chignell et al. (Eds.): The Smart Internet, LNCS 6400, pp. 137–151, 2010.

less technical details than programming, are potentially closer to the problem domain, and can be better supported by tools because they are more constrained. The shift towards a development model based on composition is in line with the shift towards rapid, opportunistic development of situated applications with short lifespan aimed at small audiences [2]. This style of development provides immediate rewards for the users and avoids difficult technological challenges such as scalability. Furthermore, the web as a platform facilitates sharing mashups and community building.

Since 2006, several commercial mashup development environments such as Microsoft Popfly, Yahoo! Pipes and IBM Mashup Center have been created. These environments target end users, web developers and business users. Simultaneously, research on mashups and mashup development environments began. Since then, both mashup research and mashup tool development have progressed rapidly, and many features have been explored. Our goal in this paper is to compare how these features support end users in developing mashups.

The rest of this chapter is structured as follows. First, an overview of the background and related work is given. Second, the methodology of this tool survey is explained and the reviewed mashup development environments are described. Third, the results of our tool survey are presented. Fourth, implications and connections to other EUD research are discussed. Fifth, we look at how mashup development environments fit into the smart internet and where they fall short. Sixth, we describe the limitations of this work and what we have done to alleviate them. Finally, we conclude the paper with a summary of our contributions and possibilities for future work.

2 Background and Related Work

The web and the way it is used evolve constantly. This makes it difficult to define mashups. The original definition of mashups refers to web-based applications that mix two or more different web-based data sources [3, 4] and reflects the ideas of remixing services and using the web as the underlying platform. The scope of this definition has been broadened by several authors [2, 5] to different devices and environments. Rapid development, situated applications and end user focus can be considered central concepts to mashups as well [6].

For this review, we define a mashup as an *end user driven recombination of web-based data and functionality*. This definition is close to the original definition while emphasizing our end user development perspective. It is less restrictive than the original definition because it does not require that the mashups are web applications. Therefore, mashup development environments are *tools that support users in the development of mashups*. The related research comes from three areas: research on mashups, research on web page customizations and research on EUD in general.

Research on mashups has focused mostly on tools and methods to support mashup development. Marmite [7] combines a visual data-flow language with incremental execution and previews of intermediate results. Karma [8] is a programming-by-example system that integrates data retrieval, modeling, cleaning, and integration. D.mix [3] supports automatic website-to-webservice mapping and combines selecting service samples from websites with remixing them in a wiki. C3W [9] combines programming-by-example for extracting actions from web pages with the spreadsheet paradigm. Through other research on mashups, researchers have explored patterns in mashups [5], the background and experiences of mashup developers [4], and the process of mashup design [2].

Research on web page customization focuses on modifying and personalizing existing web pages instead of creating new ones. Chickenfoot is such a tool for customizing web pages using scripts that run in the browser [10]. It extends the browsers' basic scripting language with special commands for web site customization, especially selecting elements from a web page based on their visual appearance.

There is a large body of literature on general EUD research. Several introductions, overviews and books are available (e.g. [11, 12, 13, 14, 15]). The concept of a gentle slope of complexity [16] and the model of different barriers in programming systems [17] are especially relevant for this review of mashup development environments. Creating systems with a gentle slope of complexity is the concept of allowing the user to learn new functionality step-by-step, without requiring major learning efforts lacking immediate results [16]. Ko et al. identified six types of learning barriers (design, selection, coordination, use, understanding, and information barriers) by studying how non-programmers learned VisualBasic using Visual Studio [17].

3 Methodology

The objective of the research underlying this chapter is to discover, organize and summarize the features and approaches of current mashup development environments from an EUD perspective. Our research methodology is a qualitative, exploratory tool analysis.

Six mashup development environments developed by major companies such as Microsoft, IBM and Google were reviewed (see Table 1). We grouped them by the kind of mashup they can generate. **Information mashups** retrieve data from one or several data sources, process those data, and publish the results either as feeds or in widgets. **Process mashups** automate processes by orchestrating services, forms and other resources in a workflow, and often include data entry. **Website mashups** change websites by removing elements, adding additional widgets, and changing their appearances.

Each reviewed mashup development environment was used and evaluated for three to six hours in the summer of 2008. During the evaluation, mashups were created, the different parts of the system were explored and used, and related documentation and tutorials were read. Features relevant to the themes were added to a feature matrix (see Table 2) as they were discovered during this evaluation.

We have chosen to review the mashup development environments based on six themes. These themes emerged from research on EUD (*EUD*) [11, 17, 12, 16, 13, 14, 15], research on mashups (*MASH*) [2, 6, 5, 4] and research on mashup development environments (*MM*) [18, 10, 19, 9, 3, 8, 7], as well as from our previous experience with mashup development environments (*EXP*), as indicated below by the abbreviations for each theme. The themes are used to guide the tool evaluations. Each theme has one or more guiding questions.

- **Levels of Abstraction** (*EUD, MASH, EXP*). What levels of abstraction are supported? What notations are used on the different levels of abstraction? How are they integrated?
- **Learning Support** (*EUD, MASH, MM*). What documentation is available? What support besides the documentation is provided? How is the concept of a gentle slope of complexity supported? What barriers exist when working with the mashup development environment?
- **Community Features** (*EUD, EXP*). How do mashup development environments support collaboration between users?
- **Discoverability** (*MASH, MM*). What features help users find relevant mashups and mashup elements?
- **UI Construction** (*EXP*). How are users supported in creating the user interfaces of mashups?
- **Software Engineering Techniques** (*EUD*). What debugging support is provided by the mashup development environments? What testing features do they offer? Is version control available?

4 Reviewed Mashup Development Environments

We reviewed 6 commercial mashup development environments (Microsoft Popfly, Yahoo! Pipes, IBM Mashup Center, Google Mashup Editor, Serena Mashup Composer, and Intel MashMaker, see Table 1). We restricted ourselves to commercial environments, because these usually offer a wider variety of features than research prototypes. The chosen environments were the major commercial mashup environments as of August 2008. According to our categorization into information, process and website mashups, four of the environments supported creating information mashups, one supported process mashups, and one supported website mashups.

Microsoft Popfly[1] (Fig. 1) was a mashup development environment that combined development perspectives that exposed different levels of complexity. Its main perspective was a view in which 3D blocks could be wired together, which was essentially

Table 1. Reviewed mashup development environments.

Mashup Development Environments for Information Mashups	
Microsoft Popfly (MP)	http://www.popfly.com *(discontinued)*
Yahoo! Pipes (YP)	http://pipes.yahoo.com
IBM Mashup Center (IMC)	http://www.ibm.com/software/info/mashup-center/
Google Mashup Editor (GME)	http://editor.googlemashups.com/editor *(discontinued)*
Mashup Development Environments for Process Mashups	
Serena Mashup Composer (SMC)	http://www.serena.com/Mashups/
Mashup Development Environments for Website Mashups	
Intel MashMaker (IMM)	http://mashmaker.intel.com/web/

[1] Microsoft Popfly was discontinued in August 2009.

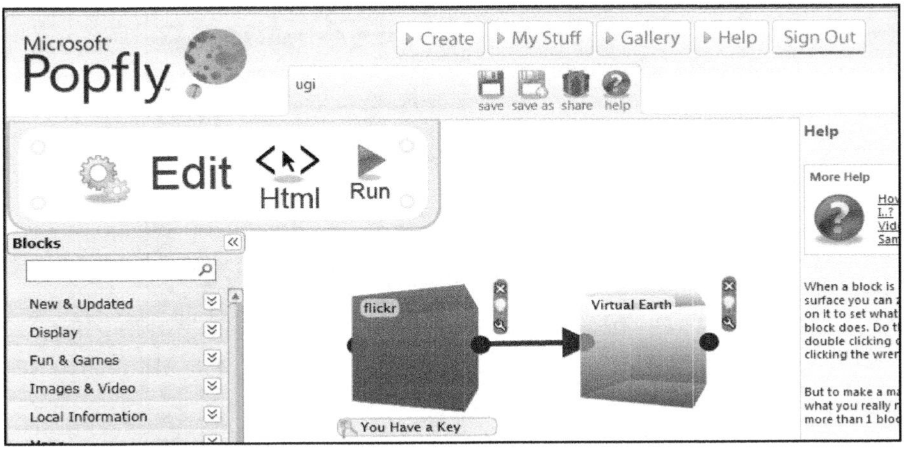

Fig. 1. Microsoft Popfly.

a visual dataflow language. Additional views allowed configuring and reusing mashups and blocks, as well as lower-level programming (including an IDE extension).

Google Mashup Editor[2] supported the creation of information mashups using a special web-based editor for a textual domain specific language that extended HTML and JavaScript. The language facilitated user interface creation and data processing.

At the time of our study, Yahoo! Pipes (Fig. 2) supported creating information mashups using a visual dataflow language. The pipes allowed users to aggregate and transform web services, pages and feeds. The results were displayed in feeds, in lists, on maps, or as photo viewers, depending on the output data.

IBM Mashup Center facilitated mashup creation using 2 sets of tools: Lotus Mashups and InfoSphere MashupHub. Lotus Mashups (Fig. 3) allowed users to layout and configure widgets and to wire the events between them. InfoSphere MashupHub contained a visual dataflow language that is similar to that of Yahoo! Pipes.

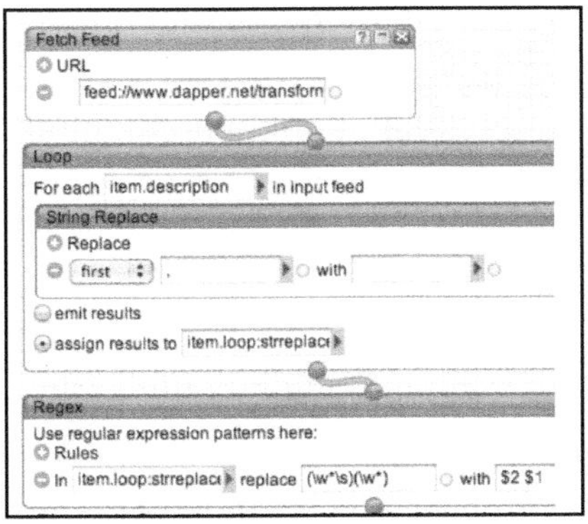

Fig. 2. Example Pipe from Yahoo! Pipes.

[2] Google Mashup Editor was discontinued in September 2009.

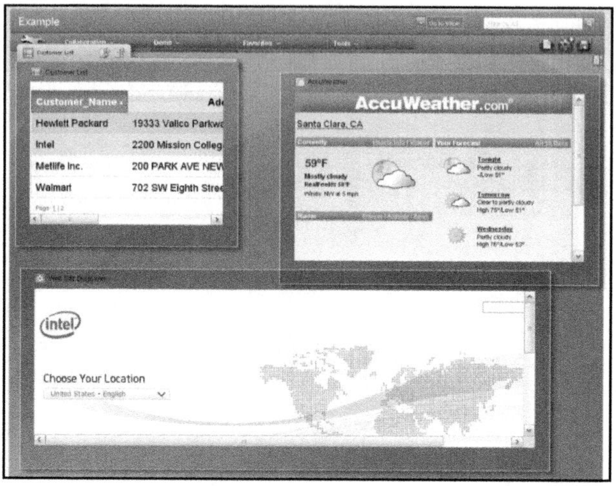

Fig. 3. IBM Mashup Center (Lotus Mashups).

Serena Business Mashups facilitated the creation of collaborative business applications, which could, for example, automate office workflows. It contained a visual workflow editor to define such workflows, and graphical UI builders similar to those offered by IDEs for developers. In addition, textual languages with domain specific extensions were provided to streamline the implementation of the workflow logic.

Intel MashMaker (Fig. 4) was a tool that supports creating website mashups. It enabled users to extract data from websites using a programming-by-example approach,

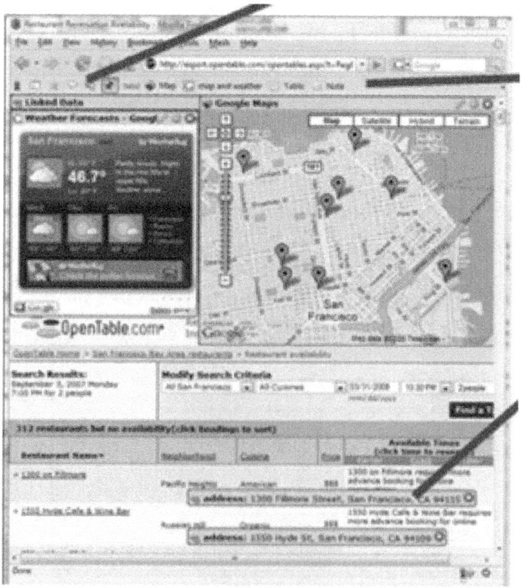

Fig. 4. Intel MashMaker (Image © Intel).

to clean the resulting data tables and trees, and to pull in additional widgets that augment the original website. For example, users were able to add a map that showed the locations referenced in the website.

5 Findings

The findings are presented according to the evaluation themes. The focus of this paper lies on summarizing the approaches in mashup development environments and not on recommending the best mashup development environments.

In this section, features are emphasized in **bold**. After each feature, the abbreviations of the mashup development environments (see Table 1) that support this feature are listed in brackets.

5.1 Levels of Abstraction

Three different levels of abstraction are used to distinguish how much programming and computer knowledge is required. There is a relationship between the required knowledge and the range of solutions that can be developed [16]. Since raising the level of abstraction requires encapsulating concepts, the number of choices available on higher levels of abstraction is usually restricted.

On a high level of abstraction, no programming knowledge is required, but the flexibility is usually restricted to reusing and configuring mashups that are developed by others. Working with a high level of abstraction is supported by the reviewed mashup development environments in several ways: **reuse of complete mashups** created by others (MP, YP, IMC, GME, SMC, IMM), high-level **mashup and widget parameterization** (MP, IMC), **automatic reuse of data extractors** (IMM) for websites, and **programming-by-example** (IMC, IMM) concepts such as extracting data by example and dragging & dropping feeds on widgets.

On an intermediate level of abstraction, knowledge about concepts such as dataflow, data types or UI widgets is required, but the technological details of these concepts are encapsulated in notations. Therefore, what can be changed or created is limited by these notations. The reviewed mashup development environments support mashup development on an intermediate level of abstraction by using mainly visual Domain Specific Languages (DSLs). **Visual dataflow languages** (MP, YP, IMC) support the users in the creation of information mashups. **Visual workflow/process orchestration languages** (SMC) support the creation of process mashups. The visual languages are used in combination with property dialogs for the parameterization of mashup elements. Data sources are primarily accessed through mashup elements in those notations. **Dialog-based wiring of widgets** (IMC) provides an alternative to visual data-flow languages that saves screen space, but depends on visual widgets. On an intermediate level of abstraction, there is typically a distinction between design and runtime mode, although the mashup development environments try to reduce this distinction, e.g. by using previews.

On a low level of abstraction, programming knowledge is required, but the greatest flexibility is achieved. **Textual DSL editors** (MP, GME, SMC) for languages such as HTML, JavaScript and custom scripting languages are used to represent mashups or elements of mashups. **Textual DSLs in dialog fields** (MP, YP, IMC, SMC, IMM) such as regular expressions enable the flexible configuration of mashup element properties. Providing **extension APIs** (MP, IMC, SMC, IMM) allows developers to use integrated development environments such as Microsoft Visual Studio for programming reusable mashup elements.

Due to the tradeoff between the level of abstraction and flexibility in designing mashups, the **integration of different abstraction levels** (MP, IMC, SMC, IMM) provides several benefits. Having several abstraction levels allows the user to choose the right level of abstraction for his goal and his skill. It also positively affects the ease of learning the functionality of a system by offering a gentle slope of complexity, and it enables reuse of elements from lower levels of abstraction in higher levels of abstraction.

5.2 Learning Support

Supporting the user in learning to master an EUD system, especially by providing a gentle slope of complexity [16], is a crucial aspect of EUD [15]. Besides the different levels of abstraction and their integration, several other mechanisms are provided by mashup development environments to aid users in their learning. Basic learning features such as **screen casts and tutorials, API documentation, and help systems** (MP, YP, IMC, GME, SMC, IMM) that explain the UI are provided by all reviewed mashup development environments. Also, community based learning support is provided in **discussion forums** (MP, YP, IMC, GME, SMC) and through **using shared artifacts as examples** (MP, YP, IMC, GME, SMC, IMM). Finally, **context-specific suggestions** (MP) offer the user hints on which mashup elements might be useful based on the current structure of the mashups.

5.3 Community Features

Supporting user communities is essential to the success of EUD tools [14]. Community members provide elements that can be reused by other members, create examples, organize artifacts, and answer questions in the forums.

Facilities for sharing mashups and mashup elements enable the reuse of those mashups and mashup elements within the community. The **shared mashups** (MP, YP, IMC, GME, SMC, IMM) can be run and copied to their workspaces for modification by other users. **Shared mashup elements** (MP, YP, IMC, SMC, IMM), e.g. building blocks in MP or feeds in IMC, can be used on the same or higher levels of abstraction. This allows less advanced users to use complicated artifacts created by more advanced users.

Collaborative categorization of user-generated mashups and mashup elements helps community members in searching for mashups and mashup elements. **Tagging** (MP, YP, IMC) is a categorization technique in which users, typically the authors, annotate items with tags to support finding. **Rating** (MP, YP, IMC, IMM) is used in different ways such as favorites, star-rating, clone-counting and user recommendations to help the user in judging the quality and usefulness of mashups and mashup elements.

Providing discussion features such as general **discussion forums** (MP, YP, IMC, GME, SMC) and **artifact-centered discussion** (MP, IMC), e.g. comments on a mashup element, enables the users to exchange ideas, help each other and build a sense of community. Artifact-centered discussions are also valuable feedback mechanisms for the authors, which assist users in judging the quality and usefulness of an artifact.

Social network systems (MP) such as Facebook have recently gained popularity. In mashup development environments, social networks help users to find mashups created by their peers, and likely increase the commitment of users to a mashup development environment by creating a stronger sense of community.

5.4 Discoverability

Searching and finding mashups and mashup elements enables users to employ artifacts created by others. **Text-based search** (MP, YP, IMC) on title, description and assigned tags is the most common mechanism for finding mashups and mashup elements. The results often include, and can be sorted by, the artifact rating. **Browsing mashups by structural properties** (YP), such as mashup elements used, helps users to find examples for their own mashups. In visual data-flow editors, a one-layer-deep **categorization of mashup elements** (MP, YP, IMC, SMC) supports users in finding the right elements. **Context-specific suggestions** (MP) can provide the needed elements to the user without requiring him to search. Using discussion features, other users can also point out relevant building blocks and example mashups when answering questions.

5.5 User Interface Construction

Since the mashup UIs determine their usability, it is important that end users can easily create the appropriate UIs for their mashups. The mashup development environments provide several different mechanisms for UI design. **Automatically generating the UI** (YP, SMC) based on the output data of the mashup, e.g. map viewers or image lists, is a convenient method for rapid UI generation, but lacks customizability. **Selecting and customizing** (MP) a single UI component provides greater flexibility, yet it requires more configuration effort. The most flexible approach is composition, which can be either **visual UI composition** (IMC, SMC, IMM) or **textual UI composition** (GME). It enables users to customize UIs to a great extent, but is more complicated than the other approaches.

5.6 Software Engineering Techniques

Given the concerns regarding security and correctness of applications developed by non-programmers [20], providing tool support for software engineering techniques for end-users is considered important in the EUD field [11]. **Debugging** (MP, YP, IMC) is only supported through consoles that print debugging output. **Version control** (IMC, SMC) is rather simple and does not contain advanced functions like branching. **Testing** and **change request management** are not supported by any reviewed mashup development environment.

5.7 Summary

Supporting end users in creating mashups requires a wide variety of software features. The reviewed mashup development environments support learning and collaboration with other users particularly well. However, while different levels of programming abstraction are usually provided, there is less support for discoverability and user interface construction. Of the 6 evaluated themes, support for software engineering techniques was neglected the most by the mashup development environments. Table 2 shows a summary of the features in the mashup development environments.

Table 2. Features of reviewed mashup development environments grouped by themes. Features that belong to several themes are shown in *italics*.

Feature	MP	YP	IMC	GME	SMC	IMM
Levels of Abstraction						
Reuse of Complete Mashups	√	√	√	√	√	√
Mashup and Widget Configuration	√		√			
Automatic Reuse of Data Extractors						√
Programming-By-Example			√			√
Visual Dataflow Languages	√	√	√			
Vis. Workflow / Process Orchestration Languages					√	
Dialog-based Wiring of Widgets			√			
Textual DSL Editors	√			√	√	
Textual DSLs in Dialog Fields	√	√	√		√	√
Extension APIs	√		√		√	√
Integration of Different Abstraction Levels	√		√		√	√
Learning Support						
Tutorials, Help, API Documentation	√	√	√	√	√	√
Discussion Forums	√	√	√	√	√	
Using Shared Artifacts as Examples	√	√	√	√	√	√
Context-Specific Suggestions	√					
Community Features						
Sharing Mashups	√	√	√	√	√	√
Sharing Mashup Elements	√	√	√		√	√
Tagging	√	√	√			
Rating	√	√	√			√
Discussion Forums	√	√	√	√	√	
Artifacts-Centered Discussion	√		√			
Social Networks	√					
Discoverability						
Text-Based Search	√	√	√			
Browsing Mashups by Structural Properties		√				
Simple Categorization of Mashup Elements	√	√	√		√	
Context-Specific Suggestions	√					
User Interface (UI) Construction						
Automatic UI Generation		√			√	
Selecting & Customizing UI	√					
Visual UI Composition			√		√	√
Textual UI Composition				√		
Software Engineering Techniques						
Debugging Output	√	√	√			
Version Control			√		√	
Testing						
Change Request Management						

6 Discussion

The reviewed mashup development environments have many features that improve the usability and learnability of mashup creation and customization. Their support for online communities, especially, is extensive; however, there are several potential areas for improvement and future research.

Although the mashup development environments provide many notations for different tasks and different complexity levels, as well as a variety of learning support features, high learning barriers still remain, especially between different levels of abstraction and different notations. These barriers can be reduced by including more specialized, intermediate notations [16], such as in MP and IMC.

Further research is required to compare different notations for the same tasks, e.g. visual dataflow languages vs. dialog-based wiring. Evaluation frameworks such as the Cognitive Dimensions of Notations [21] can be used to analyze the strengths and weaknesses of such notations, and formal user studies can compare how users perform on the same tasks using different notations.

Ko et al. described a model of six types of barriers in end user programming systems [17]. When evaluating mashup development environments, this model can be used to identify the areas that need the most improvement, as well as typical problems users encounter in developing mashups. This form of evaluation can be done via user studies.

Programming-by-example [12] is used successfully for website data extraction [9, 3], data transformations, and filtering [8], as well as for drag & drop gestures in the UI. Using it for other tasks in mashup development environments and comparing it to other notations are important research challenges. For example, programming-by-example approaches could help find of mashups and mashup elements, which is likely to be challenging in the future [8].

Regarding UI development, an integration of different design mechanisms, such as using automatic generation to provide a starting point and then being able to modify it using a visual form editor, would combine the strengths of the different approaches. Another important UI improvement is providing a means for advanced information visualization, which could help to leverage the user's perceptual system and further increase the usability of mashups.

The overall support for software engineering techniques such as testing and debugging in mashup development environments is quite limited. Given the concerns regarding security and correctness of applications developed by non-programmers [20] and the growing popularity of mashups, these shortcomings are dangerous, especially in the context of enterprise mashups. Non-programmer oriented debugging and testing facilities such as debuggers, test frameworks and assertions are researched in the area of end user software engineering (e.g. [11], [22]). Applying these concepts to mashup development environments could alleviate the dangers of incorrect and unsafe mashups.

7 Mashup Environments and the Smart Internet

Ng et al. identify the lack of integration from the user's perspective and limited user control over web pages as two of the major shortcomings of the current web [1].

Mashups and mashup development environments provide a partial solution to these shortcomings. They apply several aspects of the principle of "a user-centric model for instinctive interaction" that was proposed by Ng et al. [1]. In particular, mashup development environments enable end users to control what content is delivered and how the content is presented to them by designing interfaces and aggregating data from services.

Mashup development environments, however, are only a first step towards a smarter internet. They provide a partial solution to the lack of integration from a user's perspective, because they lack an aggregation model and framework to drive service composition [1]. Several shortcomings hinder a better integration of current mashups into the smart internet.

First, mashups are not connected to matters of concern. Instead, they are much like regular web pages in that users have to search for a mashup that fits their current matter of concern similar to searching the web. From a usage point of view, the only differences are that users are able to modify mashups if they need to and that they can construct their own mashups if they do not find an existing page or mashup that fits their needs.

Second, current mashup tools only support a single target platform, typically web browsers on regular desktop computers or notebooks. The support of additional platforms such as mobile devices and especially the support for interaction across devices, however, is a crucial part of the smart internet, which envisions that "instinctive interaction should be tailored [...] to [...] the user's systems of interaction" [1].

Third, current mashups do not take the user's profile and context explicitly into account. While mashups can be customized by users to implicitly reflect their preferences and needs, the current mashup tools fall short in applying such customization automatically.

Fourth, while current mashup tools allow the users to construct and modify mashups, they do not generate mashups automatically. This is a major barrier, because many users lack the time to construct and modify mashups for their own tasks. We believe that in order for the smart internet to become reality, mashups need to be generated automatically based on the user's task, profile, environment and context. Researchers have started looking at how services can be discovered and composed based on the users' contexts [23], [24].

Despite those shortcomings, we believe that mashup environments will be a vital part of the smart internet, if mashups are linked to matters of concern. This could be achieved by integrating mashup development environments into the infrastructure for matters of concern in a way that users can decide to create a mashup for their current task, use an existing mashup for their current task, and tailor mashups to their context and preferences. Once mashups are linked to tasks and thus to matters of concern, systems can mine those mashups to identify which data sources, aggregation workflows, and presentation elements are utilized in these tasks. This information can be used to automatically construct mashups for other users, for different devices, for related tasks, or for related contexts. By giving users the ability to modify those automatically generated mashups, they will contribute even more task-related information that can be leveraged.

8 Limitations

There are several limitations to the generalizability of this study. Other mashup development environments besides those reviewed here exist, and they may contain additional EUD features. We have chosen the reviewed mashup development environments in order to get a broad, representative feature set. As an initial exploration showed, the mashup development environments from major companies tend to be more advanced. We also made sure that all three different mashup types (information, process, and website mashups) were included in our tool survey.

Second, there was no standard way in using the mashup development environments during the evaluation. A stricter evaluation approach like trying to create the same mashup on all mashup development environments was not feasible because of the maturity of the tools and the differences in their functionality and in the kinds of mashups they generate.

Third, the tool review was conducted in July and August 2008 and reflects the tools and features available at that time.

9 Conclusion

In this chapter, we presented a survey of six mashup development environments from a EUD perspective. Six different themes that emerged from our literature review (Levels of Abstraction, Learning Support, Community Support, Discoverability, UI Design and Software Engineering Techniques) were used to guide our evaluation. The mashup development environments provide many features to support end users, but there is still much room for further improvement.

We then looked at how mashup development environments fit into the vision of the smart internet. We believe that they can be an essential part of the smart internet if mashups are connected to matters of concern. This would enable mining of mashup elements and could facilitate automatic mashup creation and customization.

Acknowledgements

This research was supported by the IBM Center of Advanced Studies (CAS) Toronto. We wish to thank Maria-Elena Hernandez, Tricia Pelz, Sean Falconer, Gargi Bougie, Bradley Blashko, Patrick Gorman and the reviewers for their helpful feedback and editing suggestions.

References

1. Ng, J.W., Chignell, M., Cordy, J.R.: The smart internet: transforming the web for the user. In: CASCON 2009: Proceedings of the 2009 Conference of the Center for Advanced Studies on Collaborative Research, pp. 285–296. ACM, New York (2009)
2. Hartmann, B., Doorley, S., Klemmer, S.R.: Hacking, Mashing, Gluing: A Study of Opportunistic Design and Development. Technical Report 2006-14, Stanford HCI Group (2006)

3. Hartmann, B., Wu, L., Collins, K., Klemmer, S.: Programming by a Sample: Rapidly Prototyping Web Applications with d.mix. In: Proceeding of the 20th Symposium on User Interface Software and Technology (UIST 2007). ACM, Newport (2007)
4. Zang, N., Rosson, M.B., Nasser, V.: Mashups: who? what? why? In: CHI 2008: CHI 2008 extended abstracts on Human factors in computing systems, pp. 3171–3176. ACM, New York (2008)
5. Wong, J., Hong, J.: What do we "mashup" when we make mashups? In: WEUSE 2008: Proceedings of the 4th International Workshop on End-user Software Engineering, pp. 35–39. ACM, New York (2008)
6. Jhingran, A.: Enterprise information mashups: integrating information, simply. In: VLDB 2006: Proceedings of the 32nd International Conference on Very Large Data Bases, VLDB Endowment, pp. 3–4 (2006)
7. Wong, J., Hong, J.: Making mashups with marmite: towards end-user programming for the web. In: CHI 2007: Proceedings of the SIGCHI Conference on Human factors in Computing Systems, pp. 1435–1444. ACM, New York (2007)
8. Tuchinda, R., Szekely, P., Knoblock, C.A.: Building Mashups by Example. In: Proceedings of the 2008 International Conference on Intelligent User Interfaces, pp. 139–148. ACM, New York (2008)
9. Fujima, J., Lunzer, A., Hornbaek, K., Tanaka, Y.: Clip, connect, clone: combining application elements to build custom interfaces for information access. In: UIST 2004: Proceedings of the 17th annual ACM Symposium on User Interface Software and Technology, pp. 175–184. ACM, New York (2004)
10. Bolin, M., Webber, M., Rha, P., Wilson, T., Miller, R.C.: Automation and customization of rendered web pages. In: UIST 2005: Proceedings of the 18th Annual ACM Symposium on User Interface Software and Technology, pp. 163–172. ACM, New York (2005)
11. Burnett, M., Cook, C., Rothermel, G.: End-user software engineering. Communications of the ACM 47(9), 53–58 (2004)
12. Lieberman, H.: Your wish is my command: programming by example. Morgan Kaufmann, San Francisco (2001)
13. Myers, B.A., Ko, A.J., Burnett, M.M.: Invited research overview: end-user programming. In: CHI 2006: CHI 2006 Extended Abstracts on Human Factors in Computing Systems, pp. 75–80. ACM, New York (2006)
14. Nardi, B.A.: A small matter of programming: perspectives on end user computing. MIT Press, Cambridge (1993)
15. Wulf, V., Klann, M., Lieberman, H., Paternó, F.: End User Development. Human-Computer Interaction Series, vol. 9. Springer, Dordrecht (2006)
16. MacLean, A., Carter, K., Lövstrand, L., Moran, T.: User-tailorable systems: pressing the issues with buttons. In: Proceedings of the SIGCHI Conference on Human Factors in Computing Systems: Empowering people, pp. 175–182. ACM, New York (1990)
17. Ko, A.J., Myers, B.A., Aung, H.H.: Six learning barriers in end-user programming systems. In: VL/HCC 2004: Proceedings of the 2004 IEEE Symposium on Visual Languages - Human Centric Computing, pp. 199–206. IEEE, Washington (2004)
18. Altinel, M., Brown, P., Cline, S., Kartha, S., Louie, S., Markl, V., Mau, L., Ng, Y.-H., Simmen, D., Singh, A.: DAMIA - A Data Mashup Fabric for Intranet Applications. In: VLDB 2007: Proceedings of the 33rd International Conference on Very Large Data Bases, pp. 1370–1373. VLDB Endowment (2007)
19. Ennals, R.J., Garofalakis, M.N.: MashMaker: mashups for the masses. In: Proceedings of the 2007 ACM SIGMOD International Conference on Management of Data, pp. 1116–1118. ACM, New York (2007)

20. Harrison, W.: From the Editor: The Dangers of End-User Programming. IEEE Software 21(4), 5–7 (2004)
21. Green, T.R.G., Petre, M.: Usability Analysis of Visual Programming Environments: A Cognitive Dimensions Framework. Journal of Visual Languages and Computing 7(2), 131–174 (1996)
22. Ko, A.J., Myers, B.A.: Designing the Whyline: a debugging interface for asking questions about program behavior. In: CHI 2004: Proceedings of the SIGCHI Conference on Human Factors in Computing Systems, pp. 151–158. ACM, New York (2004)
23. Xiao, H., Zou, Y., Ng, J., Nigul, L.: An approach for context-aware service discovery and recommendation. In: ICWS 2010: The 8th International Conference on Web Services (2010)
24. Xiao, H., Zou, Y., Tang, R., Ng, J., Nigul, L.: An automatic approach for ontology-driven service composition. In: SOCA 2009: IEEE International Conference on Service-Oriented Computing and Applications (2009)

Smart Media: Bridging Interactions and Services for the Smart Internet

Margaret-Anne Storey, Lars Grammel, and Christoph Treude*

University of Victoria, Department of Computer Science
{mstorey,lgrammel,ctreude}@uvic.ca

Abstract. This chapter describes a need for Smart Media to enhance the vision of the Smart Internet. Smart Media is introduced as a mechanism to bridge Smart Services and Smart Interactions. Smart Media extends the existing notions of Media in HCI such as Hypermedia, New Media, Adaptive Hypermedia, and Social Media. There are three main contributions from this paper: (1) A historical perspective of media in HCI and how media could benefit from smartness; (2) through some high level sample scenarios, a proposal for Smart Media to meet the vision of the Smart Internet; and (3) a detailed example of how Smart Media could play a role in software development. The paper concludes by outlining some of the key challenges that need to be faced in realizing and applying Smart Media objects.

Keywords: Smart internet, smart interactions, smart services, smart media, social media, web 2.0, intelligent user interfaces, computer supported cooperative work, human computer interaction.

1 Introduction

The vision for a smart internet, according to Ng, Chignell and Cordy [1], arises from a shift away from a server-centric model to a user-centric model. It realizes that the user's model is paramount in terms of supporting the users' interactions, and consequently a new kind of session is needed that centers on the user's perspective and context [1]. That is, a user's interaction on the web should be situated within a socio-technical perspective that involves multiple web services, context about the user, as well as collaborations with other people. Such elaborate interactions thus require a "dynamic social binding" [1] of web interactions with web applications that supports collaboration across individuals, as well as knowledge about the user's needs.

Ng *et al.*'s vision of the Smart Internet requires both "Smart Interactions" and "Smart Services". Smart Interactions focuses on developing an advanced user model on the web that captures the users' contexts and their matters of concerns. Smart Services refers to the algorithms that will orchestrate the web as a cohesive platform thus enabling the advanced user models required for smart interactions [1].

* The authors are supported by grants from the Canadian Institutes for Health Research (CIHR).

M. Chignell et al. (Eds.): The Smart Internet, LNCS 6400, pp. 152–169, 2010.

In this chapter, we explore Smart Media as a potential third component of the Smart Internet. Media, the plural of medium, sometimes refers to channels or systems of communication, information, or entertainment[1,2]. The term is also often used to refer to artifacts that are communicated along a given channel, such as a specific video clip or newspaper article.

The need for smart media on the smart internet is based on the observation that users' interactions with web services usually involve information artifacts that play a central role in the current, but also future, interactions of the users with the web. For example, when booking a flight over the web, the artifact created is an airline booking. This booking can be transmitted along various channels, such as by email or by posting on a secure website. The email and website channels are media channels that are used to mediate the users' interactions with the services, as well as mediate their interactions with other stakeholders in the booking.

In this chapter, we explore if there are potential opportunities for and potential advantages of adding "smartness" to the information artifacts themselves. Rather than referring to them as just information artifacts, we suggest referring to these enhanced information artifacts as smart media objects. Essentially, we propose that smart media objects can become a way to bridge smart interactions and smart services by reifying and aggregating the user's context with information resources and services that will satisfy the user's needs.

In order to explore the proposed concept of smart media, we look back at the history of different forms of media in Human Computer Interaction (Section 2). We then consider what the requirements may be for media that is "smart" in Section 3 and refer to some potential applications of smart media. In Section 4, we explore how smart media can be realized in the architecture of the Smart Internet. In Section 5, we present detailed scenarios of how "Smart Media" could play a role in collaborative software engineering and how developers may benefit from smart media objects. Finally, in Section 6 we articulate the many challenges that must be overcome to design smart media for the Smart Internet and outline future work. We conclude the chapter in Section 7.

2 A Brief History of the Role of Media in Human Computer Interaction

In this section, we explore the historical perspectives of media, hypermedia and the more recent phenomenon of social media.

2.1 From Media to Hypermedia

The term "Media" is often used to refer to different but related concepts. For example, media may refer to channels or systems of communication, information, or entertainment. "Mass media" more specifically refers to media that is communicated to a

---

[1] As opposed to Mass media, communication (as newspapers, radio, or television) that is designed to reach the mass of the people (http://www.merriam-webster.com/dictionary/mass+medium)

[2] Definition of medium: http://www.merriam-webster.com/dictionary/medium

wide population. Examples of mass media include newspapers, radio and television. In Human Computer Interaction systems, examples of media artifacts include text files, photographs and emails. The term "new media" is often used to refer to the emergence of digital media and networked information resources that occurred over the past 30-40 years. New media are digital artifacts such as videos that can be interactively manipulated and linked over the internet.

We note that the use of the term "Media" often blurs the distinction between **channel** (e.g. email system, youtube), **data artifacts** (a specific email or newspaper article) and the **representation** that is used to communicate the data (e.g. video, text, graphics). More succinctly, a channel is a mechanism whereby a given representation of a data artifact can be transmitted to the user. The selection of the appropriate channels and the manner in which the artifact is represented is critical in terms of meeting the user's needs. We note that it is not always possible to distinguish representation from channel, e.g. in the case of a Twitter feed, the representation is fixed (text of length 140 characters) although different tools could present the feeds in a different way (e.g. by expanding pictures or showing clips of embedded links in the feed). We provide the following high level definition of media to guide our future discussion:

Media = Artifact + representation + channel

A major challenge in HCI research has been to find suitable tools and environments for creating, searching, manipulating, consuming, annotating, sharing and analyzing digital media artifacts. As early as 1945, Vannevar Bush noted that *"publication has extended far beyond our present ability to make real use of the record"* [2]. Indeed he proposed a system called the Memex, an external memory device where individuals could store and index all their personal books, records and communications. Users could construct "trails" through the material, and annotate their resources with margin notes, comments, keywords and cross references to other material. Although the Memex concept was based on Microfilm, many saw it as a precursor to "hypertext".

The Hypertext and Hypermedia terms were later coined by Ted Nelson in 1965 [3]. Hypertext refers to a non-sequential collection of text [4]. It can be modeled as a directed graph where each node represents a certain amount of text. Hyperlinks (directed arcs) connect the nodes in the graph. Hypermedia extends the term hypertext to include graphics, audio, video, as well as text and hyperlinks, to create a "non-linear medium of information" [5]. The term multimedia is a broader concept that includes hypermedia, as well as non-interactive mixed media.

Although never fully implemented nor adopted, Nelson proposed the Xanadu system. Xanadu was to be a system that could store all the world's literature, with the ability to link from any substring to another, and where the most recent version would be retrieved (but older versions would be retained and would never be deleted). Other concepts in Xanadu included author attribution and transclusion, the inclusion of a part of a document into another document by reference. Although not fully implemented, Nelson's concepts of Hypertext and Hypermedia are fundamental concepts to all web-based information systems today. However, Nelson's disappointment in some of the limitations from today's web is evident in this quote of his: *"The 'Browser' is an extremely silly concept-- a window for looking sequentially at a large parallel structure. It does not show this structure in a useful way.*" Our observations of how users interact on the web have indicated to us that the browser is also a poor mechanism for user interaction with media artifacts that supports a user's task that crosscuts multiple sessions on the web. Part of the issue is that the user further wants to use different channels for viewing and interacting with their media artifacts, but there is currently very poor integration or awareness across these channels[3].

Despite some drawbacks with today's web, it is of course highly successful and widely used. Some of the reasons cited for its success are that it is built around an open systems approach with standardized specifications for interoperability. It is also backwards compatible (for legacy data) and control over content on the web has been decentralized [6]. Today's media artifacts are typically embedded in a hypermedia system that consists of a web of links to other media objects.

The more recent development of Web 2.0 technologies and a change in philosophy have led to a new form of media, that of Social Media.

2.2 From Hypermedia to Social Media

The emergence of Web 2.0 technologies and a change in philosophy in how users participate as authors as well as consumers over the web, have resulted in a paradigm shift in how users (and their social networks) create, gather, annotate, share and analyze information [7, 8, 9]. This new model has led to the emergence of "Social Media". Social media is often referred to as the many-to-many broadcast mechanism, and the implication of its creation along with the usage of Web 2.0 technologies are widespread, but as of yet quite poorly understood.

Web 2.0 or social software as it is often referred to, is built around an "architecture of participation" that aggregates both explicit user contributions (e.g. created artifacts) and implicit user contributions (e.g. navigation trails). Web 2.0 implies that processes and tools are socially open, and that content can be used in several different contexts. Web 2.0 tools and technologies support interactive information sharing, data interoperability and user centered design. Web 2.0 affords the creation of social media, where content (information artifacts) can be read, written, and transformed into other content by a many-to-many collaboration if desired. One of the most important implications of Web 2.0 is a significantly enhanced user experience, as well as user control over the applications that they use and the data they create.

Example social media channels include wikis, blogs, mashups and feeds, where specific artifacts are wiki articles, user blogs and instances of mashed up services. The media channels are being used by users and communities of users to help organize, manage and categorize artifacts in an informal and collaborative way.

Referring back to the airline ticket example: how could social media improve the interactions and the services underlying the ticket? Some suggestions are that it may be desirable to use social media to assist in creating the airline booking, by helping the user choose which airline or route to select during the booking (note: this is already supported by websites such as expedia.ca). But social media could also be used to enhance the experience of the booking once underway by linking in social media that informs the user as they experience their trip (e.g. reviews recently uploaded to

[3] The recent introduction of the OpenGraph protocol by Facebook and their collaborators is addressing that very issue, see http://developers.facebook.com/docs/opengraph.

tripadvisor.com or just in time transportation issues discussed on Twitter). Moreover, the user could use the booking itself as a portal to add to this user generated content if desired, and thus help other users with their travel plans in real time. Some of these enhancements to ticket bookings already exist – for example, expedia.ca ties in many of these services so that updates to the itinerary can be made in real time. However, such enhancements are made following a server centric point of view with only limited context about the user and the user's task playing a role in how new information and services are pushed to the user. This is where more "smartness" is required to put the user at center of the booking artifact, and thus greatly improve the user experience.

3 Towards Smart Media for the Smart Internet

As mentioned previously, we propose that the smart internet needs not only smart interactions and smart services, but also the notion of smart media. But what do we mean by "smart"? Here we can draw inspiration from the research community of "Intelligent User Interfaces". According to Maybury [10], *"Intelligent user interfaces (IUIs) are human-machine interfaces that aim to improve the efficiency, effectiveness, and naturalness of human-machine interaction by representing, reasoning, and acting on models of the user, domain, task, discourse and media (e.g., graphics, natural language, gesture)."* Many of the goals articulated for IUIs match those of the smart internet, thus we can learn from and build on research from that community.

"Smartness" in user interfaces these days is appearing in many forms. For example, the use of recommendations [11], adaptive interfaces [12], and the semantic web [13], are just a few areas where "intelligent" support for the user is being explored. While all these efforts are making large strides to improve the user experience, what is perhaps lacking is a cohesive plan of how interactions, media and services can together improve how the internet fulfills users' personal and social needs. Users still suffer from the lack of integration of services, difficulties in tracking tasks (especially across services) and challenges personalizing web pages to suit their needs [1]. Many of these concerns stem from insufficient knowledge about users, their social network and the tasks they need to complete.

The lack of a consistent user model across services is also a significant reason for difficulties and barriers to an effective user experience. One research area, that could be helpful in this regard, is the area of User Modeling (see http://www.um.org/), this research topic explores how to develop cognitive models of human users describing their knowledge and skills. One example of user modeling underlies "adaptive hypermedia" – hypermedia that adapts to meet the user's goals, abilities, interests and knowledge [14]. Thus, User Modeling is another community that we should look to for inspiration in developing the Smart Internet and in particular for supporting Smart Interactions. Indeed, capturing, updating and leveraging the User's Model is a crucial aspect of the proposed Smart Interactions on the web.

But how can the media artifacts and media channels offer aspects of "smartness"?

We already see examples of "smartness" emerging in media channels. Consider the youtube channel where we benefit from recommendation systems, and in email we benefit from spam detection that is improved through collaborative filters. As another example, the use of Twitter during the earthquake crisis in Haiti [15] demonstrates how the Twitter media channel can be used to harness collective intelligence in helping rescue efforts. Such examples can be further augmented through the use of agents and services, as well as information about the User's model (such as history, user preferences etc) to improve the user experience.

What we propose in this paper is to also push smartness into the media artifact itself.

Let's consider the flight booking example again. When I book my flight, I can get a copy of the booking by email, which is then added to my calendar and I can access a copy of it on a secure website. There are two or more copies (representations) of the booking. The booking as presented on the website channel is likely to be updated if changes are made, but the email version and the calendar versions will not be updated. This is one problem that can cause significant difficulties for users as they have to manage multiple versions of the booking and remember which one is valid and furthermore may miss important updates if a non-live version is used. This is not an unusual scenario, many media artifacts are often constrained to be used across just one channel, and can't easily cross the boundary between channels, and only some channels will support live updates.

Another issue is that although the website version of the booking can customize the booking according to the user's preferences stored on the website, the website channel may not be privy to information generated from other services that may impact the user's travel plans (for example, imagine that the user is waitlisted for surgery through another service, and the user does not wish to carry through with their travel plans if it conflicts with a surgical opening that arises).

Rather than requiring all services to know about all other services that may be relevant to a user, the currently proposed model of the smart internet assumes there is a user model that the services access. The services thus update the artifacts as needed according to the user's model which should ensure that consistency is achieved across all the services and media artifacts relevant to the user.

What we propose is that some of the smartness required should be pushed into the media artifact itself, and that the media artifact should play an intermediary role between the User's Model (smart interactions) and the services they use. If some of the "smartness" is pushed down into the artifact, the artifact that is created by, for or with the user can adapt to and transform a user's needs. This is achieved by having a model of how the artifact should behave. The artifact behavior is made possible through the use of services and by interacting with the User's model.

Rather than the term "artifact", a better term may now be *smart media object* – to emphasize that it represents data, representation options, channels and intelligent services. The smartness comes from the fact that a smart media object has a model that describes how it should behave to meet the users' needs, it can access information about the User's Model and leverage services that matter to the user. From the user's point of view, there is just one booking artifact that can be displayed on different channels (using different representation techniques if desired), and it can be updated through a variety of means so that *just-in-time* information that matters to the user will be available. Such an approach would reduce friction in how the user interacts with the internet but would also greatly enhance the user's experience through additional service integration.

We now revisit our high level definition of media from above, and expand on it to provide a high level definition of smart media object as follows:

Smart media object = Data + representation + channel + *intelligence*

The following provides natural language definitions of the terms *smart media object* and *smart media channel:*

> ***Smart media objects** are socio-technical artifacts that are aware of user(s) context(s), they aggregate data from one or more services and through the use of services and through dependencies with other smart media objects can anticipate, participate in, adapt to, react to, evolve and transform user(s) needs.*
> ***Smart media channels** are used to transmit data between the user's devices and the smart media objects that are linked to the user.*

We expect these definitions to evolve as we explore these concepts, but for now they at least capture the intent underlying the proposed benefits of smart media to support the Smart Internet.

The concept of smart media is of course not entirely new; adaptive hypermedia that adapts to a student's learning needs exhibits some characteristics of "smart" media that we propose and there are very likely other examples of this concept. What we propose is that a unified and widely adopted concept of a smart media object can support an improved mediation of the user's interactions with smart services. We emphasize that the smart media objects should not be tightly coupled to specific services nor dependent on specific channels, but according to the user's needs can be accessible anyhow, dynamically updated and be live on the channel that is most appropriate for the user's task and context.

Although this proposal may seem a utopia in HCI, there are many current research efforts that lead us in this direction, such as Web 2.0, the semantic web, service oriented architectures, cloud computing and advanced user modeling techniques. In the next section of this chapter, we present a potential architecture that fits with this vision.

4 A Proposed Architecture for the Smart Internet That Supports Smart Media

So far we have described what we believe could be the benefits from having smart media objects for improving the user experience on the web, but not discussed much how these smart media objects would interface with smart services and smart interactions. In Figure 1, we first show a high level architecture of the proposed Smart Internet.

In Figure 2, we add to this architecture and propose how Smart Media Objects could fit into this architecture. Smart interactions are implemented using the notion of a personal agent bound to a model of the user. There is one such agent and model for each user; the model is updated using information sent to it through media channels that the user opts to use, through service updates and through sensor inputs to the model. The agent will use the user's model to decide which data captured by the smart media objects should be communicated to the user, and which media channels should be used for communicating that information.

To relate our previous example of a flight booking to this architecture, we describe how it could be instantiated using the model in Figure 2. The travelers booking their

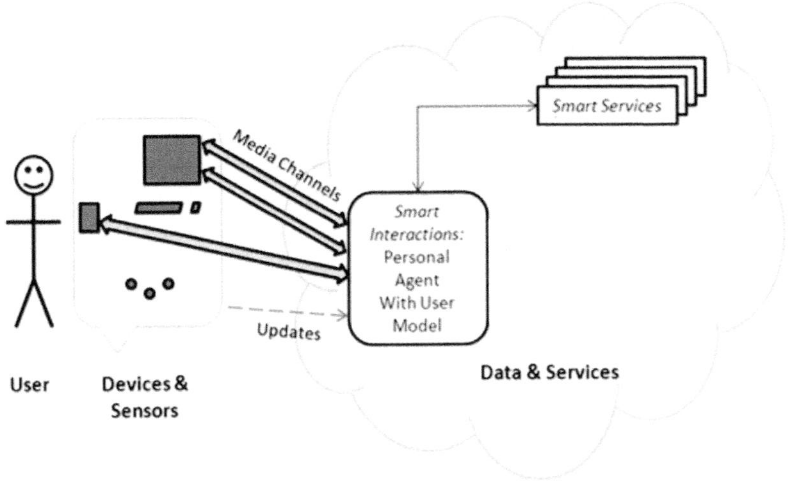

Fig. 1. Architecture for the Smart Internet.

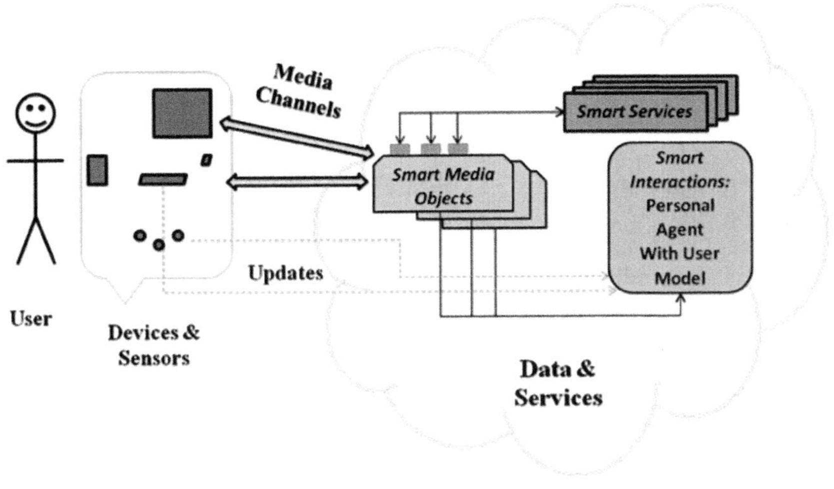

Fig. 2. Smart Internet Architecture with Smart Media Objects.

travel are instances of the user. Users have a smartphone (with GPS services) and a laptop as devices at their disposal. They have previously booked their flight using expedia.ca and their flight booking is now represented as a smart media object. The user's model captures the preferences of a particular user, including the fact that the user prefers an aisle seat whenever possible. The flight booking object notes that the user is currently assigned to a window seat and using one of the smart services associated with the booking object, periodically polls to see if an aisle seat comes available. When an aisle seat is available, the flight booking data is updated to reveal a new seat has been assigned. The booking object refers to the User's model and notes that the user wants to be informed when a change is made to the seat assignment using an instant message channel connected to the User's smartphone.

This last example demonstrates how the media object *pushes* information to the user and makes changes to the artifact (the flight booking) to benefit the user. In order to "know" which changes should be made, the media object has an internal model keeping track of the state of the user (that is relevant to the artifact), the state of the booking itself and references to services that it may pull information from, or registered services that can push information to the media object. The smart media object's model is not represented in Figure 2, but the services it uses for both pushing and pulling information from the services are shown as connectors to the Smart Media Object.

In order to demonstrate more aspects of the architecture, we present a second scenario based on user-initiated *pull* operations. Assume the user is at the airport and has not checked in her baggage yet. The user initiates looking at the booking through her smartphone. The personal agent passes the context (smartphone, location at airport, time) into the view operation of the booking (which knows the user has not checked in her luggage). The booking media object returns a representation of itself that emphasizes the location and name of the check-in counter. The personal agent indicates to the booking that the user's web browser channel should be utilized to render a route from the user's current location to the check-in counter with additional information about the booking. After the user has checked in, but is not through security, the same operation would result in a map with the next security gate location, time until boarding and security instructions as well as the current average waiting time at the security gate. After the user is through security (user location has now changed), the booking would send a representation of itself also through the web browser channel that emphasizes the gate location and boarding time.

The examples just presented are to illustrate how the smart media objects can play a role in the architecture of the Smart Internet. In the next section of this chapter, we look at a specific domain, that of collaborative software development, and further explore how smart media objects could play a role in that domain.

5 Smart Media Objects for Software Development

In this section we propose that software development could be an appropriate test environment to explore the concept of smart media objects. First of all, software developers tend to be early adopters of new technologies[4]. Indeed, social media technologies are causing a paradigm shift in how software is developed. Developers routinely blog [16], use twitter [17], use social networking [18] and use social coding sites such as github.org and heroku.com[5]. When searching for information they make use of Google search and websites such as www.freshmeat.org and www.stackoverflow.com.

Secondly, modern IDEs and IDE features under research development already benefit from "smartness". The notion of "content assist" is now routinely used in search engines and development environments. Recommendation engines for code samples, developer expertise, related bugs (work items) and test bases are currently an

[4] This is particularly so for younger developers.

[5] See http://sites.google.com/site/web2se/

active area for research in software engineering[6]. Along with this, there is active research on how to improve search during development[7]. Recent research on IDE improvements investigates how more knowledge of the user and their tasks can be used to improve recommendation engines [19] and how such information could lead to an improved knowledge based IDE [20]. Chapter Four in this book further explores how smart interactions can improve interruption management in software development [21].

By partnering with groups of developers to try out the ideas underlying smart media objects, these developers can participate in helping us determine the requirements for smart media objects and furthermore provide feedback to us on the concepts underlying the smart internet. We propose that three social media artifacts from software development, work items, dashboards and feeds, can be transformed into smart media objects that will improve collaborative development activities. We consider these artifacts within the context of the Jazz development environment (an IBM product).

5.1 "Smarter" Work Items

Modern software development environments typically have explicit tool support for managing tasks. For example, Jazz[8], a collaborative IDE developed by IBM, has tool support for managing "work items", where a work item is a generalized notion of a development task (see Fig. 3). Work items are assigned to developers, are classified using predefined categories, and may be associated with other work items. Jazz work

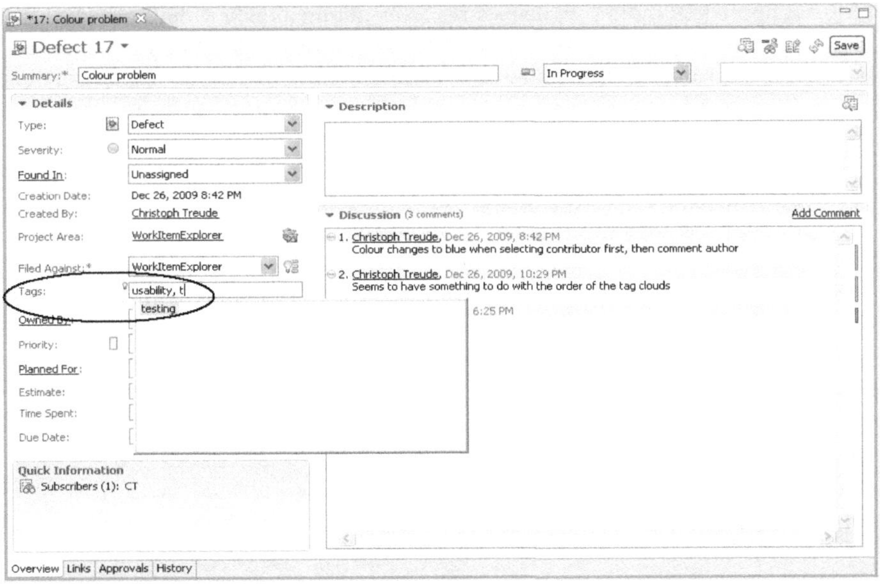

Fig. 3. Work items in Jazz, the circle shows how developers can freely tag work items.

[6] See http://sites.google.com/site/rsseresearch/rsse2010
[7] See http://scg.unibe.ch/wiki/events/suite2010
[8] www.jazz.net

items also have some web 2.0 tool support to address social aspects. Specifically, Jazz supports a discussion thread and a lightweight "tagging" mechanism. Using this latter feature, developers can freely associate user defined keywords with work items. In our previous work [22], we showed how the tagging feature of work items has been eagerly adopted by developers.

Work items can be viewed in the client application of Jazz or through a web browser. Developers can set up feeds on work item events as well as see views on the work items in dashboards. Dashboards and feeds are discussed further below.

Some of the challenges facing developers that use work items include the following:

- *Notifications:* Developers have to customize how they should receive notifications of events related to specific work items. This can be quite cumbersome to do and there is a tension between having too much information (overload) and missing out on important events that may be important to them. This latter issue relates to developers maintaining appropriate awareness during collaborative development activities. McGrenere and Li's chapter in this book investigates the related issue of interruption management [21].
- *Finding out about related work items:* There are many different possible relation types possible between work items (such as child of, depends on, and related to). The Jazz work item interface provides support for navigating related work items – but the developer has to know about the related work items to encourage this exploration. Moreover, many work items may be interrelated but no explicit relationship has been created between them. Thus support for finding related work items automatically would be a useful improvement to the tool support. The current research on recommending bugs shows promise for practical application.
- *Expertise location:* A single developer within a large software project can't possibly have expertise on all aspects of the project. As work items are created by a developer, she should be able to quickly find team members with the required expertise. Currently the developer has to manually search through the logs or ask people to find this out. There is current research on expertise location that could be used to provide this information.
- *Managing order of work, articulation of work:* Although work items are already an important cog in the wheel of team based development activities, they could be further enriched if they actively played a role in the overall work plan. Jazz currently has some support for this through a process management component, but again much of this has to be manually handled by the developer but aspects of this could be automated.

Some of the problems described above could be eliminated or at least reduced through smarter work items. But what would a smarter work item object look like? We use our definition of smart media object above to describe the architecture of a smart work item object:

Data: A work item artifact has a predefined structure with a set of fields as follows: summary (free text), priority (levels predefined), severity (from a given set of choices), component name, tags (freely assigned), comments (free text, shown in sequence), owner, creator, subscribers, state, team area, and a description (text). It also has a set of typed links to other work items and a history of how it has changed.

Channels: The work item can be displayed to the user using the Jazz client channel, or through the Web browser channel. Alternatively a feed channel may be used to communicate events on the work item.

Representations: What is represented and how it is represented depends on the channel but the representation should also be adapted to fit the user's needs. Text and graphics are used primarily in the web and client versions of the work item representation, but just text representations of some of the elements in the work item is used in a feed.

Intelligence: What we propose is that the smart work item media object should have associated with it a number of heuristics (i.e. a model) of how it should be updated and how it should send information to the user. These heuristics should work in concert with the user's model (smart interactions) as well as respond to events from services and make explicit calls to services as needed.

The above description of a smart work item object could play a role in the management of collaborative work as follows: when a work item is closed, a developer that may have related work to do should be notified. A feed can inform the developer that the work item status has changed, or alternatively, if the developer is currently reading emails, he may receive an email providing some more information on the work item that was closed. The work item should then keep track of which information has already been communicated to the developer. The work item object may further let other developers know who has been informed. The behaviours that the work item exhibits will depend on the heuristics associated with it, its own internal model of the work item model, the user's model and the available services that are associated with the work item object.

5.2 "Smarter" Dashboards

Dashboards are information resources that support distributed cognition; they are crucial to many business intelligence applications. Dashboards are also used in software development [23]. For example in the Jazz IDE, dashboards are displayed and configured using the web interface. They are intended to provide information at a glance and to allow easy navigation to more complete information (such as to a work item). By default, each project and each team within a project has their own dashboard; and an individual dashboard is created for each developer when they first open their web interface. Figure 4 shows an example dashboard.

A dashboard consists of several viewlets. Viewlets are rectangular widgets displaying information about some aspect of a project. Each viewlet is an instance of a viewlet type. The actual content shown in a viewlet depends on the viewlet type, e.g., visual representations of the current workload or a list of members on a team, as well as the way the particular instance has been configured. Developers can add viewlets to their dashboards and configure the viewlets using different parameters. Viewlets can be organized into different tabs within a single dashboard.

By default, dashboards only display general purpose viewlets containing information about developers and teams, and links to general feeds. In addition to individual customizations of dashboards, project managers or component leads can customize the default settings. Normally the development manager of a project is in charge of

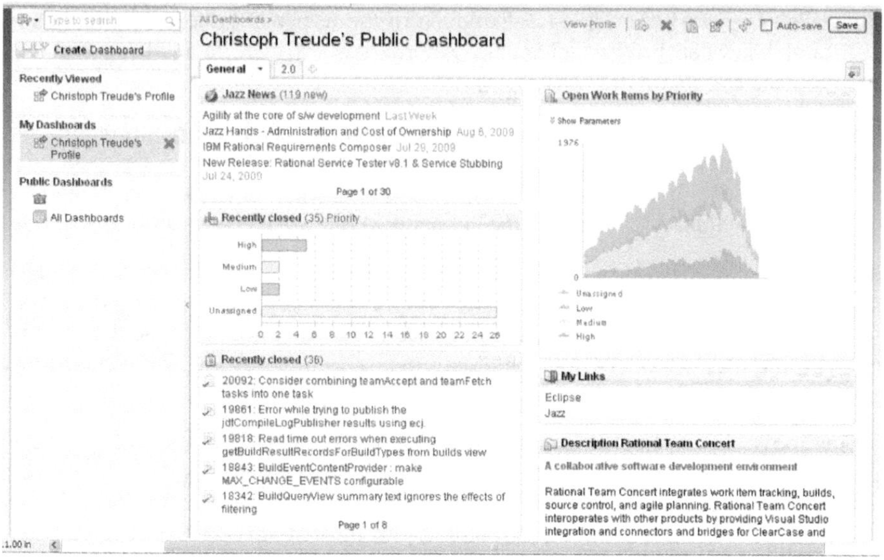

Fig. 4. Dashboards in Jazz.

updating the project dashboard, the component leads are responsible for the team dashboards, and individual developers change their own dashboards.

With dashboards, different people want to see different things depending on their role, development tasks to be supported, where the team is in an iteration (e.g. just before a release developers need to know about the must fix items), and the size of the team. We conducted a study of how dashboards are used in a collaborative development project [23], and one of the challenges with using dashboards is that users have to customize them according to their needs (as described above). Furthermore, as the project progresses, they need to further customize the dashboard as their information needs change.

Another issue is that in Jazz there is another feature called Team central views (shown within the client) that overlaps much of the information shown in the dashboard within the web browser. Ideally, these two views should be representations of the same data and once one of them is customized for the user, the other one should be customized in similar manner. Moreover, if the user has viewed information in one of these views, the other view should reflect that the information is no longer new to that user.

These issues of customization and managing state about what the user has already viewed could be solved by adding "smartness" to the dashboard. We again use the high level definition of a smart media object to help propose what a smart dashboard media object may look like:

Data: The information to be displayed by the dashboard would include data from work items, build results, team membership and development events.

Channels: In this case the relevant channels for the developer may be a view in the client IDE application, a view in a web browser, or a special view designed for a mobile device.

Representations: The representations used in the dashboard will depend both on the needs of the user, but also on the data to be represented. Currently dashboards make use of charts, tables, lists and tag clouds.

Intelligence: For smarter dashboards, we again propose that this smart media object should have associated with it a number of heuristics for how it should be updated and how it should send information to the user and a model of the dashboard object that captures its state. The dashboard object heuristics should work in concert with the user's model (smart interactions) as well as respond to events from services and make calls to the smart services. A model of the development process may also be useful in guiding how the dashboard should behave. The development model can be accessed through a service. For example, this notion of a smart dashboard object, which leverages both the user's model as well as the development process model, can be used to automatically show *mustfix* work items right before a release.

We anticipate that as dashboards become more prevalent that the user will need more tool support in specifying how it should be configured and how it should be updated over time. Currently such tool support is very limited. We suggest that some of the ideas that are currently being explored to support mashup creation by end users [24] could be applied to customizing dashboards. For more information on Mashups see the preceding Chapter by Grammel and Storey.

5.3 "Smarter" Feeds

For awareness on the basis of events, the Jazz CDE provides feeds. Feeds can either be displayed in the client application or as a viewlet as part of a web-based dashboard (discussed above). The most common way to view feeds is through the Team Central view in the client application. Figure 5 shows an example. Team Central is organized into multiple sections that are updated continually with the latest events. By default, Team Central displays a bar chart of current work for the signed-in developer by priority (see top of Fig. 5). The event log in the middle of the view's default configuration shows feeds. These are configured to include build events for all teams that the signed-in developer is part of, work item changes that are pertinent to the signed-in developer, and changes to teams.

Developers can add or remove feeds and filter events to personalize their event log, however, it can be cumbersome for the user to know which feeds and events to customize for their needs. In addition, incoming events are displayed as small popup windows in the client application, which may or may not be disruptive to the user.

A feed as described above is an example of a media channel rather than a media object. However, we suggest that a feed media object can be an instantiation of a user's query that can be delivered through various feed channels.

The *data, channels* and *representation* aspects of a smart feed object are very similar to those for the smart dashboard object (hence we do not repeat these descriptions here). In terms of *intelligence*, we believe the following behaviours could be supported by considering the user's model:

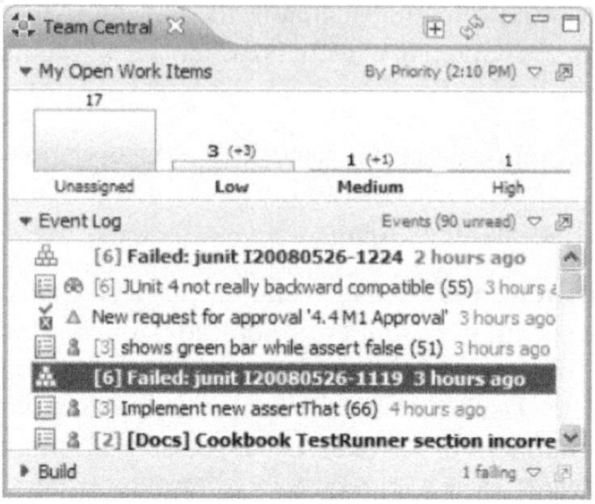

Fig. 5. Feeds in RTC Team Central.

- *Aggregation*: Grouping of related events
- *Filtering* of events that are not of interest to the user (based on their task, phase in the process etc)
- *Relevancy*: Ordering of events according to the user and process models
- *Immediacy*: Choosing a channel based on urgency and user context
- *Consistency*: Across channels

Adding "smartness" to feeds could help improve the delivery of important information to developers and also help to reduce the effects of information overload. If the user is on email, then the smart feed can use that channel first to deliver important information, and once a user has read about an event through a feed, it should appear as "read" in other channels.

5.4 Summary: Towards a "Smarter" IDE

In this section we proposed experimenting with some of the ideas for smart media objects in the domain of software engineering. We gave three examples of how media objects could be constructed and described scenarios of how "smartness" that leverages smart interactions and smart services could improve developers' tasks. We suggest the domain of software engineering because developers tend to be early adopters of new technologies and because we have access to these users and to the tools that they use. Nevertheless, there are many challenges to be overcome. We discuss these challenges in the next section.

6 Discussion of challenges

The vision of a Smart Internet is an attractive one, but many challenges will have to be overcome to meet it. In this section we explore these challenges and pose them as future research questions.

6.1 Challenge #1: User's Model

It goes without saying that the smart internet, and therefore smart media and smart interactions will require a model of the user that documents the user's matters of concern, aggregates content that is important to the user (or at least aggregates access to it) and is situated within a systems view of the user's needs. Figure 2 in this chapter shows how the User's Model can be situated in the cloud and can play a role in the proposed architecture for the Smart Internet. This is one proposal, but the important question to ask is can a common user model be developed so that all services can use it? Will the community of service providers participate in developing the common model and adopt it? How resilient to change will the model be, and will the model support change where necessary? Matching the user's model to the user's mental model will be critical in providing appropriate cognitive support to the user, otherwise they may be distracted by disruptive *interruptions* or *misleading* recommendations.

A key question to consider, in terms of smart media, is what if all parts of the model are not known for a given user, will the services still work with incomplete models? When inconsistencies arise in populating the model, can these be handled?

6.2 Challenge #2: Session

Ng *et al.*'s vision of the Smart Internet [1], advocates for a concept of the user's session that is not bound to the server, but instead may crosscut multiple services and may also be asynchronous. But how will the smart internet determine what a user session is? Will the notion of a session be stored with the User's Model or with the Smart Media Object? From the Smart Media perspective, what information should a session include, what should it exclude? Where is this information stored, and will this new concept of a session be understood by legacy services?

6.3 Challenge #3: Collaborative Interactions

Although not discussed much so far in this chapter, we project that smart media objects will have to play a larger role in collaborative interactions. Thus these questions arise: How to model these collaborative activities across multiple users' models? How to detect social networks, that once known, could improve the services delivered to the individual and group users? Once collaboration comes into play, there are then many existing concerns about internet use such as security, privacy, awareness, etc, that have to be considered. For socio-technical concerns, we need to turn to the research area of Computer Supported Cooperative Work (CSCW) [25] for assistance.

6.4 Challenge #4: Rethinking Media as Smart Objects

In order to achieve the benefits we have proposed in this paper, it requires rethinking media artifacts as first class objects that have state, heuristics, and respond to and leverage smart services. This consequently means that changes may also need to be made to media channels and media objects. For example, if a change to a ticket is made when a user retrieves an old email message containing the ticket, the message needs to be updated somehow. Another issue not discussed so far is the level of granularity of media objects. For example, should a media object contain all aspects of a travel booking such as flight, hotel and car rental? The level of granularity will in part depend on the user's model but the services that create the media objects will also need to determine this to meet the users' needs. Of course designing media objects that work well for users will require a lot of empirical work to understand how media artifacts are currently used, reused, shared and transformed.

Media objects that are "too smart" for the user's good is also at risk of damaging the user's experience – being smart ultimately means automating some steps on behalf of the user, but if the wrong steps are automated or if the right steps are automated in a bad way, this could be very disruptive for the user.

6.5 Challenge 5: Evaluating Smart Media and Smart Interactions

Another significant challenge may be how to study users when the way they use the internet services is rapidly changing. What may work one day, may not the next. More importantly, will we recognize characteristics of "smartness" when we see them? Borrowing ideas from McLuhan [26] on evaluation of media, we should consider: how will smart media *enhance*, make *obsolete*, *retrieve* and *flip* into when compared to social and other forms of media? Do smart media share many of the concepts of Boundary Objects [27], a concept from CSCW, which refers to how the same information artifacts are used in diverse ways by different communities? Will smart media objects be a form of boundary object? And if so, can we use evaluation techniques from the CSCW community to evaluate how smart media supports both individual and communities of users?

7 Conclusion

This chapter describes very preliminary thoughts on the concept of Smart Media, which we feel is needed to fulfill the vision of the Smart Internet of Smart Interactions and Smart Services. Our chapter does not offer technological solutions to the inherent challenges, but rather points to the socio-technical advantages that could arise if Smart Media did exist. In the meantime, there are many emergent activities in the research community that lean in this direction. Our goal is to study these paradigm changes, to take advantage of them, to learn from the past and hopefully help identify new opportunities for improving the user experience on the web.

Acknowledgments. This research was supported by the IBM Centres for Advanced Studies (CAS) Canada Research Labs.

References

1. Ng, J.W., Chignell, M., Cordy, J.R.: The Smart Internet: Transforming the Web for the User. In: Martin, P., Kark, A.W., Stewart, D. (eds.) Proceedings of the 2009 Conference of the Centres for Advanced Studies on Collaborative Research, CASCON 2009, Ontario, Canada, November 02-05, pp. 285–296. ACM, New York (2009)
2. Bush, V.: As we may think. The Atlantic Monthly (1945)
3. Nelson, T.H.: Complex information processing: a file structure for the complex, the changing and the indeterminate. In: ACM 1965: Proceedings of the 1965 20th National Conference, pp. 84–100. ACM, New York (1965)

4. Nielsen, J.: The art of navigating through hypertext. Commun. ACM 33(3), 296–310 (1990)
5. Tsihrintzis, G., Jain, L.: Multimedia services in intelligent environments: an introduction. In: Multimedia Services in Intelligent Environments, pp. 1–8 (2008)
6. Berners-Lee, T.: CERN (1989), `http://www.w3.org/History/1989/proposal.html`
7. Murugesan, S.: Understanding Web 2.0. IT Professional 9(4), 34–41 (2007)
8. O'Reilly, T.: What is Web 2.0: Design patterns and business models for the next generation of software (2005)
9. Raman, T.V.: Toward 2w, beyond web 2.0. Comm. ACM 52(2), 52–59 (2009)
10. Maybury, M.: Intelligent user interfaces: an introduction. In: IUI 1999: Proceedings of the 4th International Conference on Intelligent User Interfaces, pp. 3–4. ACM, New York (1999)
11. Resnick, P., Varian, H.R.: Recommender systems. Commun. ACM 40(3), 56–58 (1997)
12. Jameson, A.: Adaptive interfaces and agents. In: The Human-Computer Interaction Handbook: Fundamentals, Evolving Technologies and Emerging Applications, pp. 305–330. L. Erlbaum Associates, Mahwah (2003)
13. Berners-Lee, T.: The Semantic Web Road Map. W3C Website (1998), `http://www.w3.org/DesignIssues/Semantic.html`
14. Brusilovsky, P., Kobsa, A., Vassileva, J. (eds.): Adaptive Hypertext and Hypermedia. Kluwer Academic Publishers, Dordrecht (1998)
15. Berners-Lee, T.: The year open data went worldwide. TED Talk
16. Park, S., Maurer, F.: The role of blogging in generating a software product vision. In: ICSE Workshop on Cooperative and Human Aspects on Software Engineering, pp. 74–77 (2009)
17. Reinhardt, W.: Communication is the key – Support Durable Knowledge Sharing in Software Engineering by Microblogging. In: SENSE 2009 (2009)
18. Begel, A., De Line, R.: Codebook: Social networking over code. In: Proceedings of ICSE, NIER Track (2009)
19. Kersten, M., Murphy, G.C.: Using task context to improve programmer productivity. In: SIGSOFT FSE 2006, pp. 1–11 (2006)
20. Van Deursen, A., Mesbah, A., Cornelissen, B., Zaidman, A., Pinzger, M., Guzzi, A.: Adinda: A knowledgeable, Browser-Based IDE. In: Companion Proceedings of the 32nd International Conference on Software Engineering (ICSE NIER). ACM, New York (2010)
21. McGrenere, J., Li, J., Lo, J., Litani, E.: Designing Effective Notifications for Collaborative Development Environments. In: Chignell, M., Cordy, J., Ng, J., Yesha, Y. (eds.) The Smart Internet. LNCS, vol. 6400. Springer, Berlin
22. Treude, C., Storey, M.-A.: How tagging helps bridge the gap between social and technical aspects in software development. In: Proceedings of the 31st International Conference on Software Engineering, pp. 12–22. IEEE Computer Society, Los Alamitos (2009)
23. Treude, C., Storey, M.-A.: Awareness 2.0: staying aware of projects, developers and tasks using dashboards and feeds. In: Proceedings of the 32nd ACM/IEEE International Conference on Software Engineering, vol. 1, pp. 365–374. ACM, New York (2010)
24. Grammel, L., Treude, C., Storey, M.-A.: Mashup environments in software engineering. In: Proceedings of the 1st Workshop on Web 2.0 For Software Engineering, pp. 24–25. ACM, New York (2010)
25. Greif, I.: Computer-supported cooperative work: A book of readings. Morgan Kaufmann, San Francisco (1988)
26. McLuhan, M., McLuhan, E.: Laws of media: The new science. University of Toronto Press (1992)
27. Bowker, G.C., Star, S.L.: Sorting Things Out: Classification and its Consequences. MIT Press, Cambridge (2000)

Part III
Smart Services

Smart Services

Joanna W. Ng[1], Mark Chignell[2], James R. Cordy[3], and Yelena Yesha[4]

[1] IBM Canada
jwng@ca.ibm.com
[2] Universtiy of Toronto
chignell@utoronto.ca
[3] Queen's University
cordy@cs.queensu.ca
[4] University of Maryland
yeyesha@umbc.edu

Abstract. The aim of this chapter is to introduce the concept of smart services, along with three key issues that need to be resolved in the development of smart services. These issues are: Web models of smart services; base Web infrastructure extensions; the new Web infrastructure required by smart services. The chapter then concludes with a roadmap that introduces and briefly summarizes the remaining chapters in this section.

Keywords: Smart services, smart internet, web models.

1 Introduction

Smart interactions define new and advanced user models of the web at a macro level, providing user-centric interactions that leverage services and resources from multiple server sites. This approach will transform client and server interactions patterns. Today's client-server interactions, when abstracted as a web model, can be thought of as a *web-graph* with *nodes* being the web pages and *edges* as hypertext links [1].

The smart interactions functionality, discussed in Part 2 of this book, adds new dimensions to client-server interactions, specifically (i) server-initiated connections and interactions; (ii) batch-processing as in completing server side services without user's involvement (iii) dynamic-binding of multiple clients into the same connections for service level collaborative interactions and (iv) services flow such as sequential and parallel services; and likely others.

In this context, the goal of smart services is to transfer the web services from being under the control of web programmers to being in the hands of end users. The research agenda of smart services includes the development of abstracted web models that capture the service interactions, and formalization of algorithms to engineer the necessary web infrastructures to support the discovery, aggregation and delivery of services and resources from the web platform, under user control.

M. Chignell et al. (Eds.): The Smart Internet, LNCS 6400, pp. 173–177, 2010.

2 Issues in Smart Services Development

Research relating to *smart services* (the web model for the smart internet) should address the issues described in the following subsections.

2.1 Smart Services Web Models

Smart interactions impose new requirements on the web as a platform. The requirements of a high degree of personalization and dynamic adaptation (to real time situations and context) of web interactions for each individual user may give rise to new web models. Server side services needed for a given matter of concern (*moc)* and its web interaction artifacts are distinctly separate and independent. For example, the subset of services of a given *moc* for a user's interactions with a mobile phone that has GPS will be different from the services of the same *moc* when the user interacts using a workstation. Which subset of services for a given *moc* to make accessible on each kind of interaction device is an important issue. The combination of *mocs* needed for each context, such as persona and type of interaction device, and that matches the user's cognitive requirements and capabilities, is another important problem to solve. How to dynamically compute all of these based on a prescribed framework and rules is another key research question. More experiments and empirical studies will be required to derive and define efficient web models appropriate to the smart internet.

2.2 Base Web Infrastructure Extensions

What new requirements for web infrastructure will be required to realize smart interactions is a key research question. User-based service interaction patterns will require capabilities that the current standard web infrastructure simply does not support, and new facilities will need to be developed.

One key requirement is a Base web infrastructure for *server-side initiated connections and services.* This includes infrastructure for event processing, and asynchronous services such as reminders and scheduled tasks. The research agenda in this area includes methods and algorithms for efficient filtering and co-relations; models for client-side asynchronous interaction tailored to the user's cognitive support; performance requirements (e.g. critical medical events) and other issues.

Other components that may need to be added to the base web infrastructure include **collaborative services** and **data visualization.**

2.3 New Web Infrastructure for the Smart Internet

Apart from the base web infrastructure to support the supply of services from each server site, there is a need for a new kind of web infrastructure that manages services at the macro level. This new level must handle *mocs* in terms of their states and sessions, and the mapping of services from multiple server sites to the dynamic context of the user's device access at the time. The requirement is for a model of composed services that spans sites but is centrally managed for users as individuals. Some key ideas we can pursue in this direction are:

- Base web infrastructure for ***service level batch processing***: Service level batch processing involves the execution of a series of services in a distributed fashion without human interaction, so that the selected services can be set up to run to completion without human involvement. This implies that all the parameters required for invocation of the series services can be pre-set and saved to be processed at service run time. This problem poses many research challenges, including invocation patterns for service level batches. For example, batch invocation could be schedule-based, event-based, or based on detection of other user interactions. A key challenge here is the design of a programming model for service batches, including capture and collection of input parameters for service invocations. Service-level batch processing is a critical element for user cognitive support.
- ***Infrastructure to Support Dynamic Adaptation***: Support of smart interactions will need a richer model for adapting services to context than that supported by the current web infrastructure. The ability to specify the adaptation of presentation to devices and context while retaining the user's *mocs* will be a major research challenge.
- ***Inference Engine***: A web infrastructure component responsible for the processing of dynamic user context, using user rules and policies to infer the most appropriate aggregation of services for the purpose of dynamic personalization will be needed. Research challenges here include rule definition, validation, and interpretation. A model of life cycles of service use will be critical to the engineering of this component.
- ***Practical Ontology Infrastructure***: If the smart internet is to be sensitive to the real-world problems and contexts of the user, support for semantic ontologies must be a key component of the new web infrastructure. A framework for ontology infrastructure that allows for dynamic inference and tagging of services and batches will be a key part of smart services.
- ***Flow Engine***: In order to orchestrate user-level services with minimal user intervention, we envisage the need for a service flow engine which can support and manage both direct user interactions and batch services in a consistent, efficient and secure way. This flow engine will require intelligent methods of scheduling and sequencing tasks, issues that are considered in Chapter 7 of this book.
- ***Service Registry and Self-discovery Approach for Service Semantics***: Automating the matching of end-user intentions with services, batches and previous interactions will require a system that can automatically associate semantic tags with services (e.g., in WSDL) and components of services (such as the out message). Such a facility must work without involving the user directly, and might for example use reverse engineering techniques to infer and add tags.

There are many other key challenges, such as security models for the smart internet. It is not clear, for example, how to meet server side security requirements while relieving the user of her cognitive burdens. What is the security model for server-initiated services such as events or asynchronous service interfaces? What is the security model for service-level batch processing and collaborative services? How can we hide the diversity of security requirements across sites while simplifying the user's tasks?

Putting all these new web infrastructure components together into a consistent new web model and framework for web application development in the smart internet is itself an exciting research challenge.

3 Roadmap of This Section

The chapters in this section examine the problem of smart services development from a number of perspectives.

The following Chapter by Stroulia examines opportunities for smart service delivery that arise from the integration of sensor networks, service-oriented middleware and virtual worlds. Stroulia highlights the different kinds of interconnectedness that arise from large scale instrumentation of the world, and reviews the numerous analyses that can be carried out on interconnected data to support and inform decision making. She describes examples of smart services in the areas of healthcare, education, and manufacturing, emphasizing the properties and benefits of creating connections between real and virtual worlds. In particular, she describes the Smart Condo project [2, 3], in which a virtual world plays a major role.

Ye and Jacobsen then write about the evolution and composition of Web services. They characterize the traditional black box approach (where well defined interfaces encapsulate functionality and hide implementation details) as compromising the flexibility and adaptability of service-oriented applications. They then propose a grey box approach to compose and evolve Web services. In this approach, changes of internal states are exposed. They illustrate their approach using case studies in healthcare and e-commerce, and describe a prototype that they implemented.

Martin and Cordy address the problem of tagging Web services (to facilitate their retrieval and use) in the following chapter by proposing that techniques previously used to detect similarity in code also be used for detecting similarity in WSDL (web service description language) service descriptions. Their approach uses source transformation techniques, to reorganize WSDL descriptions so that they are both more human readable and better suited to analysis by similarity detection tools.

Joshi et al. then present their vision of the process by which future services will be automatically discovered, procured and integrated with the service consumer's technical environment. They suggest a number of new applications such as policy management and service procurement that will be needed to allow smart services to operate efficiently.

Due to their heterogeneity and scope for novel compositions, the flexibility and dynamism of smart services may potentially lead to problems with reliability and quality. Simmonds et al address these issues in their Chapter, describing a user-guided runtime monitoring and recovery framework for web services. They propose the use of runtime monitoring of conversations between partners as a means of checking behavioural correctness of the entire web service system. In their approach, if violations are found, recovery plans are automatically proposed and ranked after which a particular plan may be selected for execution.

In the final chapter on smart services, Villegas and Muller look at the problem of how to make the configuration of smart services responsive to dynamic environments. In their view, understanding, modeling, acquiring, managing, and controlling dynamic context is critical for implementing smart services and smart interactions effectively. Their chapter provides a survey of context modeling techniques and dynamic context management approaches.

4 Conclusion

The development of a Smarter Internet requires new kinds of smart services. This is a challenging topic and some of the research challenges have been introduced in this introduction to Part 3 of the book. Many of the relevant issues are discussed in more detail in the following chapters.

References

1. Kleinberg, J.: Authoritative sources in hyperlinked environment. J. ACM 46(5), 604–632 (1999)
2. Bores, N., Chodos, D., Huag, J., Gburzynski, P., Nikolaidis, I., Stroulia, E.: The smart Condo: Visualizing Independent Living Environments in a Virtual World. Journal of Virtual Worlds Research 2(1) (2009)
3. Stroulia, E., Chodos, D., Bores, N., Huag, J., Gburzynski, P., Nikolaidis, I.: Software Engineering for Health Education and Care Delivery Systems: The Smart Condo Project. In: Workshop on Software Engineering in Healthcare, at the 31st International Conference on Software Engineering, Vancouver Canada, pp. 20–28. ACM/IEEE (2009)

Smart Services Across the Real and Virtual Worlds

Eleni Stroulia

Department of Computing Science, University of Alberta,
stroulia@ualberta.ca

Abstract. Today, we are witnessing a new level of scale, complexity, and pervasiveness of software systems that are designed to support much more holistically complex processes. Much richer information is becoming available for processing, including raw data, proven facts and people's opinions. A multitude of interesting analytics methods is being developed to extract new knowledge from this plethora of data. In this paper, we examine some opportunities for smart service delivery that arise from the integration of sensor networks, service-oriented middleware and virtual worlds.

Keywords: Service-Oriented Architecture, Virtual worlds, Simulation-based training, Smart homes, Smart services, Data analytics, Knowledge management.

1 The "Smart Systems" Vision

Today, we are witnessing a new level of scale, complexity, and pervasiveness of software systems. Tiny sensors, embedded in our environment, houses, clothes, and bodies, measure an unprecedented variety of environmental and physiological parameters. Social-networking platforms enable practically everyone to socialize online and publish their knowledge and opinions, giving rise to a multitude of flexible communities, through which information is fast propagated. And, through high-level programming languages and cross-platform integration standards, legacy and new software systems are being integrated, increasing the efficiencies of complex processes (that can now be globally optimized) and generating opportunities for new services.

This constellation of technologies have brought about the vision of a new breed of software-based systems that will support *smart services* in a whole slew of domains, including education, health care, utilities, retail and manufacturing. Although the term "smart system" is by no means well defined, it is usually (see http://asmarterplanet.com/) associated with three attributes: (a) instrumented, (b) intelligent and (c) interconnected.

The term "***instrumented***" refers to the embedding of "sensing devices" in the environment where the service-delivery process occurs. Sensing devices vary widely in terms of their costs and capabilities. RFIDs (passive and active) are being increasingly embedded in objects for warehouse management and logistics applications. Sensors deployed through wireless networks are envisioned as the smart dust covering our planet and monitoring a multitude of environmental parameters. At the same time, wireless transceivers are being embedded in all types of electronic devices, making available their remote monitoring and control. Finally, many cell phones today include

M. Chignell et al. (Eds.): The Smart Internet, LNCS 6400, pp. 178–196, 2010.

accelerometers, GPS and compass, enabling a rather precise recognition of where someone is located, whether they are moving, how fast, and in what direction.

This large-scale instrumentation of the world around us is also contributing to the feature of ***interconnectedness***. We see at least four different types of interconnectedness: (a) data interconnectedness, (b) system interconnectedness and (c) people interconnectedness.

Data interconnectedness refers to the fact that multiple sources generate data that is related to each other and should be analyzed together. On one hand, multiple sensing devices collect different measurements of the same phenomena: for example, a person walking through a mall may be sensed through his cell-phone GPS as well as the Bluetooth-enabled store devices that recognize him as a loyal customer to email him offers. On the other hand, measurements collected by different agents for different purposes can potentially be analyzed together: for example, drug dispensation usage (collected primarily for the purpose of reimbursement from an insurance provider) can potentially be analyzed together with at-home drug usage (monitored by smart pillboxes) and physiological parameter recordings (collected by home-care devices) to produce information about patients' conformance with prescribed drug usage and the drugs' clinical effectiveness.

System interconnectedness refers to the large scale of intra- and inter-organization integration of hardware and software. Through hardware virtualization and task distribution heterogeneous computing resources appear as a single computing platform. Processing and storage capacity have long become available, practically as utilities, on the cloud. And increasingly, software is being migrated to the cloud. This migration is enabled through the web-service standards and technologies, which have enabled the integration of legacy and new software in flexible architectures that can be adapted to expose services tailored to clients' needs.

The last aspect of interconnectedness, namely *people interconnectedness*, refers to the social networks supported by the variety of social applications available today. Each individual may belong to a multitude of online social networks as a result of their membership to real-world organizations or online communities of interest or the more entertainment-oriented virtual worlds (VWs). These densely populated, highly overlapping networks are highly effective channels for information dissemination, annotation (with subjective opinions) integration and cross-pollination.

Finally, the term "***intelligent***" refers to the numerous analyses – both computational and interactive – that are possible on the multitude of information available and can inform and improve our decision making. Analytical and interactive data mining can enable the fusion of different types of data towards higher-order information that can support better – more informed, more context specific, more timely – decision making.

In our own recent work, we have been developing software to support several "traditional" service areas, including health care, education, and more recently manufacturing. In this work, this new breed of "smart" software-based systems is envisioned to support the whole service-delivery process. To that end, (a) they are built around a core service-oriented middleware that integrates systems (semi)automating individual process steps; (b) they include a wireless sensor-network that senses their environment and/or mobile devices through which users manipulate information as they perform their tasks in the context of the overall process; and (c) they incorporate social platforms, namely 2D wikis and 3D virtual worlds, to support the natural interactions of the people involved in the service-delivery process.

We are particularly interested in the role that virtual worlds stand to play in this generation of systems. Virtual worlds, where thousands of people can interact simultaneously within the same simulated three-dimensional space, represent a frontier in social computing with critical implications for business, education, social sciences, technological sciences, and our society at large. Members participate in virtual worlds through graphical representations of themselves, i.e., their avatars. In a virtual world, through their avatars users can engage in rich interactions with each other. They can build objects and they can exchange them for in-world money, sometimes exchangeable with real money. They can communicate through voice over a headset and microphone, they can use text chat, and they can communicate non-verbally with their avatars' gestures. They can navigate through the world by walking, running, driving vehicles, flying, and teleporting. All in all, they can "experience" the world through a rich variety of interactions with it, including dressing, changing their avatars' shapes, touching things, building and owning things, engaging in quests, doing sports, dancing, hugging, and kissing. This rich experience and the increased degree of engagement it enables create an opportunity for a new type of software systems that can enable new forms of system-user interaction.

It is exactly this opportunity that we have been exploring in the context of the three projects on which we report in this paper. In the *Smart-Condo* project, we adopt a virtual world as a rich, intuitive and interactive visualization platform. In the *simulation-based training* project, the virtual world provides the platform in which trainees can, through their avatars, apply their theoretical knowledge to practice complex procedural skills in the context of (a simulation of) the environment where these procedures will be applied in the real world. Finally, in our most recent *augmented-alternative reality games* project, the virtual world is serving as a means to communicate the narrative of the game through the game-world simulation and to support the game interactions among the players and between the players and the game world.

The rest of this paper is organized as follows. First, we briefly review the three projects, in Section 2. In Section 3, we discuss some of the major conceptual challenges in this research agenda. Finally, in Section 4, we conclude with some thoughts about the lessons we have learned to date and our future plans.

2 Service-Delivery across the Real and Virtual Worlds

To date, we have worked on three systems that exemplify three types of opportunities for service-delivery using virtual worlds. In the rest of this section, we review each of these systems, in terms of the service it is envisioned to provide, its technological and research background, its software architecture and the ways in which it implements the "smart systems" vision.

2.1 The Smart Condo

In this project, the virtual world serves as a mirror of the real world.

The service: The University of Alberta has established the Health Sciences Education Research Commons (HSERC) as an umbrella organization to advance the research agenda around the multi-disciplinary education of health professionals. Part of HSERC's mandate is to investigate the use of technology for enabling the upcoming technology-savvy generation of health professionals to deliver better care to their patients. The *Smart Condo* project is a collaborative project with colleagues in Computer Networks, Rehabilitation Medicine, Art and Design, Pharmacy, and Education [1, 2]. The long-term clinical objective is to support older adults and patients living at home or in rehabilitation facilities. Although these individuals are, by and large, able to live independently, they are still susceptible to harmful incidents related to physical infirmities and/or cognitive impairments. To that end we are designing a model Smart Condo in which patients can live assisted by software and health-care providers who can offer their services in an unobtrusive yet timely manner.

The background: The term *Smart Home* means a home that has both a set of sensors to observe the environment and a set of devices/actuators to improve the inhabitant's experience at home. A Smart Home can provide variety of services. On one end of the service-complexity spectrum are simple task automations invoked in response to sensor readings, such as controlling heating and air-conditioning appliances and light switches and blinds based on pre-defined thresholds of sensed temperature and light intensity. On the other end of the spectrum, more relevant to health care, the envisioned services assume more complex analyses of the readings of a variety of sensors to discover patterns in sensor readings corresponding to various occupants' activities. Then, recognition of instances of these patterns enables the invocation of automations in support of these activities – such as switching the bathroom lights when the occupant goes in and out of the bathroom in the night – as well as the recognition of exceptions that may indicate harmful events – such as the recognition of a stove burner switched on but not off.

Our Smart-Condo work is motivated by the latter type of health-care services. There has already been substantial research in this area. Among the earliest projects in this area is most likely Georgia Tech's *Aware Home,* which is "devoted to the multidisciplinary exploration of emerging technologies and services based in the home" [3] (p. 3675). This is an umbrella project under which a variety of distinct research activities have been carried out, most focusing on developing effective human-computer interfaces through which to support people with cognitive and memory impairments. The Sensorized Elderly Care Home [4] was installed in a nursing home in Tokyo and assumes limited patient mobility: it relies on transmitters placed on the ceiling and wheelchairs, and receivers placed in several locations in the nursing home, to monitor when patients leave their beds and move with their wheelchairs.

More recently, the MavHome project [5] exemplifies the potential of more complex analyses for activity inferencing. It uses a variety of sensors (light, temperature, humidity, motion, and door/seat status sensors) to monitor the state of the environment and analyzes the collected data to (a) identify lifestyle trends, through sequential pattern mining, (b) provide reminders to the home occupants, through prediction of future activities, and (c) detect anomalies in the current data, when the actual sensed events are considered unlikely according to the system's predictions. The Gator Tech Smart House [6] is yet another high-tech house, which recognizes the need for an extensible software architecture. The sensor-platform layer adopts the OSGi (Open Services Gateway Initiative) framework to maintain the service definitions of the underlying devices and make them available to application developers. A sensor is registered when it is powered on by sending its "service bundle definition" to OSGi. The application developers can write new services or use available services in this layer for their applications.

Finally, the Tiger Place [7] is among the longer and more mature projects in the area, having been deployed in 17 apartments for between 2 and 3 years. The system sensors (motion, bed pressure and stove on-off) communicate with the X10 protocol with a PC that collects the information from a home and pushes it in regular intervals to a central database that makes it available through a web application to care providers. The system architecture appears to have evolved as a by-product of the technologies adopted; however, the project is especially interesting because it involves a substantial team of researchers across disciplines, who have conducted very interesting case studies with their installation. Through these studies, they have empirically demonstrated the social value of such monitoring installations, as both the elderly participating in the program and their family members agreed that they had an increased peace of mind with the system than without. The researchers also raised the very important question of the clinical value of such installations being conditional upon the ability to correlate the sensor data stream with clinical observations by the health-care providers.

The system: The actual Smart Condo is located in a single large room (of approximately 850 square feet) in a building on the University of Alberta campus. The project was inspired by the independent-living suite at the Glenrose Rehabilitation Hospital in Edmonton, where patients who have had a major surgery stay for one or two days before they are released. During this stay, they are supposed to live independently, i.e., take care of themselves as if they were at home. Healthcare personnel are supposed to unobtrusively monitor them and only become involved when needed. Thus, the first milestone in the development of our Smart Condo has been to establish that through sensors only, we can record a precise picture of the condo's occupant, which can be unobtrusive and equally useful as if the healthcare personnel were actually monitoring the occupant through video cameras.

As part of an undergraduate course, teams of Industrial Design and Occupational Therapy (OT) students converted this area into a six-room condominium. Inside each room, they created prototypes for appliances, furniture, and other fixtures. Inside this space, we have deployed our wireless sensor network (WSN), which currently consists of nineteen nodes. These nodes contain four types of sensors, including (a) two types of motion sensors, (b) tactile pressure sensors, (c) reed switches, and (d) accelerometers. In terms of motion sensors, we have deployed six passive-infrared motion sensors for spot detection (Panasonic AMN43121) and seven passive-infrared motion sensors for wide-area detection (Panasonic AMN44121). Spaced throughout the condominium, the thirteen motion sensors cover the unit adequately to correctly locate the condo's occupant. Pressure sensors (FlexiForce A201, 1 pound) have been embedded in several chairs. They enable us to detect when someone sits on these chairs. We attached reed switches to the front door and the door of the microwave to determine whether they are open. Finally, we attached an accelerometer to the front door to detect knocking. We are now working towards integrating specialized home-care devices, such as a smart pillbox (alerting the patient when it is time to get a medicine and recording when the patient does so) and a watch that monitors blood pressure and heart rate. Note that the process of deploying the sensors is supported by an interactive tool that attempts to optimize the sensor coverage of the space [8].

The incoming stream of raw readings is inspected to recognize instances of patterns indicative of interesting activities in the condo. Currently these patterns are still user defined, not discovered through mining. For example, a sequence of motion-sensor readings that have appeared within a short time window are triangulated to recognize a person's location in the condo. Readings from switches are interpreted as specific interactions of the occupant with the appliances on which the switches are installed: for example, a switch can be either on or off which implies that the microwave door is either open or closed.

The sensor readings and the higher-order information extracted through the inspection of the sensor-data stream, such as the occupant's location for example, are archived in a database and is subject to further analyses. For example, based on two subsequent recorded locations and an architectural diagram of the condo and its furnishings, a path planner is invoked to infer a trajectory of how exactly the occupant moved in the space to go from the first location to the next. This information can potentially be clinically relevant as an indicator of overall daily activity.

The server exposes the collected information through a set of REST [9] APIs. To date, we have developed three clients. The first two were developed in the context of the SensorGIS project [10] that focused primarily on analyzing outdoor wireless sensor networks: one displays interactive plots of the sensor readings, through which users can visually explore data trends and statistics; the second is a wiki through which they can annotate interesting readings with their observations. The second Smart-Condo client is based on Second Life. It is composed of a conversion utility that (semi)automatically turns a 2D blueprint of a home into a 3D model of the space in Second Life, and an automated character module that controls the occupant's avatar to reflect the occupant's movements and actions in the real world.

Our use of Second Life as a means of visualizing the activities of the Smart Condo occupant is motivated by several considerations. First it enables an intuitive comparison of the correctness of the system inferences against the video recording of the space, which was the first milestone of our project. In Figure 1, a top-down view of the Second-Life Smart Condo is shown next to a camera-recorded view of the front area of the space. Through the juxtaposed views, one can see that the person's location in the video recorded image and the avatar's location in the Second-Life visualization are quite close to each other. Video recording provides a very precise record of the occupant's life but it raises many challenges, both technical with respect to storage requirements and information extraction, as well as social, around privacy. The Second Life visualization is generated through the sensor data-stream analysis and need not be stored as it can be regenerated upon demand. At the same time, it provides an intuitive interface for health professionals and family members alike, who can be aware of the occupant's activities as opposed to simply being alerted to exceptional problematic events. Even if health professionals and family members want to only be alerted upon such events, the Second-Life visualization – regenerated upon demand – can potentially provide more context about the person's activities before the event of interest. Finally, we envision Second Life will be useful, not simply as a visualization environment, but also as a bidirectional communication platform between the Smart-Condo occupant and his/her health providers and family members. We would like to encourage the occupant's friends to visit with him/her in the Second Life Smart Condo as well as enable the occupant to visit other places and potentially develop a

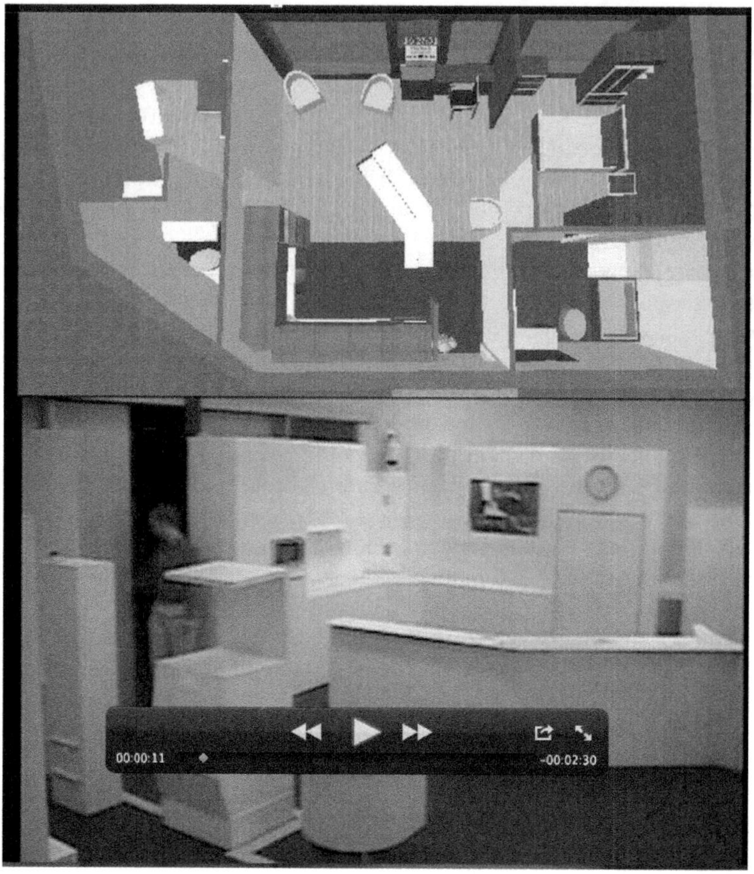

Fig. 1. Real and Virtual Smart Condo.

parasocial life in the virtual world. By no means, would we want to encourage further alienation of the elderly by "locking" them in the virtual world, as opposed to encouraging them to participate in real-world activities. However, in some cases (mobility issues, lack of family members in the vicinity, long winters), this environment can provide a rich alternative and augmentation medium of the occupant's social life.

How it is smart: The Smart-Condo system integrates a few tools that make its deployment straightforward, including support for (semi)automatically building the home's 3D model from its architectural drawings, and an interactive tool for deciding the sensors' placement. In this manner, we were able to redeploy it within a couple of hours after our space was renovated.

More importantly, it can enable several innovative types of intelligence in the context of health-care delivery.

First, it improves on the state-of-the-art in patient monitoring. When compared with video, its natural "competitor", the virtual-world view into the patient's activity is realistic and intuitive, more cost-effective in terms of required network bandwidth, while at the same time less intrusive, since personal-appearance details are not actually monitored or recorded. In this manner, healthcare professionals have a live stream of the person's activity and can be alerted to intervene at the occurrence of a harmful event. Even more importantly, this monitoring channel can be viewed as a communication channel instead: health-care professionals and family members can join the patient in their virtual home to answer questions, offer advice or simply chat, thus associating an added value to the cost of the intrusion to the patient's privacy.

Second, it provides a novel way to inform clinical practice. Sensor-based monitoring produces an information stream easier to analyze than video recordings and potentially more directly relevant to many clinical decisions. For example, our colleagues from pharmacy are interested in correlating drug-dispensation data (available at the pharmacy) with drug usage and physiological-parameter values, in order to assess the patient's compliance with their drug regimen and the effectiveness of this regimen. On the other hand, our rehabilitation-medicine colleagues are interested in examining how the environment affects the level and type of activity of their patients, in order to advance proper design standards and building codes and to come up with specialized rehabilitation regimens for their patients appropriate for their environments. In the longer run, we envision that standardized specifications of sensor-data analyses, with appropriate guarantees of information quality, may enable the collection of high-quality information that can become part of the patient's electronic health record.

2.2 Medical Simulation Training

In this activity, the virtual world is viewed as an alternative to the real world. In the virtual world, through their avatars, users can enact the same procedures as they can in the real world: they can interact with software systems, they can act upon the (simulacra of the) objects in their environment, and they communicate with each other('s avatars). It is exactly this parallelism with the real world that makes virtual worlds ideas for training people in complex activities, where the context of the physical environment and the interaction with other people is essential to the enacted procedures.

The service: Our work on medical-simulation training in a virtual world is in collaboration with colleagues from Education, Nursing and Emergency Medical Services. The stabilization of a trauma patient by EMS personnel at the scene of the accident and the handoff of the patient to the ER personnel is a complex procedure. It has to conform with many rules and meet timing constraints and it involves the handling of a variety of devices and the coordinated interactions among several people. Training students – across health disciplines – for this complex process is very expensive; it is usually done with standardized-patient scenarios in simulated scenes where a professional actor enacts the role of the patient. A virtual-world based simulation can potentially enable the training of many more students by providing a lower-cost alternative while sacrificing little of the verisimilitude of the experience.

The background: Simulation-based training has been used extensively in medical training for a long time. Medical-simulation technologies vary according to their level of fidelity [11]. *Low-tech simulators* are models or mannequins used to practice simple physical maneuvers or procedures. *Simulated/standardized patients* are actors, trained to role-play patients, with which students interact to practice their skills of history taking, conducting physical examinations, and communication. *Screen-based computer simulators* are programs used to train students in clinical knowledge and decision making. *Task trainers* are computer-driven physical models of body parts and environments that offer high-fidelity visual, audio, and touch cues. Finally, *realistic patient simulators* are computer-driven, full-length mannequins that simulate anatomy and physiology, enabling handling of complex and high-risk clinical situations.

Virtual worlds offer a rich, immersive communication and collaboration experience and can easily be integrated with existing systems; thus, they represent an opportunity for simulations of a novel category that should be introduced somewhere between the second and third types of the above taxonomy. A simulation-based training system on a virtual world can provide the student with a safe, realistic environment in which to practice, while requiring less resources than real-life techniques such as standard patient-based training or running scenarios with actors. Indeed, several projects are currently being developed within virtual worlds, such as Second Life, to educate healthcare professionals. The Second Health project [12] simulates several key points of care in a proposed model for the British healthcare system, including a hospital and a clinic. It is not intended for training but rather for providing stakeholders with an interactive view of the healthcare model. The Ann Myers Medical Centre [13] provides a meeting place for medical educators and students, in order to facilitate educational sessions in a virtual meeting space that includes some medical equipment and screens for showing presentation slides and medical images. A similar project in Duke [14] found that nursing students expressed a higher level of satisfaction with the environment and level of instruction in the virtual world, as compared with other online learning systems. The Razorback Hospital [15] uses Second Life to model healthcare logistics and to conduct usability evaluations of new devices.

Heinrichs and his colleagues [16] described the characteristics of a disaster training system, and assessed the system's effectiveness in three virtual world-based training scenarios: individual trauma cases, disaster preparedness training, and mass casualties after a disaster. They found that the scenarios are lifelike enough for students to be able to "suspend disbelief", and intuitive enough to be easily learned. This allows "repeated practice opportunities in dispersed locations with uncommon, life-threatening trauma cases in a safe, reproducible, flexible setting." Pulse!! [17] is probably the most ambitious project in this area. Its Virtual Clinical Learning Lab is "an interactive virtual environment simulating operational health-care facilities, procedures and systems". The system has been tested in the Yale School of Medicine and Johns Hopkins School of Medicine. The technology has been licensed to BreakAway Ltd., for commercial development. Another commercial product is under development by Forterra systems [18].

The system: The architecture of the MixEd Reality Integrated Training System (MERITS) framework [19, 20] mimics the three-tiered structure of traditional web-based applications. If employs a virtual world as the user interface, a BPEL[1] orchestrated set of software processes as the application logic, and a resource repository maintaining a record of the archival data of the organization and the transient data of each service-delivery process. To date, we have applied MERITS to the development

---

[1] BPEL, the Business Process Execution Language (http://www.oasis-open.org/committees/tc_home.php?wg_abbrev=wsbpel), is an XML-based executable specification of complex processes, whose individual steps are implemented with web services. In turn, these web services are accessible through their XML-specified interfaces and may be implemented in different languages and platforms and deployed across organizations.

Expert's Scene Description

Image:

Narration: Paramedics arrive on the scene and don gloves. Two EMS staff assess and stabilize the patient transport into ambulance.

Object:

- gloves
- c-spine board

Character:

- Medic1
- Medic2

NPC:

Activity:

- check airway (Medic1 Medic2)
- checks breathing (Medic1 Medic2)
- checks circulation (Medic1 Medic2)
- pace patient on a c-spine board (Medic1 + Medic2)

Fig. 2. Scene description in Annoki.

of a simulation of the handoff scenario from emergency-medical services personnel to emergency-room personnel. The prescribed procedure, including the victim assessment and stabilization activities that take place at the scene and the information communication activities among the people involved, is documented in a set of structured Annoki[2] [21] pages shown in Figure 2. It is then "translated" by software analysts into a BPEL specification. The BPEL workflows specify the behaviors of the trainees, automated characters and objects in the scenario. The workflows of the automated characters are enacted by a web-service engine. Throughout the enactment, SOAP messages issued by the engine inform the virtual world about changes in the states of the characters and the world objects with which they interact, so that they can be

[2] Annoki is a MediaWiki-based collaboration platform that we have developed. It supports collaboration by improving the organization of, managing access to, assisting in the creation of, and graphically displaying information about content stored on MediaWiki.

Fig. 3. Accident Scene in the EMS/ER Scenario.

reflected in the world. At the same time, as the students' avatars interact with the various objects in the virtual world, relevant SOAP messages are issued to the web-service engine so that it can advance the workflows of the simulated medical procedures. A scene, captured in Second Life, of an EMS technician inspecting the victim on the scene is shown in Figure 3. A complete record of the interactions is kept, both in the virtual world and in the BPEL enactment engine. At the end of the scenario, critics are applied to the record in order to recognize problematic behavioral segments. In this manner, the student participants are informed about their mistakes when their behaviors do not conform to the specified procedure.

How it is smart: As was the case with the Smart-Condo project, the MERITS project provides intelligent solutions for its deployment and, though its behavior, it also enables new intelligent services in the delivery of education materials. With respect to its deployment, MERITS provides support to an important problem in the development of training scenarios: Annoki – our suite of MediaWiki extensions – provides a collaborative repository for easy prototyping of the scenario scenes.

Of course, the fundamental contribution of this work will eventually be its broad enablement of simulation-based training. Today, simulations presuppose the synchronous availability of a skilled professional, as the facilitator – a.k.a. "director" – and a set of costly resources, including the venue, all the required props and all the required participants. This fundamentally limits the adoption of simulation as a training tool to "rich" organizations, the development of only few typical scenarios, and sometimes within a single discipline (to limit the number of participants). High-quality virtual-world simulations, with associated tools to ease the scenario specification for domain experts, will enable the treatment of many (including rare) scenarios, the participation of multiple, geographically distributed stakeholders from across disciplines.

The current application of MERITS is the simulation-based training of health professionals. In the longer run, however, our objective is to investigate the novel breed of simulation-based training that it enables: namely, training for complex *mixed* service-delivery processes, where some activities are carried out by people and some are automated. Note that these type of processes abound in all service-delivery domains and it is a long-standing objective of service scientists – from business, computing and operations research alike – to further systematize them and increase the degree of their automation [23]. The MERITS orchestration of automated web-services with people's activities in the (simulation of the) real world enables a new style of service-process modeling and auditing. Interactive and computational analyses can be applied to the process-instance traces to identify opportunities of their improved management and potential reengineering.

2.3 Alternate-Augmented Reality Games for Fun and Learning

In our nascent augmented/alternative reality education games (AARG) work, the virtual world *augments* the real world. Different but correlated (inter)actions are possible in the real and the virtual world with consequences across both worlds.

The service: In the context of a recently established collaboration with colleagues from Humanities Computing and Education, we have started to envision a technological infrastructure for creating collaborative, educational, augmented-alternate reality games (AARGs) based on a spatial metaphor. The game players will interact with the game (a) in the real world through location-specific clues (communicated to them through cell-phones, PDAs, and possibly sensors embedded in the environment) and (b) in a parallel virtual world that reflects the real-world in some dimensions –i.e., space– and augments it in others –by including (superimposing) artificial objects and characters next to (on top of) the representations of real-world elements in the game.

The background: *"Alternate Reality Games – sometimes also called pervasive games – take the substance of everyday life and weave it into narratives that layer additional meaning, depth, and interaction upon the real world. The contents of these narratives constantly intersect with actuality, but play fast and loose with fact, sometimes departing entirely from the actual or grossly warping it - yet remain inescapably interwoven."* (http://archives.igda.org/arg/resources/IGDA-AlternateRealityGames-Whitepaper-2006.pdf) A closely related form of pervasive gaming is augmented reality. Augmenting alternate-reality games with "parallel" narratives that take place on-line, possibly in the context of 3D virtual worlds similar to those of Massively-Multiplayer Online Role-playing Games, is giving rise to a new breed of alternate-augmented reality games. Some of the features of these games include the use of physical objects, such as phidgets, to control virtual environments and the superimposition of virtual layers on top of the physical environment through sensors.

The system: PicoSafari is our first AARG prototype, designed around the concept of a virtual treasure hunt. Virtual creatures, called picos, are hidden in the real world and players can hunt them using a smart phone equipped with a camera, GPS and wireless Internet connection; as soon as the player is close to the Pico, he can see it through his phone camera and capture it. In a virtual world reflecting the game locale, players can control their avatars to look for picos on-line.

The software architecture of PicoSafari includes four components. The Layar browser runs on any smart phone such as iPhone and Android and accesses a repository of points of interest (POIs) to show the ones in the player's vicinity on his phone camera. When the player is in the outdoors, the player's location is established through the phone GPS; when the player is indoors, his location is established through QR tags red by special-purpose application running on the cell phone. One of the buildings in the game has been developed in Second Life and players who move in the real-world building leave a trace in the virtual building. A database-driven web application supports typical game functionalities, i.e., player login, profile maintenance etc. It also enables the game designers to manage the pico placement and players to access information about the picos available in the system and their properties. Finally a restlet supports the game logic through a set of RESTful APIs, including managing and accessing information about picos and players.

The objective of PicoSafari is primarily entertainment, and secondarily exploration of a locale; players are supposed to be motivated to play the game simply by their desire to capture the various picos, each of which has a different appearance, story and behavior.

A separate prototype, currently under integration with the PicoSafari, involves an indoor bicycle, instrumented with SunSPOTs, through which a player can control the movement of an avatar in an Open Wonderland environment. The game was developed, in collaboration with rehabilitation therapists from the Glenrose Rehabilitation Hospital, to motivate children with cerebral palsy to go through their prescribed rehabilitation regimens. In this game, the player's cowboy avatar moves around to gather the dinosaurs that threaten his farm (very similarly to hunting picos).

How it is smart: We envision two distinct styles of AARG game narratives. In one style, which we explore in the current game, real-world play is augmented through displays synchronized with the virtual world. Cellphones (and possibly tablets or PDAs) with realistic overlay technologies (such as http://layar.com/ and possibly projection eye-ware) overlays the virtual world (picos) with the real world. In this scenario it is the creativity of the overlay and the degree to which it engages the players' imagination that makes the system compelling. This degree of engagement is what we hope to harness in the case of the CP bike game in order to motivate the players to behave in positive ways.

In the latter style, virtual-world play will allow participants to interact digitally with the environment, allowing the impact of gaming decisions to be simulated (in super-real time) in the virtual world in order to evaluate their consequences. In this scenario, it is the power of the analytical models simulating the impact of the players' actions and the realism of the virtual world effectively visualizing the simulation results that makes the system smart.

3 Research Challenges

In our work in the above three activities, we have faced several problems; some of them technical, most of them conceptual. In this section we briefly review what we consider the most intellectually interesting ones.

Service modeling: Acknowledging and modeling the complexity of service processes is essential to supporting them with smart systems. To date, there is no conceptual service-modeling framework that accounts for all aspects of social interactions, technology and physical environment parameters around a service process. In our work with MERITS, we have started examining the service-blueprinting methodology [23].

Service blueprinting concerns itself with (a) customer actions, (b) onstage/visible contact employee actions, (c) backstage/invisible contact employee actions, (d) support processes, and (e) physical evidence. This framework is broad enough but very informal. To increase its utility, it should be integrated with (i) more traditional software models of workflows (to express the orchestration of the various on-stage/backstage activities), (ii) artificial-intelligence models of behavior (to represent the behaviors of the participants' and their avatars in the virtual world), and (iii) design models of physical space (to specify the layout and affordances of the space in which the service is delivered and to represent it in the virtual world).

Separating the layers: The integration of traditional middleware with wireless sensor networks, mobile devices and highly interactive environments such as virtual worlds poses substantial software-engineering challenges. The elementary functionalities that each layer delivers and the orchestration of these functionalities are not yet well understood and delineated. For example, a wireless sensor network can be viewed either as a (set of) untrustworthy device(s) collecting raw data, or as a computational component that collects data while also computing interesting higher-order queries on them. Similarly, the behaviors of avatars in a virtual world have information processing and communication consequences of interest to the traditional workflow middleware. The question now becomes to precisely characterize the layers within which these functionalities can be organized and the APIs through which they can be composed.

There is ongoing effort for standardization of these two layers. At the sensor-network level, there are SensorML, the OpenGIS® Sensor Model Language Encoding Standard (http://www.opengeospatial.org/standards/sensorml) and OSGi (http://www.osgi.org/). The former is XML syntax for specifying the geometric, dynamic, and observational characteristics of sensors and sensor systems. On the other hand, OSGi is a Java-specific service-oriented technology to support the discovery and (dynamic) composition of a variety of networks. The OSGi Alliance has produced many standard component interfaces for common functions like HTTP servers, configuration, logging, security, user administration, XML and many more. Plug-compatible implementations of these components can be obtained from different vendors with different optimizations and costs. However, service interfaces can also be developed on a proprietary basis.

The virtual-world layer is much more in a state of flux: new worlds appear frequently and the only recognizable standard is COLLADA (http://www.collada.org), and XML framework for exchanging assets across the virtual worlds. We are also witnessing the ad-hoc development of integration modules that aim at bridging software development across virtual worlds. For example, the Scratch4SL (http://web.mit.edu/~eric_r/Public/S4SL) module compiles scripts developed for Scratch (http://scratch.mit.edu/) into SLScript, which can be imported (through cut and paste) and executed in Second Life and OpenSim. Similarly objects developed in Alice (http://www.alice.org) and their behaviors can be imported in Open Wonderland (http://openwonderland.org/).

Managing identities: In such complex multi-component systems, the user's identity is a function of his web profiles and virtual-world avatars, tool-usage history and in-world activities, and real-world behavior (as captured by wearable sensors, including mobile devices). In order to make possible the consideration of all these sources of user information within the same context, we have to develop a transparent and flexible mechanism for managing the user's identity across platforms and systems. In our work, we have been associating the various IDs of a single user with her

MediaWiki's "user" specification. We believe that wikis offer an easy to grasp metaphor for large-scale collaboration and social networking and that MediaWiki is a flexible platform for integrating resources and supporting access to them through REST APIs.

On the other hand, the *presentity* specification (http://tools.ietf.org/html/rfc2778) is aimed at capturing a user's presence at the various channels through which he may be accessible. The purpose of this specification is to manage and reason about the channels through which one is available for communication and it is unaware of the particulars of the user's representation in the environments connected to each of these channels. It seems however possible that this specification would provide the basis on which to start building a mechanism for cross-referencing information produced through each of the various channels through which a user is accessible.

Information fusion: More platforms are becoming available for information representation. The real world "generates" information through sensor readings. The web contains factual information and opinions accessible through services. In 3D virtual worlds, aspects of the real world are modeled and simulated. The challenge now becomes to recognize the semantic overlap among these information sources, to use its redundancy to increase the robustness of all tasks that rely on it, and to fuse the available multi-modal data (i.e., data of different types) on the same process into meaningful evidence for understanding it better. For example, in the Smart Condo project, we envision correlating information about the sensed patient's activity with his blog (assuming there is one) and with the comments/findings of their health providers, in order to extract high-quality evidence on their status and better manage their care. This information could eventually become part of the patient's electronic health record.

Knowledge Mining: Much of the intelligence of these systems relies on analytics. Today's distinction between data mining (where knowledge is extracted through computationally intensive processes on a database), OLAP (where users interactively manipulate and search through data sets) and stream mining (where data is analyzed in the context of other data available in the same temporal window) is rather crude.

Finer grained categories are required to appropriately characterize (a) the quality of the available input data (in terms of precision and recency), (b) the quality of the output data required to appropriately support a specific activity or decision, and (c) the cost of the computations or user interactions that can potentially accomplish this transformation.

Explicit workflows vs. emergent interactions: Some service-delivery processes are more explicitly orchestrated than others. Consider, for example, the activities of a cashier vs. a personal sales advisor. When there is no explicit "workflow" to drive the participants' interactions, it is the environment that has to engage them and guide them with appropriate cues to make progress towards their goals. To that end, we need to better understand the cognitive mechanisms of motivation and information filtering in people, and to develop methods for endowing our systems with the capacity to motivate their users. Virtual worlds can become quite faithful and realistic representations of the real world. Thus, they stand to provide a means for learning – through simulation-based practicing – complex procedures and skills relevant to a variety of professional activities.

Scalability of the software/hardware architectures of Virtual Worlds: Today, commodity worlds[3] do not easily scale to large-scale simulated environments, with complex artifact models and many concurrent users. To support acceptable levels of interactivity and performance, they place limits to the number and complexity of artifacts included in the world and the number of users simultaneously present. The mechanisms that are currently being explored to increase scalability are (a) the deployment of the virtual world on a virtualized platform – i.e., cloud – that can be extended with computational resources[4], (b) the flexible distribution of the computational load around the management and rendering of the world state between the world server and the clients' machines, and (c) the development of specialized hardware for rendering the virtual-world state. A particularly interesting design decision involved in the maintenance of the world state is the distribution metaphor adopted. The conceptually simplest choice is that of "distribution according to geography", where all activity within a geographical parcel is managed by a single computational resource. This is a rather restrictive decision, especially as the complexity of the user behaviors in the world and the simulation of their effects increases. The community is now looking at alternative models that will allow the distribution of distinct services within a region across computational resources thus supporting and enabling this increase in complexity.

In our work, as "end users" of Second Life, we have not examined this question at all, in spite of having faced several ad-hoc limitations of the platform through which we have identified potential services. For example, we had to develop a mechanism for recursive compositions of artifacts all of which move together and can be examined through their overall container in order to support the physical examination of the various body parts of the accident victim through his clothing. We also had to develop a radio transmission system to communicate information from one area in Second Life to another far away. These are just two small examples of the infrastructure services that will have to be supported by virtual worlds, which may cut across regions and, as such, will certainly challenge the simple geographic distribution model.

4 Concluding Remarks

Imagining the future of our computational systems and their embedding in our environment and life is ultimately exciting. In this paper, we have discussed our experience with the development of the three styles of real-and-virtual service systems and the services they support (health-care delivery, professional procedural training, and learning).

These three systems are at different stages in their development. The Smart Condo project has been evaluated in terms of its "technical correctness" and we are confident about the fact that it provides an accurate recording of the activities of a person living in it. We are currently extending it with a wider range of sensors that will enable the monitoring of the condo's ambient environment (such as temperature, humidity, light

---

[3] Our experience is limited to Second Life (http://secondlife.com/), OpenSim (http://opensimulator.org/) and Wonderland (http://lg3d-wonderland.dev.java.net/).

[4] Wonderland can be deployed on the cloud http://blogs.sun.com/wonderland/entry/elastic wonderland.

and noise intensity) and the occupant's physiological parameters (such as blood pressure, heart rate, weight, glucose levels, etc) in addition to the occupant's activities. At the end of this extension phase we will conduct a second study to evaluate its clinical relevance, namely the extent to which it can support clinicians to assess patients who live in such an environment. The MERITS simulation platform has recently went through its first pilot study. Four EMTs and a physician enacted the scenario and gave us their feedback on the system's usability and their view of its potential usefulness. We are currently analyzing the collected data (system logs and focus group record) using a grounded-theory methodology to help us identify the requirements for the next version, which will be evaluated in a more controlled experiment in the end of 2010. Finally, our work on augmented/alternative reality games is its infancy. A first pilot of the augmented-reality aspect of the game, where players move in the real world and interact with their game through their mobiles (both providing information to the game engine about their locations and receiving game-specific feedback from the engine as layers augmented their mobile interfaces) will be conducted in the summer of 2010.

All these systems rely, to a greater or lesser extent, on virtual worlds. We believe that this relatively new phenomenon of general-purpose (i.e., not game-focused) multi-user distributed platforms will bring about a new phase in the computer-supported work. Similar to the way the web brought about the broad information production and sharing, virtual worlds stand to revolutionize the way we communicate with each other, socialize and form communities on line, and interact. This increased sense of "being there" and "being with the partners" will improve the frequency, quality and effectiveness of distributed collaboration and will make a whole new set of activities possible. The Smart Condo is an example of "remote monitoring and analytics" activities. The MERITS platform exemplifies "distributed interdisciplinary collaborative activities". The augmented/alternative reality games platform demonstrates new opportunities of large scale, open-ended edutainment. It is only a matter of time before many more styles of systems based on virtual worlds will arise; the opportunities are vast and exciting!

This integration of traditional software systems with virtual worlds comes with its own complexities. We have also briefly mentioned some of the most interesting challenges we have faced in this work until now. Undoubtedly, these system styles will soon be viewed as just a few points in a complex space of smart systems. And the challenges put forward will be refined and redefined as the work of the research community progresses. Nevertheless, we believe that the constellation of these technologies (sensor, service-oriented middleware and virtual worlds) has huge potential to support smart services and is rich with many interesting problems to the research community.

Acknowledgements

I would like to acknowledge the generous financial support of NSERC, iCORE, IBM and Alberta Advanced Education and Technology. More importantly, I am grateful to my students and colleagues for their intellectual curiosity, enthusiasm, sense of humor, and hard work.

References

1. Boers, N., Chodos, D., Huang, J., Gburzynski, P., Nikolaidis, I., Stroulia, E.: The Smart Condo: Visualizing Independent Living Environments in a Virtual World. In: 3rd International Conference on Pervasive Computing Technologies for Healthcare, London, UK, pp. 1–8 (2009)
2. Stroulia, E., Chodos, D., Boers, N., Huang, J., Gburzynski, P., Nikolaidis, I.: Software Engineering for Health Education and Care Delivery Systems: The Smart Condo Project. In: Workshop on Software Engineering in Healthcare, at the 31st International Conference on Software Engineering, Vancouver, Canada, pp. 20–28. ACM/IEEE (2009)
3. Kientz, J.A., Patel, S.N., Jones, B., Price, E., Mynatt, E.D., Abowd, G.D.: The Georgia Tech Aware Home. In: CHI 2008: Extended Abstracts on Human Factors in Computing Systems, pp. 3675–3680 (2008)
4. Hori, T., Nishida, Y., Murakami, S.: Pervasive sensor system for evidence-based nursing-care support. In: ICRA 2006: Proceedings of the IEEE International Conference on Robotics and Automation, pp. 1680–1685 (2006)
5. Cook, D.J.: Health monitoring and assistance to support aging in place. Journal of Universal Computer Science 12(1), 15–29 (2006)
6. Helal, S., Mann, W.C., El-Zabadani, H., King, J., Kaddoura, Y., Jansen, E.: The Gator Tech Smart House: A programmable pervasive space. IEEE Computer 38(3), 50–60 (2005)
7. Skubic, M., Alexander, G., Popescu, M., Rantz, M., Keller, J.: A Smart Home Application to Eldercare: Current Status and Lessons Learned. Technology and Health Care 17(3), 183–201 (2009)
8. Huang, J.: A Service-Oriented Framework For Sensor-Based Applications. University of Alberta MSc thesis, http://repository.library.ualberta.ca/dspace/bitstream/10048/695/1/thesis.pdf
9. Fielding, R.T., Taylor, R.N.: Principled design of the modern Web architecture. ACM Transaction on Internet Technology 2(2), 115–150 (2002)
10. Huang, J., Boers, N.M., Stroulia, E., Gburzynski, P., Nikolaidis, I.: SensorGIS - An Integrated Architecture for Information Systems based on Sensor Networks. In: 6th International Conference on Web Information Systems (2010)
11. Eder-Van Hook, J.: Building a National Agenda for Simulation-based Medical Education (2004), http://www.medsim.org/articles/AIMS_2004_Report_Simulation-based_Medical_Training.pdf (Last accessed February 2009)
12. Second Health, http://secondhealth.wordpress.com (Last accessed September 2009)
13. Ann Myers Medical Centre, http://ammc.wordpress.com (Last accessed November 2009)
14. Johnson, C., Vorderstrasse, A., Shaw, R.: Virtual Worlds in Health Care Higher Education. Journal Of Virtual Worlds Research 2, 2 (2009)
15. Razorback Hospital, http://vw.ddns.uark.edu/index.php?page=overview (Last accessed January 2010)
16. Heinrichs, W.L., Youngblood, P., Harter, P.M., Dev, P.: Simulation for team training and assessment: case studies of online training with virtual worlds. World Journal of Surgery 32(2), 161–170 (2008)

17. Mcdonald, C.L.: The Pulse!! Collaboration: Academe & Industry, Building Trust. Presentation given at the 17th Medicine Meets Virtual Reality Conference, Long Beach, CA, January 19-22 (2009)
18. Armentrout, M.: Transportation Incident Management: Using 3D Virtual Worlds to Train First Responders. Published by Forterra Systems (2008)
19. Chodos, D., Naeimi, P., Stroulia, E.: A simulation-based training framework for health-science education on video and in a virtual world. Journal of Virtual Worlds Research 2(1) (2009)
20. Chodos, D., Stroulia, E., Boechler, P., King, S., Kuras, P., Carbonaro, M., deJong, E.: Healthcare Education with Virtual-World Simulations. In: 2nd Workshop on Software Engineering in Health Care, Vancouver, Canada (2010)
21. Tansey, B., Stroulia, E.: Annoki: A MediaWiki-based Collaboration Platform. In: Web2SE: First Workshop on Web 2.0 for Software Engineering, Cape Town, South Africa (2010)
22. Zysman, J.: The algorithmic revolution – the fourth service transformation. Communications of ACM 49(7), 48 (2006)
23. Bitner, M.J., Ostrom, A.L., Morgan, F.N.: Service Blueprinting: A Practical Tool for Service Innovation, Center for Services Leadership, Arizona State University (2007)

Event Exposure for Web Services: A Grey-Box Approach to Compose and Evolve Web Services

Chunyang Ye and Hans-Arno Jacobsen

University of Toronto
chunyang.ye@utoronto.ca, jacobsen@eecg.toronto.edu

Abstract. The service-oriented architecture (SOA) is an emerging software engineering paradigm for developing distributed enterprise applications. In this paradigm, Web services are encapsulated and published as black-box components accessible to service consumers following the principles of component-based design. This however restricts the flexibility and adaptability of Web services to react to changing requirements, which are commonplace today, especially in the emerging smart Internet and smart interactions domain. In this chapter, we propose a grey-box approach to compose and evolve Web services to increase their flexibility and adaptability. By exposing the services' internal state changes at runtime as events, our approach allows services involved in service compositions to share and consume events from partner services, and make use of these events to evolve and adapt their behavior. This approach is illustrated in two case studies.

1 Introduction

The service-oriented architecture (SOA) is a widely adopted software engineering paradigm to manage the complexity of software development for distributed enterprise applications. In this paradigm, service providers develop reusable software components, publish them as Web services, and register them in service registries. By composing selected services from service registries, service consumers can quickly develop collaborative applications across distributed, heterogeneous and autonomous organizations.

Traditional service composition approaches inherit the principles of component-based design and treat Web services as black-box components. These principles hide the implementation details of services and encapsulate their functionality in service interfaces (e.g., WSDL and WSCI [1] etc.). In this way, the complexity of maintaining and interoperating services in service-oriented applications is reduced, and the business concerns of service providers are protected (i.e., service implementations are not revealed.)

However, services are different from components, in the sense that a service usually describes a partial behavior whereas a component describes a whole behavior [2]. With respect to an SOA environment, services are usually developed independently by different service providers to realize some partial enterprise application functionality. Also, often participating services are executed and maintained in different heterogeneous and autonomous organizations. Therefore, services in a service composition usually have little knowledge about their partner services except a restricted view via the partners' statically exposed service interfaces. All runtime interactions are based on these statically exposed and restricted interfaces, which may not be able to handle unexpected

M. Chignell et al. (Eds.): The Smart Internet, LNCS 6400, pp. 197–215, 2010.

scenarios at runtime. As a result, these black-box solutions are inadequate for SOA applications to flexibly react and adapt to changing application domain requirements. Applications in emerging domains such as the newly developing smart Internet, smart interactions, and Web 2.0 spaces are especially prone to suffer from lack of flexibility and adaptability due to the ever changing standards and new specifications that drive these rapidly developing domains.

For example, in a healthcare application network composed of black-box services, the interactions among hospital services and pharmacy services strictly adhere to their statically exposed service interfaces (e.g., the hospital services send the electronic prescriptions to the pharmacy services). During their interactions, the hospital services have no idea of the internal execution state of the pharmacy services (e.g., what kinds of medication are in short supply). Similarly, the pharmacy services know nothing about the internal runtime state of the hospital services (e.g., the number of patients registered by the hospital services and what the kinds of medical conditions diagnosed are). The hospital services and the pharmacy services may collaborate to work well under normal operational conditions; that is without the knowledge of their partners' runtime execution state. However, such an application lacks the flexibility to quickly adapt to changing requirements. For instance, when a flu outbreaks, the number of patients would increase dramatically, but the pharmacy services may not expect such a scenario at design time and are unable to detect and handle such a scenario at runtime. As a result, the pharmacy services are unable to react more smartly by timely and pro-actively provisioning more drugs via their own suppliers.

To enable applications to react to changing requirements, service providers may need to evolve the services in a service composition. For instance, both hospital services and pharmacy services may be re-designed and re-encapsulated to extend their original interfaces with additional query functionalities. Then new interactions are developed based on these extended interfaces to cover the changing requirements (e.g., the pharmacy services can periodically retrieve the statistics on patients and update their inventory levels accordingly). However, such a solution may be less efficient to keep up with the frequently changing requirements because service providers may need to sit down and negotiate their new service interfaces before they start to evolve and redeploy their services, since they have little knowledge about their partner services. Moreover, this approach may also reduce the reusability of Web services because the extension of the interface for a service in one application may make the service unable to work in another application with differently changing requirements (which may need an altogether different service interface).

The difficulties for black-box services to efficiently handle changing requirements suggest to provide services more information about their partner services besides their statically exposed interfaces. On the other hand, the implementation details of services should be hidden to protect the business interests of service providers. These observations inspire us to go beyond black-box component-based composition approaches to explore additional runtime information from services without revealing their implementation details. In this chapter, we propose a novel grey-box approach to compose Web services and evolve them dynamically. Our approach encapsulates the internal state changes of services as *events*. For example, the hospital services may raise an event whenever the number of patients (for each type of disease) registered with the hospital services on a daily basis changes. Such events can be exposed to partner services such that these services can make use of the events to evolve and adapt their behavior to react to changing requirements. For instance, if the number of patients treated for certain diseases increases dramatically, the pharmacy services will be notified of these events. The pharmacy services will then react to the events and adapt to increase the inventory levels for specific medication used in the treatment of the disease in advance so that the response time to supply medication in response to the outbreak of the disease is shortened.

The advantage of this approach is its flexibility and ability to evolve and adapt services to react to changing requirements quickly. Services need not be re-encapsulated and re-deployed every time some domain requirement changes. Instead, services can keep their service interfaces unchanged and simply make use of events exposed from partner services to evolve and adapt their behavior. Such event-driven evolution makes the services and their interactions smarter, that is, our approach increases the flexibility and adaptability of services and reduces the services' response time as a result of changing application domain requirements. Moreover, a service can customize the encapsulation and exposure of events for different service compositions it participates in. In this way, the reusability of the service is honored, at least to a large extent.

The rest of this chapter is organized as follows: Section 2 introduces our solution methodology. Section 3 presents two case studies based on real-life examples to illustrate our approach. Section 4 analyzes the state of the art in this area. Section 5 summarizes the work, extrapolates the potential impact of this work, and presents further research questions.

2 A Grey-Box Framework for Web Service Composition

2.1 Overview

In our model, we view an *event* as a change in state [3]. A *state* of a service is defined as a snapshot of its execution at runtime (e.g., the number of patients registered today). The execution of a service can be seen as a series of transitions among its states. The transition from one state to another is denoted as a state change. For example, the hospital service updates its state –that is, the number of patients registered today– whenever a new patient is registered. Such states are usually invisible from outside the service, and thus referred to as *internal states*. In our approach, to allow collaborating partner services to become aware of each others' internal state changes, services convey internal state changes as events for different service compositions the services participate in and publish events to collaborating partners. By subscribing to events of interest, collaborating partner services may trigger corresponding adaptations (e.g., the pharmacy service increases its inventory level for certain medications) on being notified of such events. In this chapter, we refer to such adaptations as *event-driven adaptations*.

In this model, services in a service composition can not only interact with each other through the invocation of their exposed functions (via sending messages to their partners and receiving messages from their partners), but can also publish events to their partners and make adaptations on being notified of events from their partners. Note that events are different from messages. An event is raised to convey a service's internal state change. A service may publish events to other services, but it has neither an idea about who will subscribe to and therefore be notified of its events, nor how these events are handled by other services (e.g., whether they are discarded or trigger event-driven adaptations inside other services). In contrast, a message is a part of a communication protocol among services, which mandates and synchronizes the behavior of the service sending the message and the service receiving the message, regardless of a synchronous or asynchronous underlying mechanism to transfer messages. Messages must be received and handled in a certain order by a service. A service may be blocked to wait for a message from another service, but a service is not blocked to wait for an event since services are notified of events, which they may consume by triggering adaptations or simply discard.

To differentiate from traditional SOA service compositions that support only message-based interactions, we use the term *Event-Driven Service-Oriented Architecture* (EDSOA[1] for short) to describe the type of service compositions that support both message-based interaction and event propagation among services and corresponding event-driven adaptations. Fig. 1 illustrates the conceptual EDSOA model. In EDSOA, services are published, discovered and composed in the same way as in SOA. However, in addition to SOA, EDSOA services in a service composition may also publish events to and consume events from their partners.

The novel aspects of our work lie in that services are composed not only based on their statically exposed behavior interfaces, but also interact through events from their event interfaces. This additional dimension for service compositions increases the flexibility and adaptability of SOA applications. To a large extent, our approach also respects the reusability of services.

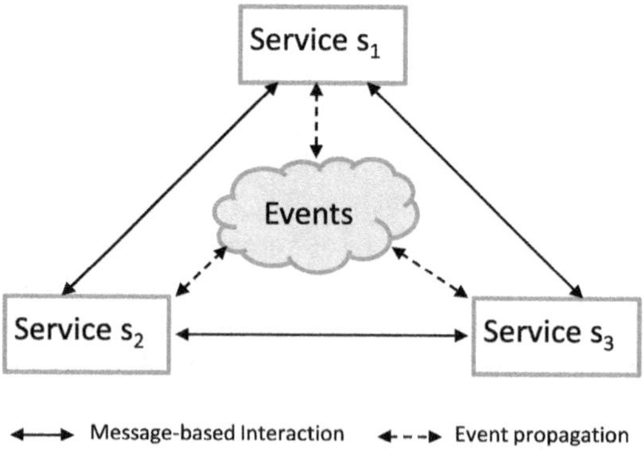

Fig. 1. Conceptual EDSOA model.

[1] Note that the term "EDSOA" used in this chapter is different from the one proposed in SOA 2.0 [4]. The difference is explained in Section 4.

2.2 Grey-Box Composition of Services

One practical concern of EDSOA is that the well-established encapsulation and modular development principles of Web services should not be breached by the integration of event-driven techniques, since events may be propagated across the boundary of services in a service composition in arbitrary ways. Therefore, it is desirable to encapsulate internal state changes of Web services as events and abstract the exchange of events among services into service interfaces as well. In our model, as illustrated in Fig. 2, a service has two interfaces: a behavior interface and an event interface. The *behavior interface* is the traditional Web service interface (e.g., WSDL and WSCI [1]), which describes the functionality of the service and its communication protocols. The *event interface* of a service on the other hand describes the types of events the service wants to expose and the types of events the service consumes from its partners.

A service composition in EDSOA concerns not only the interactions of services through behavior interfaces, but also determines the event advertisements and event subscriptions among services (defined below). The service interactions based on behavior interfaces are the same as their counterparts in SOA applications. However, the event propagation among services requires additional mechanisms. In our work, we adopt the content-based pub/sub model for event propagation [5] (WS-Eventing [1] also adopts a pub/sub model). In this model, event producers (e.g., services or software modules) advertise the types of events they will generate (also referred to as *event advertisements*); event consumers (e.g., services or software modules) subscribe to the types of events they are interested in (also referred to as *event subscriptions*). Both, event advertisements and event subscriptions can be expressed as a set of event types in event interfaces. At runtime, each event is propagated from its producer to all subscribers whose subscriptions are matched by the event's content.

Services can be composed hierarchically and incrementally to form composite services. In EDSOA, a composite service also needs to provide an event interface in addition to its behavior interface, as illustrated in Fig. 2. The composite service aggregates events from the events exposed from the event interfaces of its involved services, and

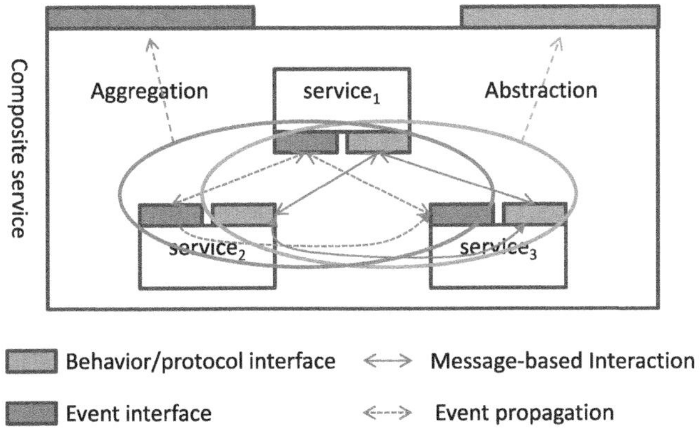

Fig. 2. Grey-Box composition of services.

exposes the aggregated events in its event interface. Similarly, the composite service may subscribe to events from its partner services in its event interface. These subscribed events will be decomposed into different events and propagated to its involved services. How exposed events are aggregated from its involved services and how subscribed events are decomposed and propagated to its involved services are determined by the business logic of the composite service.

The advantage of this approach is that services need not propagate low-level events generated inside the services to all partner services. Instead, they can customize and aggregate the low-level events into more meaningful high-level events. This not only reduces the traffic due to event propagation, but also helps to hide the implementation details of a service.

2.3 Event-Driven Service Evolution

With the support of event exposure and event propagation, services can become aware of their partner services' runtime execution states. Services can make use of these events to evolve and adapt their behavior dynamically. Fig. 3 illustrates the implementation model of event-driven service evolution.

In the model, a service is equipped with queues to store subscribed events from its partner services. To evolve a service and adapt its behavior dynamically, event-condition-action (ECA [6]) rules can be added to the rule repository of a service dynamically. Whenever the service is notified of an event matching its subscriptions, the event is put into the tail of a queue. The service can then handle the events in its queues by invoking the matching ECA rules to handle the events. For example, the pharmacy services may evolve to become aware of the number of patients reported by the hospital services by subscribing to the hospital services' events, and add ECA rules to handle the events (i.e., increasing the inventory levels for specific medication whenever the number of patients increase dramatically).

The advantage of this approach is that it increases the flexibility and adaptability of service-oriented applications, because ECA rules can be added to the services' repository

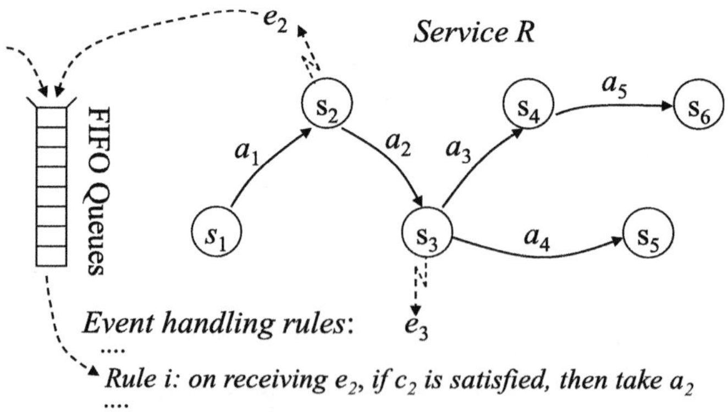

Fig. 3. Event-driven service evolution model.

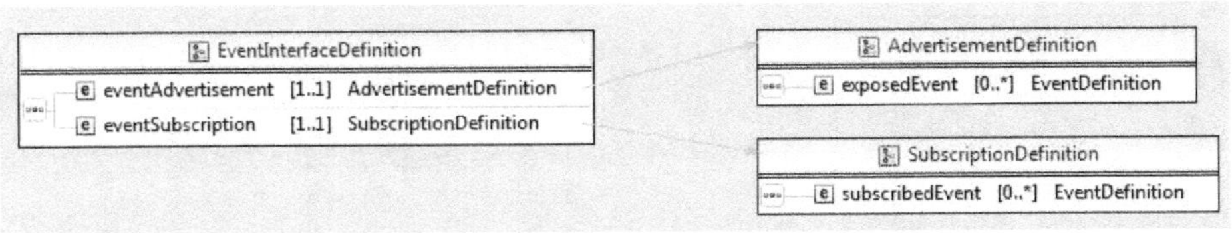

Fig. 4. Event interface description language schema.

dynamically. Moreover, the reusability of services is respected since services need not be re-designed and re-deployed; their behavior interface remains unchanged.

2.4 Implementation

As a proof of concepts, we implemented a prototype of the proposed grey-box framework. In this prototype implementation, we extended BPEL 2.0 [7] to support event exposure and event-driven adaptation for business processes. To support event interfaces, each BPEL processes is attached separated XML documents defined by our event interface language called *Event Interface Description Language* (EIDL for short). Fig. 4 describes the schema of the event interface description language.

In BPEL, users can define event handlers to handle two types of events (receiving a message or time-out alarm). We can define event handlers in BPEL to handle events from partner services at runtime. However, this implementation requires redeploying a BPEL process whenever a new ECA rule is added to this process. Moreover, different instances of a BPEL process may need different rules at runtime. Therefore, event handlers in our prototype are defined in separate documents attached to a BPEL process and encapsulated as Web services too. In this way, whenever a new ECA rule is added for a particular instance of a BPEL process, only the corresponding new event handler is deployed as a Web service, and the BPEL process and its other instances are not affected. As a result, ECA rules can be added or removed dynamically.

Our prototype implementation is built based on the open-source project called Apache ODE (Orchestration Director Engine [8]). Apache ODE is a BPEL engine for orchestrating BPEL processes. In order to support event exposure for BPEL processes, we implemented an event listener and hooked it into the Apache ODE engine. The event listener is responsible for monitoring the events generated during the execution of BPEL processes, and exposing the events defined in the event interfaces and filtering out the others. To propagate events to the partner services, we designed a pub/sub interface that can be implemented by existing pub/sub systems (e.g., Padres [9]). When an event interface is deployed, the exposed events and subscribed events defined in the event interface are converted to corresponding advertisements and subscriptions. In this way, services can publish events to and consume events from their partner services through the underlying pub/sub system at runtime. To support event-driven adaptation, we designed a rule engine and an adapter for the underlying pub/sub system. This adapter is notified of events from partner services and the rule engine evaluates whether an ECA rule can be triggered for every incoming event. If a rule can be triggered, the rule engine will invoke the corresponding event handler, which is deployed as a Web service. The architecture of the prototype is illustrated in Fig. 5.

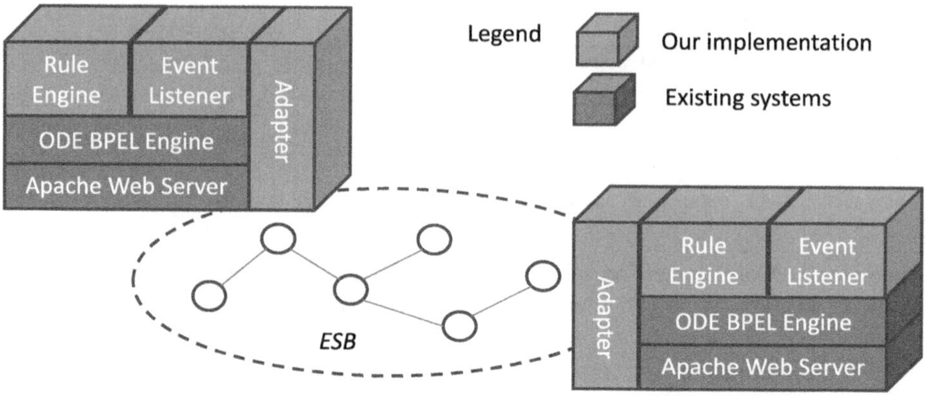

Fig. 5. Prototype architecture.

In the next section, we conduct two case studies to investigate and evaluate the advantage of our proposal and compare it to existing black-box solutions.

3 Case Studies

In this section, we present two case studies to illustrate our approach. In the case studies, we compare our solution to existing work to illustrate the flexibility of our approach.

3.1 Healthcare Application

This example is from a healthcare application, as illustrated in Fig. 6(a), where the public health center service (PHC for short) collaborates with hospital services to provide healthcare services for patients.

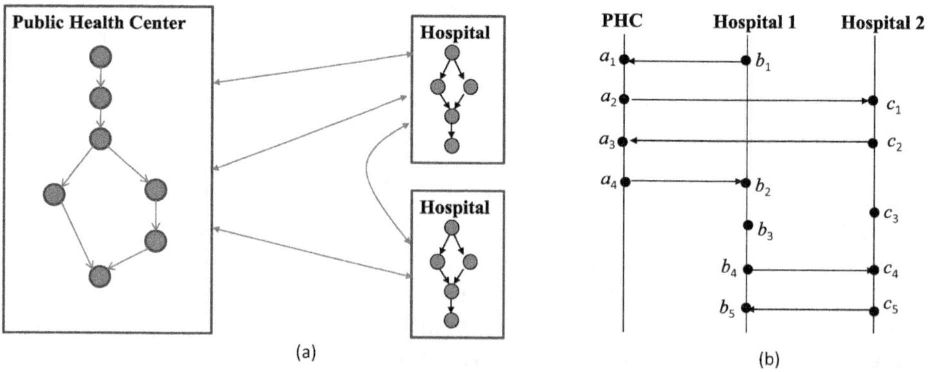

Fig. 6. Healthcare application scenario.

Let us consider a collaboration scenario in this application, as shown in Fig. 6(b). Hospital 1 sends a request message (represented as action b_1) to PHC to transfer a patient to another hospital with more adequate treatment procedures. On receiving the message (a_1), the PHC service finds that Hospital 2 satisfies the admission requirements. It then sends a patient transfer request message (a_2) to Hospital 2. If Hospital 2 agrees to receive this patient, it sends a transfer permit message to PHC (c_2), and prepares for the reception of the patient (c_3, e.g., schedules the ambulance). On receiving the permit forwarded from PHC (a_4), Hospital 1 does some preparation (b_3, e.g., physical checkup for the patient) and then sends a transfer confirmation to Hospital 2 (b_4). On receiving the transfer confirmation, Hospital 2 will arrange an ambulance to transfer the patient (c_5).

Note that this service-oriented application works well for the given scenario. To provide more qualified healthcare services for patients, new application requirements are imposed by the public health regulator, mandating healthcare services to react to emergency situation quickly (based on a specified service level). For example, in case of a flu outbreak, the hospital services should react quickly to quarantine the patients to prevent them from being cross-contaminated. With respect to above patient transferring scenario, if a flu outbreak is reported in the area of Hospital 2, Hospital 1 should not transfer the patient to Hospital 2. Instead, Hospital 1 may request remote therapy support from Hospital 2 to avoid the patient being cross-contaminated.

To address these new requirements, the services in this application need to be redesigned, re-encapsulated and re-deployed using traditional approaches. For example, Fig. 7 illustrates an implementation of these services to cover these new requirements. In order to detect the outbreak of a flu, the public health center service will monitor and periodically query the number of patients and the corresponding types of disease in the hospital services. Therefore, these services have to be re-designed and re-encapsulated to provide new operators (i.e., b_1, b_2, c_1 and c_2) in the new interfaces to support such query functionality, as illustrated in Fig. 7(a). Similarly, when Hospital 1 wants to transfer a patient to Hospital 2, new operators (i.e., a_5 and a_6) are needed in the public health center service for Hospital 1 to query whether it is risky (i.e., whether there is a flu outbreak

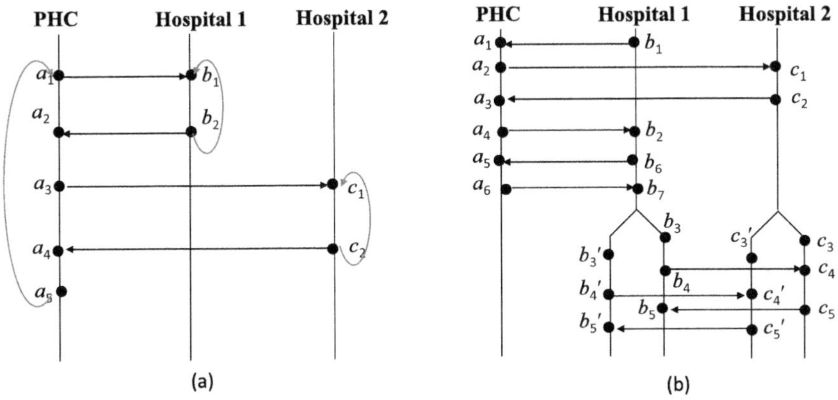

Fig. 7. Sample black-box solution.

in Hospital 2) to transfer the patient. If so, both hospital services use the re-designed functionality to provide remote therapy support for the patient, as illustrated in Fig. 7(b).

From the above sample implementation, we can observe that traditional black-box service composition solutions lack the flexibility and adaptability to handle new application requirements, because the services need to be re-designed, re-encapsulated and re-deployed. In the rapidly evolving smart Internet environments of today, the requirements of an SOA application may change frequently. Black-box solutions are unable to handle the changing requirement quickly. As a result, the quality of the services (e.g., availability of the services) is compromised. Moreover, since the service behavior interfaces also need to be re-designed, the reusability of the services is also compromised.

In contrast, our grey-box solution can address these changing requirements in a flexible way. In our solution, services expose some of their internal state changes as events and publish these events to their partner services. For example, as illustrated in Fig. 8(a), whenever the number of flu patients registered per day changes, the hospital service will publish an event to its partners, specifying the current number of flu patients registered per day. By subscribing to such events, if the PHC service is notified of an event indicating more than 50 flu patients per day (the number 50 is determined from historic data about flu outbreaks) are registered, the PHC service changes its flu alarm state from safe (i.e., $Alarm\_level \leq 3$) to risky (i.e., $Alarm\_level > 3$). Such an internal state change of the PHC service is defined as another event, a flu alarm event, and published to hospital services. On being notified of the flu alarm event, hospitals may adapt their regular flu treatment procedure (e.g., separate flu patients from others). For example, as illustrated in Fig. 8, during the preparation for patient transfer (b_3), if Hospital 1 is notified of an event e_2 from the PHC indicating that a serious flu outbreak is detected in Hospital 2, Hospital 1 will adapt its behavior (i.e., from b_3 to b'_3) to request support from Hospital 2 (b'_4) instead of transferring the patient to Hospital 2 to protect the patient from being cross-contaminated. Similarly, Hospital 2 also adapts its behavior to provide remote therapy services for Hospital 1 on being notified of event e_2.

Compared to traditional black-box solutions, the following advantages are observed in our grey-box solution: First, it increases the flexibility of the application, because the services need not be re-designed and re-deployed. Instead, only some events are defined and exposed to their partner services. In this way, event-driven adaptation rules

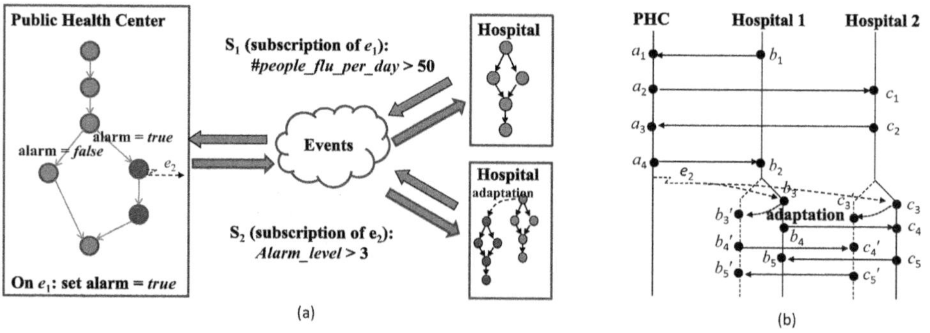

Fig. 8. Our solution.

(ECA rules) can be easily added to the application to handle new requirements. If the requirements change, services may only need to expose different events and change the ECA rules. Next, the reusability of services are respected, because the behavior interface of some services (e.g., public health center service) remains unchanged.

3.2 E-Commerce Application

This example is from an e-commerce application, where a customer with a mobile device travels to different places. The customer uses shopping services provided by merchants and pays by credit card. Fig. 9 illustrates a typical scenario. The customer uses a credit card to pay the bill from the merchants, who then transfer the payment request to the bank. On receiving the request, the bank will check the authenticity of the card holder and approve the payment if it is an authorized transaction. Sometimes, the bank may call the customer to confirm the transaction before approving the payment if the amount paid in the transaction is larger than a specified threshold.

To provide better services for customers in such a scenario, the bank may want to improve the security of its credit card services on the one hand, and provide more flexible and smarter interactions with customers on the other hand. Let us image a scenario where the customer travels to another country, and shops with a credit card. Since the payment is from another country, to improve the security of the credit card services and protect the interests of card holders, the bank may call the customer to confirm the transaction before approving the payment. The customer whose cellphone is operating under expensive roaming charges may decide not to take the call and, thus, the transaction is declined, with all the negative consequences such a situation entails. A more flexible and smarter interactions are required to resolve this dilemma. For example, if the customer travels to another country, the bank may choose to send a short message to the customer instead of dispatching a phone call. Similarly, if security concerns about the credit card are raised during the weekend or a holiday, the bank may contact the customer via his cellphone instead of his office phone.

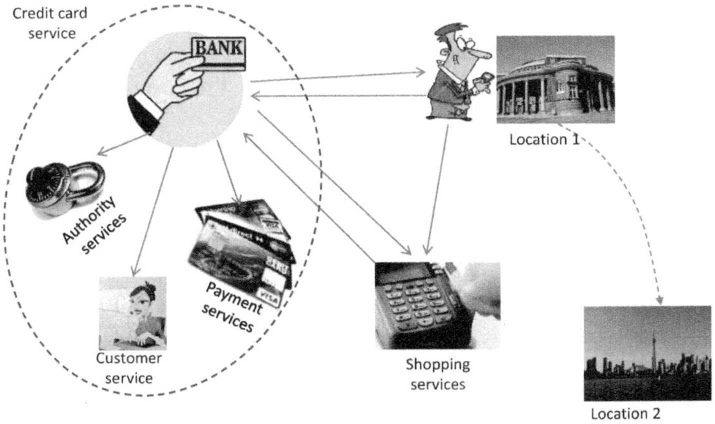

Fig. 9. E-Commerce application scenario

As explained in Section 3.1, traditional black-box approaches to enrich original services with such new functionality require refactoring or re-designing the services and re-deploying them. Such solutions lack the flexibility since whenever a new functionality is added, the services need to be re-factored or re-designed and re-deployed. This also compromises the availability of the services during the service evolution.

In the rest of this section, we illustrate our solution based on event exposure and event-driven adaptation. We show that our solution increases the flexibility and adaptability of the services for such scenarios. To implement the above described new functionality, the following events are exposed by these services:

1. $e_{location}$. In order to increase the security of the credit card services, the customer may agree to expose and publish this location change event to credit card services whenever he travels to another country. This event indicates the current location of the customer. This can be done via the GPS functionality running on the customer's mobile device.
2. e_{amount} and $e_{merchantLocation}$. These events are raised from the payment service that handles the payment transaction. These events are exposed and propagated to the card holder authenticity checking services which can make use of these events to estimate the risk of the transaction.
3. e_{alarm}. This event is raised from the authenticity services that evaluate the risk of a payment transaction. Whenever the services detect some unusual events, this event is raised and propagated to the credit card service, whose customer services will contact the card holder to confirm the transaction before approving it. Note that this event is a composite event, in the sense that it is composed of other events. For example, a payment from a location different from the current (or home) location of the card holder with an amount larger than a threshold may indicate a potential risk that the card is stolen. Therefore, this event can be defined as $e_{amount}.value > threshold \wedge e_{merchantLocation} \neq currentlocation_{customer}$. Other abnormal scenarios can be defined in a similar way.

To propagate these events, the following event interfaces are defined for the corresponding services:

1. $EI_{customer}$. This event interface is for the customer, whose mobile device service exposes event $e_{location}$ through the event interface. Other possible events may be exposed in the event interface in the future (e.g., the current state of customer: in meeting, traveling, sleeping etc.)
2. $EI_{creditcardservice}$. This is the event interface for the composite service: credit card service. The event interface subscribes to the event $e_{location}$ from customers.
3. $EI_{payment}$. This event interface is for the payment services, which expose these two events e_{amount} and $e_{merchantLocation}$.
4. $EI_{authority}$. This event interface is for the authentication services. In this event interface, two events (i.e., e_{amount} and $e_{merchantLocation}$) are subscribed to from partner services (e.g., payment services). The authority services also expose the event e_{alarm} in this event interface.
5. $EI_{customerservice}$. The customer service consumes the event e_{alarm} from the authentication services through this event interface.

Based on these exposed events and event interfaces, event-driven adaption rules can be defined to implement the new functionality, that is, increase the security and interact with customers in a flexible and smart way. Some sample rules are illustrated as follows:

1. **ECA-Rule**: *On being notified of* $e_{location}$, *set* $currentlocation_{customer} = e_{location}.value$.
   This rule is defined for the credit card service. Its intuitive meaning is to update the current location of customers.
2. **ECA-Rule**: *On being notified of* e_{alarm}, *if* $currentlocation_{customer} = location_{register}$, *call customer; else, send an SMS message.*
   This rule is defined for the customer service. The intuitive meaning is to provide a flexible and smarter way to interact with customers, that is, if the customer is traveling, then send an SMS message instead of calling him.
3. **ECA-Rule**: *On being notified of* e_{amount} *and* $e_{merchantLocation}$, *such that* $e_{amount}.value > threshold \wedge e_{merchantLocation} \neq currentlocation_{customer}$, *then raise event* e_{alarm}.
   This rule is defined for the authentication services to detect abnormal situations. Other rules can be defined to detect abnormal situations in a similar way.

In this case study, we observed the following advantages of our approach compared to existing black-box solutions: First, by making use of exposed events from partner services, it is easy to define ECA rules to support flexible and smart interactions between customers and the credit card service at low cost. Second, our solution is easy to maintain and evolve for new application requirements. For example, if a new security requirement is imposed, the services may only need to expose additional events and define new ECA rules. This exempts services from the burden to be re-designed and re-deployed. It also simplifies the design and composition of services by providing simple behavior interfaces to capture the basic business logic, leaving the frequently changing parts to be realized by event-driven adaptation rules.

3.3 Summary and Lessons Learned

In this section, we illustrate our proposal using two case studies. In the studies, new requirements are added to existing service-oriented applications. We observed that existing black-box solutions lack the flexibility and adaptability in both studies. This is because services need to be re-designed and re-deployed whenever the requirements change. Such solutions also compromise the availability and reusability of services. In contrast to black-box solutions, our solution provides an additional dimension to compose and evolve services through event exposure and corresponding event-driven adaptation. Such an additional dimension simplifies the maintenance and evolution of services, because the frequently changing behavior introduced by new requirements can be implemented by this additional dimension. As a result, services need not be re-designed and re-deployed whenever the requirement changes. This increases the flexibility and adaptability of service-oriented applications. Moreover, a service can customize different event interfaces to different service compositions and keep its behavior interface unchanged. In this way, the reusability of services is also respected.

In the study, we also learned some lessons from our solution. The additional dimension for service composition also imposes new challenges for application development. The increased flexibility and adaptability may introduce more inconsistency among services in a service composition. Services in a service composition may consume events from their partner services and make inconsistent behavior adaptations. Such inconsistent behavior adaptations may cause serious deadlock problems for a service composition at runtime which may not be expected and easily discovered.

For example, in the first case study, as illustrated in Fig. 8, if Hospital 2 does not react to event e_2 (or due to out of order event delivery), then the inconsistent adaptation between Hospital 1 and Hospital 2 will cause a deadlock, because Hospital 2 is still waiting for the transfer confirmation (i.e., c_4) from Hospital 1, whereas Hospital 1 has adapted to request a remote therapy (i.e., b'_4) from Hospital 2. As a result, both services are blocked waiting for responses from each other and thus form a deadlock.

We observed that such inconsistency issue caused by event exposure and corresponding event-driven adaptation has not been addressed in existing work. The reason is that existing work exposes only the syntax of events in the event interfaces, whereas the causality relationships among events and the effects of corresponding event-driven adaptation are missing. For example, in the industry standard Service Component Architecture (SCA) [10], event interfaces are proposed to specify event propagation among service components. W3C also proposed the WS-Eventing [1] protocol to standardize the propagation of events among services. However, the event interfaces in these standards expose only the format and syntax of events and the underlying event propagation mechanisms, ignoring how the causality relationships among events and event-driven adaptations impact the behavior of services in a service composition. With respect to the example in Fig. 8, the event interfaces generated by these approaches describe only the syntax of events e_1 and e_2. However, the event-driven adaptations in services Hospital 1 and Hospital 2 are invisible to each other. As a result, the aforementioned inconsistency issue cannot be detected based on these event interfaces.

These lessons suggest that not only the syntax of events but also their causality and effects of corresponding event-driven adaptations among services should be exposed in event interfaces. How to define and how to derive such information for event interfaces require further research efforts.

4 Related Work

In this section, we review work related to the scope of our research falling in the areas of reflection, service evolution, event-driven development, and event processing.

Software Reflection. Reflection [11] is an approach to inspect the internal state of a system and adapt its behavior dynamically. By providing programmatic access to the meta-level information about the system, the instructions of the system can be revised at runtime. Services can be implemented with reflection-oriented programming to adapt their behavior dynamically. However, this is impractical for a composite service composed of services from different organizations, because the exposure of the services' meta-level information may reveal proprietary implementation details. Our approach only needs to expose the internal runtime states of services as events and no meta-level information or other details about the implementation of services is required and revealed. The kinds of state changes revealed by events are left under the control of the service designer.

Service Evolution. The issue of service evolution has been addressed by many researchers. Casati *et al.* [12] proposed approaches to modify process descriptions and manage ongoing process instances whose description has been modified. Aalst and Basten [13] proposed to evolve services based on inheritance of workflows. A similar approach was proposed by Schrefl *et al.* [14] to evolve a class from its supertype class. All these approaches evolve services by extending or revising their behavior interfaces. Our work complements this work by evolving services from another dimension leaving the behavior interfaces unchanged.

Event-driven SOA and Event-driven BPM. The concept of "Event-driven SOA", also known as SOA 2.0, has been proposed in the community [4]. However, the meaning of this concept is different from the term "EDSOA" proposed in our work. The "Event-driven SOA" concept is proposed from the perspective of event-based business process execution and collaboration. The purpose is to define and trigger business applications based on event-driven rules instead of describing the business logic in a procedural manner. The advantage is that business applications can be executed dynamically and can react quickly to changing requirements. However, the approach proposed in our work is to provide an additional dimension to procedure-based business collaboration based on event exposure and event-driven adaptation. This additional dimension allows services to be composed and evolved in a grey-box manner. The purpose is to increase the flexibility and adaptability of SOA applications.

On the other hand, event-driven business process management has been widely adopted in enterprise applications due to the needs for increased flexibility and adaptability of business processes [15,16,17,3,18,19,20,21]. This requires effectively integrating business logic with the generation, exposure, propagation, detection and handling of events in business applications. Frei *et al.* [22] proposed to use aspect-oriented program (AOP for short) techniques to extract and expose events from legacy enterprise applications. Developers can make use of these events for refactoring the legacy applications. In addition, industry standards like BPEL [7] also support two kinds of events, namely a timeout alarm and the receiving of a message, which however are local to a BPEL process and are not propagated to other partners. The notification mechanism in BPEL is similar to event notification, but it is based on messages. BPEL processes interact through messages only. In our work, we differentiate message exchange and event propagation. More general events are supported and they can be propagated among services to support dynamic service evolution and behavior adaptation. In the SCA specification [10], events can be propagated among components, where event propagation is governed by the WS-Eventing protocol [1]. However, the causal relations between events and the effects of event-driven adaptation inside a service are not exposed in these interfaces. As a result, these event interfaces cannot be used to check the compatibility property of services. In addition, Rapide [3] applies a top-down approach to design event-driven applications. However, the methodology to compose and evolve services based on events is not addressed in these approaches.

Interfaces for services and components. In component-based development, interfaces are used to abstract the functionality of components and encapsulate their access points. The composition of components should conform to the requirements specified in their interfaces. Different interfaces may specify different requirements. For example, Beyer *et al.* [23] proposed to specify three kinds of constraints in Web service interfaces, namely signature constraints, consistency constraints, and protocol constraints. These constraints define the correctness requirements for syntax level, functionality level and collaboration level of a service. Alfaro and Henzinger [24] proposed to describe interfaces as automata to capture temporal aspects of constraints. Their approach provides a type system to check the compatibility of interface modules based on game theory. Scalability is a major concern for compatibility checking based on interface automata. To solve this problem, Emmi *et al.* [25] proposed a modular verification approach based on assume-guarantee rules. However, the effectiveness of this approach depends on how to derive the appropriate assumption for each model. The event interface proposed in our work is different from existing service interfaces. The difference is that message-styled communication is used to connect service interfaces based on message names, whereas the asynchronous content-based pub/sub event propagation model is adopted for event interfaces in our approach. In addition, interfaces of components in reactive systems [26] usually include only the input and output signals of the components, and the effects of the signal handling are left to the behavior description of the component. This is not feasible in Web services because the implementation of services is usually invisible to others. On the other hand, many equivalence relationships between two processes are defined in process algebras (e.g., CSP) [27]. These equivalence relationships can be used to derive interfaces from service implementations under different equivalence semantics. However, these relationships cannot be applied to derive event interfaces for Web services because they are based on synchronous message-based communication.

Event Processing Techniques. Currently, many middleware systems have been proposed to support event processing. Representative ones include content-based pub/sub systems [5,28,9], which can be used to store and deliver events from where they are produced to where they are consumed. In addition, some of these systems may support the processing of complex events (e.g., composite subscriptions [29]). Fiege *et al.* [30] further proposed to scope pub/sub applications to increase the flexibility. Our work supports event aggregation and decomposition for a composite service. More complex event processing can be supported by integrating new services implementing such complex event processing.

5 Conclusions and Future Work

In this chapter, we proposed a grey-box approach to compose and evolve Web services. Our approach is based on events specified in event interfaces which complement the traditional behavior interfaces of services as an additional dimension. Events capture the internal state change of a service. The advantage is that a service can make use of this information to better adapt its behavior to the internal state changes of its partner services. This increases the flexibility and adaptability of service-oriented applications to react faster to changing application requirements. This also honors the reusability of services.

However, the additional dimension for service compositions also imposes new challenges for application development. The increased flexibility and adaptability may introduce more inconsistency among services of a composition. Services in a service composition may consume events from their partner services and make inconsistent behavior adaptations. Such inconsistent behavior adaptations may cause serious deadlock problems for a service composition at runtime which may not be expected and easily discovered. In addition, a subsequent evolution with new behavior adaption inside a legacy service may also introduce deadlocks into an originally deadlock-free service composition. Therefore, the detection of deadlock and the guarantee of deadlock-free evolution of services augmented with events is an important research question. In particular, the exposure of events in event interfaces and the kind of information required for this exposure are also important concerns. We plan to study how to derive some equivalence relationships to guide the evolution of a service without violating its original properties.

Another research question pertains to the aggregation and decomposition of events inside a composite service, especially for a top-down design of a service composition. This should be reflected in a service composition specification. A methodology to consider both the behavioral aspects and event aggregation is needed. Moreover, new approaches are needed to discover and select services based on the additional dimension enabled through event exposure and event propagation. Other research questions such as a service quality-of-service, service maintainability, and service transactions may need new attention and require rethinking in sight of event exposure.

In addition, we also plan to utilize the additional information provided by event exposure to test and debug service compositions. Services in a service composition are usually tested by using black-box testing approaches due to the unavailable implementation details of services. Our approach sheds light on testing service compositions in a grey-box manner, that is, test cases may be designed to cover the service implementation in a more accurate way with the help of exposed events in the service's event interface. Moreover, these exposed events may also be helpful to diagnose faults in a service composition. We plan to study how to expose events and how to derive test cases to test service composition based on event exposure.

This work has the potential to impact the way services are developed and composed. The work opens a door for service developers and service consumers to rethink services (which have been viewed as black-box components for a long time) and the way services are composed (usually viewed as nothing new but a special case of component composition). In our work, a service is no longer a simple and "dead" black-box component with a statically exposed interface, but a "live" component that not only exposes static interfaces but also consumes and exposes dynamic information and dynamically adapts its behavior. The exposure of additional information as events will be helpful to SOA applications in many ways, such as contribute to their flexibility, adaptability, evolution, testing, and debugging and so on. The solutions to the aforementioned research issues may also encourage some current industry standards (such as WSDL and SCA) to further integrate events and event-related information into their specifications.

Acknowledgments

This research was in part supported by IBM's Center for Advanced Studies, an IBM Faculty Award, a Discovery Accelerator Supplement and a Discovery grant from the Natural Sciences and Engineering Research Council of Canada, an Ontario Early Researcher Award, and a grant from the Mathematics of Information Technology and Complex Systems research network.

References

1. W3C: WSCI, WSDL, WS-Eventing, http://www.w3.org
2. Broy, M., Krüger, I.H., Meisinger, M.: A formal model of services. ACM TOSEM 16(1), 5 (2007)
3. Luckham, D.C.: The Power of Events: An Introduction to Complex Event Processing in Distributed Enterprise Systems. Addison-Wesley, Boston (2001)
4. Wiki: SOA 2.0, http://en.wikipedia.org/wiki/Event-driven_SOA
5. Carzaniga, A., Rosenblum, D.S., Wolf, A.L.: Design and evaluation of a wide-area event notification service. ACM TOCS 19(3), 332–383 (2001)
6. Act-Net Consortium, C.: The active database management system manifesto: a rulebase of ADBMS features. SIGMOD Rec. 25(3), 40–49 (1996)
7. OASIS: BPEL 2.0, http://docs.oasis-open.org/wsbpel/2.0/wsbpel-v2.0.html
8. Apache: Apache orchestration director engine, http://ode.apache.org/index.html
9. Systems research group, M.: Padres, http://research.msrg.utoronto.ca/Padres/
10. OSOA: SCA event processing, http://www.osoa.org/
11. Smith, B.C.: Procedural Reflection in Programming Languages. PhD thesis, MIT (1982)
12. Casati, F., Ceri, S., Pernici, B., Pozzi, G.: Workflow evolution. In: Thalheim, B. (ed.) ER 1996. LNCS, vol. 1157, pp. 438–455. Springer, Heidelberg (1996)
13. van der Aalst, W.M.P., Basten, T.: Inheritance of workflows: an approach to tackling problems related to change. TCS 270(1-2), 125–203 (2002)
14. Schrefl, M., Stumptner, M.: Behavior-consistent specialization of object life cycles. ACM TOSEM 11(1), 92–148 (2002)
15. Chau, T., Muthusamy, V., Jacobsen, H.A., Litani, E., Chan, A., Coulthard, P.: Automating sla modeling. In: CASCON 2008, pp. 126–143. ACM, New York (2008)
16. Hu, S., Muthusamy, V., Li, G., Jacobsen, H.A.: Distributed automatic service composition in large-scale systems. In: DEBS 2008, pp. 233–244. ACM, New York (2008)
17. Li, G., Muthusamy, V., Jacobsen, H.A.: A distributed service-oriented architecture for business process execution. ACM Trans. Web 4(1), 1–33 (2010)
18. Muthusamy, V., Jacobsen, H.A.: BPM in cloud architectures: Business process management with SLAs and events. In: BPM 2010, Hoboken, New Jersey, USA, pp. 5–10. Springer, Heidelberg (2010)
19. Muthusamy, V., Jacobsen, H.A., Coulthard, P., Chan, A., Waterhouse, J., Litani, E.: Sla-driven business process management in soa. In: CASCON 2007, pp. 264–267. ACM, New York (2007)
20. Papazoglou, M.P., Heuvel, W.J.: Service oriented architectures: approaches, technologies and research issues. The VLDB Journal 16(3), 389–415 (2007)

21. Yan, W., Hu, S., Muthusamy, V., Jacobsen, H.A., Zha, L.: Efficient event-based resource discovery. In: DEBS 2009, pp. 1–12. ACM, New York (2009)
22. Frei, A., Popovici, A., Alonso, G.: Eventizing applications in an adaptive middleware platform. IEEE DSO 6(4), 1 (2005)
23. Beyer, D., Chakrabarti, A., Henzinger, T.A.: Web service interfaces. In: WWW 2005, pp. 148–159. ACM, New York (2005)
24. de Alfaro, L., Henzinger, T.A.: Interface automata. In: ESEC/FSE-9, pp. 109–120. ACM, New York (2001)
25. Emmi, M., Giannakopoulou, D., Păsăreanu, C.S.: Assume-guarantee verification for interface automata. In: Cuellar, J., Maibaum, T., Sere, K. (eds.) FM 2008. LNCS, vol. 5014, pp. 116–131. Springer, Heidelberg (2008)
26. Harel, D., Lachover, H., Naamad, A., Pnueli, A., Politi, M., Sherman, R., Shtul-Trauring, A.: Statemate: a working environment for the development of complex reactive systems. In: ICSE 1988, pp. 396–406. IEEE Computer Society Press, Los Alamitos (1988)
27. Bergstra, J.A.: Handbook of Process Algebra. Elsevier Science Inc., New York (2001)
28. Fabret, F., Jacobsen, H.A., Llirbat, F., Pereira, J., Ross, K.A., Shasha, D.: Filtering algorithms and implementation for very fast publish/subscribe systems. In: SIGMOD 2001, pp. 115–126 (2001)
29. Li, G., Jacobsen, H.A.: Composite subscriptions in content-based publish/subscribe systems. In: Alonso, G. (ed.) Middleware 2005. LNCS, vol. 3790, pp. 249–269. Springer, Heidelberg (2005)
30. Fiege, L., Mezini, M., Mühl, G., Buchmann, A.P.: Engineering event-based systems with scopes. In: Magnusson, B. (ed.) ECOOP 2002. LNCS, vol. 2374, pp. 309–333. Springer, Heidelberg (2002)

Towards Web Services Tagging by Similarity Detection

Doug Martin and James R. Cordy

School of Computing, Queen's University
{doug,cordy}@cs.queensu.ca

Abstract. A challenge for the Smart Internet will be the automated tagging of equivalent or similar services, both in terms of domain semantics and service protocols, in support of efficient discovery and selection of relevant alternative services for the current matters of concern. Code similarity detection is an established technique that can be brought to bear on this problem if service descriptions can be partitioned into appropriate units for comparison. Unfortunately, specifications written in Web Service Description Language (WSDL) are poorly structured for this purpose, with relevant information for each service operation scattered widely over WSDL service descriptions. In this work we describe a first step in leveraging code similarity techniques to identify and tag similarities in WSDL descriptions of web service operations. Using source transformation techniques, we describe a method for reorganizing WSDL descriptions such that they are both more human readable and better suited to analysis by similarity detection tools. We demonstrate our method by the automated identification and grouping of similar service operations using clone detection in two example WSDL systems.

Keywords: WSDL, web services, clone detection.

1 Introduction

The internet service infrastructure of the future will require rapid identification of alternative services, operations and providers, in order to allow a greater level of user-centric automation that can rapidly adapt to a user's current matters of concern. While hand-categorization of services and operations can be used to tag new services as they are developed, adaptation of the large numbers of existing services and actions will require automation to assist in categorizing and tagging them. Moreover, as new ontologies are developed and new semantic domains are added to the service portfolio, automation will be essential in adapting and tagging existing services to integrate with these new views. To assist in this automation, an important part of the Smart Internet initiative is the rapid identification and tagging of web services that are similar in semantic domain or service protocol [1].

Fortunately, code similarity tools, or *clone detectors* [2] provide a mature, scalable similarity detection technology that can be leveraged to assist in this

M. Chignell et al. (Eds.): The Smart Internet, LNCS 6400, pp. 216–233, 2010.

problem. Our aim in this work is to leverage these techniques to analyze service descriptions, written in WSDL (Web Service Description Language), for similarities that can then be more easily classified and tagged. However, WSDL service descriptions usually contain unified descriptions of all of the operations that the web service has to offer, with pieces of each operation scattered over different parts of the file. This not only makes the operation descriptions difficult to read, but it also presents a challenge for clone detection tools.

In this chapter we address this problem by utilizing source transformation in TXL [3] to restructure WSDL service descriptions by consolidating and separating complete standalone operation descriptions, which can then be analyzed by clone detection techniques to cluster them into sets of semantically and structurally similar operations. We then run a sample set of consolidated WSDL operations with NiCad [4], a clone detection tool, to evaluate the generated results and gather insight into ways we can improve our tool.

The remainder of this chapter is structured as follows. In Section 2 we review previous approaches to service similarity detection and provide a background in the code clone detection and source transformation systems on which our method is based. Section 3 reviews the basic structure of WSDL service descriptions and explains why this structure makes it difficult to detect similarities and relationships between services and operations. Section 4 introduces our consolidation method using a running example. Section 5 presents the results of an initial experiment looking for similarities among the thousands of operations in two sets of several different WSDL service descriptions. Finally, Section 6 outlines the observed strengths and limitations of our work in its current state, and plans our next steps.

2 Related Work

Our research attempts to solve a relatively new problem (finding and tagging similar web services) by approaching it from a well known problem (clone detection) using a method for manipulating code (source transformation). In this section we will: discuss some current attempts to find similar web services and how they differ from our approach (Section 2.1); give a brief background of clone detection and the clone detector we used to evaluate our consolidation method (Section 2.2); and give a brief overview of source transformation, specifically the TXL language (Section 2.3).

2.1 Service Similarity Detection

Much research has been done to identify related services from a repository of WSDL descriptions. The focus has been on developing new tools built specifically to handle the intricacies of the language.

Dong et al [5] developed a search engine called Woogle that goes beyond the conventional keyword search and provides the user with a similarity search. Once a user finds a web service that is close to meeting their needs, they may search for services that are similar to it, take similar inputs, or compose with the given service. At the heart of the algorithm supporting this similarity search is a clustering algorithm that groups the service's parameters into semantically similar concepts. This clustering algorithm uses the heuristic that parameters that occur together often tend to express the same concepts.

Syeda-Mahmood et al. [6] have explored the use of domain-independent and domain-specific ontologies when comparing service descriptions. Specifically, they looked at large company mergers or acquisitions where each company has its own set of web services that do similar things, but use different terminology. They used a number of techniques to aid in the search. First, they used word tokenization to separate multi-term parameter names (e.g. PartNumber) into its individual terms (e.g. PartNumber becomes "Part" and "Number"). Then, they used part-of-speech tagging and filtering to identify noun phrases and adjectives. Next, they expanded abbreviations (e.g. Cust becomes Customer). Finally, they used a synonym search with a thesaurus like WordNet to find synonyms for each word and assigned a similarity score based on how close the words were. They then use a matching algorithm to produce a ranked list of matching services and tested it using a domain-independent ontology, a domain-specific ontology, and none at all. What they found was that using a domain-specific ontology improved precision over a domain-independent ontology.

Stroulia et al. [7] developed a suite of methods designed to aid developers in the search for a suitable web service operation. They implemented 3 methods for this. First, when only a textual description of a service is available, they use a vector-space model to match the description with the text inside the service's `<documentation>` tags. A variation of this method uses WordNet to find synonyms (words with similar meaning), hypernyms (word parent), hyponyms (word children), and sibling senses (e.g. am, are, is) for the textual descriptions and apply scores based on how close they match. Second, when a stub of a web service is available and a structurally similar service is desired, they do structure matching. In this method, they compare data types, messages and operations of all pair-wise combinations from the source and target services. Finally, when a stub of a web service is available and a semantically similar service is desired, they do semantic structure matching. This method is an extension of the structure matching described above except instead of looking for compatible type mappings to find a syntactically similar service, they look for semantically compatible mappings to try to find a semantically similar service. This suite of methods solve the problem of service discovery based on different stages in a development process.

The main difference between the above 3 approaches and our own is that they all have designed tools specifically for finding similarities in WSDL descriptions. What we propose is a method of transforming WSDL descriptions for use in already available similarity detection tools and algorithms, like clone detection, rather than build new tools to specifically handle WSDL.

The other difference is that all 3 of these are designed from the perspective of finding a target service that is similar to a source service provided by the user. What we would like to do is organize and tag a large repository of WSDL descriptions into meaningful groups for better service discovery.

2.2 Clone Detection

Reusing a code fragment by copying and pasting with or without minor modifications is a technique frequently used by programmers, and thus software systems often have duplicate fragments of code in them. Such duplicated fragments are called *code clones* or simply *clones*. Code clones have been shown to have a significant software maintenance impact [8], and over the past decade several techniques and tools for detecting code clones have been proposed [2], called *clone detectors*.

While designed for finding copy-pasted fragments of source code, clone detectors have also been used for a range of other applications where similarity is an issue, such as plagiarism analysis and GPL auditing. In our work we leverage the generality of the NiCad clone detector [4] to identify similarities between service operations. NiCad uses an efficient and scalable hybrid parsing and text comparison technique based on the longest common subsequence (LCS) algorithm to identify "near-miss" clones, those fragments that are very similar but perhaps not identical. In our case, we apply NiCad to consolidated WSDL service operations to identify operations that are similar in functionality, vocabulary or context.

2.3 Source Transformation

Source transformation systems use rewriting rules to describe and automatically implement complex manipulations of source code. TXL [3] is a programming language explicitly designed for describing such source transformations, which has been used for a wide range of applications in academia and industry [9]. TXL's grammar-based paradigm makes the expression of structural changes both clear and efficient. In this work we use TXL to implement the consolidation of WSDL service operations as a set of rewriting rules that restructure the WSDL source code to consolidate all the dependencies and remote references in an operation description into the description itself, so that our similarity comparisons can be made in full context.

3 Web Service Description Language (WSDL)

Before we begin, it is important to understand how a web service is defined. WSDL files are XML based, which means that the only information that we have about a web service operation is the structure of its parameters along with their names. This is what makes finding similar services such a difficult problem.

In this section, we review the structure and elements of a WSDL service description and what makes it difficult to detect similarities and relationships between them. We will also introduce an example service that will be used as a running example throughout the remainder of this chapter.

3.1 Example

As an illustrative example, we use a simple hotel reservation service (Figure 1). This service consists of one operation, "ReserveRoom," defined in the portTypes section, which takes a Payment element and Room element as parameters. These two elements' types are defined further below in the types section.

3.2 Anatomy of a WSDL Description

A WSDL file contains a description of one or more operations provided by a particular web service. These descriptions are broken up into pieces and grouped based on what aspect of the operation they define. These pieces, when linked together (Figure 2), form the description of the operation.

The pieces are organized into 5 groups: types, messages, port types, bindings, and services.

Types. The types section contains type definitions for exchanging data between a requesting client and the web service using the XML Schema language. It may contain one or more of these schema, and they can be defined locally (i.e., embedded in the types section), or externally by referencing a ".xsd" file. The schema may define complexTypes, which are essentially objects that contain other elements. For example, in our simple hotel reservation service, we define a type called 'Room' containing two integers to represent the room ID and number of beds, and a boolean to represent whether the room is smoking or non-smoking. The schema also defines elements that are referenced by parts in the messages section.

Messages. Messages define the data elements corresponding to the input, output and faults of each operation. They are separated into one or more parts, which may refer to elements defined in the types section. These parts can represent parameters of the operation, but often they simply refer to an element in the types section that contains the parameters. This is the case with our example. For instance, the message named "ReserveRoomRequest" contains a part named 'body,' which refers to an element in the types section also named "ReserveRoomRequest." This element contains the operation two input parameters, *payment* and *room*.

Port Types. The port types section contains one or more operations that make up the web service. Each of these operations may contain an input or output element depending on what kind of communication takes place (e.g. request-response, notification, etc.). It may also contain any number of faults. These inputs, outputs and faults refer to messages defined elsewhere in the file. Our simple hotel reservation example contains one operation, "ReserveRoom," which has one input, one output and one fault, each referring to a message defined previously in the messages section.

```
<?xml version="1.0"?>
<definitions name="HotelReservationService"
             targetNamespace="http://myhotel.com/reservationservice.wsdl"
             xmlns:tns1="http://myhotel.com/reservationservice.xsd"
             xmlns:xsd1="http://myhotel.com/reservationservice.xsd"
             xmlns:soap="http://schemas.xmlsoap.org/wsdl/soap/"
             xmlns="http://schemas.xmlsoap.org/wsdl/">

    <types>
        <schema targetNamespace="http://myhotel.com/reservationservice.xsd"
                xmlns="http://www.w3.org/2000/10/XMLSchema">
            <element name="ReserveRoomRequest">
                <complexType>
                    <sequence>
                        <element name="payment" type="tns1:Payment"/>
                        <element name="room" type="tns1:Room"/>
                   </sequence>
               </complexType>
            </element>
            <element name="ReserveRoomResponse">
                <complexType> <sequence/> </complexType>
            </element>
            <element name="RoomNotAvailableException">
                <complexType> <sequence/> </complexType>
            </element>
            <complexType name="Room">
                <sequence>
                    <element name="roomID" type="xsd:int"/>
                    <element name="numBeds" type="xsd:int"/>
                    <element name="isSmoking" type="xsd:boolean"/>
                </sequence>
            </complexType>
            <complexType name="Payment">
                <sequence>
                    <element name="cc" type="tns1:CreditCard"/>
                </sequence>
            </complexType>
            <complexType name="CreditCard">
                <sequence>
                    <element name="ccNumber" type="xsd:Room"/>
                    <element name="cardHolder" type="xsd:string"/>
                    <element name="expiryDate" type="xsd:date"/>
                    <element name="PIN" nillable="true" type="xsd:int"/>
                </sequence>
            </complexType>
        </schema>
    </types>

    <message name="ReserveRoomRequest">
        <part name="body" element="xsd1:ReserveRoomRequest"/>
    </message>
    <message name="ReserveRoomResponse">
        <part name="body" element="xsd1:ReserveRoomResponse"/>
    </message>
    <message name="RoomNotAvailableException">
        <part name="body" element="xsd1:RoomNotAvailableException"/>
    </message>

    <portType name="HotelReservationServicePortType">
        <operation name="ReserveRoom">
           <input message="tns1:ReserveRoomRequest"/>
           <output message="tns1:ReserveRoomResponse"/>
           <fault message="tns1:RoomNotAvailableException"/>
        </operation>
    </portType>

    <binding name="HotelReservationServiceSoapBinding"
             type="tns:HotelReservationServicePortType">
        . . .
    </binding>

    <service name="HotelReservationService">
        . . .
    </service>

</definitions>
```

Fig. 1. Example WSDL service description for a hotel reservation service.

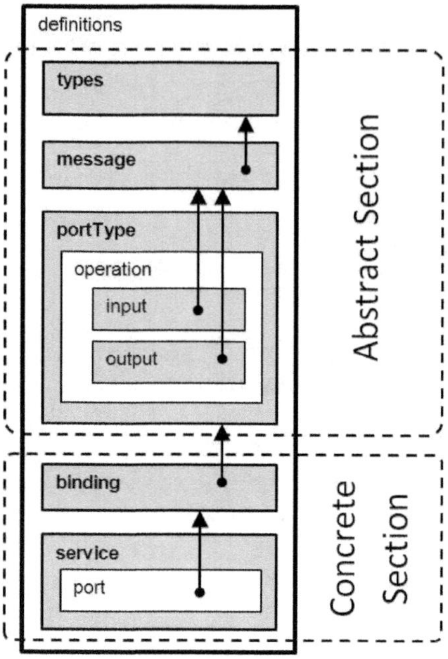

Fig. 2. Structure of a WSDL file.

Bindings. Bindings define a message format and protocol for a port type. Often this protocol is Simple Object Access Protocol (SOAP).

Services. The services section defines a group of ports. Ports define an endpoint and specify an address for a binding.

These 5 groups can be split into 2 categories. Types, messages and port types are *abstract*, while bindings and services are *concrete*. Our tool only takes the abstract groups into consideration, since the concrete groups are specific to the implementation and not necessary for comparing operations.

3.3 The Problem

The similarity detection tools we wish to use require a set of potential matches (documents, code fragments, etc.) in which to search for similarities. But what do we use for WSDL?

A WSDL description may contain descriptions of more than one operation, so using the entire file would not provide the granularity that we require. We could extract the operations from the portTypes section, but the information contained in these elements is often not enough to detect a meaningful relationship between two operations (more on this in Section 5) . What we need is a way of combining all the pieces of an operation definition into a self contained unit that can be compared with other operation definitions compiled in the same manner. This is where our tool comes in.

4 Method

As we saw in the previous section, an operation definition is spread out over the entire WSDL file. In this section, we will describe our method to consolidate these pieces into a single localized whole that can be more effectively compared to other operations for service similarity.

Our tool uses the source transformation system TXL [3] to construct a set of consolidated service operations from a WSDL description. It works by merging the pieces together to form a set of independent consolidated operation descriptions that clearly and directly identify inputs, outputs and possible faults. We can think of our method as consisting of 5 abstract phases, described below using the "ReserveRoom" operation from our example service in Section 3.1.

4.1 Phase 1: Extract Operations

The first step in the consolidation is to set up a skeleton for each operation. This acts as a base in which to integrate the contextual elements (such as messages and types) from their definitions in the other sections, and thus localize the semantics of the operations. We extract every operation from the port-Types section, which contains the operation's inputs, outputs, and faults.

Figure 3 shows an example of one such operation skeleton extracted from our hotel reservation system example.

```
<operation name="ReserveRoom">
  <input message="tns1:ReserveRoomRequest"/>
  <output message="tns1:ReserveRoomResponse"/>
  <fault message="tns1:RoomNotAvailableException"/>
</operation>
```

Fig. 3. Consolidation Phase 1: Extract operations.

4.2 Phase 2: Inject Messages

Each of the operation's inputs, outputs, and faults refers to a named message whose detailed description appears elsewhere in the service description. In the next step of our consolidation, we resolve these message references by finding the message description for each message referred to in an input, output or fault and expanding it in the corresponding tag.

The result is an enhanced operation description in which all messages are fully described inside the input, output or fault that refers to them, as shown in Figure 4.

```
<operation name="ReserveRoom" >
  <input message="tns1:ReserveRoomRequest">
    <message name="ReserveRoomRequest">
      <part name="body" element="xsd1:ReserveRoomRequest"/>
    </message>
  </input>
  <output message="tns1:ReserveRoomResponse">
    <message name="ReserveRoomResponse">
      <part name="body" element="xsd1:ReserveRoomResponse"/>
    </message>
  </output>
  <fault message="tns1:RoomNotAvailableException">
    <message name="RoomNotAvailableException">
      <part name="body" element="xsd1:RoomNotAvailableException"/>
    </message>
  </fault>
</operation>
```

Fig. 4. Consolidation Phase 2: Inject messages.

4.3 Phase 3: Inject Element into Parts

Each message itself contains a number of parts, each of which is associated with a particular data element. These elements are described separately in the WSDL types section. In the next consolidation step, we find and inject these element descriptions into the corresponding part tags, resulting in part descriptions whose element structure is fully embedded in the consolidated message descriptions.

Figure 5 shows the result of this step on our example operation. As we expand each level, we gradually reduce the dependence of the operation description on

```
<operation name="ReserveRoom" >
  <input message="tns1:ReserveRoomRequest">
    <message name="ReserveRoomRequest">
      <part name="body" element="xsd1:ReserveRoomRequest">
        <element name="ReserveRoomRequest">
          <complexType>
            <sequence>
              <element name="payment" type="tns1:Payment"/>
              <element name="room" type="tns1:Room"/>
            </sequence>
          </complexType>
        </element>
      </part>
    </message>
  </input>
  . . .
</operation>
```

Fig. 5. Consolidation Phase 3: Inject elements.

its context, localizing the necessary information to understand and compare it independently.

4.4 Phase 4: Consolidate Elements

Each element may be either a native atomic type (such as an integer or text string) or a complex type described elsewhere in the service description. In the next consolidation step, we find the type definition for each element's type, if one exists. For each such defined type, we expand the definition and elements of the type and integrate them into the parent element of the part. This same process is repeated recursively for all the elements of the expanded type, until all elements in the part have been expanded to elements of native types (eg. string, int, etc.), or no matching type definition can be found in the file.. The final result looks something like that shown for our example in Figure 6.

```
<operation name="ReserveRoom" >
  <input message="tns1:ReserveRoomRequest">
    <message name="ReserveRoomRequest">
      <part name="body" element="xsd1:ReserveRoomRequest">
        <element name="ReserveRoomRequest">
          <complexType>
            <sequence>
              <element name="payment" type="tns1:Payment">
                <element name="ccNumber" type="xsd:int"/>
                <element name="cardHolder" type="xsd:string"/>
                <element name="expiryDate" type="xsd:date"/>
                <element name="PIN" nillable="true" type="xsd:int"/>
              </element>
              <element name="room" type="tns1:Room">
                <element name="roomID" type="xsd:int"/>
                <element name="numBeds" type="xsd:int"/>
                <element name="isSmoking" type="xsd:boolen"/>
              </element>
            </sequence>
          </complexType>
        </element>
      </part>
    </message>
  </input>
  . . .
</operation>
```

Fig. 6. Consolidation Phase 4: Consolidate elements.

4.5 Phase 5: Clean Up

Some redundant tags (e.g. `<complexType>`, `<sequence>`, and so on) remain in our expansion after phases 1-4, so we remove these to make the operation definitions cleaner, simpler and easier to read and compare. The final result for our

```
<operation name="ReserveRoom" >
  <input message="tns1:ReserveRoomRequest">
    <message name="ReserveRoomRequest">
       <part name="body" element="xsd1:ReserveRoomRequest">
         <element name="ReserveRoomRequest">
           <element name="payment" type="tns1:Payment">
             <element name="ccNumber" type="xsd:int"/>
             <element name="cardHolder" type="xsd:string"/>
             <element name="expiryDate" type="xsd:date"/>
             <element name="PIN" nillable="true" type="xsd:int"/>
           </element>
           <element name="room" type="tns1:Room">
             <element name="roomID" type="xsd:int"/>
             <element name="numBeds" type="xsd:int"/>
             <element name="isSmoking" type="xsd:boolean"/>
           </element>
         </element>
       </part>
    </message>
  </input>
  <output message="tns1:ReserveRoomResponse">
    <message name="ReserveRoomResponse">
       <part name="body" element="xsd1:ReserveRoomResponse">
         <element name="ReserveRoomResponse"/>
       </part>
    </message>
  </output>
  <fault message="tns1:RoomNotAvailableException">
    <message name="RoomNotAvailableException">
      <part name="body" element="xsd1:RoomNotAvailableException">
        <element name="RoomNotAvailableException"/>
      </part>
    </message>
  </fault>
</operation>
```

Fig. 7. Consolidation Phase 5: Clean up.

hotel reservation example is shown in Figure 7, and the entire process can be visualized as illustrated in Figure 8.

What we are left with is a clear human-readable standalone representation of each operation, its required input and expected output. For example, we can see that the ReserveRoom operation in Figure 7 takes a Payment object and a Room object and returns an acknowledgement. Further, from the composition of the Payment and Room objects, we can easily tell what information is required for this service. In this expanded form we can more meaningfully test whether different operations are similar, something that we could not effectively do in their original context-dependent form.

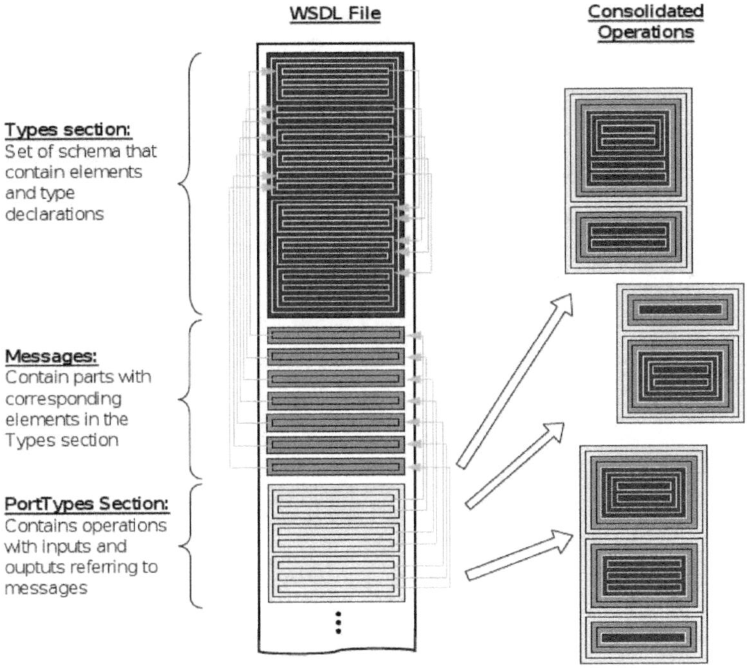

Fig. 8. Visualization of the consolidation.

5 Results

Thus far we have tested our method on two sets of WSDL service description files. *Set 1* is a system of over 200 web services containing more than 1,100 operations, many of them similar or duplicates. *Set 2* is a collection of over 500 service descriptions containing over 7,500 operations from a wide variety of domains, obtained through a web services search engine by Seekda [11].

For each set, we compared the result of clone detection at various difference thresholds on the set of consolidated operations that our tool generates against the results on the set of original non-consolidated operations present in the original service descriptions. It should be noted that the purpose of this evaluation was to test our method of consolidating operations against non-consolidated operations using clone detection. We have not tested the overall approach of using clone detection to find similar web service operations at this time.

We used the clone detection tool NiCad [4] (briefly discussed in Section 2.2) on both sets of services. NiCad produces a set of clusters of operations that it determines to be clones (i.e. similar) for a given difference tolerance or **threshold**. The threshold specifies the portion of lines that are allowed to be different between two code fragments (in our case WSDL operation descriptions) in order for them to be considered clones. For example, a threshold of 0.3 means that operation descriptions are allowed to differ in 30% of their total number of lines

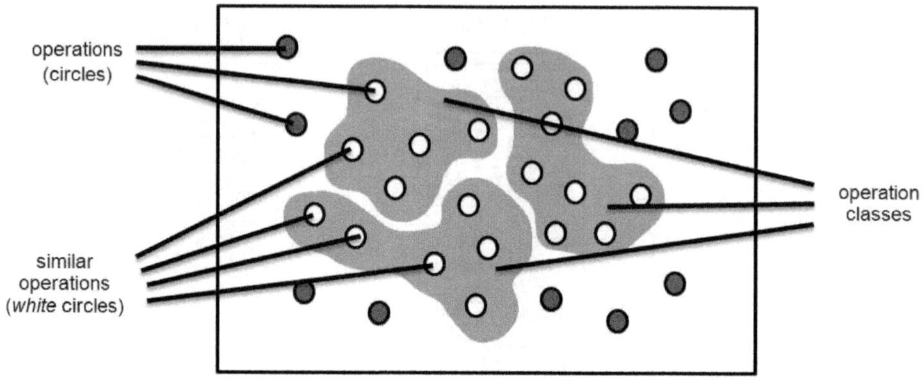

Fig. 9. Visualization of the clone detection.

(i.e., 3 lines in 10), while a threshold of 0 means that two operations must be exactly the same to be considered clones.

NiCad summarizes the results using a number of metrics, only two of which we will show here. The first metric is the number of fragments, which is the total number of code fragments (operations) for which there exists 1 or more clones (*similar operations*). The second metric is the number of clusters, or the number of groups of similar operations, which we call *operation classes*. Figure 9 provides a visualization of these definitions and how they relate to each other. Each circle inside the rectangle represents an operation in the sample set. Similar operations are shown as white circles inside there operation class, which is represented by the shaded areas surrounding them.

NiCad requires all potential clones (i.e., operation descriptions we wish to compare for similarity) to be put in a single XML file, enclosed in `<source>` tags, with attributes *file*, *startline* and *endline* specifying the original source WSDL file and the starting line number and ending line number of the original operation description within the file.

NiCad efficiently compares each potential clone (operation description) to the others looking for ones that differ by at most the number of lines allowed by the threshold described above. Based on this, it outputs XML files for each threshold with a list of `<class>` tags containing the similar operations belonging to that particular operation class.

We extracted and consolidated the operations of each of our two sets of web service descriptions. We also extracted the bare-bones non-consolidated operation elements in order to evaluate the benefits of our consolidation method over raw clone detection. Figure 10 shows the NiCad generated clone metrics for each set (non-consolidated and consolidated).

The first thing we notice, that may seem counter-intuitive at first glance, is that the number operations that are exactly the same (threshold 0.0 in Figure 10a) decreases when considering our consolidated operations over non-consolidated operations. The same can be said for similar operations that are

	Set 1		Set 2	
Difference Threshold	Non-Consolidated	Consolidated	Non-Consolidated	Consolidated
0.0	852	705	1434	1066
0.1	852	734	1434	1228
0.2	879	775	1438	1637
0.3	884	813	1469	1637

(a) Number of similar (i.e. cloned) operations

	Set 1		Set 2	
Difference Threshold	Non-Consolidated	Consolidated	Non-Consolidated	Consolidated
0.0	169	187	587	433
0.1	169	139	587	499
0.2	172	142	589	631
0.3	171	136	591	631

(b) Number of groups of similar operations

Fig. 10. Similarity Metrics produced by NiCad.

within the threshold of 0.1 and in the case of Set 1, 0.2 and even 0.3. It may appear that consolidating the operations gives worse results. However, upon deeper inspection, we see that false positives (that is, operations declared to be similar that are not) are being filtered out.

One might think that if two operations were the same non-consolidated, consolidating them (assuming that the consolidation is done the same way for each) would just add new information that was still the same for both. But this is not the case. Consider two non-consolidated operations with the same input and output tags. They may appear to be the same, however when we look at the type definitions of the parameters, we see that they use different types which may even have completely different names. An example of this can be seen in Figure 11. Here we see the description of two non-consolidated operations (Figure 11a) considered to be exactly the same. (We present the description only once because they are identical). However, when we consolidate them based on their context (Figure 11b and 11c), we see that they contextualize to have very different meanings. Specifically, we see that the word "Stock" has been used to mean inventory in one context and a financial stock quote in the other.

The second thing we noticed is that by consolidating the operations, operation classes (i.e. groups of similar operations) can be split into multiple classes. For instance, a class that contained 10 non-consolidated operations may be split into 2 classes with 5 consolidated operations in each. This tends to be the case in situations like the one described above (Figure 11) when there are operations that look similar non-consolidated, but when consolidated can be seen to have different contexts.

Finally, and most importantly, we found that consolidating operations allowed us to find similar operations with clone detection that we would never have been able to find without consolidating. For example, consider the operation class shown in Figure 12. It contains operations, all related to charting, with

```
<operation name="GetStock" >
    <input message="tns:GetStockRequest" />
    <output message="tns:GetStockResponse" />
</operation>
```

(a)

```
<operation name="GetStock" >
    <input message="tns:GetStockRequest">
        <message name="GetStockRequest">
            <part name="parameters" element="tns:GetStockRequest">
                <element name="GetStockRequest">
                    <element name="symbol" type="xsd:string" />
                </element>
            </part>
        </message>
    </input>
    <output message="tns:GetStockResponse">
        <message name="GetStockResponse">
            <part name="parameters" element="tns:GetStockResponse">
                <element name="GetStockResponse">
                    <element name="Stock">
                        <element name="date" type="xsd:string"/>
                        <element name="open" type="xsd:float"/>
                        <element name="high" type="xsd:float"/>
                        <element name="low" type="xsd:float"/>
                        <element name="close" type="xsd:float"/>
                        <element name="volume" type="xsd:float"/>
                    </element>
                </element>
            </part>
        </message>
    </output>
</operation>
```

(b)

```
<operation name="GetStock" >
    <input message="tns:GetStockRequest">
        <message name="GetStockRequest">
            <part name="parameters" element="tns:GetStockRequest">
                <element name="GetStockRequest">
                    <element name="InventoryNumber" type="xsd:int" />
                </element>
            </part>
        </message>
    </input>
    <output message="tns:GetStockResponse">
        <message name="GetStockResponse">
            <part name="parameters" element="tns:GetStockResponse">
                <element name="GetStockResponse">
                    <element name="Stock">
                        <element name="Supplier" type="s:string"/>
                        <element name="Warehouse" type="s:string"/>
                        <element name="OnHand" type="s:string"/>
                        <element name="OnOrder" type="s:string"/>
                        <element name="Demand" type="s:string"/>
                    </element>
                </element>
            </part>
        </message>
    </output>
</operation>
```

(c)

Fig. 11. Two operations considered to be exactly the same before consolidation (a), but not after (b and c).

```
<wsdl:operation name="DrawDoubleTechnicalChartCustom">
  <wsdl:input message="tns:DrawDoubleTechnicalChartCustomSoapIn" />
  <wsdl:output message="tns:DrawDoubleTechnicalChartCustomSoapOut" />
</wsdl:operation>

<wsdl:operation name="DrawSingleTechnicalChartCustom">
  <wsdl:input message="tns:DrawSingleTechnicalChartCustomSoapIn" />
  <wsdl:output message="tns:DrawSingleTechnicalChartCustomSoapOut" />
</wsdl:operation>

<wsdl:operation name="GetHistoricalEnergyFutureChartCustom">
  <wsdl:input message="tns:GetHistoricalEnergyFutureChartCustomSoapIn" />
  <wsdl:output message="tns:GetHistoricalEnergyFutureChartCustomSoapOut" />
</wsdl:operation>

<wsdl:operation name="GetRealChartCustom">
  <wsdl:input message="tns:GetRealChartCustomSoapIn" />
  <wsdl:output message="tns:GetRealChartCustomSoapOut" />
</wsdl:operation>

<wsdl:operation name="GetLastSaleChartCustom">
  <wsdl:input message="tns:GetLastSaleChartCustomSoapIn" />
  <wsdl:output message="tns:GetLastSaleChartCustomSoapOut" />
</wsdl:operation>

<wsdl:operation name="DrawHistoricalChartCustom">
  <wsdl:input message="tns:DrawHistoricalChartCustomSoapIn" />
  <wsdl:output message="tns:DrawHistoricalChartCustomSoapOut" />
</wsdl:operation>

<wsdl:operation name="DrawIntraDayChartCustom">
  <wsdl:input message="tns:DrawIntraDayChartCustomSoapIn" />
  <wsdl:output message="tns:DrawIntraDayChartCustomSoapOut" />
</wsdl:operation>

<wsdl:operation name="GetIntradayEnergyFutureChartCustom">
  <wsdl:input message="tns:GetIntradayEnergyFutureChartCustomSoapIn" />
  <wsdl:output message="tns:GetIntradayEnergyFutureChartCustomSoapOut" />
</wsdl:operation>

<wsdl:operation name="GetDelayedChartCustom">
  <wsdl:input message="tns:GetDelayedChartCustomSoapIn" />
  <wsdl:output message="tns:GetDelayedChartCustomSoapOut" />
</wsdl:operation>

<wsdl:operation name="GetHistoricalEnergyCommodityChartCustom">
  <wsdl:input message="tns:GetHistoricalEnergyCommodityChartCustomSoapIn" />
  <wsdl:output message="tns:GetHistoricalEnergyCommodityChartCustomSoapOut" />
</wsdl:operation>

<wsdl:operation name="DrawCapitalizationChartCustom">
  <wsdl:input message="tns:DrawCapitalizationChartCustomSoapIn" />
  <wsdl:output message="tns:DrawCapitalizationChartCustomSoapOut" />
</wsdl:operation>

<wsdl:operation name="GetTopicBinaryChartCustom">
  <wsdl:input message="tns:GetTopicBinaryChartCustomSoapIn" />
  <wsdl:output message="tns:GetTopicBinaryChartCustomSoapOut" />
</wsdl:operation>

<wsdl:operation name="GetTopicChartCustom">
  <wsdl:input message="tns:GetTopicChartCustomSoapIn" />
  <wsdl:output message="tns:GetTopicChartCustomSoapOut" />
</wsdl:operation>

<wsdl:operation name="DrawRateChartCustom">
  <wsdl:input message="tns:DrawRateChartCustomSoapIn" />
  <wsdl:output message="tns:DrawRateChartCustomSoapOut" />
</wsdl:operation>

<wsdl:operation name="DrawYieldCurveCustom">
  <wsdl:input message="tns:DrawYieldCurveCustomSoapIn" />
  <wsdl:output message="tns:DrawYieldCurveCustomSoapOut" />
</wsdl:operation>

<wsdl:operation name="DrawRateChartCustom">
  <wsdl:input message="tns:DrawRateChartCustomSoapIn" />
  <wsdl:output message="tns:DrawRateChartCustomSoapOut" />
</wsdl:operation>
```

Fig. 12. A sample operation class that can only be found with consolidation.

completely different names that could not be recognized as related by clone detection if they were not consolidated. Some, such as "DrawYieldCurveCustom", don't even have "chart" in their name. The reason these are recognized as being similar by NiCad is that the consolidation expands all type definitions into the operation description, and all of these operations actually contain very similar elements.

We believe that examples like this validate our initial belief that consolidating operation descriptions can allow us to more effectively find similar operations. It contextualizes an otherwise sparse operation description, which allows standard clone detection tools like NiCad to match based on context.

6 Conclusions and Future Work

WSDL descriptions of web services pose problems for finding similarities. In this work we have shown how we can leverage code clone detection techniques to identify and cluster similar services by restructuring service descriptions to consolidate remote information. Our consolidation makes WSDL descriptions both more human readable and more amenable to analysis using code similarity techniques. The consolidation not only refines the results generated by clone detection to avoid identifying services that while similar on the surface actually have very different meanings, but also produces results identifying similar services that could not be found without consolidation.

In our work thus far we have concentrated only on service operations, and ignored most other aspects of service descriptions. Based on the promising results so far, it is time to extend our consolidation and similarity detection to a broader range of WSDL service description features and versions. For example, thus far we do not handle WSDL 2.0, and some aspects of XML schemas are ignored. We can also now begin to attack the real goal of our work, the automated tagging of alternative services and operations for a given purpose or to match a given protocol or domain ontology. Using the results of our clone detection-based similarity analysis, we can further leverage our source transformation methods to tag and classify similar services and operations.

A side effect of our work is the discovery of a new class of code clones - those that are hidden in the original source text, but may be uncovered by contextual consolidation similar to what we have done for WSDL. This new idea of *contextual clones* holds promise for other languages as well, and we are currently beginning new research in using the technique for concept analysis in other languages.

Acknowledgements

This work is supported in part by an IBM Faculty Award, by an IBM Canada Centre for Advanced Studies Fellowship, and by the Natural Sciences and Engineering Research Council of Canada.

References

1. Ng, J.W., Chignell, M., Cordy, J.R.: The Smart Internet: Transforming the Web to Fit User Needs. In: Proc. CASCON 2009, pp. 285–296. ACM, New York (2009)
2. Roy, C.K., Cordy, J.R.: Comparison and Evaluation of Code Clone Detection Techniques and Tools: A Qualitative Approach. Sci. Comput. Program 74(7), 470–495 (2009)
3. Cordy, J.R.: The TXL Source Transformation Language. Sci. Comput. Program 61(3), 190–210 (2006)
4. Roy, C.K., Cordy, J.R.: NiCad: Accurate Detection of Near-Miss Intentional Clones Using Flexible Pretty-Printing and Code Normalization. In: Proc. of the International Conference on Program Comprehension 2008, pp. 172–181 (2008)
5. Dong, X., Halevy, A., Madhaven, J., Nemes, E., Zhang, J.: Similarity Search for Web Services. In: Proc. of the 30th VLDB Conference 2004, pp. 372–383 (2004)
6. Syeda-Mahmood, T., Shah, G., Akkiraju, R., Ivan, A., Goodwin, R.: Searching Service Repositories by Combining Semantic and Ontological Matching. In: Proc. ICWS 2005, pp. 13–20 (2005)
7. Stroulia, E., Wang, Y.: Structural and Semantic Matching for Assessing Web-Service Similarity. International Journal of Cooperative Information Systems 14(4), 407–437 (2005)
8. Juergens, E., Deissenboeck, F., Hummel, B., Wagner, S.: Do Code Clones Matter? In: Proc. of the International Conference on Software Engineering 2009, pp. 485–495 (2009)
9. Cordy, J.R., Dean, T.R., Malton, A.J., Schneider, K.A.: Source Transformation in Software Engineering using the TXL Transformation System. Journal of Information and Software Technology 44(13), 827–837 (2002)
10. Christensen, E., Curbera, F., Meredith, G., Weerawarana, S.: Web Services Description Language (WSDL) 1.1. World Wide Web Consortium (W3C) (2001), `http://www.w3.org/TR/wsdl` [Accessed: April 16, 2010]
11. Web Services Search Engine, `http://webservices.seekda.com/`

User-Centric Smart Services in the Cloud

Karuna P. Joshi[1], Yelena Yesha[1], Ant A. Ozok[2], Yaacov Yesha[1], Ashwini Lahane[1], Hari Kalva[3], Ankur Agarwal[3], and Borko Furht[3]

[1] Computer Science and Electrical Engineering Department,
[2] Information Systems Department
{kjoshi1,yeyesha,ozok,yayesha,alahane1}@umbc.edu
[3] Computer & Electrical Engineering and Computer Science Department
{hari,ankur,borko}@cse.fau.edu

Abstract. In this chapter we describe our vision for the next generation of IT services. Services will be automatically discovered, procured and integrated with the service consumer's technical environment. This whole process will be determined by the policies defined by the consumer and will be transparent to the consumer. We also define the new applications of Policy Manager, Service Manager, Service Procurer and Service Integrator that will allow Smart Services to operate efficiently on the Smart Internet. Usability and User issues are also identified. We illustrate the Smart Services with examples from the health care and multimedia domains.

Keywords: Smart Internet, Smart Services, Services automation.

1 Introduction

TIt is increasingly being recognized that the Internet in its current state is server-centric where the content, control and performance lies with the servers running the websites. The onus is on the consumer to search for the required data/information across various websites and combine it as needed. The next generation of the Internet, termed Smart Internet [1], advocates a user-centric model for the web instead of the server-centric model that exists today. The Smart Internet addresses the technological gaps due to lack of integration, individualization, user control, collaborative services that exist in the current rendition of the Internet.

In this chapter, we articulate a similar vision for services, specially virtualized services on the cloud. Virtualized service models are emerging and IT development and maintenance which was previously either in-house or outsourced is being replaced by this new delivery model where businesses purchase IT components, like software, hardware or network bandwidth, as services from providers distributed globally. In such scenarios, multiple providers often collaborate to create a single service for an organization. In some cases, organizations utilize multiple service providers to mitigate risks associated with a single provider. In other cases, they may utilize a single provider who in turn utilizes the services of other providers. Moreover, the component service of a provider could simultaneously participate in several composed service orchestrations. This model has also been termed Service Virtualization [2].

M. Chignell et al. (Eds.): The Smart Internet, LNCS 6400, pp. 234–249, 2010.

Virtualization implies that the service with which an end customer interacts may be composed of many others, and each service in turn could depend on backend applications (database, web server) and resources (storage, bandwidth, CPU). It could be delivered remotely to the consumer via a computing grid or cloud. The service, in effect, is virtualized on the cloud. This virtualized model of service delivery potentially allows easier service customization, better resource utilization and greater responsiveness on part of the service providers. In this model, the service is acquired through the "on demand" pull technology. This is true of services that are purely IT in nature (e.g. Software as a Service (SaaS) or Infrastructure as a Service (IaaS)), as well as services that are IT enabled (ITeS) but involve human contact (e.g. those provided via contact centers). It is possible in these scenarios that neither the hardware infrastructure, nor the software; and not even the people running these services belong to the organization that uses the service.

Creation of a user-centric model for virtualized services presents new challenges. While the concept of 'Service on demand', i.e. a user requesting service or its components when needed, is promising; there appears to be no rush from organizations to adopt this new model. One of the key barriers is the lack of infrastructure to enable automatic management, procurement and integration of services. Smart Internet is essential to realize the full benefit of the virtualized delivery model. In this paper we describe our vision of how services will be more automatically managed in a Smart Internet environment. Another barrier is the Usability and User related issues of on-demand services. In this chapter we also look into this in detail and identify the open issues that will need to be addressed in the Smart Internet. We have provided examples from multimedia and the health care domain to illustrate our vision. Additional discussions of the healthcare domain may be found in the earlier Chapters by Yu et al., Weber-Jahnke and Williams, and Spence and Marziali, respectively.

We review related work in this area in section 2 and detail the proposed service flow in section 3. We look into the Usability issues that will arise for such services in section 4. Section 5 and 6 provides some examples from the healthcare and multimedia domain respectively and list the open issues that will need to be addressed for services on the Smart Internet. We conclude in section 7 and provide an overview of our ongoing work.

2 Related Work

A user-centric model of the Internet mandates the capability of individualizing or personalizing websites for each user based on their preferences, traversal patterns, functional domain, services consumed etc. Personalization of the web has been extensively researched. Researchers have tried to enhance it by improving upon Internet searching capabilities. Joshi and Jiang [3] had proposed an algorithm to cluster search results to provide users with a personalized view of their web queries. Stanford NLP group [4] have developed PageRank algorithm to decide the ranking of web pages returned after a search. More recently, Balke and Wagner [5] have proposed an algorithm featuring the expansion of service requests by user-specific demands to enable personalized selection of web services. However, most of these approaches have been based on the current server-centric model on the Internet.

Researchers have also concentrated on developing methodologies for virtualized services. Papazoglou and Van Den Heuvel [6] have proposed a methodology for developing and deploying web services using service oriented architectures. Their approach, however, is limited to the creation and deployment of web services and does not account for virtualized environment where services are composed on demand. Providers may need to combine their services with other resources or providers' services to meet consumer needs. Other methodologies, like that proposed by Bianchini et al. [7], do not provide this flexibility and are limited to cases where a single service provider provides one service. Zeng et al. [8] address the quality based selection of composite services via a global planning approach but do not cover the human factors in quality metrics used for selecting the components. Maximilien and Singh [9] propose an ontology to capture quality of a web service so that quality attributes can be used while selecting a service. Their ontology is limited by the fact that it considers single web services, rather than service compositions. Black et al. [10] have proposed an integrated model for IT service management. Their model is limited to managing the service from the service provider's perspective. Milanovic et al. [11] have summarized the key issues in web services composition. Dustdar et. al [12] have presented several different composition strategies and have reviewed the dynamic web service composition approach which is relevant to the on-demand service composition.

In a virtualized service-oriented environment, consumers and providers need to be able to exchange information, queries, and requests pertaining to the data and policies with some assurance that they share a common meaning. One possible approach to this issue is to employ Semantic Web techniques for modeling and reasoning about services related information. Semantic Web is an enhancement of the World Wide Web that deals primarily with data instead of documents. It enables data to be annotated with machine understandable metadata, allowing the automation of their retrieval and their usage in correct contexts. Semantic Web technologies include languages such as Resource Description Framework (RDF) [13] and Web Ontology Language (OWL) [14] for defining ontologies and describing metadata using these ontologies as well as tools for reasoning over these descriptions. Web Services Description Language (WSDL) [15] is an XML based language that provides a model for describing web services. It defines services as collections of network endpoints, or ports operating on messages containing either document-oriented or procedure-oriented information. Business Process Execution Language (BPEL) [16] is a standard executable language for specifying business process behavior based on web services. Its messaging facilities depend on WSDL. Semantic web technologies can be used to provide common semantics of service information and policies enabling all agents who understand basic Semantic Web technologies to communicate and use each other's data and services effectively.

3 Services on Demand

Existing methodologies for designing and deploying web based services put the control in the hands of the service providers who plan and design the service, decide its composition, delivery mode and then wait for consumer request of the service. Services are mainly developed by using the semantic web technologies. While semantic web languages are easier to read compared to computer languages, like C or Java; they still require the consumers to possess technical expertise in semantic web languages to be able to consume the services.

We envision that with the development of the Smart Internet and further adoption of virtualized services and cloud computing models, the next generation of service lifecycle will be fully automated. It will be transparent to the consumer and services needed will be automatically identified by the service environment, discovered and procured in the cloud and seamlessly integrated back with the consumer's service environment. Figure 1 illustrates the flow of information in automated services. The consumer's services environment will consist of three new applications/toolsets that will completely automate how services are acquired, consumed and managed in a Smart Internet environment. The service environment will consist of a Service Manager, Policy Manager, Service Monitor and Service log that will help manage the services consumed in an organization. Service procurer will automatically acquire the desired services from the service cloud. Service Integrator will seamlessly integrate the acquired service into the existing service environment. We describe the applications and the lifecycle of smart services in detail below.

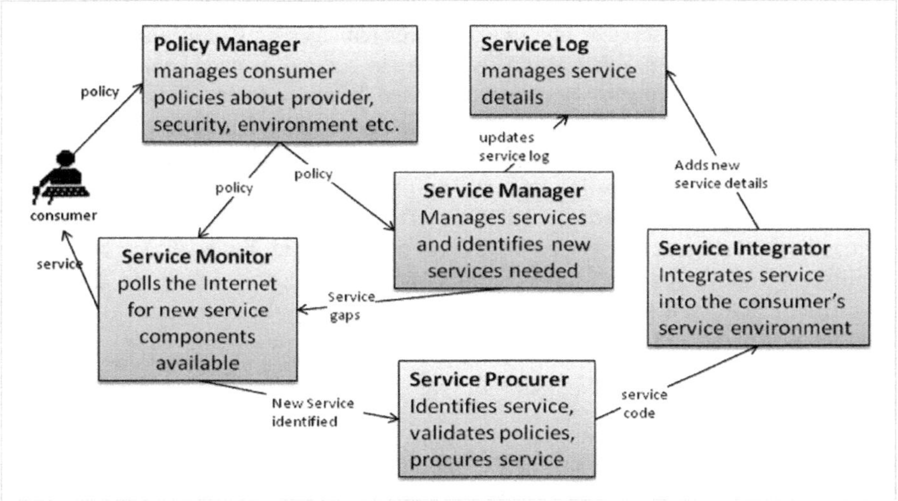

Fig. 1. Smart services will consist of service manager, service monitor, service procurer and service integrator applications built into the service infrastructure.

3.1 Smart Services Consumer Environment

Current design of the Internet requires the consumers to manually search/discover and procure a service available on the web and then integrate it within their IT environment. This approach is cumbersome for the consumers and also prone to guess work on the user's part as to which service is needed. Smart Internet in the future would enable automation of this step by dynamically identifying the services that a user needs and automatically procuring them. This would be similar to the existing upgrade utility on computers that automatically checks the software versions installed and then runs the update in the background after confirming with the user. For instance, if a user is consuming a service that provides financial information, then additional services that are either missing or could enhance the information displayed would be automatically identified and procured for the consumer depending on the service procurement policies that the consumer has defined. Smart services infrastructure running on the consumer's IT environment will include the applications listed below.

3.2 Service Manager

Service Manager manages the services by tracking their quality and performance. It also identifies gaps in the services and inform the Service Monitor of them so that the Monitor could search for services that can fill the gap. If a service does not meet the desired performance levels, the service manager will send alerts to humans or automatically terminate the service and send instructions to the service monitor to poll for another service.

Many software providers like Microsoft [17], IBM [18], Hewlett Packard [19], Oracle [20] etc. have released basic versions of service managers in the market. However these products are platform specific. For instance, the Microsoft service manager manages only Windows specific services and Oracle server manages only Oracle services. Due to this the consumer has to either manually integrate service management across various platforms or write a proprietary program to manage the service flow across platforms. We envision that in Smart Services, the Service Manager application will be platform independent and will provide a user-centric aggregated view of all the services in the consumer's IT environment regardless of service provider.

Service Manager will also consist of a Service Log that will manage a list of all services in the consumer's service environment. It will track the service by its functionality, provider, dependent services/components and technical features. The service log will also act as an audit for each service by logging the number of times it was used, the user name and cost to the organization.

3.3 Service Monitor

The current state of art of the Internet requires that the consumer first identify the service that s/he wishes to use and then discover a provider on the cloud who will be able to compose the service to match their requirements. Smart services will consist of a Service Monitor program to regularly poll the cloud and identify any new services or service upgrades that have been released. Service Monitor will refer to the policies stored in the policy manager to determine the domains and constraints that it should filter off. For instance, if the consumer is using a document management service to manage their organizational files, then the service monitor will poll the service cloud for other similar services that might be available at reduced cost. This functionality is similar to the update application available on Windows environment which lets the users know as soon as a security patch is available to update their operating system. The service monitor will also protect the service environment from being inundated by sample services or advertisement spam sent by service providers.

When the service monitor identifies a service that needs to be procured, it sends the list of requirements along with the associated policies determining the service constraints to the Service Procurer.

3.4 Policy Manager

Policy Manager manages the policies decided by the consumer on service discovery and procurement along with the policies pertaining to business rules. For instance, the consumer may specify a limited list of providers for service discovery; or may want to limit service discovery to a geographical location. Similarly the consumer may specify the budgetary, security or language constraints as part of their procurement policy. The Service Policy Master would ideally contain all the business rules and IT policies of the organization that should be considered by the consumer before procuring a service.

The collection of consumer's policies is translated to a description using semantic web languages such as RDF and OWL. We plan to use the Rei policy framework [21] (http://rei.umbc.edu) to develop the policies. This will ensure that the Service Policy Master uses a standard interface, and replacing it does not require reentering the policies.

The collection of consumer's policies is translated to a description using semantic web languages such as RDF and OWL. Examples of policy frameworks that may be used are Web Services Policy Framework [22], that includes WS-Policy assertions and WS-Policy Attachments and the Rei policy framework [21] (http://rei.umbc.edu) to develop the policies. This will ensure that the Service Policy Master uses a standard framework and that policies can be easily reused and shared when this is desirable

3.5 Service Procurer

Service procurer searches for services on the cloud that match the specified service. The discovery is constrained by functional and technical attributes identified by the Service monitor, and also by the budgetary, security, data quality and agent policies of the consumer defined in the policy master. One approach that the service procurer could take for discovering services would be to run a query against the services registered with a central registry or governing body. Alternatively, it could limit the service search to a set of providers specified in the consumer's provider policy. While discovering the service, the procurer will need references for providers that match the requirements, especially if the provider is not a part of the preferred vendor list defined in the policy. Service procurer will be able to get certification for the service provider by contacting a central registry, like UDDI [23].

If the service procurer identifies the exact service matching the specifications and constraints then it automatically procures it and transfers the control to the service integrator. If the procurer discovers multiple providers for the service, each meeting the consumer's policies, then it creates an aggregated view of the search results providing instantaneous comparison of the services available, their cost, their constraints and the service gap. The control is then transferred to the consumer who finalizes the service provider. While the existing Internet infrastructure does not allow aggregation of website from multiple servers or transfer of control to the user, Smart Internet has been envisioned to enable this. After the consumer finalizes the service provider, service procurer begins contract negotiation with the provider. Service Level Agreements

(SLAs) are finalized during this negotiation. SLAs define the service data, delivery mode, agent details, compliance policy, quality and cost of the service.

After the service procurer acquires the service, it transfers control to the service integrator.

3.6 Service Integrator

Once the service is procured, the next step is to integrate it into the IT environment that exists on the consumer's side. Currently web services require a skilled administrator at the consumer end to integrate the service with other existing applications. This adds to the overall cost as well as the maintenance of the service and is a major disincentive for organizations to adopt services technology.

We envision that in the Smart Internet, there will be a Service Integrator program that will automatically integrate the new service procured into the consumer's existing service infrastructure, thereby removing the need of manual integration. Often different services procured could be combined to form a single service. In other instances, the service procured could be integrated into multiple services. For instance, a currency converter service procured could be integrated with multiple financial application services. Either way, this integration would be transparent and seamless to the end user. Service integrator will also update the service manager, service monitor and the service log with the details of the new service procured.

4 Usability and User Issues

As the "on demand" service systems deal with users, human-computer interaction issues need to be taken into consideration in design, implementation, and maintenance phases of the system and beyond. In designing such software systems with a service focus, emphasis on usability and user issues may be critical for maintaining optimal user and satisfaction. Variations of usability design guidelines initially created by Shneiderman [24] and Nielsen [25] can be adopted for service oriented systems and its components. Time-critical tasks can be run more effectively on systems with optimally usable interfaces that present the relevant content in a user friendly design.

The concept of "smart services" may bring with it a number of issues that previously may not have been noted by researchers. It should be noted that the concepts of cloud computing and smart services are fairly new, and human-computer interaction aspects of cloud computing are scarcely defined. The personalization aspects of cloud computing may require that user-specific aspects of the cloud services need to be given attention to allow a smooth interaction between all users and their interactive interfaces.

Shneiderman [24] defines a usable interface as an interface that allows, among others, easy learnability and guidance. The challenge to provide these concepts in the cloud rather stems from the variety of the customized interfaces that can be and are required to be provided to a wide variety of user groups. For example, one user group using cloud services may consist of technology professional experts in artificial intelligence while another may consist of teenage shoppers. To provide usable interfaces that allow a smooth human-computer interaction, user requirements and demographics may need to be determined in a way that can allow for easy design adjustments.

Other usability principles from Shneiderman and Nielsen are also to some extent applicable to services in cloud computing, especially with the increase in mobile device use. Clear documentation of each mistake made while using the services and systems may usually be difficult to provide in the cloud environment, but future service provision systems may need to pay attention to this documentation issue in design. The same attention would need to be paid to the provision of error messages in the cloud for services. Additionally, if the user intends to move away from a particular service, this should be made possible via clearly marked exits. Consistency in cloud computing is a difficult issue but cloud providers can attempt to making sure that different services are offered via consistent interfaces to allow for higher satisfaction as well as transfer of knowledge from one system to another. Service providers need to determine the specific group of users who are likely to use their services and in some cases tailor their interfaces based on the cognitive and physical needs and limitations for this group. For example, if a service caters to the elderly population, more attention should be given to the screen design in terms of contrast, colors, and font and image sizes.

One other issue where human computer interaction and usability in design may play a critical role may be administrators that use the cloud. Administrators can be at a position where they may need to access a number of different interfaces for the purposes of exchanging, sharing, manipulating and using information. To allow for a usable customer interface environment to be presented to the administrators, their job and interface requirements will need to be determined in order to determine the user requirements on their part, which can be followed by designs tailored for administrators and their specific needs on their jobs, which can vary from database to network administration and more. In the following sections, first, general personalization issues in cloud computing are discussed. This is followed by an overview of methods to gather user requirements for usability design and evaluation. Finally, challenges in cloud computing and delivery services as they relate to usability and design are discussed.

4.1 Personalization in Cloud Computing and Smart Services

As the name indicates, smart services allow consumers to manually and easily search for and locate the services they are looking for. An analogy can be made between smart services and e-commerce retail where easy searches are done with the search box provided on e-commerce retail Web pages. Moreover, Web pages are able to give recommendations to consumers based on the shopping, browsing and searching habits of consumers. A recent study by Ozok, Fang and Norcio [26] indicated that a compact set of information with a small number of recommendations with the ability to get more information on these recommendations work best for the users. Similarly in smart services, a small number of consumer-targeted service choices with targeted service recommendations may work best in cloud computing. Personalization can be provided to users on an on-demand basis, with the interfaces offered with a default look and being able to be personalized if the service users wish to personalize them. Today, the Web, especially news-related pages, offer a number of personalization options where users can reach the relevant information and organize it according to their wishes. However, in return, some pages also ask for information on demographics, among others. Cloud service providers can use the information they gathered on their clients to tailor the interfaces to their clients' specific needs, but this should be done with permission from the clients.

4.2 Administrators, Personalization and Usability

Administrators work with the cloud by managing different applications that are most suitable for a single user or a group of users. Presenting them with a usable interface can allow administrators to work in an environment where they can maximize their performance and satisfaction with their managing and administrating duties. While service managers are software programs, a user-friendly interface can allow the controllers of such interfaces to obtain and use the relevant managing information easily from these systems. For this to happen, human factors research can allow the interfaces to be tailored to the needs of the administrators and human controllers of the manager information.

4.3 Consistency of Interfaces

Ozok and Salvendy [27] indicated that consistency plays a crucial role in computer interface design. Allowing consumers to present consistent interfaces for different applications can allow user performance and satisfaction to improve. Therefore, cloud providers can offer interface consistency for their applications to allow for consistent interfaces in the cloud. While this may be technically difficult to realize, organizations can provide at the very least a basic level of consistency to allow for smooth services and satisfied consumers.

4.4 Methods for Measuring Usability in Cloud Computing

While measuring consumer performance is almost impossible in the cloud arena, cloud users can be offered surveys to determine the usability environment of the services they are offered. Ozok [28] offered a number of usability measurement techniques using surveys. A sample representative group of cloud consumers can be given surveys to determine the critical success factors in usability as they relate to the particular cloud environment. Cloud services are variable and differ significantly between applications. However, explicit surveys that can be administered online can be used as input in usability design of the cloud environment.

4.5 Usability Challenges in Cloud Computing and Service Delivery

Cloud services widely vary in the capabilities they can offer to their consumers. A smart service can also learn from user behaviors and present user interfaces consistent with the users' cognitive capabilities, desires and satisfaction factors. Success in terms of usability in cloud computing is challenging due to the variety of services offered. However, determining the user base of the cloud, the capabilities, limitations and desires of the average cloud user can help in better interface design in the cloud environment. Relevant cloud content can be presented based on user-centric approaches that start with user requirements gathering, and that involve design, evaluation and testing in terms of usability. Sample user interfaces in the cloud can also be tested in laboratory environments on small samples. While usability issues in the cloud can be expected to come more to the foreground with the advent of cloud computing and services, at this stage in development, usability can be seen as an important factor in smart services and on-demand application delivery.

5 Healthcare Services on the Smart Internet

The user-centric model of the Internet described so far involves the customization of websites for each user based on their preferences, functional domains, traversal patterns etc. The Internet is flooded with websites containing large volumes of data and every moment more data is being generated, distributed and made accessible all over the world. To be able to make efficient use of this data we need to apply intelligence in iterations over the data to extract information, knowledge and ultimately wisdom. The capability of customizing the website to suit individual use at the client side and extraction of useful information from data is achieved by use of smart services. They facilitate automatic detection and procurement of essential services thus proving to be beneficial to a wide variety of fields and professionals.

Health services contain extremely personalized and sensitive data and hence require a highly secure environment with high availability and accessibility. A health service system should measure for disaster recovery and fault tolerance while maintaining the high standard of data integrity. Another important aspect of executing healthcare applications is its integration with standards and compliance with Health Insurance Portability and Accountability Act (HIPAA). Some of the applications in health care that would benefit from Smart services that use Smart Internet are listed in the sections below.

5.1 Surgery

Personalized Smart service could be an extremely important tool for surgeons and physicians that would help them locate the exact article/ reference to a video or some piece of information they might want to look up urgently for the success of the surgery. While performing the surgery, a surgeon might need to refer to a similar previously recorded surgical procedure/ complication. It is extremely important for the surgeon to be able to immediately locate the required recording without having to click on each of the links returned by a text based search. The user-centric smart service used in this case can be customized to return results from medical domain. It would internally use Smart internet for an image/ video based search that would allow the surgeon to view the video of his interest at a single click. It could be further personalized based on the type of surgery or the specialization of the surgeon. For instance, in case of a cardiac surgeon performing a heart bypass surgery, the Smart service would list only videos archived under Heart Bypass Surgery category and further refine the search to result into Traditional Coronary Artery Bypass Grafting, Off-Pump Coronary Artery Bypass Grafting or Minimally Invasive Direct Coronary Artery Bypass Grafting depending on the type of bypass being currently performed on the patient. This auto-refinement of search can drastically improve the way surgeries are performed by saving the surgeons search time in critical situations and allowing to concentrate more on the surgical complication rather than worrying about find the exact piece of information from a huge amounts of data.

5.2 Neonatal Ward

One of the important goals of health care has been to reduce child mortality. According to UNICEF's records more than 70 per cent of almost 11 million child deaths every year are attributable to six causes: diarrhea, malaria, neonatal infection, pneumonia, preterm delivery, or lack of oxygen at birth. In order to help doctors to detect any life threatening infections in babies at an earlier stage, "smart" neonatal wards are used. Each heartbeat, movement of the baby in this neonatal ward is a piece of information. A Smart service in conjunction with such a neo natal ward will enable quicker knowledge gathering from the large amount of data being captured every second in the ward. It will use the information acquired from the data on Smart Internet to efficiently match the information generated in the neonatal ward and the archive of symptoms that are likely to be seen in case of life threatening infections that babies are vulnerable to. Thus it can analyze the data and predict what can happen, faster and help doctors take action earlier. Thus smart services can be effectively used in preventive cure of diseases by diagnosing symptoms and suggesting appropriate preventive treatment to avoid the disease.

5.3 Medical Record Synchronization

Traditionally medical records have been written on paper and kept in folders. The advent of electronic medical records has not only changed the format of medical records but has also increased accessibility of files. In case of an emergency situation where a patient is brought into a hospital that doesn't hold his previous medical record, acquiring this information can be a time-consuming job. In cases where the patient is allergic to a particular medicine, it is very important to have his previous medical record handy before being administered any drug. Smart services can play a big role in this situation. It can allow a service provider to maintain a person's medical record right from birth along with links to family's medical history. This record gets augmented with more information with his every visit to a doctor. Such a record will be a one-stop medical database for that patient. When the person is hospitalized, hospital with legal authority can use the Smart service to access his medical records. Thus doctors can immediately get an entire picture of the patient's medical history, allergic conditions, medications being taken etc. Moreover, the smart service will also use the patient's family member's medical records and suggest the doctor of a potential risk the patient might face due to heredity even though it doesn't show in his records. This can save the doctor's valuable time by being able to link trees of data, helping them diagnose the potential problems and decide on the safest treatment thus ensuring higher chances of success in saving lives. The challenge faced in developing such an application would be having centralized patient data available for use at any time.

5.4 Telesurgery

Telesurgery (also known as Remote surgery) allows a surgeon to perform surgery on a patient who may not be physically present in the same location. It combines elements of robotics, communication technology such as high-speed data connections and management information systems. Smart services coupled with the telesurgical equipment could sense the current state of the surgical procedure, lookup the medical records of the patient, search similar surgeries previously performed and suggest the surgeon of alternative steps he could follow in the surgery. This is analogous to having another "experienced" surgeon in the room to assist the operating surgeon with the right knowledge of the surgery and the patient. An example of this would be a cardio surgeon looking up a video of previously performed bypass surgery for reference, on the internet, while performing a remote surgery. The accurate result of the lookup must be obtained very quickly considering the time criticality of the current surgery. The smart services pre-customized to the surgeon's search pattern and requirements would eliminate a large amount of time required to return the desired video. The smart service would not just return the correct reference but also provide suggestions for controlling the telesurgical equipment under gives circumstance. Thus a smart service can be customized to every user's needs and specifications allowing the user to get desired results. The challenge faced in such an application would be the development of an efficient filtering mechanism that allows the smart service to return the most accurate and relevant results and a control mechanism that coordinates with the surgical equipments.

5.5 Cloud Based Medical Image Visualization

Cloud based medical image visualization is a unique concept of centralizing and sharing all radiology images such as CT-Scans, MRIs, X-rays, ultrasound among others in a secured environment. Such cloud based environment can seamlessly integrate all medical imaging with electronic patient records that can be accessed from any location and reviewed by any authorized user. In such scenario, it is extremely important to store and transmit medical records in a secured and safe environment with a very high standard of data integrity, protecting patient privacy and complying with all security and HIPAA regulations.

Medical images are large files (Digital Imaging and Communication in Medicine (DICOM) objects) and therefore, it is difficult to share among several care delivery organizations. There is significant amount of delay involved in sharing these medical images. Such delays often result in repetition of medical procedures and increased cost of healthcare to the patients, insurance companies and federal government. In addition to the cost saving, sharing of medical records, specifically radiology imaging databases, can drastically reduce medical redundancies and exposure to radiations. A DICOM object viewer and the Picture Archiving and Communication System (PACS) server can reside in a cloud computing environment.

A key requirement for DICOM viewers is lossless image coding; users accessing DICOM images should receive lossless image to rule out any compression artifacts. The views rendered by the DICOM viewer have to be communicated to the users remotely accessing the image. Commercial remote access tools such as Citrix use lossy compression for remote viewing and hence are not suitable for medical imaging application. The use of lossy compression may not be an acceptable solution under several medical conditions. For instance, a lossy compression may provide wrong information about the size of a cancer cells that may be growing in any part of a body. Since the stage of a cancer is determined by the volume of the cancer cells; a lossy image may show a reduced volume by removing some pixels.

A lossless virtual presentation layer can then be developed to reside on cloud. This component can allow a radiologist to annotate the image through a web based viewer and store it back into the distributed cloud based database. Therefore, an instantaneous lossless access to all DICOM objects can be achieved to eliminate the download time.

6 Multimedia Services on the Smart Internet

In a user centric model for content access on the Internet, content is adapted and customized for the user needs. The multimedia nature of the content makes the adaptation problem complex – computationally as well as algorithmically complex. Customizing a website to suit individual use requires user context awareness and the customization possible depends on type of content used on the website. Customizing content such as video is highly resource intensive. We showed that customization based on computational model of human attention is a bandwidth conserving solution but requires large computational resources [29]. This section presents challenges and possible approaches to overcome the challenges in offering video services over cloud infrastructure. The Smart Internet would adapt one of these approaches.

Multimedia content accessed by the users is either stored or real-time. Stored media is pre-recorded and hence can be pre-processed to enable rapid customization when users access such content. Real-time media, on the other hand, is generated in real-time and requires real-time computing resources to perform the desired customization. In the case of video and audio, customization typically implies changes to one or more of bit rate, resolution, quality, and modality [30]. Customization could also involve knowledge extraction which in turn will help in customizing related content and services.

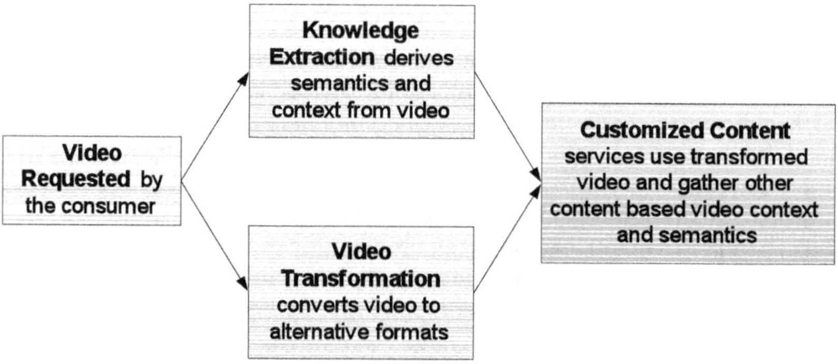

Fig. 2. User centric customization of video content.

Video is data intensive media with large computational requirements for processing and can potentially benefit from cloud computing infrastructure. The parallelism inherent to video processing problems depends on the processing at hand and the format of the video. Since video is necessarily compressed for transmission and storage, any video processed by the cloud is typically compressed. Video compression, while reducing storage and bandwidth requirements, creates dependencies that could affect the granularity of parallelism possible in a given video processing task. For example, predictive coding modes in video use previously coded frames to improve compression efficiency but create dependencies that are undesirable in distributed computing. A key challenge is balancing the tradeoffs between compression efficiency and the possibilities for parallelism.

Smart Internet infrastructure would be able to customize user centric video services by rapidly transforming videos to suite the current user context and also use the knowledge from videos to create a better experience for users. For customizing stored video, the challenge is to reduce the turnaround time. Typically turnaround time can be reduced by increasing the computing resources – e.g., number of machine instances on the cloud dedicated to the given task. A map-reduce framework such as Hadoop can thus be used to reduce the turnaround time. In the case of video, the number of machine instances cannot be increased arbitrarily and is limited by the number of video segments that can be independently processed. The performance and scalability of a video processing problem is thus influenced by the video compression features used (e.g. number of I frames as I frames typically create independent video segments). This also implies that the framework for workload distribution on the cloud has to be media aware.

Real-time video is generated by a single source and improving the throughput, i.e., increasing the number of streams processed, is a key performance consideration for a service provider. Depending on the type of service, real-time video services allow a few seconds of delay and the buffered video can be used to parallelize the problem and increase the throughput. The real-time nature of the video data stream puts constraints on how the performance can be improved. Solutions such as load balancing are more appropriate and distributed computing frameworks such as Hadoop are not suitable.

7 Conclusion and Ongoing Work

User-centric smart services will create a paradigm shift in the way management perceives IT in the organization. In this chapter we have detailed our vision for services lifecycle in the Smart Internet. We have described the service manager, monitor, procurer and integrator applications that will need to be developed. To the best of our knowledge, this is the first such effort, and it provides a description of the new applications needed to automate discovery, acquisition and deployment of services. As part of our ongoing work, we are developing policies for service procurer using the Semantic Web technologies. Usability issues in cloud computing also need to be explored further to provide environments for cloud service users that are more effective, efficient and user friendly.

Acknowledgments

The authors would like to acknowledge the support of IBM CAS Toronto and MURI grant 00003857 from the Air Force Office of Scientific Research.

References

1. Ng, J.W., Chignell, M., Cordy, J.R.: The Smart Internet: Transforming the Web for the User. In: Martin, P., Kark, A.W., Stewart, D. (eds.) Proceedings of the 2009 Conference of the Centres for Advanced Studies on Collaborative Research, CASCON 2009, Ontario, Canada, November 02-05, pp. 285–296. ACM, New York (2009)
2. Xu, M., Hu, Z., Long, W., Liu, W.: Service virtualization: Infrastructure and applications - The Grid: Blueprint for a New Computing Infrastructure by Ian Foster, Carl Kesselman. Morgan Kaufman, San Francisco (2004)
3. Joshi, A., Jiang, Z.: Retriever: Improving Web Search Engine Results Using Clustering. In: Gangopadhyay, A. (ed.) Managing Business with Electronic Commerce: Issues and Trends. Idea Press (2001)
4. Stanford Personalized PageRank Project, `http://nlp.stanford.edu/projects/pagerank.shtml`, last retrieved on October 12 (2009)
5. Balke, W.T., Wagner, M.: Towards personalized selection of web services, (WWW 2003) Alternate Track on Web Services (2003)
6. Papazoglou, M., Van Den Heuvel, W.: Service-oriented design and development methodology. International Journal of Web Engineering and Technology 2(4), 412–442 (2006)
7. Bianchini, D., De Antonellis, V., Pernici, B., Plebani, P.: Ontology-based methodology for e-service discovery. International Journal of Information Systems, The Semantic Web and Web Services 31(4-5), 361–380 (2006)
8. Zeng, L., Benatallah, B., Dumas, M., Kalagnanam, J., Sheng, Q.: Quality driven web services composition. In: Proceedings of the 12th International Conference on World Wide Web, pp. 411–421 (2003)
9. Maximilien, E.M., Singh, M.: A Framework and Ontology for Dynamic Web Services Selection. IEEE Internet Computing 8(5), 84–93 (2004)
10. Black, J., et al.: An integration model for organizing IT service Management. IBM Systems Journal 46(3) (2007)
11. Milanovic, N., Malek, M.: Current solutions for Web service composition. IEEE Internet Computing 8(6), 51–59 (2004)
12. Dustdar, S., Schreiner, W.: A Survey on web services composition. Int. Journal on Web and Grid Services, InderScience 1(1), 1–30 (2005)
13. Lassila, O., Swick, R., and others.: Resource Description Framework (RDF) Model and Syntax Specification. In: World Wide Web Consortium (1999)
14. McGuinness, D., Van Harmelen, F., et al.: OWL web ontology language overview. In: W3C recommendation, World Wide Web Consortium (2004)
15. Web Services Description Language (WSDL) 1.1 March (2001), `http://www.w3.org/TR/wsdl`
16. Web Services Business Execution Language (WS-BPEL) 2.0, `http://docs.oasis-open.org/wsbpel/2.0/wsbpel-v2.0.pdf`
17. Microsoft System Center: Service Manager, `http://www.microsoft.com/systemcenter/en/us/servicemanager.aspx`, retrieved April 5 (2010)
18. IBM Service Management, `http://www-01.ibm.com/software/tivoli/solutions/`, retrieved April 5 (2010)

19. Hewlett-Packard Service Manager software, retrieved April 5 (2010), https://h10078.www1.hp.com/cda/hpms/display/main/hpms_content.jsp?zn=bto&cp=1-11-8512473_4000_100__&jumpid=reg_R1002_USEN
20. Oracle Web Services Manager, http://www.oracle.com/appserver/web-services-manager.html, retrieved April 5 (2010)
21. Kagal, L., Finin, T., Joshi, A.: A Policy Based Approach to Security for the Semantic Web. In: Fensel, D., Sycara, K., Mylopoulos, J. (eds.) ISWC 2003. LNCS, vol. 2870, pp. 402–418. Springer, Heidelberg (2003)
22. Web Services Policy Framework, Contributed by IBM, BEA Systems, Microsoft, SAP AG, Sonic Software, VeriSign, http://www.ibm.com/developerworks/library/specification/ws-polfram/, retrieved on April 26 (2010)
23. Ran, S.: A model for web services discovery with QoS. ACM SIGecom Exchanges 4(1), 1–10 (2003)
24. Shneiderman, B.: Designing the User Interface: Strategies for Effective Human-Computer Interaction. Addison-Wesley, New York (1992)
25. Nielsen, J.: Usability Engineering. Morgan Kaufmann Publishers Inc., San Francisco (1993)
26. Ozok, A.A., Fan, Q., Norcio, A.: Design Guidelines for Effective Recommender System Interfaces Based on a Usability Criteria Conceptual Model. Behaviour and Information Technology 29(1), 57–83
27. Ozok, A.A., Salvendy, G.: How Consistent is Your Web Design? Behaviour and Information Technology 20(6), 433–447
28. Ozok, A.A.: Survey Design and Implementation in Human Computer Interaction. In: Jacko, J., Sears, A. (eds.) The Human-Computer Interaction Handbook, 2nd edn., pp. 1151–1169. Lawrence Erlbaum Associates, Mahwah
29. Jillani, R., Kalva, H.: Exploiting spatio-temporal characteristics of human vision for mobile video applications. In: Proceedings of SPIE Volume 7073, Applications of Digital Image Processing XXXI, part of SPIE Optics + Photonics, San Diego, CA (2008) (Invited Paper)
30. Vetro, A., Kalva, H.: Technologies and Standards for Universal Multimedia Access. In: Furht, B. (ed.) Handbook of Video Databases. CRC Press, Boca Raton (2003), ISBN 0-8493-7006-X

Monitoring and Recovery of Web Service Applications

Jocelyn Simmonds, Shoham Ben-David, and Marsha Chechik

Department of Computer Science, University of Toronto
{jsimmond,shoham,chechik}@cs.toronto.edu

Abstract. For a system of distributed processes, correctness can be ensured by (statically) checking whether their composition satisfies properties of interest. However, web services are distributed processes that dynamically discover properties of other web services. Since the overall system may not be available statically and since each business process is supposed to be relatively simple, we propose to use (on-line) runtime monitoring of conversations between partners as a means of checking behavioural correctness of the entire web service system. Our framework allows application developers to specify behavioural correctness properties. By transforming these properties to finite-state automata, we enable conformance checking of finite execution traces of web services described in BPEL against the specification. Moreover, when violations are discovered at runtime, we automatically propose and rank recovery plans which users of the system can then select for execution. For some of the violations, such plans essentially involve "going back" – compensating the occurred actions until an alternative behaviour of the application is possible. For other violations, such plans include both "going back" and "re-planning" – guiding the application towards a desired behaviour. We report on the implementation and experience with our monitoring and recovery system, and discuss the implications that the move to "smart internet" [1] may have on our approach.

1 Introduction

Recent years have seen an emergence of the field of web services, which use Service-Oriented Architectures (SOA) to dynamically discover and bind to services in order to increase the flexibility of business interactions. Each service consists of *components* and can discover other components using published interfaces. An SOA component can be written in a traditional compiled language such as Java™, or in an XML-centric language such as BPEL [2]. An SOA *module* is made up of multiple SOA components which are commonly referred to as web services.

Since each web service is a relatively simple process, analysis can concentrate on the message exchange between partners – their *conversations*. For a classical system of distributed processes, correctness can be ensured by statically checking their composition against properties of interest. The same approach has been taken by several researchers in the context of web services as well, e.g., [3, 4, 5, 6, 7]. While static analysis is very appealing – errors are discovered ahead of time and without the need to exercise the system, this approach has several major limitations:

M. Chignell et al. (Eds.): The Smart Internet, LNCS 6400, pp. 250–288, 2010.

- Web services are distributed systems, where partners are dynamically discovered and are going on- and off-line as the application runs.
- Web services typically communicate via infinite-length channels, so the problem is decidable only under certain conditions [8].
- Web applications usually interact with web services developed by partners. Partners are only required to make web service interfaces public, not the code.
- Realistic web services exchange many types of messages: some synchronous, some asynchronous, and some with acknowledgements and priorities.
- Web services are typically heterogeneous, i.e., each component can be implemented in a different programming language.

Instead, we concentrate on the dynamic analysis via *runtime monitoring*, which tries to ensure the quality of an application through the analysis of runtime events. *Online* monitoring – during the execution of the application – concentrates on monitoring *predefined properties*, collecting just those events which are related to the given properties. Moreover, monitoring as the system runs provides a chance to recover from an error once a problem has been detected.

This chapter describes a user-guided runtime monitoring and recovery framework for web services expressed in BPEL. Our motivation was the traditional web services model, where services reside on the server and communicate with other partners or with the user. We discuss the implications that the move towards *smart internet*, described in [1], has on our approach at the end of the paper, in Section 10.

In the "traditional" web service model, properties describe behavior, specifically, interactions between service partners. Such properties are effectively scenarios that the system should exhibit and those that the system should not exhibit. Such desired and forbidden behaviors can come from use-cases, global invariants, simulation, or a variety of other sources. In this chapter, we express behavioural correctness properties using the Specification Pattern System (SPS) [9], converting the high-level patterns into quantified regular expressions (QRE) and then to finite-state automata. We then use the automata to enable conformance checking of finite execution traces and recovery, should a violation be detected.

Motivating Example. Consider a simple web-based Trip Advisor System (TAS). In a typical scenario, a customer either chooses to arrive at her destination via a rental car (and thus books it), or via an air/ground transportation combination, combining the flight with either a rental car from the airport or a limo. The requirement of the system is to make sure the customer has the transportation needed to get to her destination (this is a desired behavior which we refer to as P_1) while keeping the costs down, i.e., she is not allowed by her company to reserve an expensive flight and a limo (this is a forbidden behavior which we refer to as P_2).

Figure 1 presents an assembly diagram depicting interactions between the main TAS process and its partners – the Car system (which offers two web services: one to reserve cars and and another to reserve limos) and the Flight system (which offers two web services: one to reserve flights and another to check whether the flights are cheap or expensive). This is depicted in Figure 1 by two sets of connections between TAS and each of the Flight and the Car components. Since the TAS system is a composition of several distributed business processes, its correctness depends on the correctness of its

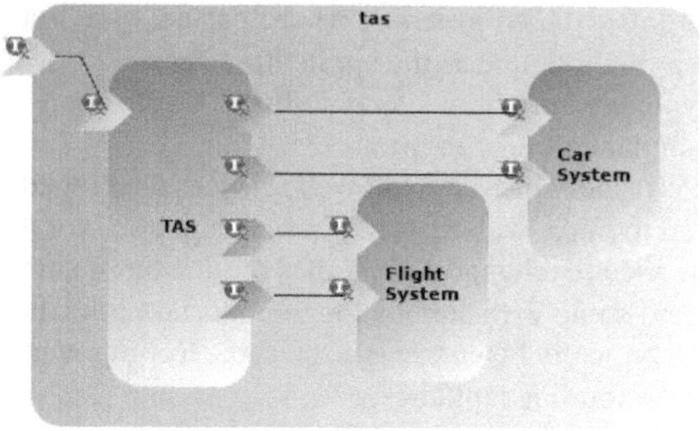

Fig. 1. Assembly diagram describing interactions between the main TAS process and its partners.

partners and their interactions. For example, the Car system can go down while the user attempts to book ground transportation, thus preventing the entire system from getting the user to her destination.

2 Overview of the Approach

The overview of the approach is given in Figure 2.

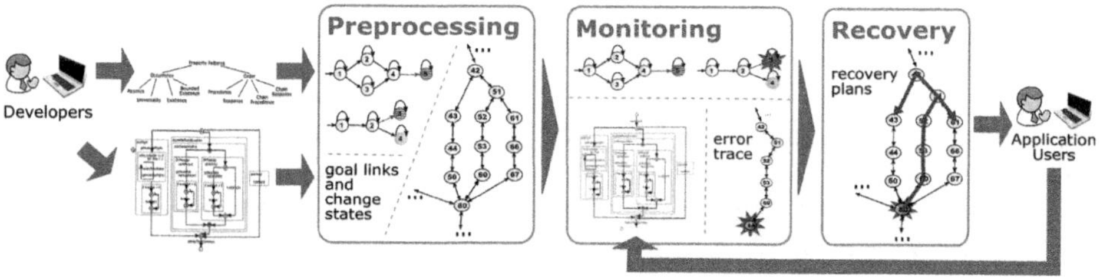

Fig. 2. Overview of our approach.

Failures of web services can be caused by bugs in the service orchestration, e.g., due to faulty logic and bad data manipulation, or by problems with hardware, network or system software, or by incorrect invocations of services. With runtime failures of web services inevitable, infrastructures for running them typically include the ability to define faults and compensatory actions for dealing with exceptional situations. Specifically, the *compensation* mechanism is the application-specific way of reversing completed activities. For example, the compensation for booking a car would be to cancel the booking.

In our approach, developers supply a BPEL program and a set of behavioral correctness properties (expressed using property patterns) that need to be maintained by the program as it runs. The BPEL program is enriched (by its developers) with the compensation mechanism which allows us to undo some of the actions of the program.

In the Preprocessing phase, the correctness properties are turned into finite-state automata (monitors), and the BPEL program is turned into a labeled transition system. These are then passed to the Runtime monitoring phase which runs the monitors in parallel with the BPEL application, stopping when one of the monitors is about to enter its error state. The use of high-level properties allows us to detect the violation, and our event interception mechanism allows us to stop the application *right before* the violation occurs and begin the Recovery phase.

In the Recovery phase, we identify and optionally rank a set of possible plans that recover from runtime errors. Given an application path which led to a failure and a monitor which detected it, our goal is to compute a set of suggestions, i.e., *plans*, for recovering from these failures. For violations of properties capturing undesired behavior, such plans use compensation actions to allow the application to "go back" to an earlier state at which an alternative path that potentially avoids the fault is available. We call such states "change states"; these include user choices and certain partner calls. For example, if the TAS system described in Section 1 produces an itinerary that is too expensive, a potential recovery plan might be to undo the limo reservation (so that a car can now be booked) or to undo the flight reservation and see if a cheaper one can be found.

Yet just merely going back is insufficient to ensure that the system can produce a desired behavior. Thus, for properties capturing such a behavior we aim to compute plans that redirect the application towards executing new activities, those that lead to goal satisfaction. For example, if the flight reservation partner fails (and thus the air/ground combination is not available), the recovery plans would be to provide transportation to the user's destination (her "goal" state) either by calling the flight reservation again or by undoing the reserved ground transportation from the airport, if any, and try to reserve the rental car from home instead. The overall recovery planning problem is then stated as follows:

> From the current state in the system, find a plan to achieve the goal that goes through a change state.

When there are multiple recovery plans available, we automatically rank them based on user preferences (e.g., the shortest, the cheapest, the one that involves the minimal compensation, etc.) and enable the application user to choose among them.

In the rest of this chapter, we further describe and evaluate the above approach. Specifically, we describe inputs to our system, BPEL models and correctness properties, in Section 3. We define the representation of BPEL models as Labeled Transition Systems (LTS) and show how to use these representations for *static* identification of change states and goal transitions in Section 4. In this section, we also discuss how to convert behavioral correctness properties into finite-state automata. We discuss runtime monitoring in Section 5 and describe recovery from violations of behavioral properties in Section 6. We report on our implementation (Section 7) and use it to compute recovery plans for several web service examples (Section 8). We then compare our work with related approaches in Section 9. Finally, in Section 10, we summarize the chapter, give suggestions for future work, and discuss the relationship between our approach and the smart internet vision articulated in [1].

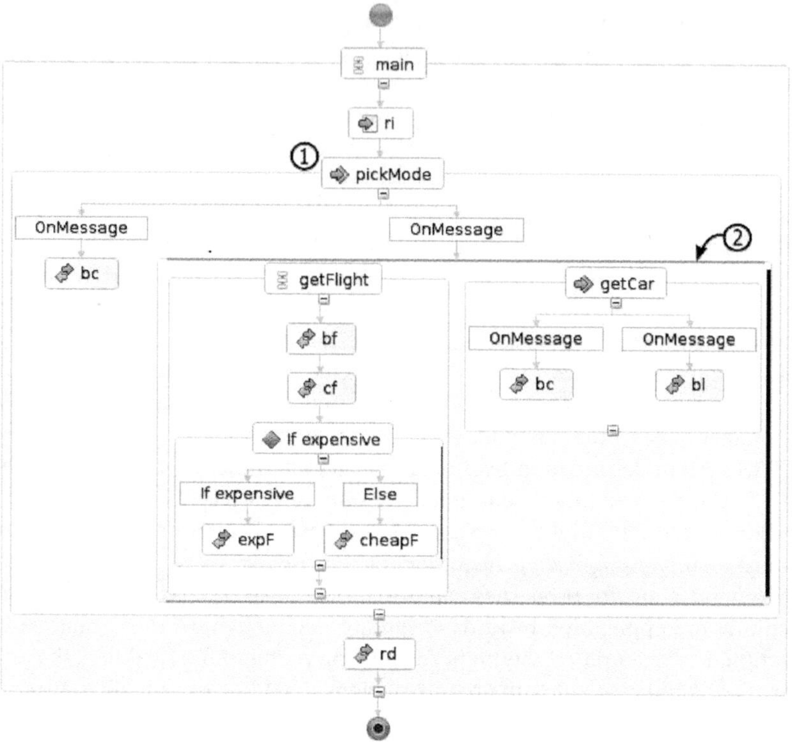

(a)

```
<scope name="bf">
   <invoke ... operation = "bf" ... outputVariable = "flightConf" />
   <compensationHandler cost = "9">
       <invoke ... operation = "cancelF" inputVariable = "flightConf"/>
   </compensationHandler>
</scope>
```

(b)

Fig. 3. (a) Workflow of TAS; (b) Compensation for booking a flight (bf).

3 Input

Inputs to our system are a BPEL program enriched with compensation actions and a set of behavioral correctness properties described as property patterns. We describe these below.

3.1 BPEL Programs

BPEL [2] is a standard for implementing orchestrations of web services (provided by partners) by specifying an executable workflow using predefined activities. The basic BPEL activities for interacting with partner web services are <receive>, <invoke> and

<reply>, which are used to receive messages, execute web services and return values, respectively. Conditional activities are used to define the control flow of the application: <while>, <if> and <pick>. The <while> and <if> activities model internal choice, as conditions are expressions over process variables. The <pick> activity is used to model external choice: the application waits for one of several possible messages (specified using <onMessage>) to occur, executing the associated child activity. The <pick> activity completes when the child activity completes.

The structural activities <sequence> and <flow> are used to specify sequential and parallel composition of the enclosed activities, respectively. The <scope> activity is used to define a nested activity. In IBM WebSphere Integration Developer v7, developers can also add <collaboration> scopes, inspired by the work on dynamic workflows [10], which can be used to alter the application logic at runtime.

Figure 3a shows the BPEL-expressed workflow of the Trip Advisor System (TAS), introduced in Section 1. We use the Eclipse BPEL Project notation[1]. TAS interacts with four external services: 1) book a rental car (bc), 2) book a limo (bl), 3) book a flight (bf), and 4) check price of the flight (cf). The result of cf is then passed to local services to determine whether it is expensive (expF) or cheap (cheapF). Service interactions are preceded by a symbol.

The workflow begins with <receive>'ing input (ri), followed by <pick>'ing (indicated by labeled ①) either the car rental (onMessage onlyCar) or the air/ground transportation combination (onMessage carAndFlight). The latter choice is modeled using a <flow> (scope enclosed in bold, blue lines —, labeled ②) since air (getFlight) and ground transportation (getCar) can be arranged independently, so they are executed in isolation. The air branch sequentially books a flight, checks if it is expensive and updates the state of the system accordingly. The ground branch <pick>'s between booking a rental car and a limo. The end of the workflow is marked by a <reply> activity, reporting that the destination has been reached (rd).

Compensation. BPEL's *compensation* mechanism allows the definition of the application-specific reversal of completed activities. For example, the compensation for booking a flight (bf) is to cancel the booking (cancelF). This is described in BPEL as shown in Figure 3b: the <invoke> and its compensation are enclosed in a named <scope> (the scope's name is later used to execute compensation).

Compensation handlers (CH) are attached to <scope> and <invoke> activities (a <scope> activity is used to logically group activities) and are executed by fault, termination and compensation via the <compensate> and <compensateScope> activities. The default compensation respects the forward order of execution of the scopes being compensated:

> If a and b are two activities, where a completed execution before b, then compensate($a; b$) is compensate(b); compensate(a).

An attempt to compensate a scope for which the CH either has not been installed, or has been installed and executed, is treated as executing an <empty> activity (we denote these by τ).

[1] `http://www.eclipse.org/bpel/index.php`.

We further extended BPEL to allow application developers to associate compensations with different costs, e.g., to indicate that canceling a flight might be significantly more expensive than canceling a car. We do this by adding an extra attribute cost to the definition of <compensationHandler>. For example, the flight booking compensation defined in Figure 3b has been assigned a cost of 9 (out of 10), indicating that this is an expensive compensation and should be avoided if possible.

3.2 Specifying Properties

The second input to our system is a set of properties that the application must satisfy. These properties, provided by the developer, are then used to monitor the run, detect errors and guide the production of recovery plans. We assume that the properties are specified using the *Specification Pattern System* (SPS). This system (described below), has been advocated as a standard tool for measuring the practical usefulness and expressive power of specification languages, e.g., [11, 12].

Our framework also includes an (optional) ranking of the properties in the order of importance. As with any other property-based specification, it is possible that the property list is incomplete (i.e., some system requirements are not captured) or even inconsistent (i.e., satisfying the entire set of requirements is not possible).

Specification Patterns. The *Specification Pattern System* (SPS), proposed by Dwyer et al. [13], is a pattern-based approach to the presentation, codification, and reuse of property specifications. The system allows patterns like "event P is absent between events Q and S" or "S precedes P between Q and R" to be easily expressed in and translated between linear-time temporal logic (LTL) [14], computational tree logic (CTL) [15], quantified regular expressions (QRE) [16] and other state-based and event-based formalisms.

The property patterns are organized into a hierarchy based on the kinds of system behaviors they describe (see Figure 4a): **Occurrence** patterns talk about the occurrence of a given event/state during system execution, and **Order** patterns specify relative order in which multiple events/states occur during system execution. The patterns are described in Table 1.

Table 1. SPS patterns

Absence	An event does not occur within a given scope;
Existence	An event must occur within a given scope;
Bounded Existence	An event can occur at most a certain number of times within a given scope;
Universality	An event must occur throughout a given scope;
Response	An event must always be followed by another within a scope;
Response Chain	A chain of events must always be followed by another chain of events within a scope;
Precedence	An event must always be preceded by another within a scope;
Precedence Chain	A chain of events must always be preceded by another chain of events within a scope.

Each pattern is associated with *scopes* – the regions of interest over which the pattern must hold. There are five basic kinds of scopes: **Global**, **Before**, **After**, **Between** and **After-Until**. Definitions of these are given in Table 2 and pictorially described in Figure 4b.

Table 2. SPS scopes

Global	The entire program execution;
Before R	The execution up to event R;
After Q	The execution after event Q;
Between Q **and** R	All parts of the execution between events Q and R;
After Q **until** R	Similar to **Between**, except that the designated part of the execution continues even if the second event does not occur.

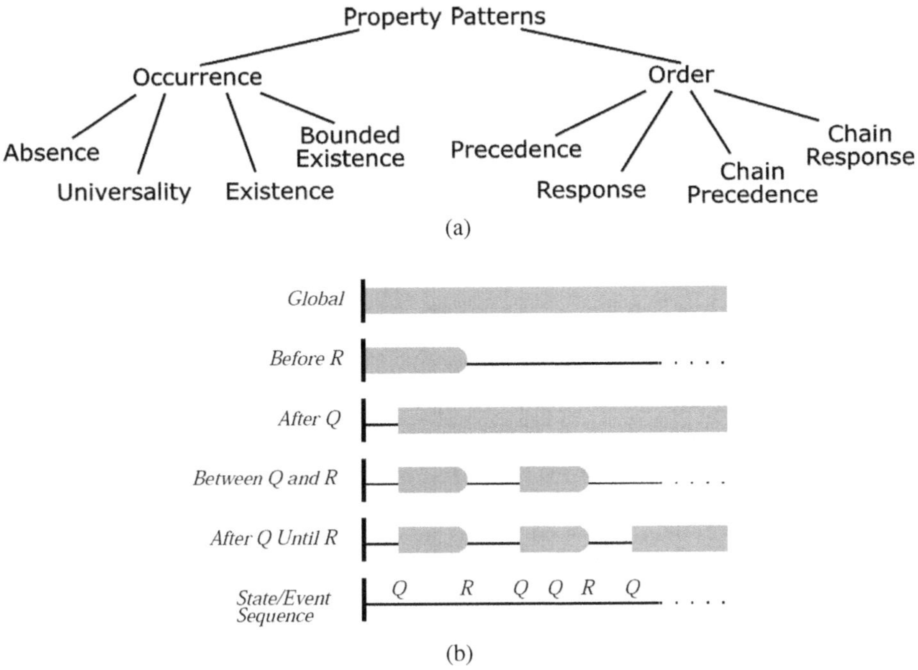

Fig. 4. Specification property system: (a) a pattern hierarchy and (b) pattern scopes.

Using the Patterns System. To use the pattern system, the specifier begins with a property of interest expressed in natural language. She then identifies atomic actions in the property, then determines a pattern and a scope and chooses a desired output language. For example, the two requirements of the TAS system are to make sure that the customer has the transportation needed to get to her destination, while keeping the costs down. More formally, they become "P_1: if requested (ri), TAS will guarantee that the transportation booked reaches the customer's destination (rd), regardless of the type of transportation chosen". This is the **Response** pattern in a **Global** scope. We now look up the pattern and the scope in the table. We use the QRE encoding that is easily translatable into monitors as shown in Section 4.2. For our example, the resulting QRE property is

$$P_1 = [-\mathsf{ri}] * \cdot(\mathsf{ri} \cdot [-\mathsf{rd}] * \cdot \mathsf{rd} \cdot [-\mathsf{ri}]*)*$$

Formalizing the second requirement, we get "P_2: the user cannot book both a limousine (bl) and an expensive flight (expF)". To express this using patterns, we use two instances of the **Absence** pattern in the **After** scope: A limousine should never be booked (bl) after an expensive flight has been booked (expF) and vice versa. In QRE, we get a pair of properties:

$$P_{2a} = [-\mathsf{bl}] * \cdot (\mathsf{bl} \cdot [-\mathsf{expF}]*)?$$

$$P_{2b} = [-\mathsf{expF}] * \cdot (\mathsf{expF} \cdot [-\mathsf{bl}]*)?$$

When monitoring the application, we need to make sure that both P_{2a} and P_{2b} hold in order to comply with the requirement P_2.

Since we use specifications to establish runtime correctness of a set of conversations between BPEL-expressed partners, we need to determine it using finite traces. Thus, not all patterns are appropriate for this view, since some use future events as preconditions. For example, the scope **Before R** requires that the pattern holds only if **R** eventually occurs on the evaluated path. The same problem occurs with the scope **Between Q and R**. In our setting, the monitoring is performed on the current execution, without looking ahead, and thus those scopes are not supported.

Positive and Negative Behaviors. We differentiate between properties describing *negative* behaviors (that should not appear in the application), and properties describing *positive* behaviors (that the system must posses). For example, property P_1 above describes a positive behavior (the destination must be reached), while P_2 describes a negative scenario that should be avoided (a limousine and an expensive flight are booked). Negative scenarios are commonly called *safety* properties, and require a finite sequence of actions to witness their violations. For property P_2, one such violating witness is "book an expensive flight, and then book a limo". For safety properties, no finite sequence of actions can show satisfaction.

Positive behaviors, on the other hand, can also be (locally) satisfied. This happens when the desired sequence is fully seen even though the property calls for repeated sequences of desired behaviour. For example, for property P_1, if rd has been seen, and a new ri was not yet initiated, the specification is locally satisfied. In many cases, properties may have both a negative and a positive component, and thus we refer to such properties as *mixed*[2].

4 Preprocessing

Inputs to the preprocessing stage are the BPEL program B and the set of properties written in QRE. We begin with converting B into a formal representation, L(B), which is a labeled transition system (LTS). We then enrich it with transitions on compensation actions to get $\mathsf{L_C(B)}$ (see Section 4.1). In Section 4.2, we discuss the translation of a given QRE specification into a monitor. Finally, in Section 4.3 we formalize *change states* and potential *goal* transitions and provide an algorithm for computing these statically on $\mathsf{L_C(B)}$.

[2] Formally, mixed properties are either finitary liveness properties or a mixture of finitery liveness and safety properties.

4.1 BPEL to LTS

In order to reason about BPEL applications, we need to represent them formally, so as to make precise the meaning of "taking a transition", "reading in an event", etc. Several formalisms for representing BPEL models have been suggested [4,17,18]. In this work, we build on Foster's [19] approach of using an LTS as the underlying formalism.

Definition 1 (Labeled Transition Systems). *A* Labeled Transition System *LTS is a quadruple* (S, Σ, δ, I), *where* S *is a set of states,* Σ *is a set of labels,* $\delta \subseteq S \times \Sigma \times S$ *is a transition relation, and* $I \subseteq S$ *is a set of initial states.*

Effectively, LTSs are state machine models, where transitions are labeled whereas states are not. We often use the notation $s \xrightarrow{a} s'$ to stand for $(s, a, s') \in \delta$. An *execution*, or a *trace*, of an LTS is a sequence $\mathsf{T} = s_0 a_0 s_1 a_1 s_2 ... a_{n-1} s_n$ such that $\forall i, 0 \leq i < n$, $s_i \in S$, $a_i \in \Sigma$ and $s_i \xrightarrow{a_i} s_{i+1}$.

Existing Translation. [19] specifies mapping of all BPEL 1.0 activities into LTS. For example, Figure 4.1 shows the translation of the <invoke> activity bf which returns a confirmation number. The activity is a sequence of two transitions: the actual service invocation (invoke_bf) and its return (receive_bf)[3]. Conditional activities like <while> and <if> are represented as states with two outgoing transitions, one for each valuation of the condition. The LTSs for these two activities are shown in Figure 5a. Note that both LTSs have two transitions from state 1: $1 \xrightarrow{\mathsf{expr\_true}} 2$ and $1 \xrightarrow{\mathsf{expr\_false}} 3$. <pick> is also a conditional activity, but can have one or more outgoing transitions: one for each <onMessage> branch (there are two of these in the example in Figure 5a. <sequence> and <flow> activities result in the sequential and the parallel composition of the enclosed activities, respectively (see Figure 5b).

Thus, formally, we are going from a BPEL program B to its LTS translation L(B). The set of labels Σ of L(B) is derived from the possible events in B: service invocations and returns, <onMessage> events, <scope> entries, and condition valuations. It also includes the new system event TER, modeling termination. The set of states S in L(B) consists of the states produced by the translation as well as a new state t. This state is reached from any state of S via a TER event: $\forall s \in S \setminus \{\mathsf{t}\}, (s, \mathsf{TER}, \mathsf{t}) \in \delta$.

Formalizing Compensation. In order to capture BPEL's compensation mechanism, we introduce additional, backwards transitions. For example, the compensation for bf, specified in Figure 3b, is captured by adding the transition $3 \xrightarrow{\mathsf{invoke\_cancelF}} 1$ as shown in Figure 4.1. Taking this transition effectively leaves the application in a state where bf has not been executed. We denote by τ an 'empty' action, allowing undoing of an action without requiring an explicit compensation action.

Note that we have made a major assumption that compensation returns the application to one of the states that has been previously seen. Thus, given a BPEL program B and its translation to LTS $\mathsf{L(B)} = (S, \Sigma, \delta, I)$, we translate B with compensation into an LTS $\mathsf{L_C(B)} = (S, \Sigma \cup \Sigma_c, \delta \cup \delta_c, I)$, where Σ_c is the set of compensation actions (including τ) and δ_c is the set of compensation transitions.

[3] Foster's translation uses names to include traceability information to the BPEL's scopes. We omit these in this chapter for simplicity.

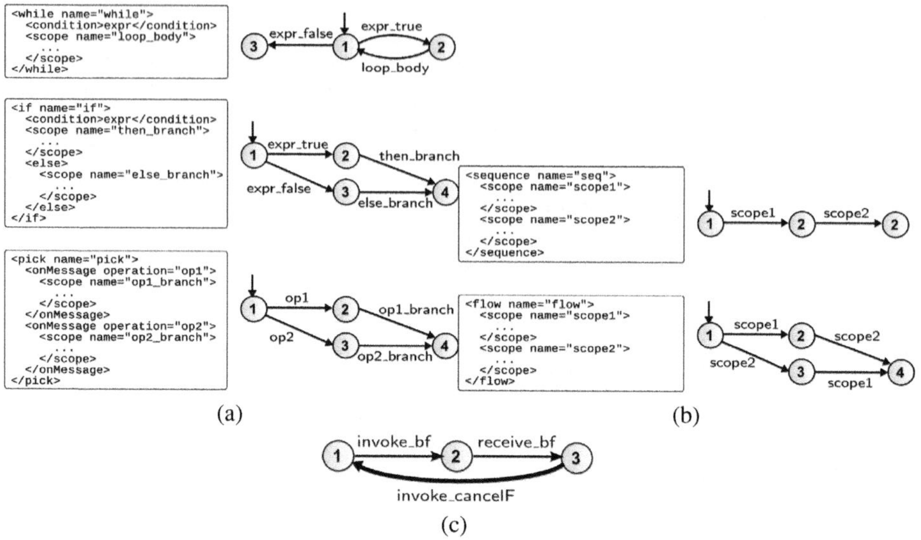

Fig. 5. (a) BPEL conditional activities and their corresponding LTSs; (b) BPEL structural activities and their corresponding LTSs; (c) LTS translation of the <invoke> activity bf and its compensation (bold).

Figure 6a shows $\mathsf{L_C}(\mathtt{TAS})$. To increase legibility, we do not show the termination state t and transitions to it. Also, we only show one transition for each service invocation, abstracting the return transition and state. In this notation, the LTS in Figure 4.1 has two transitions: $1 \xrightarrow{\mathsf{bf}} 3$ and $3 \xrightarrow{\mathsf{cancelF}} 1$. This allows us to visually combine an action and its compensation into one transition, labeled in the form $a/\bar{a}$, where a is the application activity and $\bar{a}$ is its compensation. In other words, each transition $s \xleftrightarrow{a/\bar{a}} t$ in Figure 6a represents two transitions: $(s, a, t) \in \delta$ and $(t, \bar{a}, s) \in \delta_c$.

The <pick> activity (➪ labeled ① in Figure 3a) corresponds to state 2 of Figure 6a. The choice between onlyCar and carAndFlight is represented by two outgoing transitions from this state: (2, onlyCar, 3) and (2, carAndFlight, 6). Since these actions do not affect the state of the application, they are compensated by τ. The <flow> activity (scope enclosed in bold, blue lines — labeled ② in Figure 3a) results in two branches, depending on the order in which the air and ground transportation are executed. The compensation for these events is also τ.

4.2 From Properties to Monitors

In order to be verified, properties are translated into deterministic finite state machines (FSMs) that we call "monitors". Different algorithms to perform such a translation from a QRE formula exist in the literature [20]. The translation we use generates a monitor that accepts the *bad* computations of the application – those on which the property fails to hold.

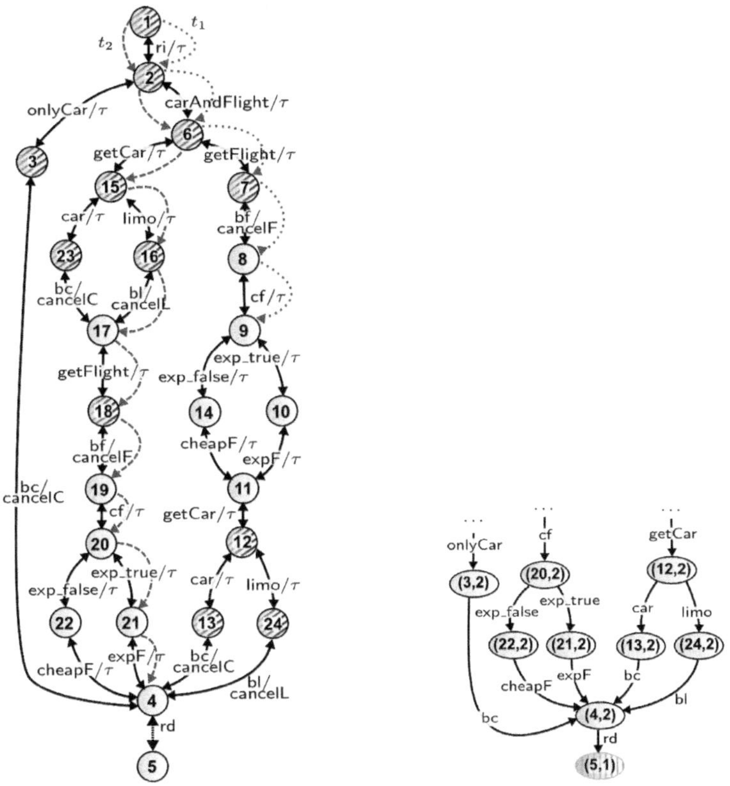

(a) (b)

Fig. 6. (a) LTS $\mathsf{L}_\mathsf{C}(\mathtt{TAS})$, showing traces t_1 (dotted) and t_2 (dashed); (b) a fragment of $\mathsf{L}(\mathtt{TAS}) \times \mathtt{A}_1$.

For example, Figure 7c shows the monitor built for the property pattern: "s responds to p after q until r". State 4 of the monitor (colored red and shaded horizontally) is an accepting state, since if we reach it, a violation has been seen: there was a q and later a p (bringing the monitor to state 3), but this p was not followed by s either because r appeared first, or because the application terminated. State 2 (colored green and shaded vertically) is a good state: if we reach it after p was seen, it means that a response by s occurred as needed. Σ is the alphabet of the monitor, i.e., it includes every event occurring in the application, as defined in Section 4.1.

Similar monitors are built for our example properties P_1 and P_2. Monitor $\mathtt{A}_1$ in Figure 7a represents P_1: if the application terminates before rd appears, the monitor moves to the (error) state 3. State 1 is a good state since the monitor enters it once the booked transportations reach the destination (rd). Monitor $\mathtt{A}_2$ in Figure 7b represents both P_{2a} and P_{2b} (defined in Section 3.2). It enters its error state (4) when either a limo was booked and later an expensive flight (corresponding to the violation of P_{2a}), or an expensive flight was booked first and then a limo (violating P_{2b}). We formalize (colored) monitors below.

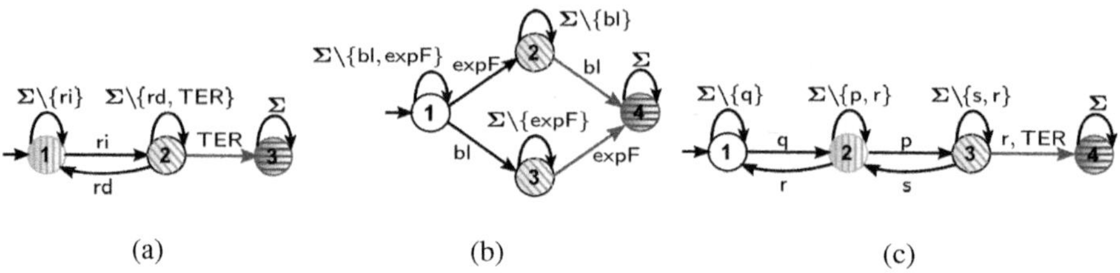

Fig. 7. Monitors: (a) A_1, (b) A_2, and (c) for a property pattern "s responds to p after q until r". Red states are shaded horizontally, green states are shaded vertically, and yellow states are shaded diagonally.

Definition 2 (monitor). *A* monitor *is a 5-tuple* $A = (S, \Sigma, \delta, I, F)$*, where* (S, Σ, δ, I) *is an LTS and* $F \subseteq S$ *is a set of final states.*

We say that A *accepts* a word $a_0a_1a_2...a_{n-1} \in \Sigma^*$ iff there exists an execution $s_0a_0s_1a_1s_2...a_{n-1}s_n$ of A such that $a_0 \in I$ and $s_n \in F$. In our case, the accepted words correspond to *bad* computations, and the set F of accepting states represents error states.

Let $A = (S, \Sigma, \delta, I, F)$ be a monitor. In order to facilitate recovery, we assign colors to states in S. Accepting states are colored red, signaling violation of the property. State 3 of Figure 7a and state 4 in Figures 7b and 7c are red states. Yellow states are those from which a red state can be reached through a single transition. Formally, for a state $s \in S$,

$$\textit{color}(s) = \text{yellow if } \exists a \in \Sigma, s' \in F \cdot (s, a, s') \in \delta.$$

In addition, we also color yellow those states whose successors are all yellow.

$$\textit{color}(s) = \text{yellow if } \forall a \in \Sigma, \forall s' \in S \cdot (s, a, s') \in \delta \Rightarrow \textit{color}(s') = \text{yellow}.$$

State 2 in Figure 7a, states 2 and 3 in Figure 7b and state 3 in Figure 7c are yellow states.

The green color is used for states that can serve as good places to which a recovery plan can be directed. We define green states to be those states that are not red or yellow, but that can be reached through a single transition from a yellow state. Formally,

$$\begin{aligned}\textit{color}(s) = \text{green iff } &(\textit{color}(s) \neq \text{red}) \wedge (\textit{color}(s) \neq \text{yellow}) \wedge \\ &(\exists a \in \Sigma, \exists s' \in S \cdot (\textit{color}(s') = \text{yellow}) \wedge ((s', a, s) \in \delta)).\end{aligned}$$

State 1 in Figure 7a, as well as state 2 in Figure 7c are colored green. Note that not all monitors have green states. For example, in A_2 of Figure 7b every yellow state (2 and 3) has outgoing transitions only to yellow or red states. Thus these states are "inescapable", and the monitor has no green states. A monitor with no green states is called a *safety* monitor. Otherwise, it is called a *mixed* monitor.

Given specification properties $\Phi_1 - \Phi_n$, we translate them to a set $A = \{A_1, ..., A_n\}$ of monitors, denoting by A_S the subset of A that includes all safety monitors.

4.3 Identifying Change States and Goal Transitions

The second part of the preprocessing phase *statically* identifies strategic behaviors of the application L(B), aimed to help find an efficient recovery plan when a violation is encountered (see Section 6).

Goal Transitions. In order to find a good recovery plan, we first need to compute a set of *goal transitions*, that is, transitions taken by the application which (immediately) result in some properties reaching a green state. We compute these on a per-property basis. Recall that not all monitors have green states; thus, we define goal transitions only for monitors that do include green states. Let $\mathsf{A_i} = (S_i, \Sigma, \delta_i, I_i, F_i)$ be such a monitor. We are looking for transitions in $\mathsf{L(B)} = (S, \Sigma, \delta, I)$ which correspond to $\mathsf{A_i}$ moving from a yellow state and entering a green state. To find those, we compute the cross-product $\mathsf{L(B)} \times \mathsf{A_i}$. $(s, a, s') \in \delta$ is a *goal transition* iff $\exists q, q' \in S_i \cdot (s, q) \xrightarrow{a} (s', q') \wedge \mathit{color}(q) = \text{yellow} \wedge \mathit{color}(q') = \text{green}$. That is, $s \xrightarrow{a} s'$ corresponds to taking a transition on a from a yellow state into a green state of $\mathsf{A_i}$. The resulting set of goal transitions is denoted by $\mathsf{G(B, A_i)}$.

For example, consider a fragment of $\mathsf{L(TAS)} \times \mathtt{A_1}$ shown in Figure 6b. The green state of $\mathtt{A_1}$ is state 1, with a transition on rd leading to it from state 2, which is a yellow state. The only transition in $\mathsf{L(TAS)} \times \mathtt{A_1}$ satisfying the above definition is $(4, 2) \xrightarrow{\mathsf{rd}} (5, 1)$, and thus $\mathsf{G(TAS, A_1)} = \{(4, \mathsf{rd}, 5)\}$ (depicted by tiny-dashed transitions in Figure 6a).

When computing recovery plans, we need to direct the application towards taking its goal transitions. While the process of identification of goal transitions requires a cross-product computation between the system and each monitor, this computation is done off-line and thus does not affect performance of the overall recovery framework.

Change States. Given an erroneous run, how far back do we need to compensate before resuming forward computation? If we want to avoid repeating the same error again, we need the application to take an alternative path. States of L(B) that have actions executing which can potentially produce a branch in control flow of the application are called *change states*.

Flow-changing actions are user choices, states modeling the <flow> activity (since each pass through this state may produce a different interleaving of actions), and those service calls whose outcomes are not completely determined by their input parameters but instead depend on the implicit state "of the world". This characteristics of services is sometimes referred to as *idempotence*, since multiple invocations of the same service yield the same results. Thus, non-idempotent service calls also identify change states. For example, cheapF is a call to determine whether a given flight is cheap and, unless the specification of what cheap means changes, returns the same answer for a given flight. On the other hand, bf books an available flight, and each successive call to this service can produce different results. Non-idempotent service calls are identified by the BPEL developer as XML attributes in the BPEL program.

Let C(B) denote the set of all change states of the LTS of the application B. For example, in the LTS in Figure 6a, state 6 corresponds to the <flow> activity and represents the different serialization order of the branches. States 2, 12 and 15 model user choices. Non-idempotent partner calls are bf, bc, bl, and thus

$$\mathsf{C}(\mathtt{TAS}) = \{1, 2, 3, 6, 7, 12, 13, 15, 16, 18, 23, 24\},$$

identified in Figure 6a by shading.

A recovery plan should pass through at least one change state, to allow a change in the execution.

5 Runtime Monitoring

The runtime monitoring phase uses the set of monitors to analyze the BPEL program B as it runs on a BPEL-specific Application Server. The runtime monitoring component of our recovery framework is based on that of [21], which has been implemented within the IBM WebSphere business integration products[4]. We capture events in Σ as they pass between the application server and the program, and use these events to update the state of the monitors and store them as part of the execution trace T. Monitors can be dynamically enabled (e.g., to monitor new properties) and disabled (e.g., to reduce monitoring overhead). Since the application properties are specified separately from the BPEL program, no code instrumentation is required in this step, enabling non-intrusive (and scalable) online monitoring.

The *interception mechanism* used in [21] has been *eavesdropping* – watching events as they pass between partners and updating monitors accordingly. While adequate for identifying and reporting property violations, it is insufficient for recovery. For example, we do not want to execute a TER event before knowing whether its execution causes any monitor violations, since we cannot reverse application termination. We also want to avoid executing other events that may directly lead to monitor violation, since these events will be inevitably compensated during recovery. Thus, instead of allowing all events to pass, our monitoring component delays the delivery of events that cause termination or property violation. If no violation is detected during analysis, the event is delivered and execution continues as usual. Otherwise, the event is not delivered and recovery is initiated (see Section 7 for details).

For the LTS of the application $\mathsf{L}(\mathsf{B}) = (S, \Sigma, \delta, I)$, we store the trace of the execution:

$$\mathsf{T} = s_0 \xrightarrow{a_0} s_1 \xrightarrow{a_1} \ldots \xrightarrow{a_{n-1}} s_n.$$

We say that T is a *successful* trace iff $\forall \mathsf{A_i} \in \mathsf{A}$, $a_0 a_1 \ldots a_{n-1}$ is rejected by $\mathsf{A_i}$. T is a *failure* (or an *error*) trace iff $\exists \mathsf{A_i} \in \mathsf{A}$ s.t. $a_0 a_1 \ldots a_{n-1}$ is accepted by $\mathsf{A_i}$. In such a case, state s_n is an *error state* of the application. In addition to T, we also store traces $\mathsf{T}^{\mathsf{A_1}} \ldots \mathsf{T}^{\mathsf{A_n}}$ that correspond to the executions of the *monitors* $\mathsf{A}_1 \ldots \mathsf{A}_\mathsf{n}$, respectively. These are used in the recovery phase (see Section 6). Note that all traces corresponding to a single execution differ in their *states* (e.g., application states are different from states of each monitor) but agree on the *events* which got executed. In what follows, traces corresponding to the application have no superscripts, whereas monitor traces are superscripted.

[4] `http://www-306.ibm.com/software/info1/websphere/index.jsp?tab=products/businessint.`

For example, consider the execution of TAS in which the customer chooses the air/ground option (carAndFlight), and then tries to book the flight before the car. In this example, there is a communication problem with the flight system partner, and the invocation of the cf service time outs. This scenario corresponds to the trace t_1, depicted by dotted transitions in Figure 6a. In addition to t_1, our tool stores $t_1^{A_1}$ and $t_1^{A_2}$ – the corresponding traces of the enabled monitors:

$$t_1 = 1 \xrightarrow{\mathsf{ri}} 2 \xrightarrow{\mathsf{carAndFlight}} 6 \xrightarrow{\mathsf{getFlight}} 7 \xrightarrow{\mathsf{bf}} 8 \xrightarrow{\mathsf{cf}} 9,$$
$$t_1^{A_1} = 1 \xrightarrow{\mathsf{ri}} 2 \xrightarrow{\mathsf{carAndFlight}} 2, \xrightarrow{\mathsf{getFlight}} 2 \xrightarrow{\mathsf{bf}} 2 \xrightarrow{\mathsf{cf}} 2,$$
$$t_1^{A_2} = 1 \xrightarrow{\mathsf{ri}} 1 \xrightarrow{\mathsf{carAndFlight}} 1 \xrightarrow{\mathsf{getFlight}} 1 \xrightarrow{\mathsf{bf}} 1 \xrightarrow{\mathsf{cf}} 1.$$

The application server detects that the cf invocation timed out, and sends a TER event (not shown in Figure 6a) to the application. Our framework intercepts this TER event and determines that executing it turns t_1 into a failing trace, because the monitor A_1 would enter its error (red) state 3. In response, our framework does not deliver the TER event to the application, and instead initiates recovery.

In another scenario, the customer attempts to arrive at her destination via a limo (bl) and an expensive flight (expF). This corresponds to the trace t_2, depicted by dashed transitions in Figure 6a (the traces of the monitors are omitted):

$$t_2 = 1 \xrightarrow{\mathsf{ri}} 2 \xrightarrow{\mathsf{carAndFlight}} 6 \xrightarrow{\mathsf{getCar}} 15 \xrightarrow{\mathsf{limo}} 16 \xrightarrow{\mathsf{bl}} 17 \xrightarrow{\mathsf{getFlight}} 18 \xrightarrow{\mathsf{bf}} 19 \xrightarrow{\mathsf{cf}} 20 \xrightarrow{\mathsf{exp\_true}} 21 \xrightarrow{\mathsf{expF}} 4.$$

As the monitor A_2 has a transition on expF to an error state, our framework delays the execution of this event from application state 21. In this example, executing expF will make A_2 enter its error state 4, so t_2 is also a failing trace. The expF event is not delivered, and the recovery phase is activated.

6 Recovery from Violations

Once an error has been detected during runtime monitoring, the goal of the recovery phase is to suggest a number of *recovery plans* that would lead the application away from the error.

Definition 3 (Plan). *A* plan *is a sequence of actions. A* BPEL recovery plan *is a sequence of actions consisting of user interactions, compensations (empty or not) and calls to service partners.*

Recovery plans differ depending on the type of property which failed. In Section 6.1, we discuss recovery from violations of a safety monitor (i.e., the one without a green state), and in Section 6.2, we consider mixed monitors.

6.1 Recovery from Safety Monitor Violations

The recovery procedure for a safety property violation receives $L_C(B)$ – the LTS of the running application B with compensations (see Section 4.1), T – the executed trace ending in an error state e (see Section 5) and C(B) – the set of change states (see Section 4.3).

(a)
$$r_{18} = 4 \xrightarrow{\tau} 21 \xrightarrow{\tau} 20 \xrightarrow{\tau} 19 \xrightarrow{\mathsf{cancelF}} 18 \qquad r_6 = r_{15} \xrightarrow{\tau} 6$$
$$r_{16} = r_{18} \xrightarrow{\tau} 17 \xrightarrow{\mathsf{cancelL}} 16 \qquad r_2 = r_6 \xrightarrow{\tau} 2$$
$$r_{15} = r_{16} \xrightarrow{\tau} 15 \qquad r_1 = r_2 \xrightarrow{\tau} 1$$

(b)
$$p_0 = 9 \xrightarrow{\tau} 8 \xrightarrow{\mathsf{cancelF}} 7 \xrightarrow{\tau} 6 \xrightarrow{\tau} 2 \xrightarrow{\mathsf{onlyCar}} 3 \xrightarrow{\mathsf{bc}} 4$$
$$p_1 = 9 \xrightarrow{\tau} 8 \xrightarrow{\mathsf{cancelF}} 7 \xrightarrow{\mathsf{bf}} 8 \xrightarrow{\mathsf{cf}} 9 \xrightarrow{\mathsf{exp\_true}} 10 \xrightarrow{\mathsf{expF}} 11 \xrightarrow{\mathsf{getCar}} 12 \xrightarrow{\mathsf{car}} 13 \xrightarrow{\mathsf{bc}} 4$$
$$p_2 = 9 \xrightarrow{\tau} 8 \xrightarrow{\mathsf{cancelF}} 7 \xrightarrow{\mathsf{bf}} 8 \xrightarrow{\mathsf{cf}} 9 \xrightarrow{\mathsf{exp\_false}} 14 \xrightarrow{\mathsf{cheapF}} 11 \xrightarrow{\mathsf{getCar}} 12 \xrightarrow{\mathsf{car}} 13 \xrightarrow{\mathsf{bc}} 4$$

Fig. 8. Recovery plans for TAS: (a) plans for the safety violation of trace t_2; (b) plans of length ≤ 10 for recovery from the mixed property violation of trace t_1.

```
<sequence name="r18">
  <compensateScope target="expF" />
  <compensateScope target="exp_true" />
  <compensateScope target="cf" />
  <compensateScope target="bf" />
</sequence>
```

(a)

```
<sequence name="p0">
  <compensateScope target="cf" />
  <compensateScope target="bf" />
  <compensateScope target="getFlight" />
  <compensateScope target="carAndFlight" />
  <pick name="transport" ... >
     <onMessage operation="onlyCar" ... >
       ...
     </onMessage>
  </pick>
  <invoke operation="bc" ... />
</sequence>
```

(b)

Fig. 9. XML versions of recovery plans in Figure 8: (a) for r_{18}; (b) for p_0.

In order to recover, we need to "undo" a part of the execution trace, executing available compensation actions, as specified by δ_c. We do this until we either reach a state in $\mathsf{C(B)}$ or the initial state of $\mathsf{L_C(B)}$. Multiple change states can be encountered along the way, thus leading to the computation of multiple plans.

For example, consider the error trace t_2 described in Section 5 and shown in Figure 6a. $\{1, 2, 6, 15, 16, 18\}$ are the change states seen along t_2. This leads to the recovery plans shown in Figure 8a. We add state names between transitions for clarity and refer to plans p_s to mean "recovery to state s". A given plan can also become a prefix for the follow-on one. This is indicated by using the former's name as part of definition of the latter. For example, recovery to state 16 starts with recovery to state 18 and then includes two more backward transitions, the last one with a non-empty compensation. Plan r_{18} can avoid the error if, after its application, the user chooses a cheap flight instead of an expensive one. Executing plan r_{15} gives the user the option of changing the limousine to a rental car, and plan r_2 – the option of changing from an air/ground combination to just renting a car. Both of these behaviours do not cause the violation of $\mathsf{A_2}$.

Computed plans are then converted to BPEL for presentation to the user. For example, plan r_{18} is shown in Figure 9a. The chosen plan can then be applied (see Section 7), allowing the program to continue its execution from the resulting change state.

The exact number of plans is determined by the number of change states encountered along the trace. Since each new plan includes the previous one, the maximum number of plans computed by our tool is set by user preferences either directly ("compute no more than 3 plans") or indirectly ("compute plans of up to length 20" or "compute plans while the overall sum of compensation actions is less than 10").

Discussion. Note that plan r_{16} which cancels the limo, would lead to rebooking it right away which may still leave the possibility of booking an expensive flight and violating the property P_2. The reason why this plan might not be as useful as others is that computation of change states in Section 4.3 treats all non-idempotent service calls as the same, whereas not all might be *relevant* to the satisfaction of properties of interest. See [22] for a description of computation and evaluation of effectiveness of relevant change states.

6.2 Recovery from Mixed Monitor Violations

When a monitor with a green state detects a violation during execution (i.e., it is in a red state), we attempt to direct the execution towards one of its green states.

The recovery procedure receives A – the monitor that identified the violation, $\mathsf{L_C(B)}$ – the LTS of the application, $\mathsf{G(B,A)}$ – the set of goal transitions corresponding to A, T – the executed trace ending in an error state e, and $\mathsf{C(B)}$ – the set of change states.

A recovery plan effectively "undoes" actions along T, starting with e and ending in a change state (otherwise, the plan would not be executable!) and then "re-plans" the behavior to reach the goal while avoiding redundant loops (i.e., when some actions are executed and then immediately compensated). Our solution adapts techniques from the field of *planning* [23], described below.

Recovery as a planning problem. A *planning problem* is a triple $P = (D, i, G)$, where D is the domain D, i is the initial state in D, and G is a set of goal states in G.

In addition to P, a planner often gets as input k – the length of the longest plan to search for, and applies various search algorithms to find a plan of actions of length $\leq k$, starting from i and ending in one of the states in G. Typically, the plan is found using heuristics and is not guaranteed to be the shortest available. If no plan is found, the bound k can be increased in order to look for longer plans.

To convert a problem of recovery from mixed monitor violations into a planning problem, we use $\mathsf{L_C(B)}$ as the domain and e as the initial state. The third component needed is a set of goal states. Recall that $\mathsf{G(B,A)}$ is a set of goal *transitions*. We define $\mathsf{G_s(B,A)} = \{s \mid \exists a, s' \cdot (s, a, s') \in \mathsf{G(B,A)}\}$. That is, $\mathsf{G_s(B,A)}$ is a set of *sources* of transitions in $\mathsf{G(B,A)}$. We can now define the planning problem

$$\mathsf{P(B,A,T)} = (\mathsf{L_C(B)}, \mathsf{e}, \mathsf{G_s(B,A)}).$$

Note that when a plan p to a goal state s is computed, we need to extend it with an additional transition, $p \xrightarrow{a} s'$ to account for $(s, a, s') \in \mathsf{G(B,A)}$. For example, consider the trace t_1 of Figure 6a, described in Section 5, in which monitor $\mathtt{A_1}$ fails. We define the planning problem $\mathsf{P}(\mathtt{TAS}, \mathtt{A_1}, t_1) = (\mathsf{L_C}(\mathtt{TAS}), 9, \{4\})$, where 9 is the initial state (see Figure 6a) and $\mathsf{G_s}(\mathtt{TAS}, \mathtt{A_1}) = \{4\}$ (see Section 4.3), and its result, p, should be expanded to $p \xrightarrow{\mathsf{rd}} 5$.

Unfortunately, we cannot simply use a planner as a "black box", for two main reasons. First, not every trace returned by solving $\mathsf{P(B,A,T)}$ is acceptable: our recovery

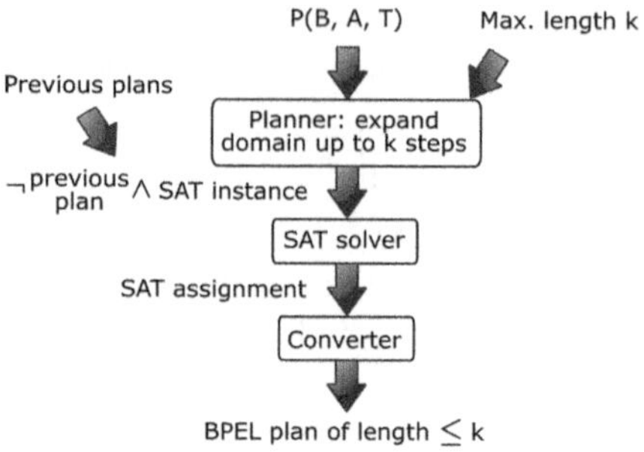

Fig. 10. Planning Diagram.

plans must visit change states. Second, we may want to produce multiple recovery plans to let the user select the best – a requirement that is not supported by planners.

Instead, we look at how planners encode the planning graph and then manipulate the produced encoding directly, to add additional constraints. Several existing planners, such as BlackBox [24], translate the planning graph into a CNF formula and then use a SAT solver, such as SAT4J[5], to find a satisfying assignment for it. Such an assignment, if found, represents a plan. We use a planner to translate a planning problem into a SAT instance, and then modify this instance for our needs.

Figure 10 gives a schematic overview of our method. The planning domain as well as the maximum length k of required plans are fed into a planner, which we use only for producing a CNF formula. We then modify the CNF formula to account for change states, and iteratively restrict it further to disallow already seen plans. The modified formula is then given as input to a SAT solver, and the satisfying assignment it produces is converted back into a BPEL plan. A detailed explanation of the modifications made to the CNF formula can be found in [25].

For example, consider the TAS problem and the error trace t_1 shown in Figure 6a (ending in state 9). Looking for plans up to length 10, we get plans p_0, p_1 and p_2 shown in Figure 8b. And, as mentioned earlier, each plan is extended with the last goal transition $4 \xrightarrow{\text{rd}} 5$.

Plan p_0 is the shortest: if unable to obtain a price for the flight, cancel the flight and reserve the car instead. Plans p_1 and p_2 also cancel the flight (since 8 is not a change state whereas 7 is) and then proceed to re-book it and then book the car, regardless of the flight's cost. Increasing the plan length, we also get the option of taking the getCar transition out of state 6, book the car and then the flight.

The produced plans are than ranked based on the length of the plan and the cost of compensation actions in it:

$$\text{cost}(p) = c_1 \times \text{length}(p) + c_2 \times \Sigma_{i=1}^{\text{length}(p)} \text{compensation-cost}_i(p),$$

where c_1 and c_2 are constants, length(p) is the number of events in the plan p and compensation-cost$_i$ is a cost of the ith compensation action. For example:

[5] http://www.sat4j.org/

$$\text{cost}(p_0) = 8 + 6 = 14,$$

assuming $c_1 = c_2 = 1$, and cost(p_1)=cost(p_2) = 17. Thus, p_0 is ranked the highest and presented first. Of course, the cost function does not take into account the time the user will spend driving rather than flying should she select plan p_0, so she may choose one of the alternative plans instead.

Chosen plans are then converted to BPEL for execution. The compensation part of the plan is similar to the one shown in Figure 9a, and the re-planning part consists of a sequence of BPEL <invoke> and <pick> operations (see the XML translation of plan p_0 in Figure 9b).

In addition, we can aim to limit the number of recovery plans computed by taking two issues into consideration: (a) making sure that the plan goes through only "relevant" change states, i.e., those that affect the computation of the violating trace, and (b) removing those plans that result in the violation of one of the safety properties (see [22]).

Discussion. *Controlling unnecessary compensations.* Plans p_1 and p_2 seem to be doing an unnecessary compensation: why cancel a flight and then re-book it if the check flight service call failed? The reason is that the application developer identified service call cf as idempotent. That is, she decided that executing this service again cannot change the flow of control of the application, and thus further compensations are necessary.

Of course, every service call can fail, and thus none are truly idempotent. Yet, having too many change states would undermine the effectiveness of our framework. We believe that the tradeoff we have made in this chapter is reasonable but intend to revisit this issue as we gain more experience with the approach.

Can generated plans still fail? There are a number of reasons our plans can fail. The first one, addressed earlier in this section, is due to the inherent imprecision of our handling of required event sequences. The second reason is that any service in the recovery plan can fail; thus, the application will be unable to reach its goal, prompting further planning and recovery. Finally, for recovery of safety properties, it is possible that all paths from a change state may still lead the application to an error state. This problem can likely be addressed using additional static analysis.

7 Tool Support

We have implemented the process described in this chapter using a series of publicly available tools and several short (200-300 lines) new Python or Java scripts. The preprocessing and runtime monitoring phases of our framework are the same for both safety and mixed properties, but different components are required for generating plans from the two types of properties. We show the architecture of our framework in Figure 11. In this diagram, rectangles are components of our framework, and ovals are artifacts. We have also grouped the components and artifacts by phase: preprocessing – green, with a ★ symbol; runtime monitoring – yellow, with a ◆ symbol; and recovery – blue, with a ✚ symbol. Artifacts with with a black border are the initial inputs to our framework.

Developers create properties for their web services using property patterns and system events. During the preprocessing phase, the *Property Translator* (PT) component

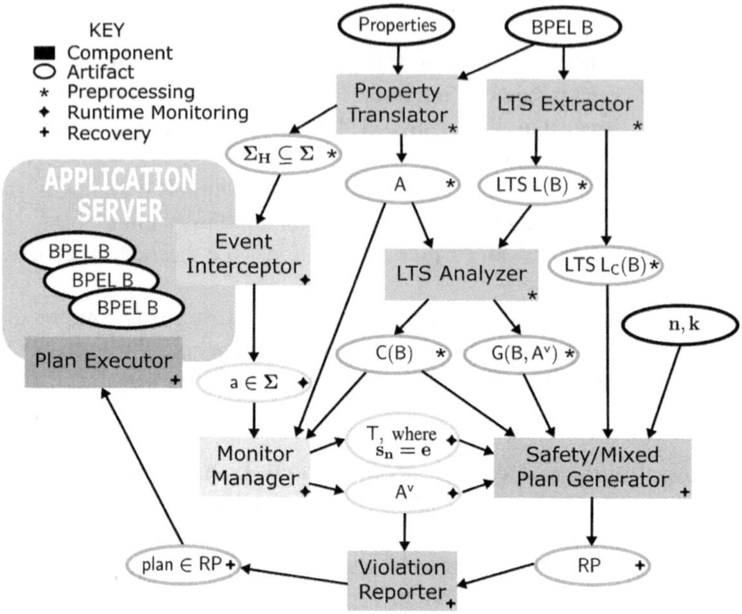

Fig. 11. Architecture of the framework.

receives the specified properties and turns them into monitors (as described in Section 4.2). The *LTS Extractor* (LE) component extracts an LTS model from the BPEL program and creates a second LTS model with compensation (both processes are described in Section 4.1). The *LTS Analyzer* (LA) computes goal links and change states using the techniques described in Section 4.3.

During the execution of the application, the *Event Interceptor* (EI) component intercepts application events and sends them to the *Monitor Manager* (MM) for analysis (see Section 5 for details). MM updates the state of each active monitor, until an error has been found (which activates the recovery phase) or all partners terminate. MM also stores the intercepted events for recovery.

During the recovery phase, artifacts from both the preprocessing and the runtime monitoring phases are used to generate recovery plans. In the case of safety properties, the *Safety Plan Generator* generates recovery plans that can only compensate executed activities (see Section 6.1). For mixed properties, plans can compensate executed activities and execute new activities. In this case, the *Mixed Plan Generator* first generates the corresponding planning problem and then modifies it in order to generate as many plans as required (see Section 6.2).

All computed plans are presented to the application user through the *Violation Reporter* (VR), and the chosen plan is executed by the *Plan Executor* (PE). If no monitor is violated during the execution of the chosen plan (MM updates the states of the active monitors during the plan execution), the framework switches back to runtime monitoring. We describe these components in more detail below.

7.1 Preprocessing

As the developer is responsible for the preprocessing phase, we have implemented this part of our framework as a WebSphere Integration Developer plugin.

Property Translator provides a graphical interface for specifying properties using property patterns and application events. Properties are translated into QREs, from which we generate a set of monitors A, as explained in Section 4.2. These monitors are stored in the Aldebaran [26] format for use by the rest of the components.

LTS Extractor receives as input a BPEL program B in the BPEL4WS XML format. We use the WS-Engineer extension [27] to LTSA [28] to translate B into an LTS L(B) and then export it in the Aldebaran format [26], with an `.aut` extension. Since WS-Engineer does not support the full handling of BPEL compensations, we built our own `.aut-to-.aut` Python script (`add_comp.py`) which uses B and L(B) to produce $L_C(B)$ as described in Section 4.1. Traceability between the BPEL and the resulting LTS is established by the WS-Engineer's encoding of BPEL scopes into names of LTS actions. This traceability allows us to convert the computed plans back to BPEL.

LTS Analyzer receives as input the application monitors and LTS L(B) (both in the Aldebaran format). We wrote a script `compute_cp.py` that computes the cross-product between the application and each A_i in $A \setminus A_S$ and uses these cross-products to identify goal links, as described in Section 4.3. This component also checks which service invocations of B have been marked as non-idempotent, and uses this information to identify the application change states (as described in Section 4.3).

7.2 Runtime Monitoring

The monitoring phase is implemented on top of the IBM WebSphere Process Server, a BPEL-compliant process engine for executing BPEL processes and a built-in Service Component Architecture (SCA), which is a particular instantiation of SOA.

The *Event Interceptor* (EI) is deployed on the process server and establishes a bridge through which our runtime monitoring framework communicates with the server to obtain information about the web service execution. On the process server, SCA is responsible for the invocation of native SCA service components and for the binding and interaction with external services. EI monitors interactions within the SCA application server runtime environment, and is responsible for observing and routing these invocation requests and responses to MM. If EI observes an event that may cause termination or a property violation (in other words, a monitor currently in a yellow state transitions to a red state on that event), the event is first forwarded to MM for analysis. If no violation is detected, the execution continues as normal. Otherwise, EI stops forwarding events to the corresponding application instance until a recovery plan is executed.

Monitor Manager receives A – the set of monitors produced by the PT component. During execution, monitors can be enabled/disabled through MM. A new copy of each active monitor is created for each new instance of the application. The MM component registers itself as a listener to EI, updating the state of all active monitors when a new event is received. MM also stores the current execution trace for each application instance. In the case of a monitor violation, MM broadcasts the violated monitor A^v and the corresponding error trace T, initiating recovery.

7.3 Recovery

The recovery phase is also implemented on top of the IBM WebSphere Process Server. This allows us to avoid recomputing recovery plans by keeping a centralized hash of property violations and computed recovery plans. The maximum plan length (k) and the maximum number of plans (n) are the configuration parameters of the framework.

Safety Plan Generator receives as input k, n, $\mathsf{L_C(B)}$, $\mathsf{C(B)}$, and T. We use our own script (`gen_safe_plan.py`) to determine which visited change states are reachable from the error state e on $\mathsf{L_C(B)}$, within the maximum plan length, and the set of recovery plans RP is produced as a by-product of this check.

Mixed Plan Generator receives as input k, n, $\mathsf{L_C(B)}$, $\mathsf{C(B)}$, $\mathsf{G(B, A_v)}$, $\mathsf{A_v}$, and T. We use our own script (`gen_plan_prob.py`) to translate $\mathsf{L_C(B)}$ into a planning problem $(\mathsf{L_C(B)}, \mathsf{e}, \mathsf{G_s(B, A^v)})$ (see Section 6.2). The planning problem is expressed in STRIPS [29] – an input language to the planner Blackbox [24] which we use to convert it into a SAT instance. The maximum plan length is used to limit the size of the planning graph generated by Blackbox, effectively limiting the size of the plans that can be produced. We use another new script (`GenPlans.java`) to successively modify the initial SAT instance in order to produce alternative plans. It calls the satisfiability solver SAT4J, extracts plans from the satisfying assignments produced by SAT4J, ranks them and converts them to the BPEL4WS XML format for displaying and execution. SAT4J is an *incremental* SAT solver, i.e., it saves results from one search and uses them for the next. For our method of generating multiple plans, where each SAT instance is more restricted than the previous one, this is particularly useful, leading to efficient analysis.

Violation Reporter (VR) receives as input $\mathsf{A_v}$ and a list of BPEL plans RP. VR generates a web page snippet with violation information, as well as a form for selecting a recovery plan. A snippet generated for a violation of P_1 is shown in Figure 12a. Developers must include this snippet in the default error page, so that the computed recovery plans can be shown when an error is detected. Figure 12b shows the (simplified) source code of such an error reporting page, where the bolded line has the instruction to include the snippet. After the recovery plans have been computed, the snippet is displayed as part of the application, and the user must pick a plan to continue execution (r in the case of safety properties, p otherwise). Figure 12c shows a screen shot of `error.jsp` after recovery plans for P_1 have been computed.

Plan Executor receives as input a BPEL plan. Statically, we add a <collaboration> scope to each process before execution, and the BPEL plan chosen by the user is set as the logic of this scope. EI also intercepts application events during the execution of the recovery plan, and a new recovery plan must be chosen if the current one causes a monitor violation.

Because web services are distributed and allow asynchronous message communication, messages may get delivered and received out of order. To handle out-of-order events, we annotate each event with two timestamps: one at invocation and one at reception. When events arrive at the message queue of MM, these timestamps are used to check if the invocation ordering is consistent with the reception ordering. If the orderings are not consistent, detected errors may be caused by network delays rather than incorrect conversations. Currently, all timestamps are generated by the same WebSphere Process Server.

snippet.jsp

```
<p><strong>Reason:</strong> The system was unable to check
            the status of the selected flight.</p>

<h1 class="title">Recovery options</h1>
<br>
<html:form name="recovery_option" action="execute_plan.do" ...>
<table width="100%">
 <tr>
  <td width="10%"><html:radio property="plans" value="p0" /></td>
  <td width="10%" align="center">A</td>
  <td>Cancel existing flight and switch to "car only" mode</td>
 </tr>
 <tr>
  <td><html:radio property="plans" value="p1" /></td>
  <td align="center">B</td>
  <td>Cancel existing flight reservation. Then try to book a new
      flight and request a rental car</td>
 </tr>
 <tr><td></td><td></td>
  <td align="center"><html:submit value="Fix it!"/></td>
 </tr>
</table>
</html:form>
```

(a)

error.jsp

```
<%@ taglib uri="/WEB-INF/struts-html.tld" prefix="html" %>
<html>
<head>...</head>
<body>
 <h1 class="title">We're sorry...</h1>
 <div class="content">
  <p>We could not complete your booking as requested:</p>
  <br>
  <table width="80%">
   <tr><th>Travel dates:</th><td>...</td></tr>
   <tr><th>Flight:       </th><td>...</td></tr>
   <tr><th>Preference:   </th><td>...</td></tr>
  </table>
  <br>
 </div>
 <%@ include file = "snippet.jsp" %>
</body>
```

(b)

(c)

Fig. 12. Violation reporting: (a) `snippet.jsp`, automatically generated snippet that contains recovery plans; (b) `error.jsp`, the application error handling page; (c) `error.jsp` displayed on a browser.

8 Case Studies

We have applied our framework to several web service applications and report on our experience on recovery from property violations. In the first case study (see Section 8.1), we show how to recover from multiple problems seeded in the Travel Booking System (TBS) (adapted from [30]). Experience with this larger, more complex case study shows that our approach is both effective and scalable.

In Section 8.2 we report on an experiment running our method on the *Flickr* system (see Carzaniga et al. [31]). In [31], several aspects of this system are modeled as finite-state machines, and the paper shows how to use redundancies in the system in order to "work around" some vulnerabilities. We reverse-engineered BPEL applications from the finite-state models presented in [31], and we compare our recovery plans to the method presented in [31].

8.1 Travel Booking System (TBS)

The Travel Booking system (TBS) provides travel booking services over the web. In a typical scenario, a customer enters the expected travel dates, the destination city and the rental car location – airport or hotel. The system searches for the available flights, hotel rooms and rental cars, placing holds on the resources that best satisfy the customer preferences. If the customer chooses to rent a car at the hotel, the system also books the shuttle between the airport and the hotel. If the customer likes the itinerary presented to him/her, the holds are turned into bookings; otherwise, the holds are released. Figure 13 shows the BPEL implementation of this system.

Implementation. TBS interacts with three partners (FlightSystem, HotelSystem and CarSystem), each offering the services to find an available resource (flight, hotel room, car and shuttle), place a hold on it, release a hold on it, book it and cancel it. Booking a resource is compensated by canceling it (at a cost of 8 out of 10), and placing a hold is compensated by a release (at a cost of 2). All external service calls are non-idempotent.

The workflow begins by <receive>'ing input (receiveInput), followed by <flow> with two branches, as the flight and hotel reservations can be made independently. The branches are labeled ① and ②: ①) find and place a hold on a flight, ②) place a hold on a hotel room (this branch has been simplified in this case study). If there are no flights available on the given dates, the system will prompt the user for new dates and then search again (up to three tries). After making the hotel and flight reservations, the system tries to arrange transportation (see the <pick> activity labeled ③): the user <pick>'s a rental location (pickAirport or pickHotel) and the system tries to place holds on the required resources (car at airport, or car at hotel and a shuttle between the airport and hotel).

Once ground transportation has been arranged, the reserved itinerary is displayed to the user (displayTravelSummary), and at this point, the user must <pick> to either book or cancel the itinerary. The book option has a <flow> activity that invokes the booking services in parallel, and then calls two local services: one that checks that the hotel and flight dates are consistent (checkDates), and another that generates an invoice (generateInvoice). The result of checkDates is then passed to local services to determine whether the dates are the same (sameDates) or not (notSameDates). The cancel option is just a <flow> activity that invokes the corresponding release services. Whichever option is picked by the user, the system finally invokes another local service to inform the user about the outcome of the travel request (informCustomer).

Properties. Some behavioural correctness properties of TBS are P_3: "there shouldn't be a mismatch between flight and hotel dates", and P_4: "a car reservation request will be fulfilled regardless of the location (i.e., airport or hotel) chosen". We can express these properties using patterns:

> P_3: **Absence** of a date mismatch event (notSameDate) **After** both a flight and hotel have been booked (bookFlight and bookHotel, in any order),

and

> P_4: **Globally** place a hold on a car (holdCar) in **Response** to a rental location selection (pickHotel or pickAirport).

Note that P_3 is a safety property, describing a forbidden scenario, while P_4 has also a desired component and it is thus a mixed property.

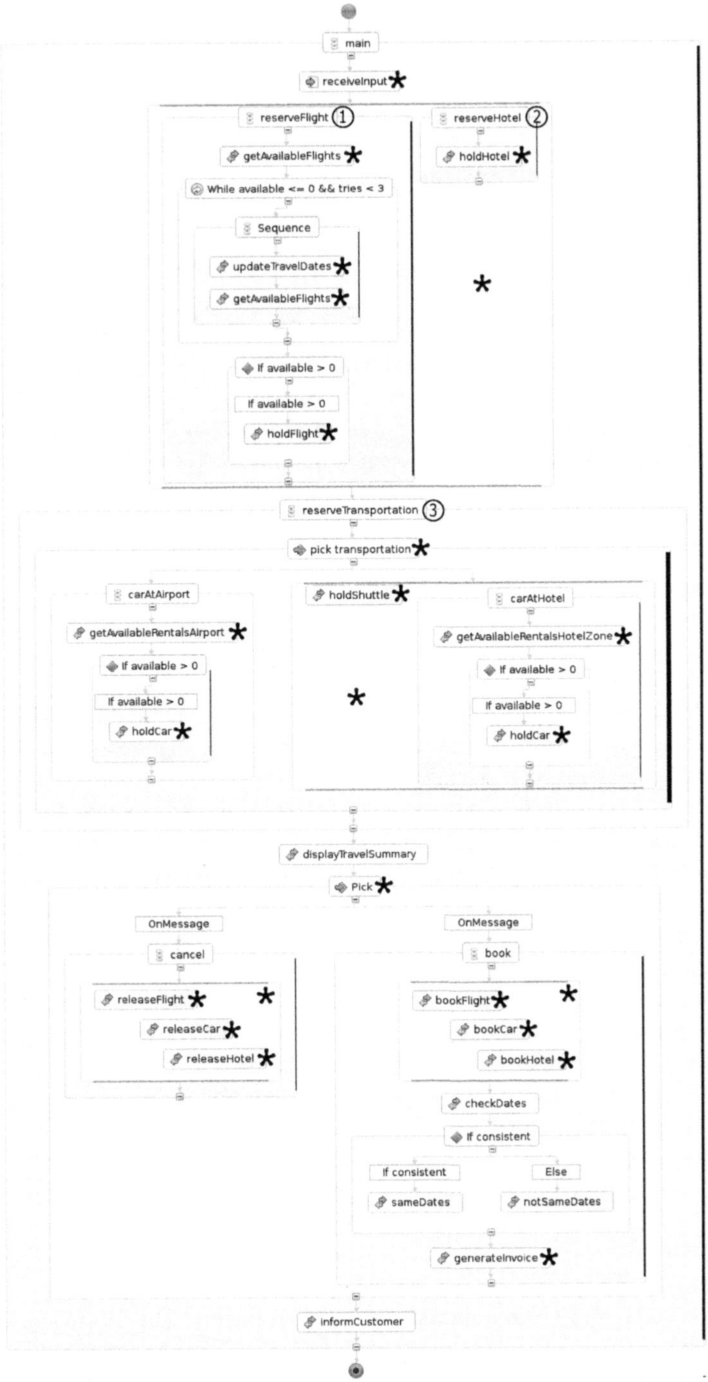

Fig. 13. BPEL implementation of the Travel Booking System.

Preprocessing. We translated the two properties into monitoring automata: P_3 (P_4) has 5 (3) states and 10 (6) transitions. P_3 (P_4) has 0 (1) green, 1 (1) yellow, and 1 (1) red states, so we could compute safety plans for P_3 and mixed plans for P_4. The LTS L(TBS) has 52 states and 67 transitions, and $|\Sigma| = 33$, which makes TBS double the size of the TAS example. 20 of the BPEL activities (highlighted with a ★ symbol in Figure 13) yield a total of 35 change states in the LTS. P_4 is a mixed property, with three goal links corresponding to it.

Experience: Recovery from a safety property violation. We generated a recovery plan for the following scenario (called trace t_3, of length 21) which violates property P_3: The application first makes a hotel reservation (holdHotel) and then prompts the user for new travel dates (updateTravelDates), since there were no flights available on the current travel dates. The car rental location is the airport (pickAirport). The system displays the itinerary (displayTravelSummary) but the user does not notice the date inconsistency and decides to book it. The TBS makes the bookings (bookFlight, bookHotel and bookCar) and then checks for date consistency (checkDates). In this case, the dates are not the same (notSameDates), which allows us to detect the violation of P_3 and initiate recovery.

We generated plans starting with length $k = 5$ and going to $k = 30$ in increments of 5. In order to generate all possible plans for each k, we chose n – the maximum number of plans generated – to be MAX_INT. Table 3 summarizes the results. A total of 13 plans were generated, and the longest plan, which reaches the initial state, is of length 21 (and thus the rows corresponding to $k = 25$ and $k = 30$ contain identical information). Since t_3 violates a safety property, no SAT instances were generated, and the running time of the plan generation is trivial.

The following plans turn t_3 into a successful trace: p^3_A – cancel the flight reservation and pick a new flight using the original travel dates, and p^3_B – cancel the hotel reservation and pick a new hotel room for the new travel dates. Our tool generated both of these plans, but ranked them 11th and 12th (out of 13), respectively. They were assigned a low rank due to the interplay between the following two characteristics of our case study: (i) the actual error occurs at the beginning of the scenario (in the flight and hotel reservation <flow>), but the property violation was only detected near the end of the workflow (in the book flow), and (ii) t_3 passes through a relatively large number of change states, and thus many recovery plans are possible.

The first of these causes could be potentially fixed by writing "better" properties – the ones that allows us to catch an error as soon as it occurs. We recognize, of course, that this can be difficult to do. The second stems from the fact that not all service calls marked as non-idempotent are relevant to P_3 or its violation. In the future, we intend to explore this direction by trying to rank change states w.r.t. their relevance to the property, with the hope of reducing the occurrences of cases like this.

Experience: Recovery from a mixed property violation. The following scenario (we call it trace t_4, with length 14), violates property P_4. Consider an execution where the user has chosen to rent the car at the hotel (pickHotel), but no cars are available at that hotel. TBS makes flight, hotel and shuttle reservations (holdFlight and holdHotel), but never makes a car reservation (holdCar). The user does not notice the missing reservation in the displayed itinerary (displayTravelSummary) and decides to book it. The TBS tries to complete the bookings, first booking the hotel (bookHotel) and then the car (bookCar). When the application attempts to invoke bookCar, the BPEL engine detects that the application tries to access a non-initialized process variable (since there is no car reservation), and issues a TER event. Rather than delivering the TER event to the application, we initiate recovery.

We are again using n = MAX_INT and varying k between 5 and 30, in increments of 5, summarizing the results in Table 3. The first thing to note is that our approach generated a relatively large number of plans (over 60) as k approached 30. While in general, the further we move away from a goal link, the more alternative paths lead back to it, this was especially true for TBS which had a number of <flow> activities. The second is that our analysis remained tractable even as the length of the plan and the number of plans generated grow (around 1 min for the most expensive configulation).

Executing one of the following plans would leave TBS in a desired state: p^4_A – attempt the car rental at the hotel again, and p^4_A – cancel the shuttle from the airport to the hotel and attempt to rent a car at the airport. Unlike t_3, the error in this scenario was discovered soon after its occurrence, so plans p^4_A and p^4_B are the first ones generated by our approach. p^4_A actually corresponds to two plans, since the application logic for reserving a car at a hotel is in a <flow> activity, enabling two ways of reaching the same goal link. Plan p^4_B was the 3rd plan generated.

The rest of the plans we generated compensate various parts of t_4, and then try to reach one of the three goal links. While these longer plans include more compensations and are ranked lower than p^4_A and p^4_B, we still feel that it may be difficult to the user to sift through all of them. We are currently actively pursuing the problem of reducing the number of plans generated to recover from mixed properties. One of the approaches is to remove those plans that (necessarily) lead to violations of safety properties. For now, this remains "work in progress" and is not presented in this chapter.

8.2 Comparisons with a Related Approach

While in the Travel Booking System, we were comparing the effectiveness of the generated plans to our expectations, in the set of examples that follow, we compare the effectiveness of the plans we generate with a related approach – that of Carzaniga et. al [31]. In each case, we describe the example from [31], discuss our experience translating it to BPEL and expressing correctness properties and then report on the plans we generate and the relevant statistics.

Flickr visibility. Flickr is a web-based photo-management application. Photos are initially uploaded as either *public*, *family* or *private*, and a photo's visibility should be changeable anytime using the setPerm function. The identified vulnerability is "when a photo is initially loaded as *private*, its visibility cannot be changed to *family* at a later date".

We created the Flickr visibility system (FV) by reverse-engineering the behavioral model in Figure 14a (given in [31]) and expressing it in BPEL (see Figure 14b). The behavioral model has four states: notOnFlickr, public, private and family. notOnFlickr is the initial state, executing the upload() operation (with a visibility parameter) from

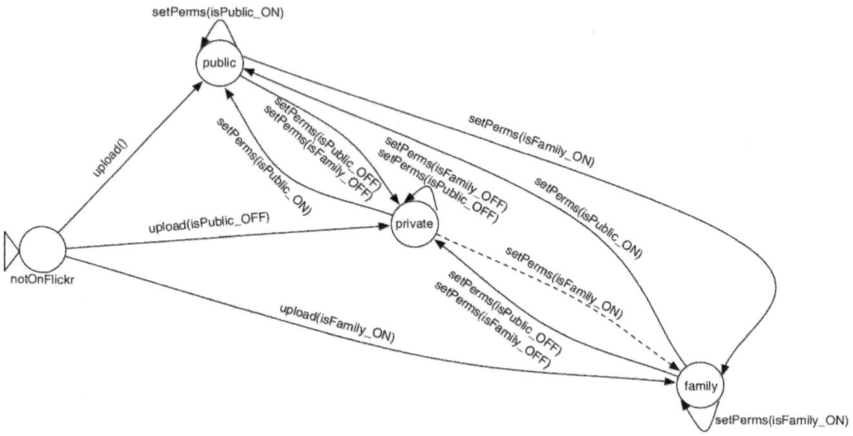

(a)

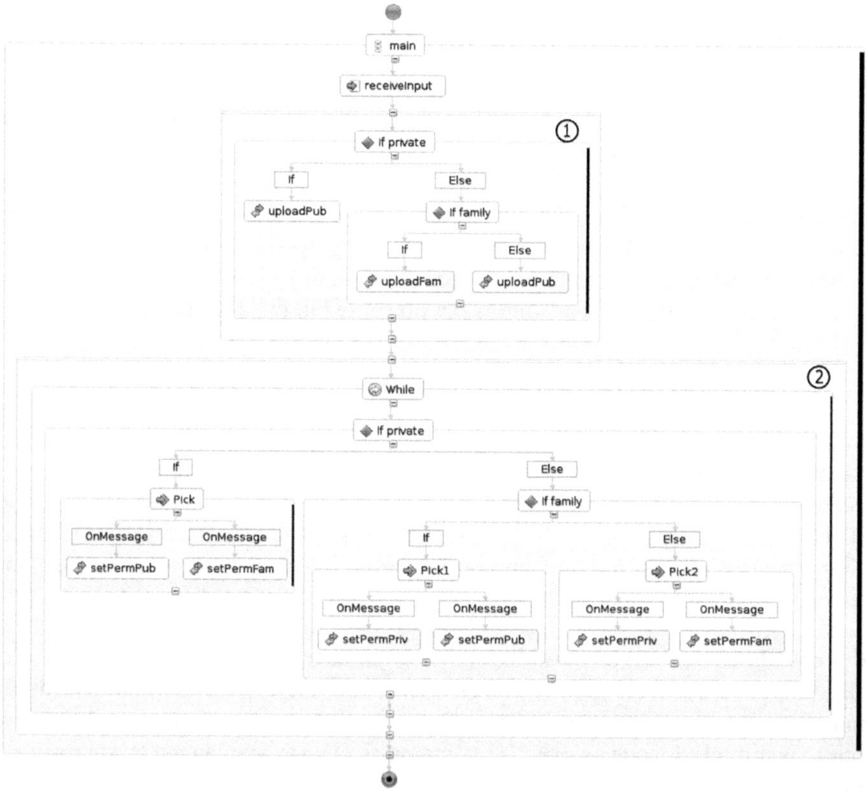

(b)

Fig. 14. FV: (a) behavioral model from [31], (b) BPEL FV.

this state leads to one of the three other states (visibility states). The BPEL model FV, consists of 20 activities (6 with explicit compensations).

In Figure 14b, the transitions from the initial state are modeled in the <scope> called upload (labeled ①). In this scope, we call three different upload services depending on the upload visibility: uploadPub, uploadPriv and uploadFam (equivalent to upload(), upload(isPublic_OFF) and upload(isFamily_ON), respectively).

The transition relation between the visibility states specifies valid changes in the photo visibility. This has been modeled using case statements in the <scope> called changePerm (labeled ②). In this scope, setPermPub, setPermPriv and setPermFam are equivalent to setPerm(isPublic_ON), {setPerm(isPublic_OFF), setPerm (isFamily_OFF)} and setPerm(isFamily_ON), respectively.

We also defined compensation for FV. Since there were no transitions back to state notOnFlickr, we assumed that the upload services do not have compensation. However, compensation for the setPerm services is obvious – reverse the permission setting, e.g., setPerm(isPublic_ON) is compensated by setPerm(isPublic_OFF). The upload and setPerm service calls are non-idempotent.

Converted to LTS, the resulting model has 28 states and 37 transitions. L(FV) is larger than the original behavioral model since the LTS includes BPEL-induced actions such as entering scopes, and we used case statements to model operation parameters.

We then expressed properties of the FV system: "If a user tries to set a photo's visibility to X, Flickr will guarantee that the photo will have the visibility X", where X is each of the possible visibilities. These became separate properties expressed using the **Response** pattern. An instance with $X = family$ will "catch" the identified vulnerability in the case where a photo is initially loaded as *private*.

Flickr comments. Flickr lets users comment on uploaded photos. While any user can add a comment to a *public* photo, only authorized users can comment on *private* and *family* photos. The identified vulnerability is "after uploading a photo as *public*, no comments could be added". Using the same process as for FV, we created the BPEL model FC (see [32]), consisting of 16 activities (6 with compensations). The resulting LTS model has 18 states and 22 transitions. We expressed FC's property "if a user adds a comment to a *public* photo that has comments enabled, the comment should be successfully added to the photo's comments" using the **Response** pattern.

Experience. The number of recovery plans generated for failed traces of FV and FC is shown in Table 3. For example, for the plan length up to 26, we have generated 8 plans for FV. The longest plan was of length 42. We now look at the effectiveness of the plan generation process. For FV, one of the plans we generate for $k = 22$ is "compensate changes in visibility until the photo becomes *private* again, set the photo visibility to *public* and change visibility to *family*", which corresponds to the workaround plan chosen by [31]. For FC, the plan corresponding to the chosen workaround is "delete the problematic comment, toggle the comments permission and then try to add the comment again", generated when $k = 12$.

To compare the precision of our approach, i.e., the number of plans generated, we look at the list of workaround sequences computed by [31] (see Table 3). The work in [31] modeled the Flickr behavior directly and the model did not include BPEL-induced

Table 3. Plan generation data. "–" mark cases which are not applicable, such as references to SAT for recovery from safety property violations.

	Our approach					[31]	
App.	**k**	**vars**	**clauses**	**plans**	**time (s)**	**length**	**plans**
TAS	6	135	254	1	0.01	-	-
	8	798	10,355	5	0.13	-	-
	13	1,398	25,023	13	0.27	-	-
TBS	5	-	-	2	0.01	-	-
t_3	10	-	-	5	0.02	-	-
	15	-	-	8	0.02	-	-
	20	-	-	12	0.02	-	-
	25	-	-	13	0.02	-	-
	30	-	-	13	0.02	-	-
TBS	5	108	464	0	0.01	-	-
t_4	10	883	30,524	2	0.14	-	-
	15	1,456	74,932	8	1.37	-	-
	20	2,141	135,047	18	4.72	-	-
	25	3,298	246,210	60	29.16	-	-
	30	5,288	464,654	68	61.34	-	-
FV	15	797	16,198	2	0.04	≤ 2	1
	22	1,436	33,954	4	0.74	≤ 3	5
	26	1,804	44,262	8	1.14	≤ 4	13
	42	3,276	85,494	40	3.12	≤ 8	412
FC	4	42	159	1	0.01	≤ 1	0
	6	95	592	2	0.02	≤ 2	2
	12	321	3,248	4	0.15	≤ 3	8
	16	554	7,393	5	0.27	≤ 4	22
	20	856	14,427	13	1.38	≤ 8	484

actions such as entering scopes. Further, the workaround sequences did not include the "going back" part – they were plans on how to execute a task starting from the initial state. Thus, the plans we generate are somewhat longer. For example, the workaround sequences of length ≤ 2 correspond to our plans of length $k = 15$. With this adjustment, Table 3 shows that we generate significantly fewer plans of the corresponding length. We also generate every plan marked by [31] as desired.

Our experience with the Flickr examples suggests that combining simple properties with the compensation mechanism is effective for producing recovery plans.

8.3 Scalability

To check whether SAT-solving done as part of the planning is the bottleneck of our approach, we measured sizes of SAT problems for FV, FC, TBS, and our running example, TAS, listing them in Table 3. For all four systems, the number of variables and the number of clauses grows linearly with the length of the plan, as expected, and the running time of the SAT solver remains in seconds.

While the web applications we have analyzed have been relatively small, our experience suggests that SAT instances used in plan generation remain small and simple and scale well as length of the plan grows. Given that modern SAT solvers can often handle millions of clauses and given that individual web services are intended to be relatively compact (with tens rather than thousands of partner calls), we have a good reason to believe that our approach to plan generation is scalable to realistic systems.

9 Related Work

Our work deals with monitoring web applications and, when violations found, uses planning techniques to propose recovery measures. This work is different from the approach of monitoring web services for quality assurance (e.g., [33, 34, 35]). The reason is that we rely on an implicit model for behavioural correctness (expressed using properties) and do our checking only w.r.t. the behaviour rather than other attributes such as the mean response time of external services.

In Section 9.1, we survey other (behavioural) monitoring frameworks, and in Section 9.2, we compare our method to other self-healing approaches for web applications. Note that the area of monitoring web services for quality assurance has been.

9.1 Runtime Monitoring of Web Services

Monitoring techniques for web services can be roughly divided into *offline* techniques (for example, [36, 37, 38]), that analyze system events *after* execution, and *online* techniques [39,40,41,42,43,44] that, like in our method, monitor the system as it executes. These techniques differ in the types of properties they can handle. *Global properties* allow the analysis of orchestrated obligations. These obligations are expressed from the point of view of the orchestrating service, but also include events from the other services involved in the conversation being monitored. *Local properties* are restricted to monitoring the events of a single service. Furthermore, some techniques concentrate on *state* properties, whereas others allow the developer to express *sequences* of events.

The approach introduced by Pistore et al. [42] is the closest to our monitoring framework. It can be used to check global properties that are specified in LTL, and thus it is somewhat more expressive than our input properties (although may prove more difficult to use [9]). However, the main interest of [42] is the synthesis of a BPEL composition, and it does not deal with recovery.

The frameworks described in [39, 40, 41, 43, 44] are restricted to local properties. Li et al. [44] specify properties using Interaction Constraints (IC) [45] – a language based, like our method, on Dwyer's Specification Pattern System [9]. Unlike our automata though, IC does not allow pattern nesting. Thus, new events must be introduced in order to reason about sequences of events. The rest of the local property frameworks check state formulas, specified using simple predicate logic. Specifically, Baresi et al. [40,41] and Lohmann et al. [43] check service pre- and postconditions associated to external service invocations, while Lazovik et al. [39] check local assertions.

Offline techniques can handle both global and local properties. In Mahbub et al. [36, 37], properties are expressed using event calculus [46]. Van der Aalst et al. [38]

introduce DerSecFlow, a graphical language that can be used to express properties similar to our patterns, but without pattern nesting.

Various techniques are used for *checking* properties. [39] and [42] rely on planning techniques to create service compositions. [42] analyzes the application once the composition has been obtained, by instrumenting the system to include Java code that checks LTL monitors during runtime. [39] iteratively replaces the violated service with another one, with weaker assertions, continuing the process until there are no more violations, or the composition is not possible.

In the case of service pre- and postconditions, [40, 41] modify the original BPEL diagram, introducing new BPEL activities that check the contract during external service calls. [43] proposes a similar, but more intrusive framework, as JML contracts are integrated at the source code level. [36, 37] use temporal deductive databases to store and reason about events generated during runtime, while [38] analyzes low-level event logs using an LTL checker.

Techniques used in the work of Li et al. [44] are the closest to ours. Like us, they take an automata-based approach for monitoring communications between partners and enable graphical display of violations.

9.2 Recovery and Self-healing

The advantage of online techniques is that it is possible for the system to react once a problem has been detected. Existing infrastructures for web services, e.g., the BPEL engine [2], include mechanisms for fault definition, for specification of compensation actions, and for dealing with termination. When an error is detected at runtime, they typically try to compensate all completed activities for which compensations are defined, with the default compensation being the reversal of the most recently completed action. Instead, our approach allows for a *guided* recovery. While using the compensation mechanism to reverse activities, we also direct the application forward, towards a goal state.

In [40,41], BPEL exception handlers can be attached to the properties being checked. If such an exception handler is not provided, the execution terminates when a violation occurs. As [42, 43] are Java-based, they can use Java's exception handling handling mechanism for recovery actions; however, this approach is highly intrusive.

Several works have suggested "self-healing" mechanisms for web-service applications. The Dynamo framework [47] uses *annotation rules* in BPEL in order to allow recovery once a fault has been detected. Such rules need to be installed by the developers before the system can function. In contrast, our work uses an existing compensation mechanism and requires no extra effort from developers.

[48] proposes a framework for self-healing web services, where all possible faults and their repair actions are pre-defined in a special registry. This approach relies on being able to identify and create recovery from all available faults. Our approach uses compensations for *individual* actions and can dynamically recover from errors as they are detected.

[49] uses fault tolerance patterns to transform the original BPEL process into a fault-tolerant one at compile time. It is done by adding redundant behavior to the application which may result in a significantly bigger, and slower, program. Our work is non-intrusive and does not slow down the application if no errors are found.

An emerging research area in recent years is that of *self-adaptive* and *self-managed* systems (see [50, 51, 52, 53] for a partial list). A system is considered self-adaptive if it is capable of adjusting itself in response to a changing environment. This approach is different from ours, since in our framework no change is made to the system itself, and recovery plans are discovered and executed using the original application. However, some similarities do exist. For example, a major issue in our approach is the identification of a goal state, which should become the target of the recovery plan. The problem of finding a *desired* or *correct* state [52] to which a system should evolve, is a concern in the field of self-adaptive system as well.

The work of Carzaniga et al. [31] is the closest to ours in spirit. It exploits redundancy in web applications to find workarounds when errors occur, assuming that the application is given as a finite-state machine, with an identified error state as well as the "fallback" state to which the application should return. The approach generates all possible recovery plans, without prioritizing them. In contrast, our framework not only detects runtime errors but also calculates goal and change states and in addition automatically filters out unusable recovery plans (those that do not include change states) and ranks the remaining ones. See Section 8 for a detailed comparison.

10 Conclusion, Discussion and Future Work

In this chapter, we described our framework for runtime monitoring and recovery of web service conversations. The monitoring portion is non-intrusive, running in parallel with the monitored system and intercepting interaction events during runtime. It does not require any code instrumentation, does not significantly affect the performance of the monitored system, and enables reasoning about partners expressed in different languages. We have then used BPEL's compensation mechanism to define and implement an online system for suggesting, ranking and executing recovery plans. Our experience has shown that this approach computes a small number of highly relevant plans, doing so quickly and effectively. In what follows, we discuss limitations of our approach and venues for future research. We also speculate about how the move towards the "smart" internet – the vision articulated in [1] – will affect our approach.

Limitations and Future Work. We have evaluated our approach on relatively small and simple examples. While we expect web service applications to be small, it is still important to conduct further case studies to assess scalability and, more importantly, usability of our approach. Furthermore, throughout the chapter we have identified several precision issues related to the identification of goals and change states. We intend to apply static analysis techniques to help improve it and conduct further experiments to better understand the tradeoffs between the more expensive analyses and the effective computation of recovery plans.

Another limitation of our approach is that we model compensations as going back to states visited earlier in the run. While this model is simple, clean and enables effective analysis, the compensation mechanism in languages like BPEL allows the user to execute an arbitrary operation and thus end up in a principally different state. In fact, our approach will encounter this situation as soon as we start modeling data in addition to control. For example, if we model the amount of money the user has as part of the state, then booking and then canceling a flight brings her to a different state – the one where she has less money and no flight. Thus, extending our framework to situations where compensation affects data remains a challenge.

In fact, reasoning about properties which involve the actual *data* exchanged by conversation participants may be challenging from the perspective of expressing the properties and converting them into monitoring automata as well as from the scalability perspective (e.g., computing the goal links, expressing the formal model of BPEL with data as a state machine, etc.).

Finally, our work so far has assumed that all partners operate within the same process server and thus a centralized monitoring and recovery is a viable option. In practice, most web services are distributed, requiring distributed monitoring and recovery. Techniques for turning a centralized monitor into a set of distributed ones, running in different process servers, have been investigated by the DESERT project [54], but we leave the problem of distributed plan generation and execution for future work.

Monitoring and Recovery for Smart Web Service Interactions. In this chapter, we have described how to monitor and recover from violations in the traditional web service model, where applications are predefined and are deployed on the server.

The emerging paradigm of smart internet and thus smart interactions, described elsewhere in the current volume [1], would shift the emphasis towards the user, who maintains a list of personal goals (defined in [1] as *matters of concern* (MOC)) which persists between individual sessions with various services.

The move to smart internet would affect our proposed framework as follows:

1. User MOCs are obvious candidates for liveness properties for our framework. They essentially describe user desires to get something accomplished, e.g., making a purchase of a great gift. In addition, users operate under a variety of constraints, such as making sure that they stay within their budget or that the gift's arrival day is before Christmas. Thus, we feel that user properties in the smart internet model are effectively MOCs subject to constraints. In our model, constraints are described using safety properties and MOCs – using liveness properties.

   However, our approach, as presented, has a limitation: the properties need to be expressible by end users. While the pattern-based approach certainly makes property expression easier than the traditional, logic-based approach, it still may not be appropriate for the end users.
2. In our approach, compensation and its cost is defined statically in BPEL. In order to move our approach to the smart internet model, compensation and its cost should be user-specified (e.g., to account for cases where some users pay smaller fees for a transaction cancellation, be that for a stop payment or for canceling a flight). Unfortunately, we are not aware of existing technology which allow such dynamic, user-centered compensation definition and configuration.
3. Finally, in the traditional model of internet, applications are created and tested by software developers. In the smart internet domain, the standard notion of testing as means of quality assurance cannot be applied, since each user has her own version of the application, with its own MOC, constraints and compensation. Thus, monitoring is the only way to ensure correctness of such applications. Furthermore,

monitoring and recovery has to be conducted on the user side rather than on the central server.

Overall, while there are a number of hurdles to overcome to make behavioural monitoring and recovery truly usable for the smart internet paradigm, we feel that this approach is a promising way (perhaps, the only way!) of ensuring quality of user-centric web systems where the level of customization does not allow effective testing. Thus, we intend to join forces with the other groups who contributed to this volume to make the smart internet vision a reality, allowing users to engage in non-trivial, meaningful and non error-prone interactions with the web.

Acknowledgements

Several people contributed to the ideas presented in this chapter: Shiva Nejati, Yuan Gan and Jonathan Amir were involved in various aspects of defining and building the runtime monitoring framework. Various people at IBM CAS Toronto, specifically, Bill O'Farrell, Julie Watermark, Elena Litani and Leho Nigel have been working with us over the years, and Bill is responsible for shaping this project into its present form, including the suggestion that we work on recovery from runtime failure. We are also grateful to members of the IFIP Working Group 2.9 for their helpful feedback on this work and Alessandra Gorla for sharing her examples and data with us. This research has been funded by NSERC, IBM Toronto, MITACS Accelerate, and by the Ontario Post-Doctoral Fellowship program.

References

1. Ng, J.W., Chignell, M., Cordy, J.R.: The Smart Internet: Transforming the Web for the User. In: CASCON 2009: Proceedings of the 2009 Conference of the Center for Advanced Studies on Collaborative Research, New York, NY, USA, pp. 285–296 (2009)
2. OASIS: WS-BPEL Version 2.0, `http://docs.oasis-open.org/wsbpel/2.0/OS/wsbpel-v2.0-OS.html` (Accessed January 2009)
3. Fu, X., Bultan, T., Su, J.: Conversation Protocols: A Formalism for Specification and Verification of Reactive Electronic Services. In: Ibarra, O.H., Dang, Z. (eds.) CIAA 2003. LNCS, vol. 2759, pp. 188–200. Springer, Heidelberg (2003)
4. Fu, X., Bultan, T., Su, J.: Analysis of Interacting BPEL Web Services. In: Proceedings of the 13th international conference on World Wide Web (WWW 2004), pp. 621–630 (May 2004)
5. Kazhamiakin, R., Pistore, M.: A Parametric Communication Model for the Verification of BPEL4WS Compositions. In: Bravetti, M., Kloul, L., Zavattaro, G. (eds.) EPEW/WS-EM 2005. LNCS, vol. 3670, pp. 318–332. Springer, Heidelberg (2005)
6. Baldoni, M., Baroglio, C., Martelli, A., Patti, V., Schifanella, C.: Verifying the Conformance of Web Services to Global Interaction Protocols: A First Step. In: Bravetti, M., Kloul, L., Zavattaro, G. (eds.) EPEW/WS-EM 2005. LNCS, vol. 3670, pp. 257–271. Springer, Heidelberg (2005)
7. Foster, H., Uchitel, S., Magee, J., Kramer, J.: Model-based Verification of Web Service Compositions. In: Proceedings of 18th IEEE International Conference on Automated Software Engineering (ASE 2003), pp. 152–163. IEEE Computer Society, Los Alamitos (2003)

8. Ghafari, N., Gurfinkel, A., Klarlund, N., Trefler, R.: Algorithmic Analysis of Piecewise FIFO Systems. In: Proceedings of 7th International Conference on Formal Methods in Computer-Aided Design (FMCAD 2007), pp. 45–52 (November 2007)
9. Dwyer, M., Avrunin, G., Corbett, J.: Patterns in Property Specifications for Finite-State Verification. In: Proceedings of 21st International Conference on Software Engineering (ICSE 1999), pp. 411–420 (May 1999)
10. van der Aalst, W.M.P., Weske, M.: Case Handling: a New Paradigm for Business Process Support. Data Knowledge Engineering 53(2), 129–162 (2005)
11. Autili, M., Inverardi, P., Pelliccione, P.: A Scenario Based Notation for Specifying Temporal Properties. In: Proceedings of the 2006 ICSE International Workshop on Scenarios and State Machines: Models, Algorithms, and Tools (SCESM 2006), pp. 21–28 (2006)
12. Yu, J., Manh, T.P., Han, J., Jin, Y., Han, Y., Wang, J.: Pattern Based Property Specification and Verification for Service Composition. In: Aberer, K., Peng, Z., Rundensteiner, E.A., Zhang, Y., Li, X. (eds.) WISE 2006. LNCS, vol. 4255, pp. 156–168. Springer, Heidelberg (2006)
13. Dwyer, M.B., Avrunin, G.S., Corbett, J.C.: Property Specification Patterns for Finite-state Verification. In: Proceedings of 2nd Workshop on Formal Methods in Software Practice (FMSP 1998) (March 1998)
14. Pnueli, A.: The Temporal Logic of Programs. In: Proceedings of 18th Annual Symposium on the Foundations of Computer Science (FOCS 1977), pp. 46–57 (1977)
15. Clarke, E., Grumberg, O., Peled, D.: Model Checking. MIT Press, Cambridge (1999)
16. Olender, K.M., Osterweil, L.J.: Cecil: A Sequencing Constraint Language for Automatic Static Analysis Generation. IEEE Transactions on Software Engineering 16(3), 268–280 (1990)
17. Hinz, S., Schmidt, K., Stahl, C.: Transforming BPEL to Petri Nets. In: van der Aalst, W.M.P., Benatallah, B., Casati, F., Curbera, F. (eds.) BPM 2005. LNCS, vol. 3649, pp. 220–235. Springer, Heidelberg (2005)
18. Ouyang, C., Verbeek, E., van der Aalst, W.M.P., Breutel, S., Dumas, M., ter Hofstede, A.H.M.: Formal Semantics and Analysis of Control Flow in WS-BPEL. Science of Computer Programming 67(2-3), 162–198 (2007)
19. Foster, H.: A Rigorous Approach to Engineering Web Service Compositions. PhD thesis, Imperial College (2006)
20. Hopcroft, J.E., Ullman, J.D.: Introduction to Automata Theory, Languages and Computation. Addison-Wesley, Reading (1979)
21. Simmonds, J., Gan, Y., Chechik, M., Nejati, S., O'Farrell, B., Litani, E., Waterhouse, J.: Runtime Monitoring of Web Service Conversations. IEEE Transactions on Service Computing (2009)
22. Simmonds, J., Ben-David, S., Chechik, M.: Optimizing Computation of Recovery Plans for BPEL Applications. In: Proceedings of the 2010 Workshop on Testing, Analysis and Verification of Web Software, TAV-WEB 2010 (to appear, 2010)
23. Giunchiglia, F., Traverso, P.: Planning as Model Checking. In: Biundo, S., Fox, M. (eds.) ECP 1999. LNCS, vol. 1809, pp. 1–20. Springer, Heidelberg (2000)
24. Kautz, H.A., Selman, B.: Unifying SAT-based and Graph-based Planning. In: Proceedings of the 16th International Joint Conference on Artificial Intelligence (IJCAI 1999), pp. 318–325 (1999)
25. Simmonds, J., Ben-David, S., Chechik, M.: Guided Recovery for Web Service Applications. In: Proceedings of Eighteenth International Symposium on the Foundations of Software Engineering, FSE 2010 (to appear, 2010)
26. Bozga, M., Fernandez, J.C., Kerbrat, A., Mounier, L.: Protocol Verification with the ALDÉBARAN Toolset. International Journal on Software Tools for Technology Transfer 1(1-2), 166–184 (1997)

27. Foster, H., Uchitel, S., Magee, J., Kramer, J.: LTSA-WS: a Tool for Model-Based Verification of Web Service Compositions and Choreography. In: Proceedings of the 28th International Conference on Software Engineering (ICSE 2006), pp. 771–774 (May 2006)
28. Magee, J., Kramer, J.: Concurrency - State Models and Java Programs. John Wiley, Chichester (1999)
29. Fikes, R., Nilsson, N.J.: STRIPS: A New Approach to the Application of Theorem Proving to Problem Solving. Journal of Artificial Intelligence 2(3/4), 189–208 (1971)
30. Gan, Y.: Runtime Monitoring of Web Service Conversations. Master's thesis, University of Toronto, Department of Computer Science (March 2007)
31. Carzaniga, A., Gorla, A., Pezze, M.: Healing Web Applications through Automatic Workarounds. International Journal on Software Tools for Technology Transfer 10(6), 493–502 (2008)
32. Simmonds, J.: Dynamic Analysis of Web Services. PhD thesis, Department of Computer Science, University of Toronto (2010) (in preparation)
33. Sahai, A., Machiraju, V., Wursterl, K.: Monitoring and Controlling Internet Based E-Services. In: Proceedings of the Second IEEE Workshop on Internet Applications (WIAPP 2001), Washington, DC, USA, p. 41. IEEE Computer Society, Los Alamitos (2001)
34. Keller, A., Ludwig, H.: The WSLA Framework: Specifying and Monitoring Service Level Agreements for Web Services. Journal of Network and Systems Management 11(1), 57–81 (2003)
35. Zulkernine, F.H., Martin, P., Wilson, K.: A Middleware Solution to Monitoring Composite Web Services-Based Processes. In: Proceedings of the 2008 IEEE Congress on Services Part II (SERVICES-2 2008), Washington, DC, USA, pp. 149–156. IEEE Computer Society, Los Alamitos (2008)
36. Mahbub, K., Spanoudakis, G.: A Framework for Requirements Monitoring of Service Based Systems. In: Proceedings of the 2nd International Conference on Service Oriented Computing (ICSOC 2004), pp. 84–93. ACM, New York (2004)
37. Mahbub, K., Spanoudakis, G.: Run-time Monitoring of Requirements for Systems Composed of Web-Services: Initial Implementation and Evaluation Experience. In: Proceedings of International Conference on Web Services (ICWS 2005), pp. 257–265 (July 2005)
38. van der Aalst, W.M.P., Pesic, M.: Specifying and Monitoring Service Flows: Making Web Services Process-Aware. In: Baresi, L., Nitto, E.D. (eds.) Test and Analysis of Web Services, pp. 11–55. Springer, Heidelberg (2007)
39. Lazovik, A., Aiello, M., Papazoglou, M.P.: Associating Assertions with Business Processes and Monitoring Their Execution. In: Proceedings of 2nd International Conference on Service Oriented Computing (ICSOC 2004), pp. 94–104 (November 2004)
40. Baresi, L., Ghezzi, C., Guinea, S.: Smart Monitors for Composed Services. In: Proceedings of 2nd International Conference on Service Oriented Computing (ICSOC 2004), pp. 193–202 (November 2004)
41. Baresi, L., Guinea, S.: Towards Dynamic Monitoring of WS-BPEL Processes. In: Benatallah, B., Casati, F., Traverso, P. (eds.) ICSOC 2005. LNCS, vol. 3826, pp. 269–282. Springer, Heidelberg (2005)
42. Pistore, M., Traverso, P.: Assumption-Based Composition and Monitoring of Web Services. In: Baresi, L., Nitto, E.D. (eds.) Test and Analysis of Web Services, pp. 307–335. Springer, Heidelberg (2007)
43. Lohmann, M., Mariani, L., Heckel, R.: A Model-Driven Approach to Discovery, Testing and Monitoring of Web Services. In: Test and Analysis of Web Services, pp. 173–204. Springer, Heidelberg (2007)

44. Li, Z., Jin, Y., Han, J.: A Runtime Monitoring and Validation Framework for Web Service Interactions. In: Proceedings of the 17th Australian Software Engineering Conference (ASWEC 2006), pp. 70–79. IEEE Computer Society, Los Alamitos (2006)
45. Li, Z., Han, J., Jin, Y.: Pattern-Based Specification and Validation of Web Services Interaction Properties. In: Benatallah, B., Casati, F., Traverso, P. (eds.) ICSOC 2005. LNCS, vol. 3826, pp. 73–86. Springer, Heidelberg (2005)
46. Shanahan, M.: The Event Calculus Explained. In: Veloso, M.M., Wooldridge, M.J. (eds.) Artificial Intelligence Today. LNCS (LNAI), vol. 1600, pp. 409–430. Springer, Heidelberg (1999)
47. Baresi, L., Guinea, S.: Dynamo and Self-Healing BPEL Compositions (research demonstration). In: Proceedings of the 29th International Conference on Software Engineering (ICSE 2007), pp. 69–70. IEEE Computer Society, Los Alamitos (2007) (companion volume)
48. Fugini, M.G., Mussi, E.: Recovery of Faulty Web Applications through Service Discovery. In: Proceedings of the 1st SMR-VLDB Workshop, Matchmaking and Approximate Semantic-based Retrieval: Issues and Perspectives, 32nd International Conference on Very Large Databases, pp. 67–80 (September 2006)
49. Dobson, G.: Using WS-BPEL to Implement Software Fault Tolerance for Web Services. In: 32nd EUROMICRO Conference on Software Engineering and Advanced Applications (EUROMICRO-SEAA 2006), pp. 126–133 (August 2006)
50. Brun, Y., Medvidovic, N.: Fault and Adversary Tolerance as an Emergent Property of Distributed Systems' Software Architectures. In: Proceedings of the 2007 Workshop on Engineering Fault Tolerant Systems (EFTS 2007), pp. 1–7 (September 2007)
51. Kramer, J., Magee, J.: Self-Managed Systems: an Architectural Challenge. In: The ICSE 2007 Workshop on the Future of Software Engineering (FOSE 2007), pp. 259–268 (May 2007)
52. Cheng, B.H.C., de Lemos, R., Giese, H., Inverardi, P., Magee, J., Andersson, J., Becker, B., Bencomo, N., Brun, Y., Cukic, B., Serugendo, G.D.M., Dustdar, S., Finkelstein, A., Gacek, C., Geihs, K., Grassi, V., Karsai, G., Kienle, H.M., Kramer, J., Litoiu, M., Malek, S., Mirandola, R., Müller, H.A., Park, S., Shaw, M., Tichy, M., Tivoli, M., Weyns, D., Whittle, J.: Software Engineering for Self-Adaptive Systems: A Research Roadmap. In: Software Engineering for Self-Adaptive Systems, pp. 1–26 (2009)
53. Cheng, B.H.C., de Lemos, R., Garlan, D., Giese, H., Litoiu, M., Magee, J., Müller, H.A., Taylor, R.: Seams 2009: Software engineering for adaptive and self-managing systems. In: 31st International Conference on Software Engineering (ICSE 2009), pp. 463–464 (May 2009) (companion volume)
54. Inverardi, P., Mostarda, L., Tivoli, M., Autili, M.: Synthesis of Correct and Distributed Adaptors for Component-Based Systems: an Automatic Approach. In: Proceedings of the 20th International Conference on Automated Software Engineering (ASE 2005), pp. 405–409 (2005)

Managing Dynamic Context to Optimize Smart Interactions and Services

Norha M. Villegas[1,2] and Hausi A. Müller[1]

[1] University of Victoria
hausi@cs.uvic.ca
[2] Icesi University
nvillega@cs.uvic.ca

Abstract. With the rapid growth of socio-technical ecosystems, smart interactions and services are permeating every walk of life. As smart interactions must managed automatically and interactively in response to evolving user's matters of concern, the smart Internet requires creative approaches where services and interactions are implemented with awareness of, and dynamic adaptation to, users, computational environments, changing policies and unknown requirements. Consequently, modeling and managing dynamic context is critical for implementing smart services and smart interactions effectively. Thus, smart interactions need infrastructure to acquire, compose, and distribute context information to multiple execution endpoints. Moreover, context management must be controlled and governed to optimize system properties. This chapter surveys context modeling and management approaches intended for the optimization of smart interactions and services, discusses the main challenges and requirements of context-awareness in the smart Internet, and provides a feature-based framework useful for the evaluation and implementation of context modeling and management mechanisms.

Keywords: dynamic context, context-awareness, context modeling, dynamic context management, feature-based context characterization survey, feedback control, smart interactions, smart services, smart Internet.

1 Introduction

Nowadays, systems are evolving from software intensive systems to socio-technical ecosystems, where dynamic groups of users, stakeholders, businesses, and software and hardware infrastructures, have to cooperate in complex and changing environments [1]. The World Wide Web is a good representative of such systems. Generally, its stakeholders have uncertain, conflicting, and changing requirements; furthermore, its control is highly complex and decentralized, and its users project an increasing need for dynamic and personalized services.

In this endeavour of providing dynamic applications centered on the user's goals, several researchers have made important contributions. One such initiative is the notion of *Smart Internet* introduced at the Smart Internet Technologies Working

M. Chignell et al. (Eds.): The Smart Internet, LNCS 6400, pp. 289–318, 2010.

Conference (SITCON) at CASCON 2009.[1] The Smart Internet includes two specific areas of research. *Smart Interactions*, which deal with aspects related to the discovery, aggregation, and delivery of resources from the Internet (e.g., the automatic deployment of components to provide personalized services to a person—traveler—who plans a trip involving transportation, accommodation, dining, and shopping); and *Smart Services*, which focus on providing the suitable infrastructure to support smart interactions (e.g., the required functionality to support the dynamic adaptation of the system, based on the traveler's environment and preferences) [2]. In order to support smart interactions and smart services, a system should be able to reason about its current state and provide functionality based on its context and the current user's matters of concern (*mocs*). In other words, such a system has to be reflective and context-aware. Thus, dynamic, user-centric applications require context management infrastructures able to provision context information by implementing self-managing interactions and services for supporting policy-based composition of context facts. We advocate creative approaches not just to acquire, model and distribute context information to multiple endpoints, but also to control and govern its provisioning, maintenance, and evolution [3].

This chapter reports on the results of a survey of context modeling and context management approaches in different problem domains. This study was performed with the motivation of identifying context modeling and management requirements for supporting smart interactions and services, and guided by four main research questions related to the challenges of context-awareness in the light of the smart Internet: (i) How to identify relevant context and the corresponding context management objectives for a particular set of interactions involved in a *moc*? (ii) How to acquire, compose, and distribute context information to multiple execution endpoints in an efficient manner? (iii) How to manage the dynamic nature of context information and the uncertainty of the context-aware system's requirements? (iv) How to control and govern context management by ensuring its provisioning according to the user's *mocs* and system's requirements?

To conduct this exploration, we propose an operational definition of context derived from three important existing definitions. The first one is the classic definition proposed by Dey et al. [4]. The second one is the operational extension of this definition given by Zimmermann et al. [5]. Our operational definition is a combination of these two definitions and the notion of *context life cycle* applied by Hynes [6]. An operational definition has the advantage of being more concrete and directly implementable than just abstract/conceptual definitions. Furthermore, we propose a context taxonomy based on previous classifications of context information. According to our taxonomy, context information can be classified into five fundamental categories: *individuality, time, location, activity* and *relational* (i.e., social, functional and compositional relationships among the first four types). To conduct our survey, we applied the method of Feature-Oriented Domain Analysis (FODA) proposed by researchers of Carnegie Mellon Software Engineering Institute (CMU SEI) [7]. The main focus of this method is the identification of prominent or distinctive features of software systems in a

[1] http://research.cs.queensu.ca/~cordy/SITCON/

domain. Using this method, we identified relevant features of context modeling and context management approaches, as well as, context modeling and management requirements for supporting context-awareness in the smart Internet. In each case, a set of feature diagrams is presented in the form of a hierarchy of common and variable features characterizing the selected context modeling and context management approaches.

The contributions of our study are as follows. First, we propose an operational definition of dynamic context information and its classification. This definition is suitable for managing context-awareness in the smart Internet, and its classification is valuable for identifying the context types involved in smart interactions. Second, we propose a set of feature models and requirements for context representation and management. These feature-based models constitute (i) a framework for the identification of context modeling and management requirements, (ii) a useful tool to evaluate and apply existing approaches, and (iii) define new context modeling techniques and context management infrastructures to realize the context requirements for the smart Internet. Third, we provide a comprehensive characterization of this domain useful to guide researchers in the investigation of new approaches related to this topic.

The remainder of this chapter is organized as follows. Section 2 describes an application scenario that is used throughout the chapter to illustrate the requirements and challenges of context modeling and management in the smart Internet. Section 3 presents our proposed operational definition of context information and its classification. Section 4 provides our feature-based characterization of context modeling and context management approaches and the requirements for addressing context-awareness in the smart Internet. Section 5 summarizes our survey by presenting its methodological aspects. Finally, Section 6 concludes the chapter with our perspective and future direction on context management for supporting smart services and smart interactions.

2 Application Scenario

To illustrate the various components of context modeling and management in the smart Internet, we use the scenario of a traveler staying at a hotel. Imagine a woman, who is taking a taxi from the airport to a hotel. While in the taxi, she receives a mobile check-in request from her booked hotel's automated desk service. While she fills-in the web form to check in, the automated desk service notifies the hotel guests information system about this new arrival. This system in turn sends a message to the traveler's mobile device for downloading a context-aware application for hotel services, such as indoor and outdoor facilities, dinning or meeting schedules, and tourist and shopping information. Once accepted for download and execution, the application asks the traveler for preferences and priorities about the kind of information and services she would like to use. Naturally, if she is a frequent guest, the system is aware of her preferences already. When she arrives at her hotel room, her favorite designer's fashion boutique, which has shops in this city, takes advantage of the traveler's location and her agenda and sends a custom dress catalog. As the woman is already registered in the boutique's system, she performs an on-line order buying that new fancy dress she wanted to wear for an important dinner that night. She also uses the smart Internet for ordering shoes and accessories suitable for her nice new dress. As the frequent traveler strolls through the hotel facilities, the dynamic adaptation capability of the downloaded context-aware application displays information and provides services. As in the case of the boutique, these services are provided according to nearby facilities, the traveler's preferences, and her agenda for this visit. Finally, before leaving the hotel, she uses her mobile device to check out and pay for the hotel service. All these functionalities are provided by composing various components of the hotel guests information system and other available services.[2] Clearly, the services required by the traveler in the scenario described above are highly dynamic and personalized.

This scenario evidences the importance of context information for improving many shortcomings in current Internet interactions. On the one hand, high levels of context-aware individualization should be supported for delivering functionality like the custom dress catalog or other services related to the user's *mocs* (e.g., registering for a spa session, paying the hotel bill with her credit card, collaborating with her friends to decide about her new dress). Moreover, based on her current *moc*, a fancy dinner that night, she should be able to drive service composition according to her needs. For instance, for ordering adequate shoes and accessories for her new dress from other on-line stores, she can compose functionality from the boutique's service with the other vendor's services. Many server-initiated connections are required to support automated services in this scenario; for example, to deploy components on the client side to provision services about nearby facilities, to facilitate the hotel's check-in service, and to deliver the personalized dress catalog. For supporting these smart interactions, context models must represent not only the current user's *mocs* and the corresponding context control objectives, but also support their dynamic adaptation as the situation changes. Consequently, the infrastructure to acquire, compose, handle and provision this information must adapt accordingly. It is worth pointing out that it is not only important the user's context, but also the context of the involved web resources. In the same way, context is crucial for supporting service level collaborations when the woman wants to ask her friends for advice about her new attire. Finally, the user control over web resources must be supported, as our traveler can select the desired set of services and decide about remote or local interactions.

The following sections discuss, using this illustrative scenario and our feature-based context characterization, requirements and challenges of context modeling and context management for supporting the smart interactions and services.

---

[2] This scenario was adapted from a research proposal by the DRISO research team at Icesi University, Cali, Colombia [8].

3 Characterization of Context Information

In order to optimize smart services and smart interactions, an operational definition of context must guide the identification of relevant features for the purpose of context modeling and context management and the corresponding requirements for the smart Internet. Therefore, the following characterization of context is based on three important contributions, which as a whole, provide the aforementioned foundation. In the first place, the definition proposed by Dey et al. states important user-centric elements [4]:

> *Context is any information that can be used to characterize the situation of an entity. An entity is a person, place or object that is considered relevant to the interaction between an user and an application, including the user and the application themselves.*

Clearly, this definition emphasizes the interaction between the user and the system. Generally, this interaction is completely related to users and their tasks.

Seven years later, in 2007, Zimmermann et al. extended Dey's definition by including two important additional dimensions [5]. The first one deals with the categorization of the design space of context models; and the second one with the dynamic behavior of context information. According to Zimmermann, the dynamic nature of context is evidenced on the transitions among contexts of one isolated entity, and the sharing of situational information among several entities. In other words, the context of a subject is constantly changing not only because the individual situation is evolving, but also because new information emerges from the interaction among different subjects.

The third foundation of this operational definition is the notion of context life cycle [6]. According to Hynes, context information can be managed by controlling its flow across a set of six stages: *acquisition, classification, handling, dissemination, maintenance and disposal.* Finally, our proposed operational definition is as follows:

> *Context is any information useful to characterize the state of individual entities and the relationships among them. An entity is any subject which can affect the behavior of the system and/or its interaction with the user. This context information must be modeled in such a way that it can be pre-processed after its acquisition from the environment, classified according to the corresponding domain, handled to be provisioned based on the system's requirements, and maintained to support its dynamic evolution.*

In summary, three important aspects constitute the foundation of our operational definition of context. The information which characterizes the situation of relevant subjects for the interactions between users and systems, the models required to represent such information, and the management and change of the information along its life cycle.

3.1 Classification of Context Information

In order to control and govern context information in a smart environment, it is useful to characterize context information types and management categories. Context information can be organized along several axes from static to dynamic, from nonvolatile to volatile, from nontransient to transient, and many others. Moreover, the dimensions for such classification can vary from one domain to another.

According to our classification, context information can be organized along five main categories, however, many other categories can be derived by combining the categories presented in Fig. 1 below. Table 1 below presents additional examples for each context category to illustrate the taxonomy in the light of the smart Internet scenario described in Sect. 2.

The first one, *individual context*, includes anything that can be observed about an isolated subject (i.e., the state of the subject). In the same way, one subject can expose more than one individual context depending on whether or not it plays multiple roles. Moreover, individual context can also be sub-classified depending on the subject type into *natural, human, artificial,* or *groups of entities* [5]. The first subcategory, *natural context,* is related to living and non-living entities which are not the direct result of any human activity (e.g., weather conditions). The second one, *human context,* refers to any information about the user behavior and his or her preferences, such as security profiles, language preferences, and his or her way of interacting with the system (e.g., the woman's security profile that enables the gathering of location information). The third one, *artificial context,* describes the state of entities resulting from human actions or technical processes. Some instances of artificial context are information related to buildings, hardware and software configurations (e.g., the dynamic architecture for deploying web resources on the woman's mobile device). Individual context can emerge from *groups of subjects,* which share common characteristics, but not necessarily interact with each other. Most importantly, membership to groups may emerge dynamically at run-time (e.g., available services that provide information about shopping stores

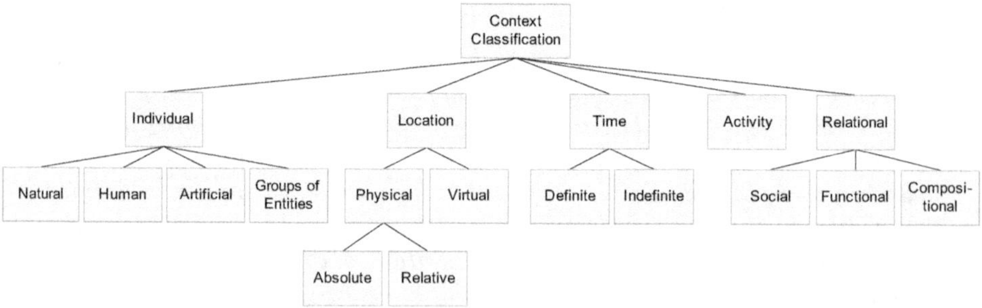

Fig. 1. Classification of context information. *Individual context* is related to information observed from independent entities or groups of them that are not interacting with others. *Time, location* and *activity* refer to the *when, where* and *what* of the user's situation. *Relational context* emerges from the relationship among the other types. Shadowed frames differentiate these nodes from feature-based models explained in Sect. 4.

Table 1. Examples of context categories for the scenario described in Sect. 2

Individual context	**Natural**	weather conditions relevant for recommending outdoor facilities
	Human	the traveler's meal preferences or her dress preferences (quality, designer, color, size)
	Artificial	the state of the traveler's mobile device battery
	Groups	services that provide information about shopping stores according to the user's preferences
Location context	**Physical Absolute**	4691 West Avenue: the hotel's address
	Physical Relative	the directions to reach the hotel from the airport or from the fashion store
	Virtual	uniform resources identifiers (URIs) of services or software components
Time context	**Definite**	the schedule of the traveler's activities for this visit
	Indefinite	the lenght of time from the traveler placed her online order until she received the dress
Activity context		The traveler's dinner at that night. A particular executable unit of one of the software components involved in the situation (the component in charge of managing the traveller's bill)
Relational context	**Social**	common affiliation among travelers who are registered to the same fashion store and are buying on-line (human, artificial and activity context involved in this social relation)
	Functional	the traveler typing her food preferences by using her mobile device when she arrived the hotel (human, artificial, time and activity location involved in this functional relation)
	Compositional	the software architecture which describes the composition of components in this situation (artificial context). The bindings restrictions between two context provisioning services

according to the user's preferences). Finally, social interests, computing power, cultural background, software architectures, and network topologies are examples of context inferred from such dynamic interactions.

Many aspects of the smart interaction between users and systems are related to the second category. *Location*, physical or virtual, involves all the information about the place of settlement or activity of an object. Instances of a physical location are absolute coordinates of the user's location (e.g., the hotel's address), the position of an object with respect to another (e.g., the directions to reach the hotel from the fashion store), or the city where our scenario is happening. An example of virtual location is the notion of Uniform Resource Identifier (URI).

Time context is the third classification as illustrated in Fig. 1. Most interactions between users and systems are influenced by this dimension in one form or another. Time information not only provides context about a specific date and time, but also categorical information such as holidays, working days, and meeting schedules. Dey and Abowd proposed an initial categorization of context based on primary and secondary information. In this former classification, secondary context can be inferred from the attributes of entities with primary context [4]. Thus, managing time context is important for obtaining secondary context (i.e., through context handling and reasoning). As an example, the fashion store application correlates the user's preferences with time context for sending custom offers. The application could suggest to the user a future activity, based on past experience of the same type of activity (e.g., a recommender system). In the same way, a dynamic context management infrastructure could use monitored information about time observations to predict future conditions and support system adaptation accordingly. Time context can be either *definite* or *indefinite.* The former represents time frames with specific begin and end points (i.e., a definite duration). In contrast, the latter expresses a recurrent event which is happening while another situation is taking place. In other words, it is not possible to know its duration in advance. Generally, user activities have not a clear beginning or end; interruptions are are natural and expected, and multiple activities take place concurrently. Thus, the ability to represent intervals of time also constitutes an important requirement for context modeling and management [5]. The fourth category, *activity context*, answers questions regarding future, current, and past goals as well as actions and tasks of an object (e.g., the traveler's dinner that night).

According to Zimmerman et al., all these context categories can be related to each other based on the three relational subcategories depicted in Fig. 1: *social, functional,* and *compositional* [5]. An operational representation of context must provide mechanisms to express semantic dependencies between two or more instances of context information. Social context emerges from the interrelation among individual human and group context. Samples of this relational context are affiliations, colleagues, and customers. Functional context refers to the information related to the usage that an object can make of another (e.g., the personalized functionalities exposed by the boutique's service to the woman). Finally, aggregation and association define the category of compositional relations.

Fundamental categories of context information have been identified in this taxonomy. Different categories can be combined to obtain new context information. These combinations correspond to social, functional, or compositional relations among relevant objects for the interaction between users and systems. Such interactions arise from individual objects which cooperate to achieve a common goal, within a definite or indefinite time and at a physical or virtual location (e.g., individual services that cooperate to achieve the user's goals according to the woman's *mocs*).

4 A Feature-Based Characterization of Context Modeling and Management Approaches

Our survey was based on the method of *Feature-Oriented Domain Analysis* (FODA) proposed by SEI [7]. The main focus of this method is the identification of prominent or distinctive features of software systems in a domain. Moreover, feature models have been applied to different areas in the fields of Computer Science and Software Engineering. In particular, in the domain of software product lines, Czarnecki and Helsen have expertly applied FODA to the characterization of model transformation approaches [9].

The feature-based models proposed in this chapter correspond to hierarchical compositions of common characteristics of the context modeling and management approaches studied in our survey. These features provide a useful conceptual tool to guide the application of existing and new approaches to context modeling and management as required by the smart Internet. One instance of the application of our feature models is the use of the features presented in Fig. 6 to define a smart Internet context meta-model that supports the generation of models able to represent the context information and the context management objectives for the interactions described in our application scenario (cf. Table 1). In other words, such a context meta-model must support the representation of granularity levels, different context types, properties and constraints of context entities, relationships among context entities, and spatial and scope representation. Similarly, for proposing a context management service infrastructure, features such as the ones depicted in Fig. 10 are valuable to guide the definition of strategies for the acquisition of relevant context (e.g., pulling or pushing and levels of indirection as communication mechanisms for context gathering).

The first big challenge related to context-awareness in the smart Internet is the identification of context requirements for a specific set of interactions or user *mocs*. Then, the second challenge is the modeling of these requirements in such a way that the representation of context is able to dynamically adapt itself as the application's environment and the user's *mocs* change. Once relevant context and context management objectives are modeled, the third challenge is to design a dynamic context management infrastructure able to support the gathering, handling, and exploitation of context according to the model. Moreover, managing context for supporting smart interactions also implies the dynamic monitoring of context control objectives to support, for instance, automatic server-initiated connections or service discovery tailored to the user's needs. Finally, as smart interactions and services need infrastructure to acquire, compose, and distribute context information to multiple execution endpoints, it seems logical to address the characterization of context modeling and context management by taking into account the central aspects of context life cycle presented in Fig. 2. With the exception of the context modeling node at the second level of this figure, the remaining nodes correspond to the central aspects of context management.

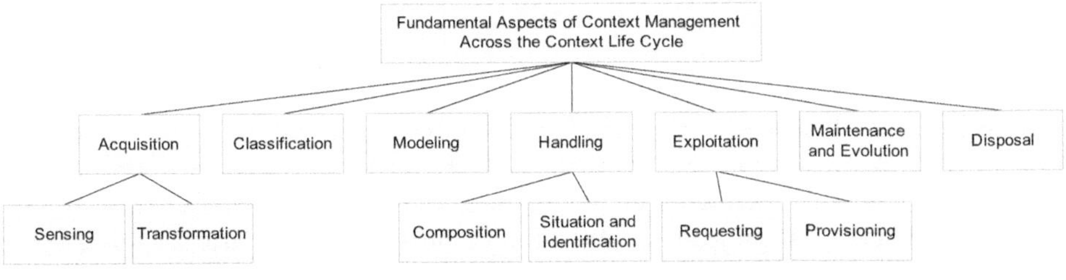

Fig. 2. Central aspects of context management across the context life cycle. Feature models defined in our survey were based on these aspects of the life cycle. Shadowed frames differentiate these nodes from feature-based models depicted in Figs. 4-13.

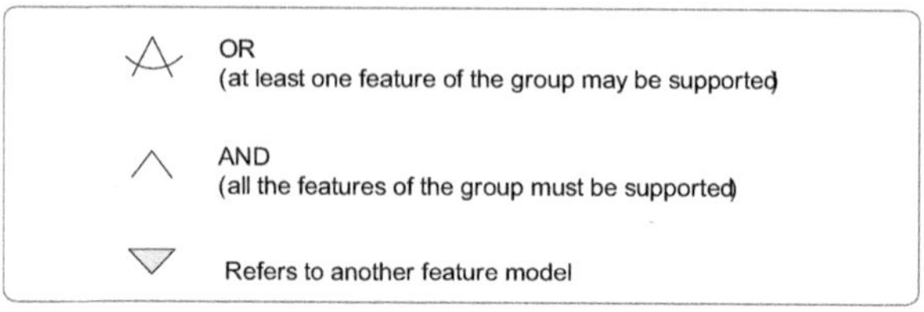

Fig. 3. Legend for feature diagrams of context modeling and management approaches. Note that this legend does not apply to Figs. 1 and 2 as they are not feature-based models.

Notational elements for the feature models presented in Sect(s). 4.1-4.3 are explained in Fig. 3.

4.1 Context Modeling

Context modeling is an important component of the context information life cycle. Context models represent the relevant aspects of entities which affect the interactions between users and systems, as well as the situations that trigger dynamic changes in such interactions. Control loops play a crucial role for monitoring context in supporting smart interactions and services. We use the term *context control objectives* to refer the aspects of context that must be monitored to support system adaptation. These aspects include not only information regarding individual, time, location, and activity context, but also relations among them. For our application scenario, important control objectives are related to the monitoring of changes in the woman's location. For instance, when the woman arrives at her destination, new interactions are automatically initiated to assist her in the hotel check-in process or in the acquisition of a new dress for her fancy dinner. Most importantly, once raw context data is pre-processed in the acquisition stage, it acquires the form defined by the context model. Context models are also required to provide higher level context information—for instance, to represent the quality of context data.

Several approaches of context representation have been proposed in recent years. In particular, many of them have been analyzed by Bettini et al. [10], Moore [11], and Strang and Popien [12]. Figure 4 presents selected features from existing context modeling approaches and context management infrastructures. In the first place, the *approach-type* feature represents any of the possible ways of representing context such as logic-based and ontology-based models. The second group of features, *context entities and situations representation*, is concerned with the modeling of important aspects such as granularity, properties, constraints, and relationships. The third one, *timeliness modeling*, refers to the representation of past and future states. The fourth set of features, *quality modeling*, corresponds to meta-data for representing quality attributes of context information. Finally, the *software engineering* set of features includes tools to support context requirements analysis, context model design, code generation, and run-time processing.

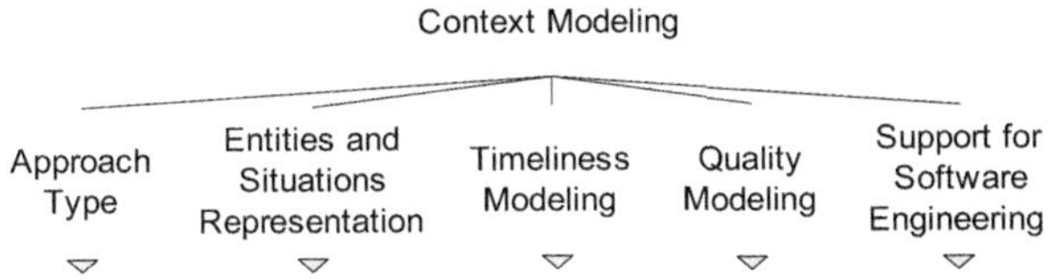

Fig. 4. Feature model of context modeling. Appropriate context models must support features of each of these six categories.

Context Modeling Techniques. Figure 5 depicts the most common approaches of context representation. According to this figure, at least one of these approaches is used in context-awareness and they can complement each other. Strang and Popien presented a comprehensive evaluation of context representation approaches and discussed implementation examples for many of them [12]. Their evaluation strategy was in terms of a set of requirements for context modeling: *distributed composition, partial validation, richness and quality of information, incompleteness and ambiguity, level of formality,* and *applicability to existing environments.* Later, Bettini et al. extended this set with selected new requirements. Requirements, such as *representation of relationships and dependencies* and *efficient context provisioning,* were used to evaluate these context representation approaches from the perspective of their expressiveness and support for reasoning [10].

Following the order presented in Fig. 5, the two first features are known as the early approaches. *Key-value pairs* are used to represent context information as a list of attributes with their corresponding values. *Markup models* generally are in the form of XML models, which represent a hierarchical data structure of tags with attributes and values. The remaining features suggest more applied approaches for context modeling. *Object-oriented models* are based on the object-oriented paradigm to face the representation of dynamic characteristics of context [13], [14]. *Meta-model-based models* emerged recently in Model Driven Engineering (MDE) domains to support the dynamic generation of new model instances based on meta-models defined at design-time [15], [16], [17], [18]. *Logic-based* and *ontology-based models* are used to define formal specifications of context entities and the relations among them in a particular domain [19], [20]. Finally, *fact-based models*, such as the object-role approach applied by Henricksen et al., emerged from the necessity of providing formal models that are able to support query processing and reasoning [21].

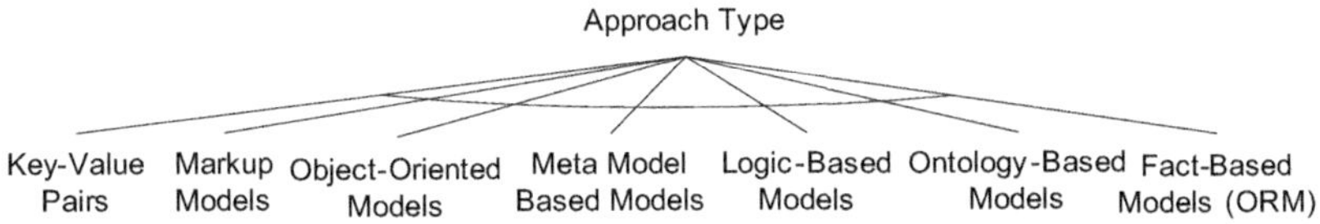

Fig. 5. Context modeling approaches. These approaches can be combined to produce more comprehensive sets of context modeling features as depicted in Fig. 4.

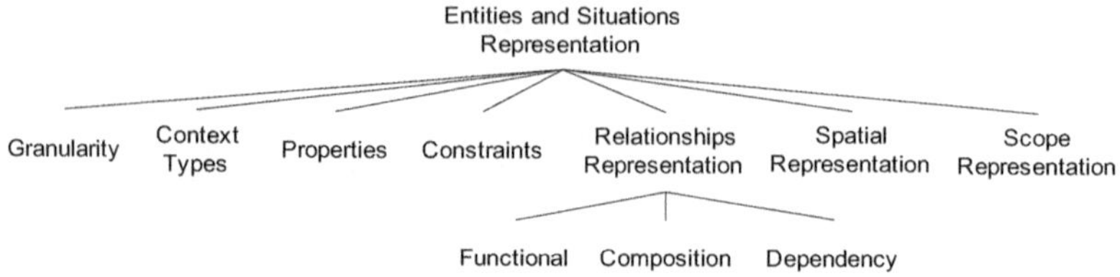

Fig. 6. Representation of context entities and situations. Reasoning about dynamic context depends on the suitability of context models to express these features.

Representation of Context Entities and Situations. The set of features depicted in Fig. 6 is related to important attributes for the representation of context entities and situations. Appropriate context models must support the detection of conditions for moving between situations and contexts. Moreover, they must be able to represent context information types, as well as different levels of granularity, constraints, relations among context entities, and spatial and scope information about the specific context. The first feature within this group is *granularity,* which is related to the level of detail of context data and the scope of this information. Moreover, the abstraction and derivation of context facts are affected by the different levels of granularity of context information [5]. In our scenario, levels of granularity in location context affect the capability of the infrastructure to provide services according to the current user's needs (e.g., services for providing functionality based on nearby facilities require finest levels of granularity).

Context type and *context property* features refer to the capability of models for representing the raw context data after its preprocessing during the acquisition process. Thus, reasoning about dynamic context depends on the suitability of such models to express data gathered from the environment. Moreover, a context model must represent different types of context information and the context management system must provide management of this information depending on its type [10].

The capability of expressing *constraints* of context entities and relationships among them is also a key factor for modeling context information. In particular, from the perspective of the smart Internet, expressing relationships and its constraints among services is important for the dynamic configuration of a context management service infrastructure (e.g., the discovery of appropriate services for supporting tasks such as credit card payments or possible service compositions to gather the required context). Context modeling techniques are required to support both, consistency verification of the model and context reasoning techniques. Moreover, they must assist the context management infrastructure in dealing with incomplete or conflicting context information. Thus, constraints are necessary for consistency verification. In the same way, the *representation of relationships* among context entities can be used to derive new context facts from existing context observations (e.g., activity and time context derived from the fact *a fancy dinner that night*, and location context from the fact *the woman arrived in a different city* are correlated to infer new context facts such as the necessity of a new dress or a hairdressing appointment) as ell as reason about context abstractions that model real world situations [10].

Finally, spatial and scope representation are useful for quality-based reasoning, management, and provisioning. In particular, *spatial representation* is useful to establish boundaries whenever it is necessary to limit the reasoning space to avoid performance degradation (e.g., the reasoning space for the boutique's service to select offers to be included in the catalog sent to the woman should be limited to the available stock in the current city). Similarly, *scope representation* is useful to enforce policies such as privacy of context information [12].

To illustrate the application of these features to context modeling, consider the MUSIC framework [16]. Context information is abstracted by context elements which provide information about entities and their scope. Moreover, these context entities can be composed of other context elements and contain a number of context values. In this model, proposed by Reichle et al., context information characterizes an entity of the world (e.g., laptop, device, or user) with a certain type or scope of information (e.g., location, current situation, or battery status), and in a certain representation (e.g., GPS coordinates in the case of location) [16].

Timeliness and Quality Modeling. The representation of past and future states of context information and its quality attributes are also important features of context modeling techniques (cf. Fig. 7). Context-aware applications need information regarding past and future states of their relevant context entities. Therefore, the *timeliness* feature, proposed by Bettini et al., needs to be captured by context models and managed by context management systems. Nevertheless, the management of historical information is challenging if the context is highly dynamic. It may not be feasible to store every variation along the time dimension. Consequently, summarization techniques, such as the use of historical synopsis of data, must be applied [10]. Due to imperfection, which is an intrinsic characteristic of context, data gathered from the environment can have different levels of quality or can even be incorrect. Krause and Hochstatter state

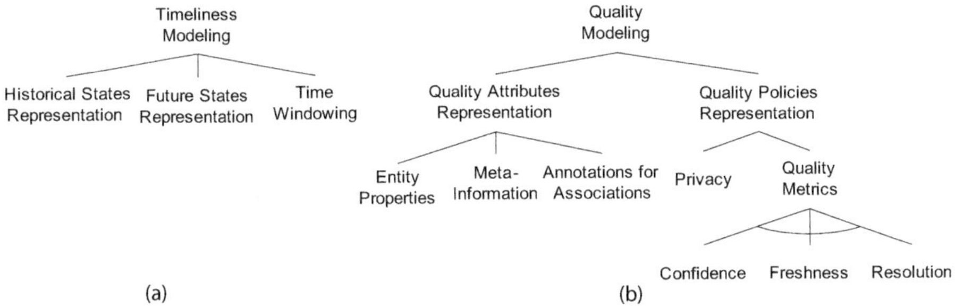

Fig. 7. Timeliness and quality modeling. Reasoning and derivation of context facts are based on information regarding past, present, and future states. Moreover, user-centric interactions must be based on quality of context information.

some possible quality problems of context information: (i) Context data could be out-dated and no longer applicable to a particular situation; (ii) default profile information could not apply to the current situation or physical constraints; and (iii) temporary effects could limit the precision of sensors [22]. Therefore, *quality modeling* must express both, information about the quality of the data that they are modeling (i.e., quality attributes), and information about quality policies and metrics (e.g., confidence, freshness, or resolution).

Support for Software Engineering. Features depicted in Fig. 8 are related to tools for supporting *analysis of context requirements, design of context models, code generation,* and *run-time processing.* According to Reichle et al., support for software development is an important requirement for context modeling [16]. Henricksen et al. proposed a similar fact-based model as an attempt to provide modeling constructs suitable for software engineering tasks such as analysis and design [21], [23]. Moreover, the framework proposed by Zimmermann et al. includes a set of tools for supporting the design of context-aware applications and the implementation of fundamental context management components [24].

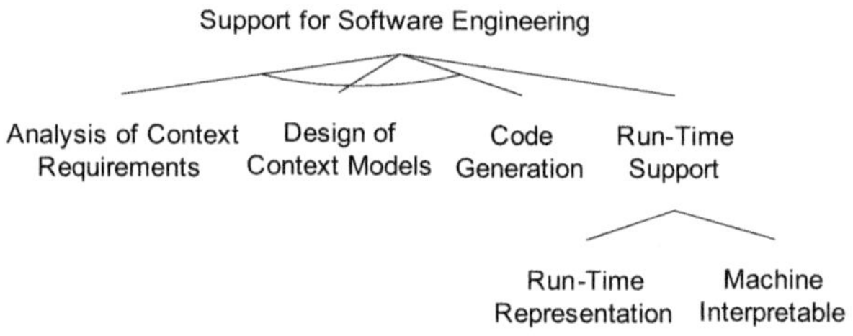

Fig. 8. Support for software engineering. Ideally, context modeling should be supported by tools and software infrastructures for the analysis of context requirements, the design of context models, code generation, and run-time processing.

4.2 Context Modeling Requirements in the Smart Internet

For supporting smart interactions, smart services infrastructures require the definition of dynamic models that characterize the situation of users and web resources involved in their *mocs*. This characterization involves properties, relationships among users and web resources, and context facts that affect the behaviour of these entities. In light of this, given a specific *moc*, context models for supporting smart interactions and services are required to (i) represent the variety of context information that characterizes the state of entities that affect the interaction between users and web resources in the *moc*; (ii) represent the context control objectives required to monitor the situations that affect the dynamic adaptation of web resources involved in the *moc*; (iii) adapt according to dynamic changes in the *moc* or in the state of its relevant entities, to ensure a consistent representation of context information. Our operational definition of context and our feature-based characterization are valuable to address these requirements. In the first place, context models should support the representation of context types presented in our context classification (cf. Fig. 1). In the second place, the features presented in Fig. 5 are useful to guide the evaluation and selection of appropriate context modeling approaches. In the third place, these requirements require that context models be compliant with the features for representing entities and situations depicted in Fig. 6, including timeliness and quality modeling features presented in Fig. 7. Finally, context models for the smart Internet must provide mechanisms for run-time representation and processing, for assisting users in its design and evolution, and many other desirable engineering features such as the ones presented in Fig. 8.

4.3 Context Management

Smart interactions deal with factors that impact the discovery, aggregation, and delivery of web resources and contents related to users and their tasks [2]. Smart services provide the computing infrastructure to support smart interactions. The combination of smart interactions and smart services feed into the notion of a smart environment and a smart Internet. From a smart environment, we expect that it is able to detect its current state or context and determine what interactions to perform or how to tailor services based on its context. Moreover, an infrastructure to support smart services and interactions must provide context services accessible from anywhere on the planet [25]. Features of context management infrastructures belong to any of the six groups depicted in Fig. 9. It is important to note the correspondence between these groups of features and the definition of context explained in Sect. 3. Refined feature diagrams for the identified context management groups are depicted in Figs. 10-13.

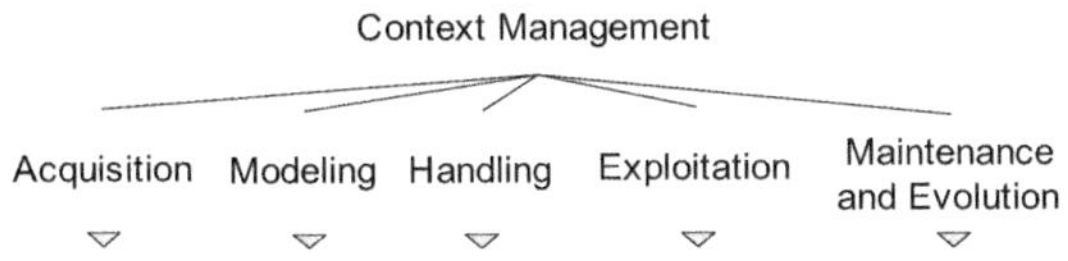

Fig. 9. Identified top level features of context management approaches. The second group, modeling features, was presented in Fig. 4 and explained in Sect. 4.1.

Context Acquisition. Context acquisition refers to the gathering of primary context from the environment. Context management infrastructures must implement mechanisms to generate numeric observables from physical sensors, and determine comparable measures by performing basic transformations.

Figure 10 depicts context acquisition feature groups. The first group represents the *distributed nature of context sources*. According to this set of features, context management infrastructures can obtain context information from one, or more than one, of these subtypes. Thus, due to this distributed character of context information, such infrastructures must implement context source discovery mechanisms. *Source discovery mechanisms* based on standards and services constitute the second group of features of context acquisition. Standards, such as the family of IEEE 1451 standards[3] and SensorML[4] provide a way of describing sensor specifications for supporting opportunistic discovery [26]. For example, the context management infrastructure propose by Hu et al. takes advantage of these standards [23], [27].

As an illustration of the third group of features, *gathering*, the service-based infrastructure proposed by Hynes et al. implements both pulling and pushing as mechanisms to receive context data. Context management infrastructures should be able to gather context information by implementing these mechanisms. That means, retrieving data and receiving unsolicited information from the source. Similarly, the implementation of *levels of indirection* is a highly desirable feature for context gathering. However, even when context-aware applications are supported by context management infrastructures, generally, context is acquired by linking the management infrastructure to each particular context source. Instances of mechanisms to implement levels of indirection are standards like Management Using Web Services (MUWS) and Management of Web Services (MOWS), which were proposed by the Oasis Web Services Distributed Management (WSDM) Technical Committee [28]. These specifications are an important milestone for implementing autonomic features because they provide standardization for manageability endpoints [29]. From the perspective of context management, MUWS and MOWS are useful to support the management and orchestration of context sources by implementing endpoints as web services.

Finally, *pre-processing* features such as *filtering* and *classification* are related to basic transformations of context information to provide symbolic observables at the appropriate level of abstraction [30], [31]. The context management system proposed by Hu et al. supports pre-processing of raw context data by implementing chains of *atomic processes*. Atomic processes are SensorML descriptions of sensors and models for processing sensor observations. Chains of atomic processes are composed by matching the outputs of processes to the inputs of other existing processes. At run-time, the pre-processing algorithm extracts a subset of this graph of atomic processes. This subset must satisfy the requirements of the application context model [27].

Context Handling. Smart applications use environmental information to decide whether or not to adapt their behavior. Thus, context management infrastructures must support smart interactions by implementing mechanisms to infer context information from sensed context, and reason about high level context abstractions (i.e., derivation of context facts). Most importantly, context information must be handled regardless of the supported context acquisition mechanisms to enforce separation of concerns between application semantics and context acquisition.

Features of context handling are depicted in Fig. 11. *Derivation of context facts* is the first feature of this group. In the multi-tier reference framework

[3] http://ieee1451.nist.gov
[4] http://vast.nsstc.uah.edu/SensorML/

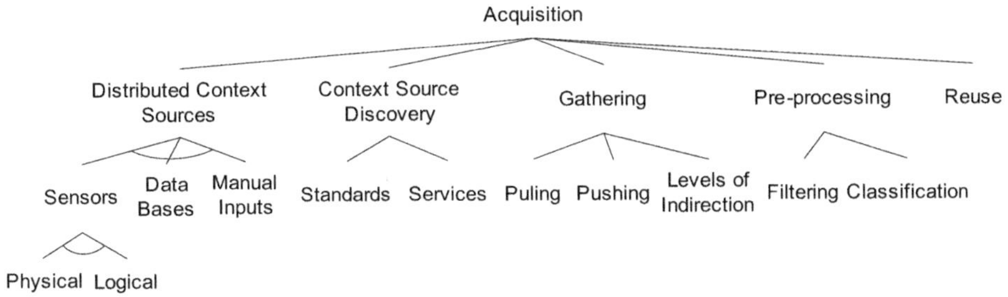

Fig. 10. Feature model of context acquisition. Context is gathered from heterogeneous and distributed sources using different mechanisms such as puling and pushing. Raw context must be pre-processed and classified before being manipulated at higher levels of abstraction.

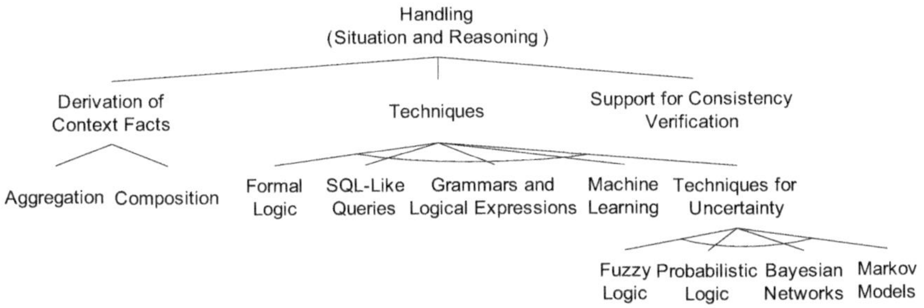

Fig. 11. Feature model of context handling. Handling is about mechanisms to infer context information from sensed data, and reason about high level context abstractions. Handling techniques can be further refined by implementing derivations of context facts as well as supporting context validation and verification.

proposed by Coutaz et al., the derivation of context facts is performed by the situation and context identification layer by reasoning about the observables generated in the acquisition phase of the context life cycle [25]. To be able to reason about observables, these measures are represented in terms of context models. The second group of features describes *techniques* for supporting context handling. Depending on the specific application domain, context management infrastructures studied in our survey support at least one of these techniques. Context handling techniques are used to reason about the information represented in a context model. Moreover, a context management infrastructure must implement *consistency verification* of the context model for supporting the dynamic adaptation of such models [10].

Context Exploitation. Context exploitation is related to the request and provision of environmental information. Context management infrastructures must provide services to support the gathering of context information from the sources and its provisioning to multiple endpoints.

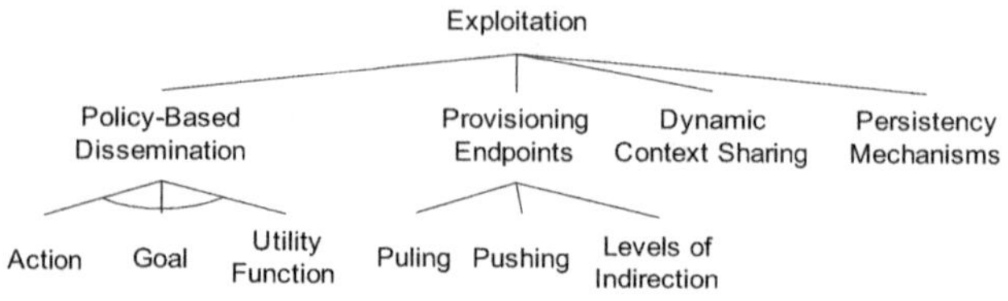

Fig. 12. Feature model of context exploitation. These features concern the provisioning of ambient information to context-aware applications.

User and business goals are continuously evolving according to their changing environment. Consequently, smart interactions and smart services have the challenge of supporting the user's tasks and stakeholders' needs, even when their requirements are highly dynamic and uncertain. Figure 12 illustrates the selected features of context exploitation. According to the first branch, context information must be disseminated by implementing *policy-based mechanisms*, as it was proposed by Salomie et al. [32], Strassner et al. [33], and Samaan et al. [14]. Thus, control policies can be applied to acquire, handle, store, and disseminate context information. A promising research direction in the area of service oriented architecture (SOA) is to establish a level of indirection to govern policies using control loops (i.e., SOA governance) [29], [34]. In fact, context management infrastructures must make decisions on behalf of their context clients by selecting and composing policies, and executing tasks based on action policies as proposed by Samaan et al. [14]; or goal and utility function policies as used by the autonomic computing community [35].

PACMAN is an example of policy-based middleware for context management in ambient networks [14]. This infrastructure uses a policy-based model to represent context. PACMAN can evolve to support new context types and new applications requirements through the dynamic generation of policies based on context transformation, context filtering and context aggregation policies. Furthermore, context control policies in PACMAN define strategies and rules for acquisition, dissemination, storage and update of context information. A policy manager is the brain of this infrastructure, which is in charge of interpreting acquired context, managing stored context, and evaluating context policies according to context level agreements. COSMOS is another instance of a policy-based context provider [13]. This component-based framework, proposed by Conan et al., offers tools to collect, interpret, and process context data.

The second feature, *provisioning endpoints*, is related to the communication mechanisms between context-aware services and context management infrastructures. For instance, ACoMS, the context management system proposed by Hu et al., supports either, querying (i.e., pulling) and publish/subscribe (i.e., pushing) mechanisms. Furthermore, ACoMS can merge different application context requests based on common quality requirements [27]. Similarly, CA3M, a middleware proposed by Taconet et al., implements two mechanisms for context provisioning. The first one, *observation mode*, corresponds to top-down interactions where applications synchronously request context observations. The second one, *notification mode*, transmits context information to applications based on conditions defined in contracts [15]. Finally, context must be considered independently from applications [25]. Thus, the more flexible the communication mechanisms are, the better is the interoperability between context management infrastructures and context-aware applications.

Dynamic context sharing is the third feature of context exploitation. Even when the context can be related to a specific domain, fundamental context categories such as *individual, time,* and *location* can be shared by a group of different applications. This feature optimizes the use of resources and the quality of the information provided to context-aware systems and supports the dynamic collaboration among services as demanded by the smart Internet community. In particular, ConServ, a Web service for context management proposed by Hynes et al., addresses the sharing of context data among smart spaces and, as a result, facilitates the creation of new smart spaces. Data related to a user's location, calendar, habits, relationships among entities, and privacy policies are combined to provide rich context data [36]. Paspallis et al. proposed a similar architecture to enable the MADAM middleware to share at run-time context information among a set of distributed mobile devices [37]. Finally, context exploitation requires efficient *persistence mechanisms* as environmental information is managed along the time dimension.

Maintenance and Evolution of Context Management Infrastructures. Coutaz et al. discuss the issue of dynamic context evolution [25]. This set of features relates to the capability of context management infrastructures to evolve, as required by the dynamic nature of context. For instance, by reconfiguring their architecture to support new context requirements, providers or consumers, that can change context control objectives at run-time. These features are depicted in Fig. 13. Generally, most context management approaches support features such as *context disposition* and *data management*, rather than *fault tolerance, scalability,* and *autonomicity.* However, several research efforts have made important contributions for the latter three features [32], [27], [26], [38], [39].

Context disposal refers to the fully or semi-automatic disposal of context information when it is not useful anymore. Policies and enforcement mechanisms can be defined to manage the disposal of context information according to certain conditions such as freshness, location or context sources [6]. Context data must also be managed to ensure the persistence of valuable information for context reasoning. Furthermore, the second feature, *management of context data*, must be based on practical considerations such as performance, computational cost, and distributed storage. Most importantly, maintenance of context data in distributed environments involves tradeoffs between persistence, processing, and communication mechanisms. For instance, storage mechanisms for context information related to the location of users, who are traveling on high speed trains must carefully monitor the cost of multiple retrievals and updates. In particular, the context management system proposed by Strimpakou et al. deals with the management of context data, by implementing a mechanism based on a federation of context repositories [18].

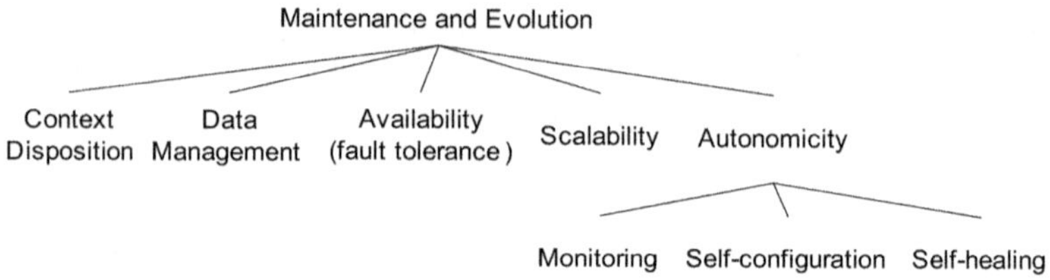

Fig. 13. Feature model of maintenance and evolution. These features are important to manage context in dynamic, uncertain, and continuously evolving environments.

The *scalability* feature is a direct result of the distributed nature of context information. In light of this, a context management infrastructure must monitor its performance to manage its degradation as the number of context sources and context consumers increases [37]. Hu et al. discuss the importance of implementing features such as *self-configuring* and *self-healing*, in context management infrastructures. They proposed an autonomic context manager that provides self-configuration of context sources and run-time replacement of failed or disconnected context sources based on redundancy mechanisms [27]. Thus, autonomic context management systems should implement (i) dynamic reconfiguration to support new types, sources, and consumers of context information and (ii) monitoring mechanisms to support failures as a normal state of their infrastructure.

4.4 Context Management Requirements in the Smart Internet

Smart services require models and infrastructure to support the three dimensions of the smart Internet: instinctive user model, sessions for users and their matter of concerns, and collective and collaborative web interactions [2]. For instinctive interactions to be user-centric, it is necessary that the management of context information be relevant for the user's *mocs*. Moreover, collaborative and collective web interactions require high levels of context-awareness to infer, for instance, opportunities of collaboration among users with similar interests. As a result, for a particular *moc* and its corresponding context model, dynamic web-based context management infrastructures are required to (i) Identify context control objectives, and define context management strategies based on the characterization of relevant context represented by the model. Most importantly, a context management infrastructure should be able to not only detect changes in the *moc*, but also changes in the state of the involved entities to support the adaptation of the context model dynamically; (ii) gather relevant context according to context requirements regardless of the availability of context sources; (iii) handle context facts and reason about context situations according to the context model; (iv) provide context information to multiple and distributed execution endpoints using open and technologically agnostic mechanisms; (v) be self-adaptive, and ideally self-managing, to address issues such as the dynamic deployment of new components for context acquisition—for instance, when a user provides a personalized sensor or when it is necessary to replace an existing one. Self-adaptation is crucial for supporting dynamic changes in context control objectives. Changes in a *moc* can impact context control objectives thus requiring the reconfiguration of the infrastructure to guarantee handling and monitoring pertinence with respect to the new situation. Finally, a context management infrastructure is required to monitor itself for regulating the satisfaction of context control requirements.

Our feature-based models for context management are applicable to satisfy the requirements of context management infrastructures in the smart Internet. Firstly, top level features as depicted in Fig. 9 define the base functionality for managing the context life cycle. Secondly, acquisition features presented in Fig. 10 summarize distributed context sources types, characterize context discovery, gathering and pre-processing mechanisms, and define other sub-requirements for context gathering. Thirdly, handling and exploitation features presented in Figs. 11 and 12 define sub-requirements and summarize useful techniques for addressing the requirements (iii) and (iv). Finally, features presented in Fig. 13 define fundamental aspects for implementing self-adaptive and self-managing context management infrastructures.

5 Survey Summary

This section summarizes our survey by presenting data related to the selected references and the research communities involved in the problems of context modeling and context management. Moreover, this section details the process followed in our study (i.e., bibliographic search, filtering, and classification), and presents useful information about trends in the evolution of this research area. Most importantly, the information presented in this section is valuable to guide the SITCON community in leveraging existing research contributions in the design and implementation of suitable approaches for modeling and managing context information according to the requirements and features described in Sect. 4.

Methodological Aspects. Our survey was based on some of the guidelines proposed by Kitchenham and Charters in their *systematic review method* [40] and its application proposed by Chen et al. [41]. The first activity of this process was our bibliographic search. Based on our set of research questions related to context definition, modeling, and management, we defined a list of keywords and search strings used for our investigation. The second step involved the filtering and classification of the results obtained from the previous activity. To determine whether or not a particular search result was related to the definition, modeling or management of context information, we fully reviewed the abstract and the contributions section of each paper. Then, the filtering was further refined by concentrating on contributions published in high-quality international journals and conference proceedings. Finally, a few additional papers were included into the set, after the detailed review of the related work of the selected papers.

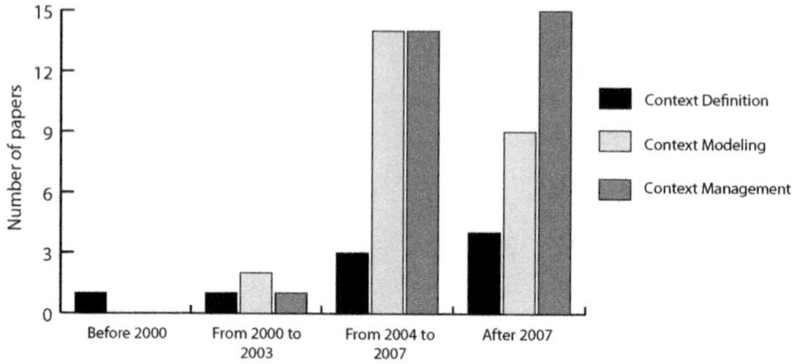

Fig. 14. Distribution of context definition, context modeling, and context management contributions by publication year. Over the past decade, the focus of the context research community has evolved from context definition to context management.

Demographic and Chronological Data. Figure 14 illustrates the distribution of context definition, context modeling, and context management contributions from 53 papers by publication year. Before 2000, context-aware and pervasive computing were emergent research areas. Most research efforts focused on the understanding of context and context-awareness [4]. In the next phase, from 2000 to 2003, researchers continued working on the understanding and definition of context, but also some efforts emerged dealing with the representation and exploitation of context information. Computer scientists, such as Dey [42], [43], Strang [19], Crowley [38],[31] and colleagues, made many valuable contributions. Finally, the last two periods of time focus on addressing the challenges inherent in the representation, acquisition, handling, and provisioning of context information. In particular, the increasing number of contributions in modeling and management can be explained with the necessity of providing context information to support several challenges in different research communities such as the SITCON community.

The survey presented in this book chapter considered the following list of papers presented by category (i.e., context definition, context modeling and context management) and in chronological order. If a paper was useful for the identification of features in more than one category, then it is listed more than once.

1. Context definition: Abowd et al. [4], Dey [43], Coutaz et al. [25], Zimmermann [24], [5], Chang [44], Kapitsaki [45], Hynes [6], Hoareau [46].
2. Context modeling: Crowley et al. [38], Strang [19], Henricksen et al. [21], Krause and Hochstatter [22], Lei and Zhang [47], Schmidt [48], Ou et al. [49], Park [50], Robinson et al. [51], Choi [52], Salomie et al. [32], Achilleos [53], Anagnostopoulos et al. [54].
3. Context management: Strang et al. [19], Krause and Hochstatter [22], Preuveneers and Berbers [55], Dey [56], Henricksen et al. [57], Chantzara and Anagnostou [30], Hu et al. [26], Paspallis et al. [37], Robinson et al. [51], Samaan et al. [14], Liu [58], Salomie et al. [32], Hu et al. [27], Dudkowski et al. [59], Paspallis et al. [60], Zhang and Hansen [61], Strassner et al. [33], Hynes et al. [36], Schmidtke and Woo [62], Abid et al. [63], Knappmeyer et al. [64]

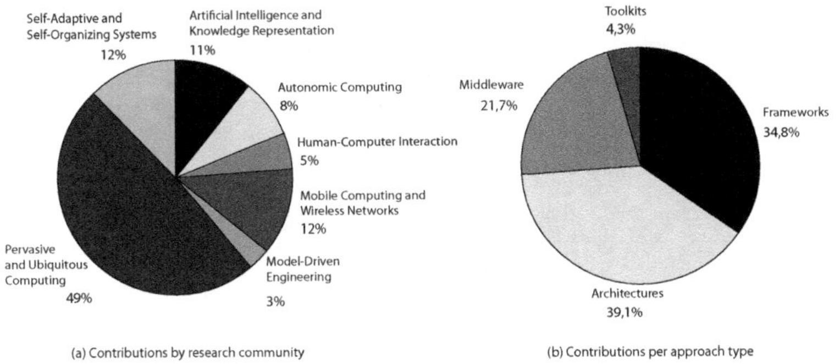

Fig. 15. (a) Overall distribution of contributions by research community; (b) Contributions per approach type.

Research Communities. Figure 15 (a) presents the overall distribution of contributions by research community. Each paper studied in our survey was classified into one of seven research communities: *artificial intelligence and knowledge representation, autonomic computing, human-computer interaction, mobile computing and wireless networks, model driven engineering, pervasive and ubiquitous computing,* and *self-adaptive and self-organizing systems.* Most approaches from autonomic computing, mobile computing, model driven engineering, and self-adaptive and self-managing systems belong to the software engineering community. It is important to note that this information does not represent an exhaustive search of the contributions in each community. Nevertheless, the graph shows the participation of each community within the set of selected papers for this survey. It is possible to conclude that before 2000, most efforts for understanding and defining context information were made by researchers in the pervasive and ubiquitous computing domain. At the turn of the century, other research communities started to contribute to this area. From 2000 to 2003, most contributions originated from the pervasive and ubiquitous computing, human-computer interaction, and mobile computing and wireless networks communities; from 2004, many valuable contributions were added by the self-adaptive and self-organizing systems, artificial intelligence and knowledge representation, autonomic computing and model driven engineering communities. The variety of the contributions has been generated in part by the increasing complexity of the problems studied by these research communities. Moreover, dealing with the dynamic nature of context information is a concern of diverse research communities in computer science, software engineering, engineering in general, health information sciences, and social sciences in general.

Context Modeling and Context Management Features. In this survey, the set of contributions related to context modeling consists of 25 papers while the set for context management includes 30. Figure 15 (b) depicts the distribution of context management contributions per approach type. Figure 16 (a) presents the distribution of modeling contributions for each top level feature detailed in

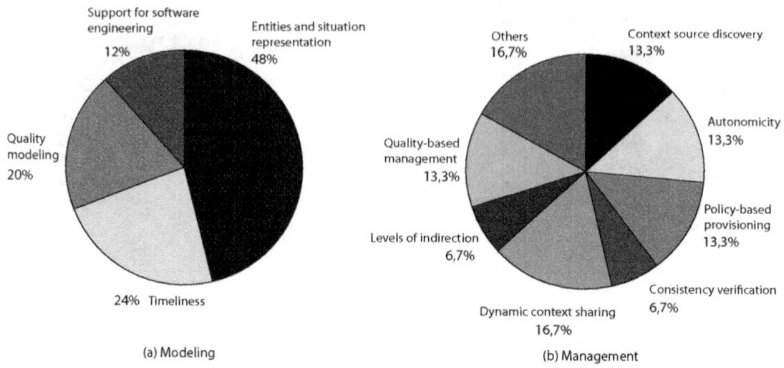

Fig. 16. (a) Distribution of contributions to top features of context modeling; (b) Selected features of context management.

Sect. 4.1. Generally, early approaches focused on the representation of entities and situations—a fundamental problem in context modeling. Fig. 16 (b) displays the distribution of contributions for a set of selected management features considered important for supporting smart interactions and smart services.

6 Conclusion and Outlook

Context-aware engineering is one of the most promising research directions for developing highly dynamic platforms for smart services and smart interactions. A system facilitating smart interactions will be able to adjust its behaviour in response to its perception of the environment and the system itself, in the form of fully or semi-automatic self-adaptation based on dynamic context information.

This book chapter posits that to take smart service and smart interaction technologies to the next level, we need to take context-awareness and context management to the next level. In particular, acquisition, leveraging, and managing of context have to be highly dynamic and self-adaptive to be able to develop highly sophisticated and smart interactions. Control loops will play a central role in monitoring and leveraging dynamic context information to smarten up services and interactions.

To optimize its functions, a smart interaction system should be extensively instrumented to keep track of useful dynamic context information figures (e.g., user clicks on search results, dynamic service attributes, location, time of day, throughput, latency, or resource consumption). The survey results presented in this chapter constitute a solid framework to organize context instrumentation that will survive the test of time. Processes that govern context-awareness can then use these figures to identify trends, adjust policies and processes, and manage service levels accordingly [65]. In particular, such processes can monitor and control the effects and outcomes of policies and processes using control loops [66], [67], [29], [68]. Selected results of context-awareness policies and processes are then fed back to a context-awareness controller, which in turn decides whether there is a need to adapt policies, control objectives and/or processes to optimize outcomes. To manage the collective context information of the smart environments described in this book, we advocate to borrow architectures, policies, and processes from the SOA governance domain. We envision an infrastructure level above the smart environment level to govern the smart interactions below.

On the one hand, the survey conducted for this chapter demonstrated that much progress has been made over the past decade in the areas of context modeling and management. In particular, existing work covers requirements related to entities and situation representation, context source discovery, and context handling and reasoning. On the other hand, many open research problems and challenges remain in the gap between the smart Internet and context-aware systems, including identifying context control objectives and relevant context from the specification of user's *mocs*; providing tools to assist users in the dynamic evolution of context models; constructing dynamic context models that support important requirements as timeliness for representing context changes along multiple Web sessions as well as expressiveness of context control objectives [12]; managing and leveraging uncertainty due to dynamic, transient and volatile context [29]; supporting the dynamic adaptation of context models and management infrastructures to ensure representation and management pertinence with current situations; categorizing control-centric architectural patterns for context-aware systems [66]; and characterizing context-management frameworks for smart interactions. Finally, to guide the following research efforts in the engineering of smart interactions and services, the SITCON community needs a comprehensive characterization of the main metaphor of the smart Internet. User's *mocs*, as the way of connecting user needs, resources and services available on the Web should be formalized by including aspects such as their life cycle, properties, classification, and types of involved entities. Furthermore, an operational specification of *mocs* for supporting smart interactions and smart services is urgently needed—for instance, for the dynamic identification of context requirements from a particular *moc*.

Acknowledgements

This work grew out of collaboration with colleagues at IBM Toronto Center for Advanced Studies, CA Labs, and Carnegie Mellon Software Engineering Institute. We are deeply indebted to many of our friends and students, who contributed significantly to our appreciation and understanding of context-awareness. In particular, we would like to thank Gabriel Tamura, Grace Lewis, Sowmya Balasubramanian, Ron Desmarais, Priyanka Gupta, Ishita Jain, Stephan Jou, Przemek Lach, Alex Lau, Serge Mankovski, Joanna Ng, Atousa Pahlevan, Dennis Smith, Kenny Wong, Qian Yang, and Qin Zhu for their continued collaboration and support. This work was funded in part by the National Sciences and Engineering Research Council (NSERC) of Canada (CRDPJ 320529-04 and CRDPJ 356154-07), IBM Corporation and CA Inc. via the CSER Consortium, as well as Icesi University, Cali, Colombia and University of Victoria, British Columbia, Canada.

References

1. Northrop, L., Feiler, P., Gabriel, R., Goodenough, J., Longstaff, T., Kazman, R., Klein, M., Schmidt, D., Sullivan, K., Wallnau, K.: Ultra-large-scale systems—The software challenge of the future. Technical report, Carnegie Mellon University Software Engineering Institute (2006)
2. Ng, J., Chignell, M.H., Cordy, J.R.: The smart Internet: Transforming the web for the user. Technical report, IBM Canada Center for Advanced Studies, Technical Report (2009)
3. Müller, H.A.: Managing dynamic context to optimize smart interactions using feedback loops and soa governance techniques. In: Pre-proceedings of SITCON 2009: The CAS/NSERC Strategic Workshop in Smart Internet Technologies, IBM CASCON 2009 (2009), `http://research.cs.queensu.ca/~cordy/SITCON`
4. Abowd, G.D., Dey, A.K., Brown, P.J., Davies, N., Smith, M., Steggles, P.: Towards a better understanding of context and context-awareness. In: Gellersen, H.-W. (ed.) HUC 1999. LNCS, vol. 1707, pp. 304–307. Springer, Heidelberg (1999)
5. Zimmermann, A., Lorenz, A., Oppermann, R.: An operational definition of context. In: Kokinov, B., Richardson, D.C., Roth-Berghofer, T.R., Vieu, L. (eds.) CONTEXT 2007. LNCS (LNAI), vol. 4635, pp. 558–571. Springer, Heidelberg (2007)
6. Hynes, G.: A context lifecycle for web-based context management services. In: Barnaghi, P., Moessner, K., Presser, M., Meissner, S. (eds.) EuroSSC 2009. LNCS, vol. 5741, pp. 51–65. Springer, Heidelberg (2009)
7. Kang, K.C., Cohen, S.G., Hess, J.A., Novak, W.E., Peterson, A.S.: Feature-oriented domain analysis (FODA): Feasibility study. Technical Report CMU/SEI-90-TR-21, Carnegie Mellon University Software Engineering Institute (1990)
8. Tamura, G.: Ubiquituous and autonomic computing: An initial exploration proposal. Technical Report Version 1.0, DRISO Research Team (October 2009)
9. Czarnecki, K.: Feature-based survey of model transformation approaches. IBM Systems Journal 45(3), 621–645 (2006)
10. Bettini, C., Brdiczka, O., Henricksen, K., Indulska, J., Nicklas, D., Ranganathan, A., Riboni, D.: A survey of context modelling and reasoning techniques. Pervasive and Mobile Computing 6, 161–180 (2009)
11. Moore, P.: A survey of context modeling for pervasive cooperative learning. In: Proceedings 1st International Symposium on Information Technologies and Applications in Education (ISITAE 2007), pp. K51–K56 (2007)
12. Strang, T., Linnhoff-Popien, C.: A context modeling survey. In: Proceedings Workshop on Advanced Context Modelling, Reasoning and Management at Sixth International Conference on Ubiquitous Computing (UbiComp 2004) (2004)
13. Conan, D., Rouvoy, R., Seinturier, L.: Scalable processing of context information with COSMOS. In: Indulska, J., Raymond, K. (eds.) DAIS 2007. LNCS, vol. 4531, pp. 210–224. Springer, Heidelberg (2007)
14. Samaan, N., Harroud, H., Karmouch, A.: PACMAN: A policy-based architecture for context management in ambient networks. In: Proceedings 4th IEEE Consumer Communications and Networking Conference (CCNC 2007), pp. 497–502. IEEE Computer Society, Los Alamitos (2007)
15. Taconet, C., Kazi-Aoul, Z., Zaier, M., Conan, D.: CA3M: A runtime model and a middleware for dynamic context management. In: Meersman, R., Dillon, T., Herrero, P. (eds.) OTM 2009. LNCS, vol. 5870, pp. 513–530. Springer, Heidelberg (2009)

16. Reichle, R.: A comprehensive context modeling framework for pervasive computing systems. In: Meier, R., Terzis, S. (eds.) DAIS 2008. LNCS, vol. 5053, pp. 281–295. Springer, Heidelberg (2008)
17. Bunt, H.: Modular partial models: A formalism for context representation. In: Blackburn, P., Ghidini, C., Turner, R.M., Giunchiglia, F. (eds.) CONTEXT 2003. LNCS, vol. 2680, pp. 427–434. Springer, Heidelberg (2004)
18. Strimpakou, M., Roussaki, I., Pils, C., Angermann, M., Robertson, P., Anagnostou, M.: Context modelling and management in ambient-aware pervasive environments. In: Strang, T., Linnhoff-Popien, C. (eds.) LoCA 2005. LNCS, vol. 3479, pp. 2–15. Springer, Heidelberg (2005)
19. Strang, T., Linnhoff-Popien, C., Frank, K.: CoOL: a context ontology language to enable contextual interoperability. In: Stefani, J.-B., Demeure, I., Hagimont, D. (eds.) DAIS 2003. LNCS, vol. 2893, pp. 236–247. Springer, Heidelberg (2003)
20. Krummenacher, R., Strang, T.: Ontology-based context modeling. In: Proceedings Third Workshop on Context-Aware Proactive Systems (CAPS 2007) (June 2007)
21. Henricksen, K., Indulska, J., McFadden, T.: Modelling context information with orm. In: Meersman, R., Tari, Z., Herrero, P. (eds.) OTM-WS 2005. LNCS, vol. 3762, pp. 626–635. Springer, Heidelberg (2005)
22. Krause, M., Hochstatter, I.: Challenges in modelling and using quality of context (QoC). In: Magedanz, T., Karmouch, A., Pierre, S., Venieris, I.S. (eds.) MATA 2005. LNCS, vol. 3744, pp. 324–333. Springer, Heidelberg (2005)
23. Henricksen, K., Indulska, J.: A software engineering framework for context-aware pervasive computing. In: Proceedings Second IEEE Annual Conference on Pervasive Computing and Communications (PerCom 2004), pp. 77–86 (March 2004)
24. Zimmermann, A., Specht, M., Lorenz, A.: Personalization and context management. User Modeling and User-Adapted Interaction 15(3-4), 275–302 (2005)
25. Coutaz, J., Crowley, J.L., Dobson, S.: Context is key. Communications of the ACM (CACM) 48(3), 49–53 (2005)
26. Hu, P., Robinson, R., Indulska, J.: Sensor standards: Overview and experiences. In: Proceedings 3rd International Conference on Intelligent Sensors, Sensor Networks and Information (ISSNIP 2007), pp. 485–490 (2007)
27. Hu, P., Indulska, J., Robinson, R.: An autonomic context management system for pervasive computing. In: Proceedings 6th Annual IEEE International Conference on Pervasive Computing and Communications (PerCom 2008), pp. 213–223 (2008)
28. OASIS Web Services Distributed Management (WSDM) Technical Committee: WSDM 1.1 OASIS Standard Specifications. Technical report, OASIS (2006)
29. Müller, H.A., Kienle, H.M., Stege, U.: Autonomic computing: Now you see it, now you don't—design and evolution of autonomic software systems. In: De Lucia, A., Ferrucci, F. (eds.) ISSSE 2006 - 2008. LNCS, vol. 5413, pp. 32–54. Springer, Heidelberg (2009)
30. Chantzara, M., Anagnostou, M.: Designing the context matching engine for evaluating and selecting context information sources. In: Roth-Berghofer, T.R., Schulz, S., Leake, D.B. (eds.) MRC 2005. LNCS (LNAI), vol. 3946, pp. 101–117. Springer, Heidelberg (2006)
31. Crowley, J.L.: Context driven observation of human activity. In: Aarts, E., Collier, R.W., van Loenen, E., de Ruyter, B. (eds.) EUSAI 2003. LNCS, vol. 2875, pp. 101–118. Springer, Heidelberg (2003)
32. Salomie, I., Anghel, I., Cioara, T., Dinsoreanu, M.: A context awareness model enhanced with autonomic features. In: Proceedings 4th International Conference on Intelligent Computer Communication and Processing (ICCP 2008), pp. 239–246 (2008)

33. Strassner, J., Hong, J.W.-k., van der Meer, S.: The design of a novel context-aware policy model to support machine-based learning and reasoning. Cluster Computing 12(1), 17–43 (2009)
34. Hinchey, G., Sterritt, R., Corteś, A.R.: Building and implementing policies in autonomous and autonomic systems using MaCMAS. Innovations in Systems and Software Engineering 3(1), 17–31 (2007)
35. Kephart, J.O., Chess, D.M.: The vision of autonomic computing. Computer 36(1), 41–50 (2003)
36. Hynes, G., Reynolds, V., Hauswirth, M.: Enabling mobility between context-aware smart spaces. In: Proceedings International Conference on Advanced Information Networking and Applications Workshops (WAINA 2009), pp. 255–260 (2009)
37. Paspallis, N., Chimaris, A., Papadopoulos, G.A.: Experiences from developing a distributed context management system for enabling adaptivity. In: Indulska, J., Raymond, K. (eds.) DAIS 2007. LNCS, vol. 4531, pp. 225–238. Springer, Heidelberg (2007)
38. Crowley, J.L., Coutaz, J., Rey, G., Reignier, P.: Perceptual components for context aware computing. In: Borriello, G., Holmquist, L.E. (eds.) UbiComp 2002. LNCS, vol. 2498, pp. 117–134. Springer, Heidelberg (2002)
39. Euzenat, J., Pierson, J., Ramparani, F.: Dynamic context management for pervasive applications. Knowledge Engineering Review 23(1), 21–49 (2008)
40. Kitchenham, B., Charters, S.: Guidelines for performing systematic literature reviews in software engineering. Technical Report EBSE 2007-001, Keele University and Durham University Joint Report (2007)
41. Chen, L., Babar, M.A., Ali, N.: Variability management in software product lines: A systematic review. In: Proceedings 13th International Software Product Line Conference (SPLC 2009), pp. 81–90. Carnegie Mellon University Software Engineering Institute, Pittsburgh (August 2009)
42. Dey, A.K.: A conceptual framework and a toolkit for supporting the rapid prototyping of context-aware applications. Human-Computer Interaction 16(2-4), 97–166 (2001)
43. Dey, A.K.: Understanding and using context. Personal and Ubiquitous Computing 5(1), 4–7 (2001)
44. Chang, H.: Modeling context life cycle for building smarter applications in ubiquitous computing environments. In: Meersman, R., Tari, Z., Herrero, P. (eds.) OTM-WS 2008. LNCS, vol. 5333, pp. 851–860. Springer, Heidelberg (2008)
45. Kapitsaki, G.M.: Context-aware service engineering: A survey. Journal of Systems and Software 82(8), 1285–1297 (2009)
46. Hoareau, C.: Modeling and processing information for context-aware computing: A survey. New Generation Computing 27(3), 177–196 (2009)
47. Lei, S., Zhang, R.: Mobile context modelling using conceptual graphs. In: Proceedings IEEE International Conference on Wireless and Mobile Computing, Networking and Communications (WiMob 2005), vol. 4, pp. 131–138. IEEE Computer Society, Los Alamitos (2005)
48. Schmidt, A.: A layered model for user context management with controlled aging and imperfection handling. In: Roth-Berghofer, T.R., Schulz, S., Leake, D.B. (eds.) MRC 2005. LNCS (LNAI), vol. 3946, pp. 86–100. Springer, Heidelberg (2005)
49. Ou, S., Georgalas, N., Azmoodeh, M., Yang, K., Sun, X.: A model driven integration architecture for ontology-based context modelling and context-aware application development. In: Rensink, A., Warmer, J. (eds.) ECMDA-FA 2006. LNCS, vol. 4066, pp. 188–197. Springer, Heidelberg (2006)

50. Park, M., Gu, M., Ryu, K.: Context information model using ontologies and rules based on spatial object. Communications in Computer and Information Science 2, 107–114 (2007)
51. Robinson, R., Henricksen, K., Indulska, J.: XCML: A runtime representation for the context modelling language. In: Proceedings Fifth Annual IEEE International Conference on Pervasive Computing and Communications (PerCom 2007), pp. 20–26. IEEE Computer Society, Los Alamitos (2007)
52. Choi, O.: A meta data model of context information for dynamic service adaptation on user centric environment. In: Proceedings International Conference on Multimedia and Ubiquitous Engineering (MUE 2007), pp. 108–113 (April 2007)
53. Achilleos, A., Yanga, K., Georgalas, N.: Context modelling and a context-aware framework for pervasive service creation: A model-driven approach. In: 8th IEEE International Conference on Pervasive and Mobile Computing (PerCom 2010), pp. 281–296 (March/April 2010)
54. Anagnostopoulos, T., Anagnostopoulos, C., Hadjiefthymiades, S.: An online adaptive model for location prediction. In: Proceedings Third International ICST Conference Autonomic Computing and Communications Systems (Autonomics 2009), pp. 64–78 (September 2009)
55. Preuveneers, D., Berbers, Y.: Adaptive context management using a component-based approach. In: Kutvonen, L., Alonistioti, N. (eds.) DAIS 2005. LNCS, vol. 3543, pp. 14–26. Springer, Heidelberg (2005)
56. Dey, A.K., Mankoff, J.: Designing mediation for context-aware applications. ACM Transactions on Computer-Human Interaction (TOCHI) 12(1), 53–80 (2005)
57. Henricksen, K., Indulska, J., McFadden, T., Balasubramaniam, S.: Middleware for distributed context-aware systems. In: Meersman, R., Tari, Z. (eds.) OTM 2005. LNCS, vol. 3760, pp. 846–863. Springer, Heidelberg (2005)
58. Liu, Q.: A novel platform for context maintenance and discovery in a ubiquitous environment. In: Proceedings 5th International Conference on Embedded and Ubiquitous Computing (EUC 2008), pp. 565–570 (2008)
59. Dudkowski, D., Weinschrott, H., Marron, P.: Design and implementation of a reference model for context management in mobile ad-hoc networks. In: Proceedings 22nd International Conference on Advanced Information Networking and Applications (AINAW 2008), pp. 832–837. IEEE Computer Society, Los Alamitos (2008)
60. Paspallis, N., Rouvoy, R., Barone, P., Papadopoulos, G.A., Eliassen, F., Mamelli, A.: A pluggable and reconfigurable architecture for a context-aware enabling middleware system. In: Meersman, R., Tari, Z. (eds.) OTM 2008, Part I. LNCS, vol. 5331, pp. 553–570. Springer, Heidelberg (2008)
61. Zhang, W., Hansen, K.M.: Semantic web based self-management for a pervasive service middleware. In: Second IEEE International Conference on Self-Adaptive and Self-Organizing Systems (SASO 2008), pp. 245–254 (2008)
62. Schmidtke, H.R., Woo, W.: Towards ontology-based formal verification methods for context aware systems. In: Proceedings Seventh Annual IEEE International Conference on Pervasive Computing and Communications (PerCom 2009), vol. 5538, pp. 309–326. IEEE Computer Society, Los Alamitos (2009)
63. Abid, Z., Chabridon, S., Conan, D.: A framework for quality of context management. In: Rothermel, K., Fritsch, D., Blochinger, W., Dürr, F. (eds.) QuaCon 2009. LNCS, vol. 5786, pp. 120–131. Springer, Heidelberg (2009)
64. Knappmeyer, M., Baker, N., Liaquat, S., Tönjes, R.: A context provisioning framework to support pervasive and ubiquitous applications. In: Barnaghi, P., Moessner, K., Presser, M., Meissner, S. (eds.) EuroSSC 2009. LNCS, vol. 5741, pp. 93–106. Springer, Heidelberg (2009)

65. Bianco, P., Lewis, G., Merson, P.: Service level agreements in service-oriented architecture environments. Technical Report CMU/SEI-2008-TN-021, Carnegie Mellon University Software Engineering Institute (2008)
66. Müller, H., Pezzè, M., Shaw, M.: Visibility of control in adaptive systems. In: Proceedings 2nd International Workshop on Ultra-Large-Scale Software-Intensive Systems (ULSSIS 2008), Workshop at 30th IEEE/ACM International Conference on Software Engineering (ICSE 2008), Leipzig, Germany, pp. 23–26 (2008)
67. Giese, H., Brun, Y., Serugendo, J.D.M., Gacek, C., Kienle, H., Müller, H., Pezzè, M., Shaw, M.: Engineering self-adaptive and self-managing systems. In: Cheng, B.H.C., de Lemos, R., Giese, H., Inverardi, P., Magee, J. (eds.) Software Engineering for Self-Adaptive Systems. LNCS, vol. 5525, pp. 47–69. Springer, Heidelberg (2009)
68. Salehie, M., Tahvildari, L.: Self-adaptive software: Landscape and research challenges. ACM Transactions on Autonomous and Adaptive Systems (TAAS) 4(2), 14.1–14.42 (2009)

Author Index

GPSR Compliance

The European Union's (EU) General Product Safety Regulation (GPSR) is a set of rules that requires consumer products to be safe and our obligations to ensure this.

If you have any concerns about our products, you can contact us on ProductSafety@springernature.com

In case Publisher is established outside the EU, the EU authorized representative is:

Springer Nature Customer Service Center GmbH
Europaplatz 3
69115 Heidelberg, Germany

Batch number: 10844619

Printed by Printforce, the Netherlands